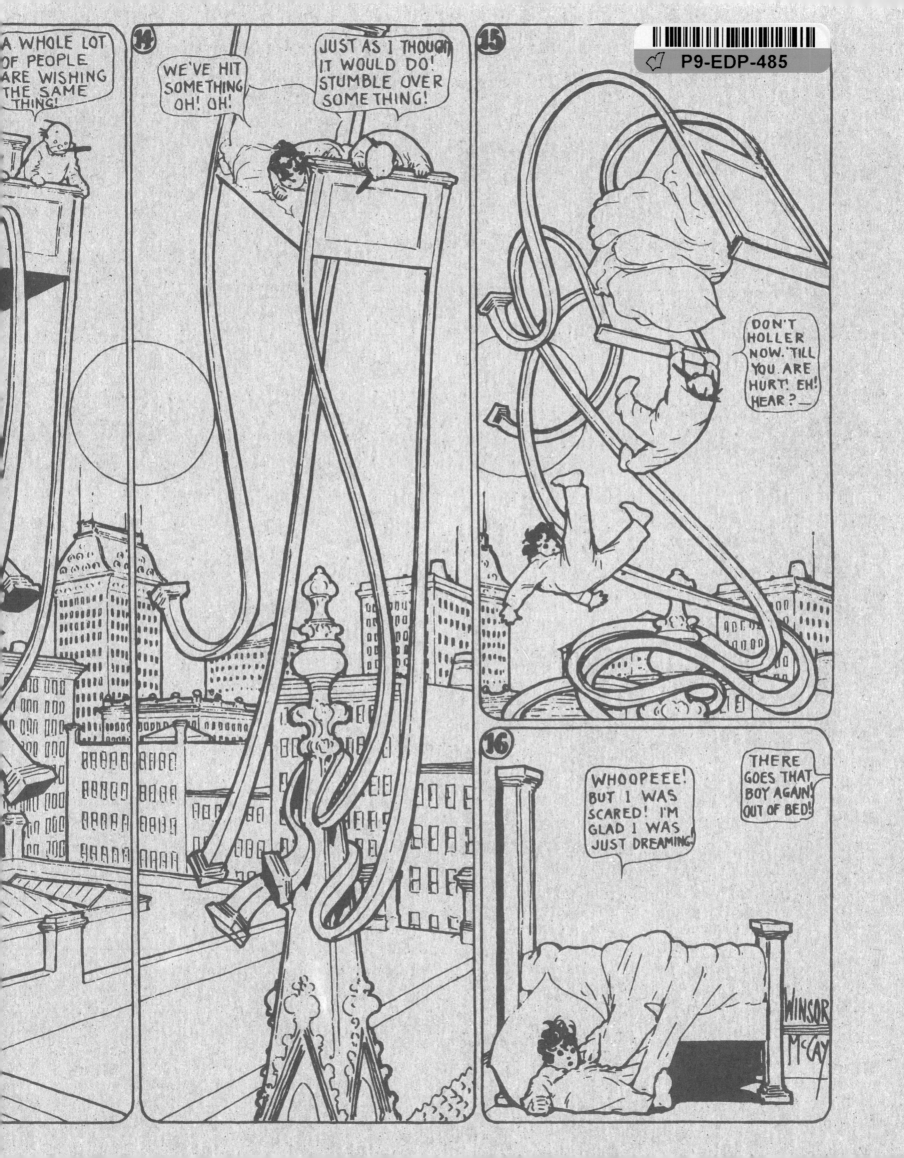

winsor mccay

his life and art • revised and expanded edition

john canemaker

FOREWORD BY MAURICE SENDAK

HARRY N. ABRAMS, INC., PUBLISHERS

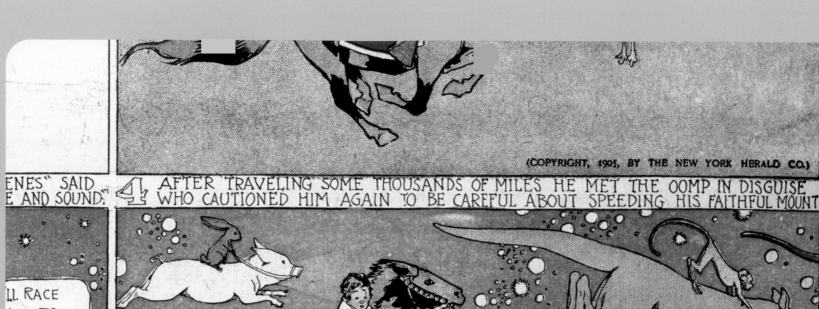

ABOVE:

October 15, 1905: The premiere episode of Little Nemo in Slumberland *in the New York Herald (detail). (Collection Robert Lesser)*

FRONTISPIECE:

The August 12, 1906, Little Nemo in Slumberland *episode is Winsor McCay's masterpiece, the single most beautiful comic strip page ever. It is a pantheistic dream, designed with the elegance and luminosity of a stained glass window. The panel shapes work in sympathy with the characters' actions—a wide rectangle accommodates six giant butterflies in the top panel, changing to a series of vertical shapes when Nemo and the Princess ascend the tree. The drawing is alive with illusions of motion: the differing poses of the butterflies imply fluttery animation, and their flight to a distant tree uses dynamic perspective to lead the eye. The point of view throughout is as mobile as if shot by a swooping camera crane in one continuous take.*

The downward direction of the insects (panel 5) signals the start of the rain, enhancing the effect. During the downpour (panel 6), McCay eliminates the usual thick Art Nouveau outlines around characters and objects, and by adding thin vertical lines he creates a diffuse, steamy summer shower of cool drops hitting hot surfaces.

The use of color is extraordinary, from the blazing red title on complementary green, to the multihued butterfly wings. The volatile sky excites us, then cools us off with its constantly changing colors. This is a peaceful world, where nature is tame and friendly—bugs do not bite and weather is truly predictable. A functional metamorphosis solves problems: a stem and leaves become a railing and stairs; a tree becomes a giant umbrella.

Only the relationship between the relentlessly boyish Nemo and his "romantic" partner, the matronly Princess, is out of synch in this leisurely, timeless utopia. They contrast in attire, energy, and attitudes: she is confident and full of polite chatter; he is concerned for his safety, preoccupied with the mechanics of the place, and bored by his hostess and her tour of marvels. "How long will this rain last, eh?" he asks with impatience. Mundane reality intrudes when the gentle rain becomes an annoying sprinkle tossed by Nemo's angry father. The dream has ended rudely and too soon, but the memory of Winsor McCay's most perfect vision will remain. (Collection John Canemaker)

for joe

contents

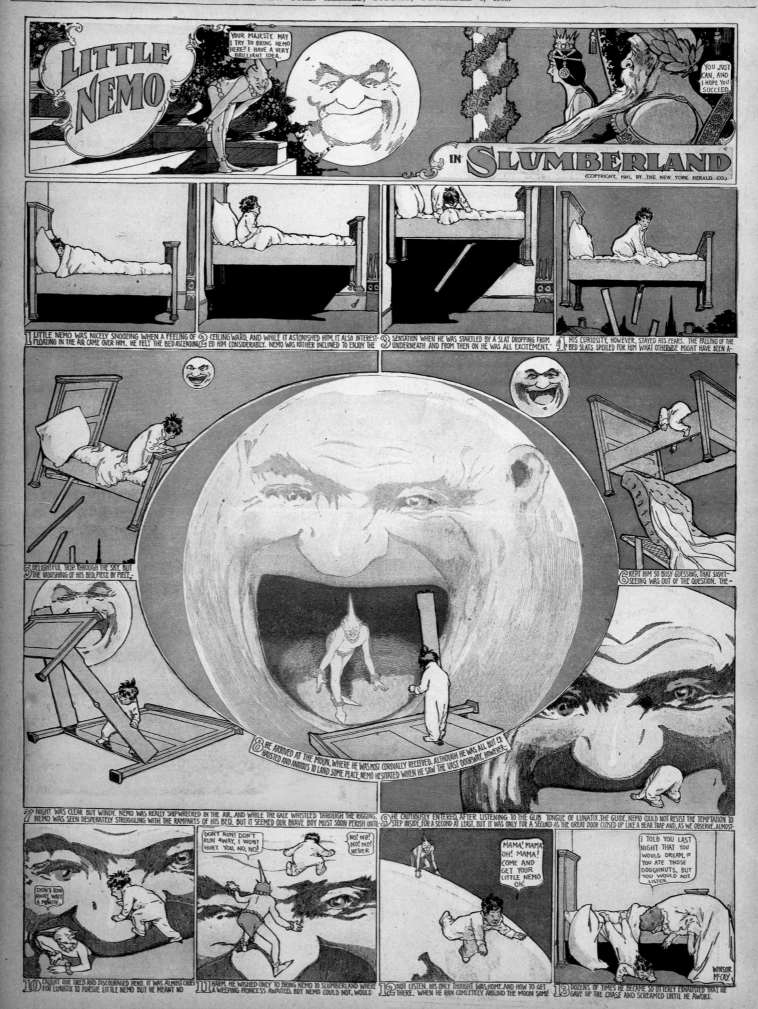

My book *In the Night Kitchen* is, in part, an homage to Winsor McCay. He and I serve the same master, our child selves. We both draw, not on the literal memory of childhood, but on the emotional memory of its stress and urgency. And neither of us forgot our childhood dreams.

Miraculously, McCay recreated dreams that we all had as children but few of us remember—or care to remember. This puts him squarely in league with Lewis Carroll and George MacDonald. His most famous creation, *Little Nemo in Slumberland*, began as a full-page Sunday comic in the *New York Herald* on October 15, 1905. But it is much more than a comic strip, especially in comparison to the debased examples of the form popular in America since the late 1930s.

An elaborate and audacious fantasy, *Little Nemo* is, in effect, a giant children's book, though no more limited to children than *Alice in Wonderland,* the Grimm tales, or any of the best books for children. Nemo's dreams, like Alice's, have the unquestionable ring of veracity. In McCay's Slumberland, as in Wonderland, irrational taboos, forbidden places, and terrifying creatures confront Little Nemo at every turn. But Nemo, unlike Alice, is afraid. He has none of her nimble wit and maddening pugnaciousness. He is dubious, suspicious, very much a miniature Buster Keaton ogling a hostile universe.

Like *Little Nemo,* McCay's *Dream of the Rarebit Fiend* is a catalogue of nightmares, a profusion of extreme fantasy images rendered with such explicit definition that the dream is captured in all its surrealistic exactitude. There are many details I suspect only children see, and those few adults who still look with a child's intelligent curiosity.

McCay's originality is confirmed by his radically personal iconography and his innovative method of visual narrative (he ignored the comic strip's traditional arrangement of panels, stretching them vertically and horizontally to get his dreamlike effects— shattering them completely in one sequence of *Little Sammy Sneeze).* He was a born architect with a breathtaking command of perspective; the elaborate structural decors that appear over and over in all his comic strips—as well as in his later editorial cartoons—are reminiscent of the architectural fantasies of the stage designers of the Baroque—and those of the creators of Dreamland and Luna Park near his home in Brooklyn. The power of his visionary landscapes and the strength of his draftsmanship override and mitigate the softening, sentimental, Art Nouveau conceits he enthusiastically took up. In fact, he injected new spirit into the agitated, voluptuous line and arbitrary, flat-color patterning of Art Nouveau design. McCay's mature style also reflects his early training, in Cincinnati and Chicago, in meeting the carnival and circus poster's demand for simple, clear shapes and showy motifs. The grandiose facades, the freaks, clowns, fancily tricked-out dancers, and comic-mirror distortions that he knew firsthand (from his days as a "lightning sketch" artist in dime museums and later in vaudeville) became the raw material from which he fashioned Nemo's world.

Little Nemo is nearly pure gold. If it falters now and again—and, at the end, repeatedly—it is a wonder that McCay could sustain his creation at its usual exalted level while producing a color comic page every week. But then, he loved to draw, and the promise of frequent escape into his child-hero's dreams must have been a helpful impetus.

John Canemaker's showcase of Winsor McCay's contributions to the popular arts—from his profound influence on comic strips and animated films to his unique work in theater, poster, and advertising design, as well as his editorial cartoons—is sufficient proof that McCay was one of America's rare, great fantasists. In a country that is ambivalent, at best, toward its volatile imaginations, further proof of his power is the fact that he could hold a mass audience for so long. But America, it seems, still doesn't take its great fantasists all that seriously. I hope this loving and scholarly book will bring Winsor McCay the recognition he deserves.

Maurice Sendak

preface and acknowledgments

I first heard of Winsor McCay in 1955 when I was twelve years old. *Disneyland,* the weekly television program, presented a show on the history of animation, and McCay was represented as an important pioneer with the showing of his 1914 cartoon film, *Gertie the Dinosaur.*

I remember being impressed with how Disney-like this early animation effort was—how fluid the movements, how naturalistic the design, and how fresh, yet familiar, the personality of the star, a charming diplodocus. Both the film and Winsor McCay's name stayed with me because of the memorable way Disney re-created the original vaudeville presentation in which the film first appeared: an actor playing "Winsor McCay" spoke commands to and cracked a whip at the cartoon character on the large movie screen behind him as the film creature obeyed with varying degrees of civility.

Almost twenty years later, I began my dual career as animator and animation historian. While I was making my own cartoon movies and delving into the history of the art to document it and its artists, Winsor McCay continually loomed as a great and influential figure. But although his work in film and newspapers still exists, facts about the man and his career were maddeningly elusive. I had many questions: how had McCay created such advanced work at so early a stage in animation's development? Who were his influences? How did animation relate to his other major accomplishments in comic strips, which were gloriously innovative? Why did he abandon both strips and films in order to concentrate on drawing editorial cartoons until the end of his life? Why did his reputation slide into near oblivion after his death in 1934? Why is this authentic American genius so little known today? What was his life like—and who *was* Winsor McCay?

As I continued my research, I had the good fortune and pleasure of meeting John A. Fitzsimmons, McCay's assistant on two of his early films, including *Gertie the Dinosaur.* In 1976, he narrated my documentary film *Remembering Winsor McCay* and was a treasure trove of information about the artist, continuing to help me up to our last meeting in 1984, two months before he died at age ninety-one.

In 1975, when I coordinated the first Winsor McCay film retrospectives in the United States, I met the family of Winsor McCay. Many people contributed to the original publication of this book in 1987, but it could not have been written without the full cooperation and encouragement of Ray Winsor Moniz (1918–2001) and his family.

Ray first suggested I write a biography of his grandfather and led me to Janet McCay Trinker (1922–1997), Winsor McCay's granddaughter, and her family (including Theresa "Tedda" McCay, widow of Robert McCay, who was Winsor's son and the model for Little Nemo). Both branches of the McCay clan generously recalled pertinent details about the life and times of Winsor McCay and allowed me to publish, for the first time, excerpts from the artist's letters, contracts, personal photos, and diaries.

Other contributors to the original 1987 version of this book include:

Robert E. Abrams; Dennis Aig; Janet Alexander; Bob Ashbrook; J. Michael Barrier; Louise Beaudet of La Cinémathèque québécoise in Montreal; Catherine Bechard of the Ontario Genealogical Society in Woodstock, Ontario; Howard Beckerman; Ann Bertagnolli; Helen Bisbee of the Grand Rapids Public Library, Michigan; R. O. Blechman; Jim Borgman; Berke Breathed; Mary Bringle; Robert N. Brotherton; Betty Jean Burr, Secretary of the Chalmers United Church of Canada at Woodstock; Mrs. Alex Cameron; Milton Caniff; Rose and John Cannizzaro; Lucy S.

Winsor McCay at work, c. 1925.

Caswell of the Library for Communication and Graphic Arts at Ohio State University in Columbus; Donald Crafton; Ken Craven of the University of Texas at Austin; Gregory D'Alessio; Maria A. Davis of the Eastern Michigan University Archives and Special Collections; Marge Devine of the National Cartoonists Society; Jim Duesing; Foster Fletcher, Ypsilanti City Historian; Eleanor B. Forlenza of Cleary College in Ypsilanti, Michigan; Woody Gelman; Tom Gill; Jack Golden; Katje de Gorog; Graham Halky; Elizabeth Hancocks; Thomas Hoffer of Florida State University; Bill Holman; Burne Hogarth; Paul T. Hudson of the Cincinnati Public Library; Jud Hurd of *Cartoonist Profiles;* M. Thomas Inge; Chuck Jones; Agatha Pfeiffer Kalkanis of the Detroit Public Library; Renée Khatami; Adrienne Knoll of *Bay News;* Jane Lahr; Debbie Le Fever of the County Clerk's Office in Stanton, Michigan; Bob Links; Linda McCabe; Mrs. M. J. Meeusen; William Moritz; Deanna Morse; Rita Moules of Cleary College; Regula Noetzli; Dorothy and Jim Noonan; Roberta Ohmer; Susan Ohmer; Neil F. Paynter of the Chicago Historical Society; Gene Phelan; John A. Pyle; Mary M. Rider; Walton Rawls; J. J. Sedelmaier; Charlotte Sheedy; Paula Sigman; Charles Silver of the Museum of Modern Art; Gary Silver; Conrad Smith; David R. Smith of the Walt Disney Archives; Vincent de Sola; Michael Sporn; Donald Spoto; Tenby Storm; Frederic B. Taraba of the Society of Illustra-

tors; Curtice Taylor; Edwin Trinker; Garry Trudeau; Renée I. Weber of Special Collections at Fairleigh Dickinson University Harry "A" Chesler Collection; Ruth Whitaker; Dorothy L. Wick of the Kenton County Historical Society, Kentucky; Jim Van Vulpen; the staffs of the Cincinnati Historical Society; New-York Historical Society; New York Public Library (newspaper and theater collections); Museum of the City of New York; Brooklyn Historical Society; and the Brooklyn Public Library.

For this new edition, I am grateful to Marco De Blois of La Cinémathèque québécoise; Larry Ruppel; G. Preston Brown; David M. Halpate; Wilber and Roy Abbott; W. Robert McCay; William Randolph Hearst, Jr.; Lew Haskins; Dennis Doros and Amy Heller of Milestone Film & Video; Tom Drysdale; Ann Butler and Marvin Taylor of the Fales Collection at New York University Bobst Library. I also wish to thank my supportive literary agent, Robert Cornfield, and the creative team at Abrams, including Eric Himmel, Céline Moulard, Michael Walsh, and the gifted designer Robert McKee.

Once again, as in 1987, I have relied on my loving and trusted friend Joseph J. Kennedy (to whom I dedicated this book) for his continuing counsel and support.

A large poster advertising the general theatrical release of McCay's popular animated film Gertie the Dinosaur *in November 1914; the film had its debut in February 1914 as part of McCay's vaudeville act. (Collection Ray Winsor Moniz)*

"Draw lines, young man, many lines, from memory or from nature; it is in this way that you will become a good artist."
—INGRES TO THE YOUNG DEGAS

"I just couldn't stop drawing anything and everything."
—WINSOR McCAY

February 2, 1914, was a bitterly cold Monday in Chicago, but the vaudeville theaters were presenting such an array of stellar attractions that full houses were assured even for the matinee. At the American Music Hall on Wabash Avenue, for example, there was vivacious Eva Tanguay, the "Cyclonic Comedienne and Her Jubilee Vaudeville Company." Over at the Garrick, Harry Lauder, billed as "The World's Greatest Entertainer" and "racy, faithful and poetic balladist of humble life," performed in Scottish tartan kilts.

At the ornate Palace Theater on Clark Street near Randolph, the Farber Sisters ("Society's Dainty Entertainers") sang, Miss Charlotte Parry ("protean actress") recited a "psychological fantasy," and the Kitaro Troupe juggled objects with their feet. The headliner at the Palace was the internationally renowned newspaper cartoonist Winsor McCay.

A veteran of eight years of intermittent touring on the vaudeville circuits, McCay was an audience favorite whose marvelous ability to sketch quickly in chalk on a blackboard never failed to please. Within minutes, through a series of lightning-fast erasures and additions, McCay would bring two facing portraits of a boy and a girl through youth, adolescence, maturity, and old age, as the pit orchestra played "Ah, Sweet Mystery of Life." Within the last three years, a new addition had been made to his mute "lightning sketch" act: he presented animated cartoon movies made by himself, based on two of his famous comic strips.

McCay's fame (and the raison d'être for his vaudeville appearances) stemmed from his prodigious output of newspaper illustrations, editorial cartoons, and, most important, comic strips. Indeed,

when the American comic strip was in its infancy, McCay became the first master of the form with two unsurpassed works of genius: *Dream of the Rarebit Fiend,* first published in the *New York Evening Telegram* in 1904, and the epic *Little Nemo in Slumberland,* begun in the *New York Herald* in 1905. Both strips dealt with the dream state, with *Rarebit Fiend* containing a decidedly adult point of view and an anticipation of surrealist conceits in its juxtaposition of fantastic occurrences in mundane settings, the instability of appearances, and the irrationality of life.

Little Nemo in Slumberland, a child's version of the mythic theme of the quest, set in a dream world, was and is quite simply the most beautiful and innovative comic strip ever drawn. McCay's style combined an Art Nouveau line with subtle yet daring coloring; stunningly rendered architectural perspectives and sequential changes of characters and settings within the borders of the strip's flexible panels reflected the artist's strong interest in motion experiments and film animation.

McCay introduced a film version of *Little Nemo* into his act in 1911, followed the next year by a delightfully gruesome animated short based on a *Rarebit Fiend* strip, entitled *How a Mosquito Operates.* Both films represented a quantum leap in the direction of the nascent animated-film art form; McCay distinguished his work from that of his contemporaries in the field by the sophistication of his elaborate graphics, the fluid movement of his characters, the attempts to inject personality traits into those characters, and the use of strong narrative continuity.

At that long-ago vaudeville matinee, Winsor McCay introduced a new film that would fascinate audiences for generations and become, as film histo-

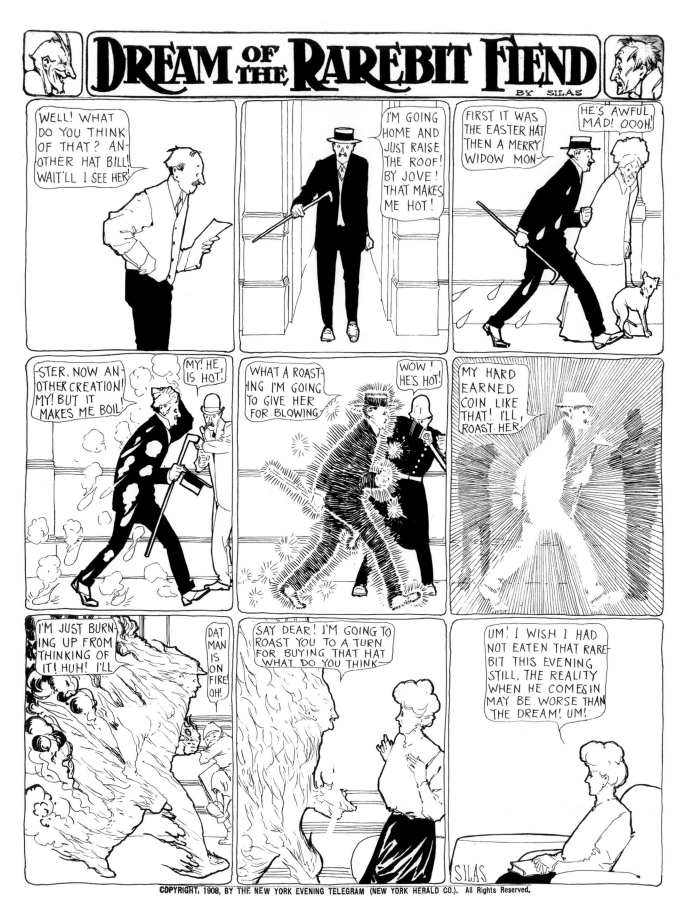

LEFT:
A man becomes literally fired with anger over the cost of his wife's new hat in a Dream of the Rarebit Fiend strip on August 14, 1908. McCay found appropriate graphic symbols to show the progressively rising temperature of the man that leads to his burning; they range from large sweat drops and boiling steam (panels 3 and 4), to radiating sparks and a glow emanating from the man's form (as if he were a match when first struck) seen in panels 5 and 6, to, finally, a full and beautiful Art Nouveau flame that engulfs the man and flows from him in a lush and sensual design. "Silas" was Winsor McCay's pseudonym for his work in the New York Evening Telegram.

OPPOSITE:
Winsor McCay in a 1906 portrait. (Collection Ray Winsor Moniz)

rian Donald Crafton put it, "the enduring master-piece of pre-Disney animation." Not until the Walt Disney studio hit its stride in 1934 (ironically, the year of McCay's death) would the animated cartoon match the high-quality draftsmanship and naturalistic motion established two decades before in *Gertie the Dinosaur.*

McCay presented *Gertie* in an impressive early version of multimedia performance art. Stepping into a spotlight next to a giant movie screen, the impeccably dressed, diminutive (five feet five, 130 pounds) McCay cracked a long bullwhip, as a circus ringmaster would. With this cue, the projectionist in the balcony area flashed the first frames of the film onto the screen. From behind some cartoon rocks hopped a large but playful diplodocus, who strode from the distance to the foreground in masterful perspective animation. Along the way, Gertie devoured a rock and part of a tree; later, she tossed a mastodon over her shoulder into a lake, which she then drank in its entirety.

Throughout the presentation, the elegant McCay barked commands at the cartoon dinosaur, demanding that she raise her foot, eat an apple, dance, behave ("Stop that crying!"), and take a bow. Gertie's reaction to the commands was based on her unique and endearing personality. Like a petulant little girl, Gertie obeyed her master in her own good time, threw a temper tantrum, and wept. The charming juxtaposition of a fragile spirit trapped inside a gargantuan body was as memorable as the mode of presentation, which is one reason why the film has had a life of its own without the physical presence of Winsor McCay.

In the final moments of his act, McCay merged reality with his fantasy world: walking out of the spotlight stage-left, he reappeared screen-right as a tiny cartoon version of himself. Gertie lowered her head gently to allow "McCay" to step into her mouth and then transferred him to her broad back. Atop his tamed monster, in total control of his imaginary universe, "McCay" took his bow as Gertie gracefully maneuvered them both off the screen.

Unfortunately for Winsor McCay, the monsters inhabiting the real world were not as easily controlled or dominated as were the fantasies existing in his pen-and-ink world. Throughout his career, McCay used his obsessively detailed drawings as a means to distance himself from problems and unpleasantness in his personal and professional life. His formidable talent for drawing was fueled by a compulsive need to draw and an overwhelming desire to give shape and direction to his life. His natural gifts included extraordinary energy, drive, and ambition; when combined with his great artistic abilities, these characteristics would lead him far from an unhappy childhood and penniless beginnings as a Midwestern poster painter for several traveling circuses, melodramas, and freak-show museums.

In 1914 Winsor McCay was forty-seven years old, at the peak of his fame and creative powers. He was employed by newspaper magnate William Randolph Hearst, who considered McCay to be the crown jewel in his fine collection of newspaper illustrators and cartoonists. McCay's salary as a "Hearst man," plus his fee as a vaudeville headliner and royalties from various merchandising and licensing deals, resulted in an annual income of between $50,000 and $100,000. He owned homes considered to be the showplaces of their neighborhoods in the fashionable resort towns of Sheepshead Bay in Brooklyn and Sea Gate near Coney Island. In winter the McCay family—Winsor, his wife, Maude, and their children, Robert and Marion—escaped the cold winds blowing off the Atlantic Ocean by moving into a suite of rooms at the Hotel St. George in Brooklyn Heights and by taking occasional trips to Miami.

McCay often joked that he had no business sense, but it was the truth. Although he could fight for and win high fees for his work, neither Winsor nor Maude saved or invested any substantial amount of money from all his years of large earnings. Despite the continuous flow of cash through their hands, money was always a prime source of irritation between the couple. To continue living the luxurious style of life to which they were accustomed, Winsor McCay literally had to work all the time.

It was true he loved to draw and once claimed that "the greatest contributing factor to my success was an absolute craving to draw pictures all the time." But the pressures of his never-ending attempts to please the demanding Maude and Hearst were beginning to tell on McCay, a man who often drew for several eighteen-hour days in a row with little outward sign of fatigue. For example, in December 1913, McCay abandoned his beloved comic strips. They were a casualty of artistic exhaustion as much as of Hearst's insistence that McCay concentrate on drawing elaborate daily half-page editorial cartoons illustrating the "average man" homilies of his dictatorial editor Arthur Brisbane, who decreed "McCay is serious, not funny."

McCay's drawing board was a constant companion on his vaudeville tours. Backstage between shows and late at night in his hotel room, the endless drawing continued. Once he began to work his pen over the white surface of the paper, McCay would be overcome by a strange peace, and he became totally immersed in the world and characters he was creating and controlling. Lovely and grotesque, grand and gaudy, the images flowed from his mind to his hand with astonishing swiftness and Mozart-like directness.

The new film addition to McCay's act received excellent notices in the Chicago papers: "Every child and its parents will want to see Gerty [sic]," wrote Ashton Stevens in the *Examiner*. And so the triumphant artist took the train back to New York, looking eagerly toward an engagement at Hammerstein's in Times Square, the country's top vaudeville house. A blizzard greeted his arrival, and snow and traffic clogged the streets so badly that the mayor eventually prayed in public for rain.

Storms of a different sort were also gathering. Maude McCay would soon be named as correspondent in a divorce suit, the second time news headlines would embarrass McCay publicly in a situation involving his considerably younger wife's attractiveness to other men.

Moreover, the unpredictable William Randolph Hearst would begin a concentrated effort to end McCay's vaudeville career, claiming McCay's "dalliance with the stage interferes with [his] regular newspaper work." Economically dependent upon Hearst and chained to an ironclad contract, McCay turned out hundreds of drawings that almost always transcended the jingoistic and pompous Arthur Brisbane editorials they illustrated. McCay's gift for composing a striking layout never abandoned him, and his art of this period was usually grand in concept, awesome in detail, and skillful in execution, reminding one of the drawings of Dürer, Daumier, and Doré.

Little by little the work that sustained McCay emotionally would disappear. First, his comic strips were discontinued, then his theatrical tours were limited to the New York area and finally ceased altogether, except for an occasional one-shot appearance. The loss of a live audience undermined his interest in making animated films; in 1921 he completed the last of only ten films, some of which were never screened publicly. McCay continued to confront the pressures of newspaper deadlines until his final escape: death from a stroke at age sixty-seven.

During his hectic but full life, Winsor McCay created perhaps a million drawings, many examples of a quality of draftsmanship unsurpassed in this century. He was a self-taught artist who survived by adapting his talents to the exigencies of the commercial marketplace, first in the popular recreational outlets of the nineteenth century—circuses, dime museums, and humor magazines—and then in the mass-production technologies of the new century—newspapers and movies—thus cementing his reputation.

In his last twenty years, when the wide horizons opened by his extraordinary gifts were diminished, McCay must often have recalled with pleasure the placid times when he could become a part of his own cartoon "Peaceable Kingdom", when he could expurgate his fears in a horrific *Rarebit Fiend* episode or, better yet, run with Little Nemo and his pals through the royal gardens and palatial halls of the king of Slumberland or, best of all, ride on the back of his very own trained dinosaur.

The McCay family of Sheepshead Bay, Brooklyn, New York, c.1907. Left to right: Maude, husband Winsor, daughter Marion, and son Robert (who was the model for Little Nemo). On the wall in the background is a photograph of Robert as an infant emerging from a lily, a quaint holdover from a nineteenth-century Victorian conceit regarding the origin of babies. (Collection Ray Winsor Moniz)

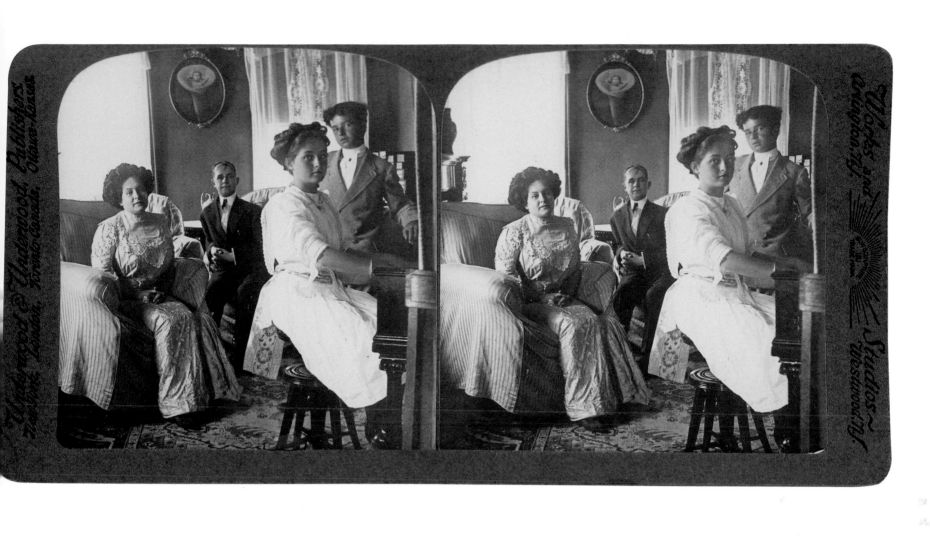

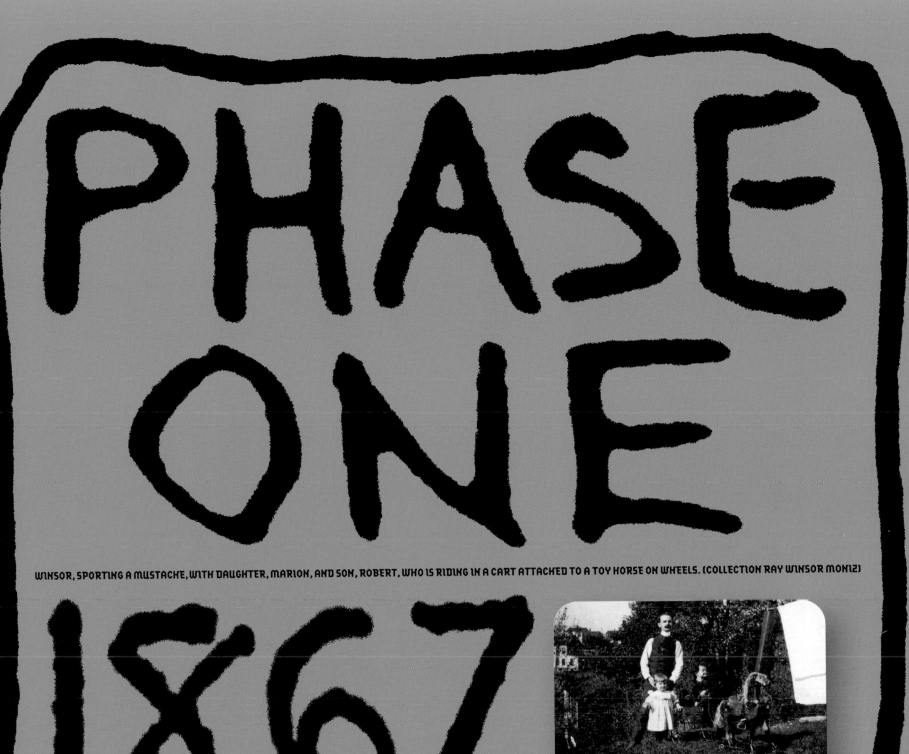

PHASE ONE

WINSOR, SPORTING A MUSTACHE, WITH DAUGHTER, MARION, AND SON, ROBERT, WHO IS RIDING IN A CART ATTACHED TO A TOY HORSE ON WHEELS. (COLLECTION RAY WINSOR MONIZ)

1867 TO 1903

chapter 1. michigan years

"Bad and good traits do not always last beyond puberty, that parting ways of dispositions."

—WINSOR McCAY'S DIARY, C. 1906–08

In the township of West Zorra, near Woodstock, Ontario, Canada, Robert McKay was born in about 1840. He was the third of six children born to Donald and Christiana McKay, farmers who immigrated from Scotland to Ontario in the mid-1830s, part of the large influx of Scottish, German, and Irish settlers eager to buy cheap land and start a new life.[1] Many of the European immigrants were disillusioned by what they found in Canada: employment opportunities were limited and the western provinces were underdeveloped. For survival they turned to America, where the burgeoning frontier offered a variety of jobs in agriculture, mining, forestry, and industry.

A PICTURE OF MY- SELF AS I APPEARED AT SCHOOL IN YPSILANTI IN THE DAYS OF AULD LANG SYNE

TAN SHOES HAD NOT BEEN INVENTED THEN, NEITHER HAD THE LOUD VEST.

SILAS IN HIS INFANCY

SILAS

On January 8, 1866, in the Methodist Episcopal Church, Robert McKay married twenty-five-year-old Janet Murray, a neighbor from East Zorra. She was the third of nine children born to Peter and Mary Murray, who were, like Robert's parents, farmers and Scottish immigrants.[2] In that year the couple crossed the border of Ontario into the United States and, in almost a straight line, traveled across the state of Michigan, heading for the township of Spring Lake on the eastern, heavily wooded shore of Lake Michigan.

The fruit industry gave Spring Lake its initial boost in population, but lumbering was equally important to the town's development. From 1860 to 1910, logging was the major nonagricultural state industry. The beautiful white pine, plentiful in Michigan, played a crucial role in the development of the prairies of middle America, making possible the building of homes and barns. As early as 1874, nine sawmills thrived within the town limits of Spring Lake.

The rapid growth of the town was noted in the *Grand Rapids Eagle* of October 4, 1871: "Four years ago this place was just struggling into notice. . . . Now the place contains about twenty-five stores, several hotels, and five or six churches, the appearances of which will at once convince the sojourner that the citizens are interested in good morals as well as fruit."

The arrival of the McKays in Spring Lake was not happenstance, for Robert had first come to America in 1862, four years before his marriage.[3] While in Canada he met and was later employed by one Zenas G. Winsor (1814–1890), an American entrepreneur involved in a number of enterprises, including manufacturing, exporting, lumber, fur trading, currency exchange for land buyers, the dry-goods trade, and Nevada silver mines. In 1866 Winsor was developing oil wells and the petroleum trade in Canada; two years later in Grand Haven, the town next to Spring Lake, he engaged in the storing, forwarding, and commission business and acted as an agent for the Chicago and Grand Rapids steamboat lines.

A contemporary sketch describes Winsor without irony as "a busy man. He could never be idle. He would always be doing something, either on his own account or for somebody else. . . ." Further, he was "genial and uniformly pleasant; a gentleman . . . enjoying the good will and wishes of everybody in this community . . . ."[4]

Certainly Robert and Janet McKay had particularly good and even deep feelings toward the older gentleman, for they named their firstborn after him: Zenas Winsor McKay.

The exact date and place of birth of the child who became Winsor McCay are uncertain because of lack of documentation. His grave marker in Brooklyn reads 1869, the same date he indicated to a 1910 Brooklyn census taker. Late in his life, however, he insisted to friends and wrote in a magazine article that he was born in Spring Lake on September 26, 1871. His birth records may have been destroyed in a disastrous fire in Spring Lake in May 1893, which burned a school, several homes and businesses, and the Baptist and Methodist churches.

A different (and probably correct) date and place of birth are found in both the 1870 and 1880 Michigan census reports, which indicate that Zenas W. McKay was born in 1867 in Canada. Apparently Janet, while pregnant, chose to make the long and arduous journey back to her family in Ontario for the birth, but a search for Canadian birth records has proved futile.

Robert McKay worked first as an unskilled "teamster," probably leading a team of horses for one of Zenas G. Winsor's several businesses. In May 1870, McKay had saved enough money to purchase a parcel of land in Spring Lake for $150 from a local businessman, Aloys Bilz. From 1879 to 1881, the Michigan Business Directory listed Robert McKay's occupation as "retail grocer," and by then his family had grown to include two more children, both born in Michigan: Arthur in 1868 and Mae in 1876.

PREVIOUS PAGE:
McCay drew this self-caricature in the February 10, 1907, New York Herald, describing it as a portrait of himself "in his infancy," living in Ypsilanti. He was actually twenty-one, but even then he was nattily dressed, complete with ever-present hat and cigarette.

ABOVE:
Robert McCay (1840?–1915), father of Winsor McCay. (Collection Ray Winsor Moniz)

FAR LEFT:
A snapshot of Robert and Janet McCay, parents of the artist, perhaps at their Michigan home, c. 1914–15. (Collection Ray Winsor Moniz)

NEAR LEFT:
Janet McCay (1840?–1927), with her son Winsor and namesake great granddaughter, c. 1923. (Collection Janet Trinker)

OPPOSITE:
Zenas G. Winsor (1814–1890), manufacturing and trading entrepreneur, after whom Zenas Winsor McCay was named. (Collection Jim Van Vulpen)

In 1885 the family moved to Stanton, a town forty miles northeast of Spring Lake, where McKay paid $100 for half of two lots. In July 1887 Robert's younger brother, Hugh McKay (1853?–1932), paid $200 for land northeast of Stanton. This was the first of many land deals over a thirty-year period involving the McKay family and the Cutler & Savidge Lumber Company, one of the most extensive and best-known lumber companies in the west.[5]

Robert McKay's gradual emergence as a real-estate agent for property owned by the large lumber firm was most fortuitous. By 1886 the lumber industry in Michigan was rapidly becoming obsolete; the forests had been depleted, virtually raped, over a fifty-year period. Log mills were dismantled, and the machinery was shipped to areas more fertile for that business. The stump-littered land was sold to farmers; hoping the plow could follow the axe, the land-sellers' rallying cry was "A farmer for every forty!" Much of the land proved unsuitable for a large agricultural return, but with extraordinary effort many of the new farmers managed to produce potatoes, livestock, and dairy products.

By 1905, Robert "McCay" was a "real-estate agent and notary public" in Edmore, Michigan. His letterhead contained a small advertisement:

> Do you want to buy a FARM on the easiest terms you ever heard of
> FROM $3 PER ACRE UP?
> I have lands of several large Lumber Firms that are anxious to sell and save paying taxes, as well as improved farms belonging to people that are never satisfied anywhere.[6]

At some point Robert McKay changed the spelling of his surname to "McCay." His son Winsor (who dropped his eccentric first name Zenas in favor of his middle name) would explain that the change was effected in order to avoid a saloon fight: "Three Scotsmen of the clan McKay were looking for a fourth member of the clan to fight four members of the Irish clan Magee. . . . 'I'm not one of you,' my father pointed out. 'You see, I'm one of the clan M-c-C-A-Y.' And that," concluded Winsor McCay, "is how I got both my name and my sense of humor."[7]

A puny, oddly named child with artistic inclinations needed more than a sense of humor to survive in the rough-hewn Michigan environment where "his boon companions were the red-shirted lumberjacks, the spike-booted drinking and rollicking fellows, who made Stanton their headquarters when 'the drive' was done." Forty years later, Winsor McCay recalled his "boon companions" in a tale of fear and survival-by-quick-thinking similar to the story of his family name change, remembering "the time the bow-legged Swede lumberman chased me and I had to jump in the river to save my hide."[8]

The story of McCay's first drawing presaged his ability to remove himself from real events and transform them through his art. Told within the McCay family for years, the story holds that one of the many fires that plagued Spring Lake destroyed the McCay house one freezing night. The family was rescued and sheltered at a neighbor's home, where young Winsor "picked up a five-penny nail which was lying on the windowsill and unthinkingly commenced to etch the catastrophe on the frosted windowpane."[9] The perhaps apocryphal story does predict McCay's abilities to work quickly in a variety of mediums, even during occasions of stress and trauma, with cool detachment. Ironically, the fragile frost drawing that soon melted anticipated the temporality of the form McCay later chose as his major vehicle of expression: the easily discarded daily newspaper.

Once discovered, McCay's interest in drawing quickly became obsessive and all-consuming. "I just couldn't stop drawing anything and everything," McCay once wrote. "I did not do this to amuse someone else or to show off how good I could draw. I drew alone to please myself. I never cared at all whether anyone else liked my drawings, nor did I get discouraged if I made a bad one. I never saved my drawings. I would give them away if anybody wanted them or would throw them away. I drew on fences, blackboards in school, old scraps of paper, slates, sides of barns—I just couldn't stop."[10]

Gene Byrnes wrote in his book *A Complete Guide to Professional Cartooning* that he asked McCay in 1925 about the source of his talent:

He said it's about 15 percent talent and 85 percent hard work. Then he explained that in learning to draw, he sketched everything he saw. If he were outdoors and a horse and a wagon happened to be near, he'd draw the horse, then the wagon. He'd look at the house across the street and draw its doorway, the gate, the fence.

A cat clawing in a garbage can as a subject was not beneath his dignity. Indoors, he'd draw furniture; chairs in different angles, lamps, fireplaces, mantel-pieces, beds, silverware, glassware. He would study the wrinkles in drapery and clothing, the differences in shoes, and the shapes of hats.

Winsor's mother once told a relative that when her eldest son was six years of age "he could draw beautifully." McCay's father corroborated his son's insatiable need to draw: "From the time he was a little fellow, all the while he was in school, he was drawing pictures. He used to get whipped in school for drawing sketches on the leaves of his books until I told the teachers it was of no use; nothing could stop him."[11] His father also attested to the technical accuracy of Winsor's drawings: "His work was true, even when he was a youngster. One day he drew a picture of a sleigh-load of logs. He got every bolthead on the side represented in its proper place in the picture, and he didn't count them either. He just stood off a way from the sleigh and drew them. He even had the owner's markings on the ends of the logs."[12]

The young artist's seemingly effortless ability to add intricate detail accurately to his graphics in fact resulted from close observation and a cognitive process he later called "memory sketching." "I have never made a drawing of a box car or a coach," McCay explained, "but if I were given the order to

make one, I'll wager I could get every important detail in the trucks as well as the rest. Why? Simply because I have studied these things with my eyes; I have put them up here in my cranium, and there they'll stay until I need them."[13] McCay's magical recall of visual details would never cease to amaze many of his newspaper colleagues.

The school records for all of Montcalm county prior to 1905 were destroyed when the courthouse burned that year, so academic records on Winsor McCay do not exist. Several anecdotes confirm that he did attend school, and an interview with a boyhood chum, H. A. Woods, pinpoints McCay's attendance when he was thirteen. Woods recalled his friend's imaginative depiction of the wreck of the steamer *Alpena* during a storm on Lake Michigan in October 1880: "Winsor here drew a picture of the wreck as he imagined it on the blackboard in our school. A photographer heard about it, came over to the school, and took a picture and then sold the pictures."[14] In 1918 McCay would reveal his version of a more famous nautical disaster in the extraordinary animated film *The Sinking of the Lusitania.*

If young Winsor's artwork impressed his classmates and peers and even the community at large, it did not have the same effect on his pragmatic father. One early account described Robert McCay as "a contractor of some wealth but crude notions and simple manners [who] thought but poorly of the higher education, and [Winsor], after he had mastered the double rule of three, and made a trifling acquaintance with Webster's spelling book, was put to work in a sawmill."[15]

"What I am sorry for is that I didn't give him an artist's education," his father once admitted. "I wanted him to have a business career and I tried to educate him for it. His uncle was a mathematician and he thought it scandalous the way the boy wasted his time drawing pictures."

BELOW LEFT:
An autograph book containing signatures from 1883 through 1887 including a sketch and signature by Winsor McCay. The book was owned by "Milo" (no last name) of Chase, Michigan. "CBC" stands for Cleary's Business College located in Ypsilanti. (Courtesy Wilber and Roy Abbott)

OPPOSITE AND THE
FOLLOWING TWO
PAGES:
Three Nemo strips—from September 29, 1907 (climbing over buildings to New York harbor, p. 25), November 18, 1906 (saving Flip from a firing squad, p. 26), and January 27, 1907 (Jack Frost's palace, p. 27)— demonstrate McCay's mastery of perspective, architectural detail, animation, and overall design and layout of a newspaper page, particularly in the way the size and shape of the strip's panels accommodate the action within them. The three strips also further define Nemo's adversarial relationship with Flip before they become buddies later in the series' run. (Collection Ray Winsor Moniz)

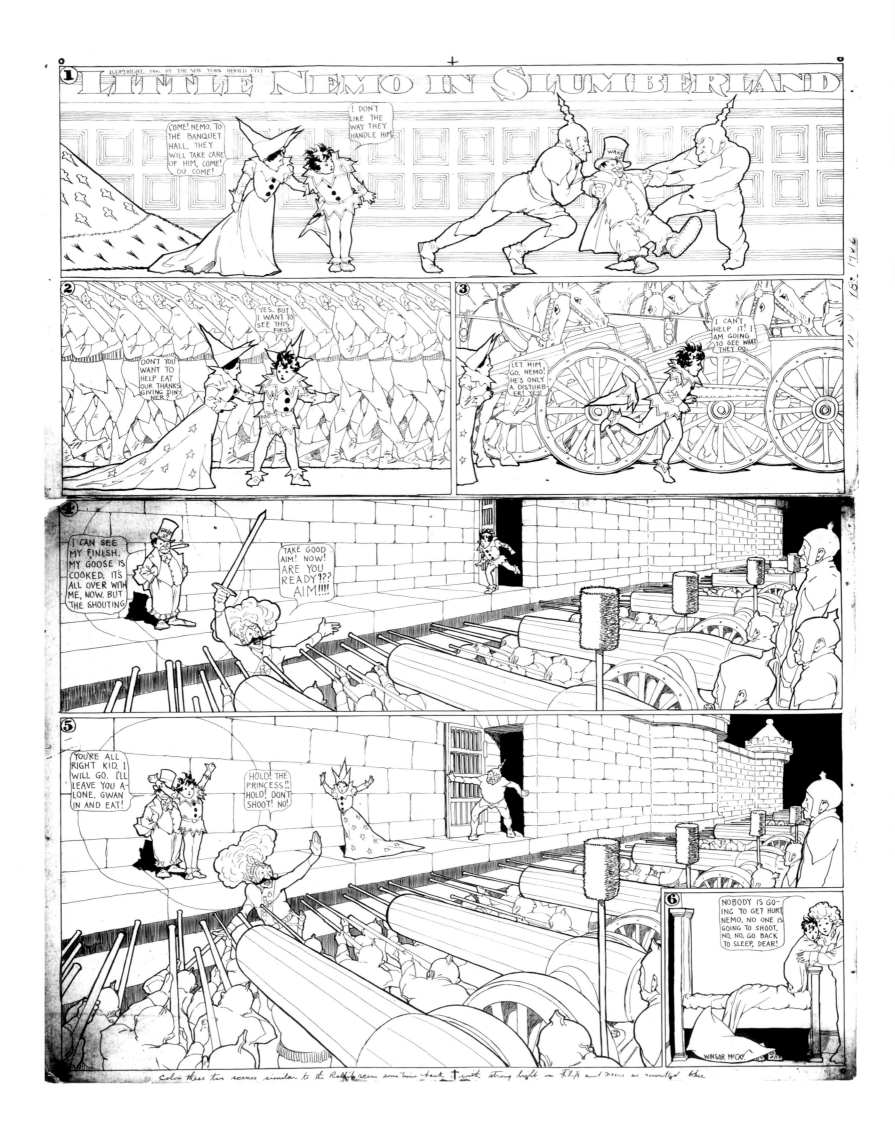

"My parents were mighty proud of my work and had dreams of my greatness," Winsor once told an interviewer in a statement that grew to a fabrication of Barnumesque proportions. "I was to be sent off to Paris to study in the ateliers."[16]

Instead, in 1886 when he was nineteen, he was packed off with four friends (who nicknamed him "Winnie") to Ypsilanti, a growing town in southeastern Michigan, to attend Cleary's Business College.[17] Years later, in one of his diaries; McCay voiced the resentment and frustration he felt as a teenager. "My parents had no more idea that I should be drawing funny pictures," he wrote, "than they did that I should fly to the moon. I don't believe they had an idea that I would amount to anything in particular."

Ypsilanti was a great deal larger than any town Winsor McCay had yet lived in. In addition to numerous small industries, there were fifteen factories manufacturing flour, plows, baseball bats, and cabinets; the largest factory turned out dress stays and bustles. Ypsilanti boasted of an opera house and a conservatory of music, two prosperous banks, and a successful Normal school. P. R. Cleary opened his business school in the fall of 1883; it survived to celebrate its centennial and continues to thrive today. At its start the institution was considered an alternative to a secondary education, and most of the students were not high school graduates. There were no entrance examinations and few age restrictions. The commercial course, which could be started at age thirteen, lasted from five months to a year, and a student could begin or end studies whenever he desired.

Perhaps an article in the June 21, 1884, *Ypsilanti Commercial Weekly* caught Robert McCay's eye. In it P. R. Cleary was depicted as a "man of enterprise" who "spares no pains to make the college one of the best in the land." Parents were advised in the article that "if they would have their sons become businessmen, they should send them where they can acquire such knowledge."[18]

Winsor and his friends rented "a large room heated with a round, cast iron wood stove and kept themselves warm with the wood they would pick up each evening on the way home."[19] For the frustrated young artist who "always had [his] heart set on a career as an illustrator or a cartoonist," attending classes in typewriting, shorthand, accounting, and office practices held no appeal. He was happy, however, to be over one hundred miles away from family tensions and the Stanton sawmills, as well as near to the big city of Detroit. His new freedom proved intoxicating, and in open rebellion against his parents, Winsor rarely attended classes nor was he ever graduated from Cleary's. Instead, while his friends worked for extra cash during the summers at the Clinker Boat Works, Winsor was hotfooting it to Detroit as often as he could to earn easy money with his drawing ability. He used to brag about his truancy: "When I was supposed to be busy with some of my studies I would skip out, catch a train for Detroit and go down to Wonderland and draw pictures."[20]

A rough pencil sketch for an early 1930s editorial cartoon shows the minimal amount of construction lines needed by McCay before he added details in pen and ink. The pencil lines indicate placement of the figure and props, and also establish the horizon line as a guide for perspective. McCay took his own advice seriously: "If you aren't familiar with the principles of perspective and try to 'get that with your eye,' you waste a lot of gray matter in nervous strain. Once you grasp the points of perspective, the rest is clear sailing. Ask yourself, 'From what vantage point will I view the thing I am about to draw?'" (Collection Ray Winsor Moniz)

Sackett & Wiggins's "Wonderland and Eden Musee" opened at Christmastime, 1886. It was a dime museum, an establishment that combined aspects of vaudeville, funhouses, and circus midway freak shows under one roof.

"I am a believer in low prices," said co-owner J. E. Sackett, who was once an associate of P. T. Barnum, whose famous prototype on Ann Street in New York inspired a flourishing of dime museums during the 1880s and 1890s.

A surviving advertisement for the week commencing Monday, October 24, 1892, offers a flavor of the kind of entertainment that delighted and influenced McCay four years earlier.

When Wonderland's doors opened from 1 to 5 P.M. and 7 to 10 P.M., visitors entered a first floor Art Gallery, Maison De Sevia Saria and Cyclorama. In the basement, wax figures posed in historical, mythical or sensational scenes, such as "Kemmler's Execution by Electricity"; "Abraham Lincoln Giving Freedom to the Slaves"; and "Rip Van Winkle Awakening from His Twenty Year's Sleep."

On the second floor, Lecture and Curio Halls contained "constantly changing" attractions. This particular week, one enjoyed Prof. Mathew's Circus of Performing Goats; Billy Wells, the "man with the Iron Skull [who] allows stones and boards to be broken on his head"; and the Family Damm Orchestra (four child violinists).

The third floor featured a Taxidermist Hall and Ladies' Parlors "fitted up for the comfort and convenience of our Lady Patrons and their escorts. A matron always in charge."

The fourth floor contained "The Finest Menagerie West of New York" where (at one time or another) one could gape at an African lion, a South American leopard, black bear, alligator, red lemur, tiger cat, red coat ocelot, lataroo tapir, badger, pig tail baboon and assorted monkeys, "Birds of all Nations," raccoons, prairie dog, skunk, iguana, and white and black rats.

Ladies entered the theater on the third floor directly from the parlors, and gentlemen entered by the theater gallery directly from the menagerie. Two afternoon and two evening performances featured an orchestra overture preceding acts such as:

Rouclere, "America's Finished Fantasist in a series of beautiful hand manipulations"; "The Dashing and Sprightly Miss Kitty Sharpe – Acknowledged to be the neatest sand dancer living"; Mildred, a mental telepathist, assisted by Rouclere, "terminating their entertainment with their original Psychognotism. First time in America"; followed by the Sisters Mendoza, "queens of the air in their startling exhibition on the aerial bars; and finishing with "The Great Salambos—Electric Dynomatic Wonders of the Age— The Sensation of all Europe."[21]

Winsor McCay's lifelong fascination with the grotesque was piqued by his exposure to dime-museum curio-hall denizens; his experiences at the Wonderland and elsewhere appeared as a *leitmotif* in all his later works.

The Wonderland gave McCay his first heady experience of making money by doing drawings. "The agreement was that I should draw pictures of patrons, sell them for 25 cents each, and get half the money. . . . I used to leave that place with my pockets bulging with money, and then I would hunt up a young telegraph operator of about my own age, who was a great friend of mine, and away we would go over to Windsor [Ontario]. My folks, of course, did not know that I made those runaway trips from Ypsilanti. And I didn't dare tell them for a long time."[22]

Equally sweet as money received in exchange for his artistic talents was the attention and admiration he attracted from his Ypsilanti schoolmates who sometimes visited Wonderland. "They immediately sighted me and swarmed about the place where I was drawing pictures." Just as ego-boosting was the dime-museum staple known as the "Old Lecturer," or "The Professor"—a loud carny barker who mounted a platform and, with grand bombastic aplomb, touted the museum's attractions. Of the young McCay, he would say: "The time will come when the pictures this young man draws of you will be valuable and you will always want to keep them. In a few years," reiterated the "Professor," "you will not want to part with the likeness which he makes of you here today."[23]

To the approval-starved young artist, this rather standard pitch sounded like a ringing endorsement of his talent and his dreams for the future. McCay would remember the barker's unremarkable spiel verbatim: "I was but a boy at the time [he was in his early twenties], and naturally to have kind things said about my drawings pleased me and the words stuck in my memory."[24]

At Wonderland McCay also learned to adapt his art to the demands of the marketplace. "A great many women and girls," he said, "had me draw their pictures, and even at that age I was wise enough to make all of them beautiful whether they were entitled to it or not. If a woman had a poor profile I would see to it that the profile in the picture was an improvement on the original, although, of course, I made it a point to get enough of a likeness to her general appearance to satisfy her that she had been the subject of [the] drawing."[25] The survival of all commercial artists depends on the appeal their art holds for the public. Throughout his career McCay always tried to give visual pleasure, whether to editors, publishers, newspaper readers, movie and vaudeville audiences, or dime-museum patrons. The wit, charm, intricacies of design, and imaginative concepts of his art stemmed from McCay's strong desire to please, to be accepted and loved, and ultimately, to survive.

McCay's growing reputation as a local artist is evident in a small notice in the *Ypsilanti Commercial* of February 10, 1888, which stated, "The work of art exhibited at the Post Office by Winsor McCay, Prof. of Drawing in Cleary's Business College, is a great credit to the young man's artistic skill." One can imagine the positive reinforcement the little exhibit and the printed review gave to McCay's confidence and pride. He certainly was not part of Cleary's teaching staff, so the sobriquet "professor" must have seemed another approbation of his talents.

Of all the positive experiences Ypsilanti offered to Winsor McCay, none would prove more important than the instruction in art he absorbed from Professor John Goodison of Michigan State Normal (now Eastern Michigan University). McCay was never a student at Normal, but his local reputation as an artist of promise brought him Goodison's attention and an offer of private lessons. Goodison's teachings constituted the only formal art education McCay would ever receive, and they profoundly influenced his work. McCay would recall, "Professor Goodeson [sic] was a great drawing teacher."[26]

John Goodison was born in 1834 in England and came to the United States in the fall of 1852. Four years later he entered Michigan State Normal, and upon graduation he taught geography and drawing there from 1860 to 1869. He left to work in the publishing business but returned in 1883 to teach until his death."[27] McCay contended that the "venerable" professor had returned to academe because he thought of "a new idea of teaching perspective," and so "with the enthusiasm of youth he gathered about him six youngsters who seemed to have a talent for drawing, the idea being 'try it on the dogs.' I was one of the 'dogs' . . . when I had a chance to receive Goodeson's [sic] instruction I jumped at it."[28]

The eager pupil learned the strict application of the perspective fundamentals to his drawings. The Normal school catalog of 1861 gives a measure of Goodison's basic approach:

> Real objects and not copies form the subjects of the lessons, and the laws of Perspective are learned by observation. The lessons include drawing the geometrical solids and objects of similar form, construction of shadows and reflections, leaf and flower forms and the elements of Linear Perspective. In addition a drill in printing on the blackboard and in drawing lines, angles and plane figures, is given.

Further details regarding the method of instruction were set down in the 1885 yearbook, which stated, "No drawing books are used. The instruction is given from the blackboard and large scale crayon drawings. The course also includes lessons in harmony and contrast of color."

To read Winsor McCay's recollection of his lessons is to hear Professor Goodison himself speaking through his most talented "dog":

If I were teaching amateur cartoonists I would set up a cone, a sphere, a cylinder and a cube before my pupils and say, "Draw nothing but these things for the next two months." When you have learned to draw them well, you will be able to draw anything—including cartoons.

For instance, if you can draw a sphere, you can draw automobile wheels and if you can draw a cube you can easily adapt it to the shape of an automobile. It is fundamentally important to understand the figures of solid geometry for every possible angle before you attempt to draw modifications of those figures. . . . Once you grasp the points of perspective, the rest is clear sailing. Ask yourself "From what vantage point will I view the thing I am about to draw?"

Any ordinary artist with an active imagination can learn to draw cartoons by first mastering perspective—lines, forms and shadows. When you draw the picture of a man standing on the ground, let him be on the ground, not somewhere up in the air. When you draw a building or a locomotive, make it look like what it's supposed to represent. You need a sixth sense—a sense of substance—which tells you, for instance, that a well-constructed table stands firmly on the floor with all four legs; its top does not jut into the air like a sliding-board.[29]

"If that young fellow doesn't smoke too many cigarettes," said Goodison of McCay, "the world is going to hear from him. He has absorbed all my teaching."[30] Professor Goodison's influence can be seen most dramatically in McCay's comic strip *Little Nemo in Slumberland*, where the diligent and masterful application of the laws of perspective supports the illusion of reality in a fantasy world and enhances its sincerity. "I admit I cannot draw any better than average," McCay once said, "but critics say my knowledge of perspective makes my drawings look snappy."[31] In both his comic strips and animated films, McCay had a pragmatic approach to fantasy, which Donald Crafton finds "profoundly consistent with the traditional concerns of American artists in general for solidity, pragmatism, and pictorial realism." The principles of perspective brought the meaning of McCay's imagery, with its "closed forms and trompe l'oeil illusionism,"[32] closer to the minds of his audience. Years later Walt Disney did the same thing in his animated feature films.

Under Goodison's tutelage McCay reinforced his powers of observation, useful for "memory sketching"; McCay's ability to make quick, dynamic blackboard sketches, like that of the *Alpena* disaster, was sharpened by Goodison's blackboard drills; his skill eventually would dazzle vaudeville audiences. McCay's bold sense of color contrast was strengthened because of Goodison's influence, for the teacher had once worked as a glass-stainer before entering Michigan State Normal. McCay also gained from Goodison a healthy respect for artists of the past, their masterpieces and discoveries.

And so McCay decided to move on. His brief time in Ypsilanti and its environs had been profitable for him in terms of self-knowledge. A career in business was out of the picture, definitely, but a life as an artist—a life his family considered a scandalous waste of time—was no longer just a dream but a real possibility. He was restless and wanted to surrender to a natural wanderlust he had only begun to explore, a nomadism that would be fully indulged during a decade on the vaudeville circuits. He wanted to try his luck in a bigger city, where a bigger audience would be waiting to appreciate his talents. He felt confident that he could survive by exploiting his drawing ability, but he was unsure where to do it outside of dime museums.

John Goodison inspired him, gave him an appetite for learning, and then advised him to seek further training at the Art Institute of Chicago. In McCay's already remarkable draftsmanship, Goodison saw a possibility for a life in art that would transcend cheap commercial exploitations of his gift. The seed of a larger dream was planted in the youth: maybe he would paint in Parisian ateliers after all. Anything was possible.

chapter 2. chicago to cincinnati

> "... the American go-getter, though he has no quarrel with the status quo, is as much a perpetual juvenile as any revolutionary."

> —ERIC HOFFER, *THE TEMPER OF OUR TIME*

Winsor McCay and a pal from Ypsilanti named Mort Touvers arrived in Chicago on an unknown date in 1889.[1] It is said that McCay passed the hat among his friends back home to pay for train fare and to protect the thirty dollars he had saved from portraiture work at the Wonderland. He dared not ask for financial help from his father; Robert McCay tolerated his son's art lessons with John Goodison in the hope that he would begin to take his business studies at Cleary's seriously. Instead, the irresponsible young man, who would be twenty-two that fall, had run off to pursue more art lessons in a sprawling metropolis of a million souls.

The rise of Chicago from the ashes of the great conflagration of 1871 was spectacular. Within three years all traces of the great fire that destroyed over 17,000 buildings and left 100,000 people homeless were gone. The year McCay arrived, 11,608 new buildings were constructed, and the city had grown to 172 square miles. The Chicago that the smalltown "boy" confronted was a brawny, busy center of industry and trade, a major railroad hub to the nation, sending wheat and beef to the East and cloth goods and farm machinery to the West.

Accounts of McCay's brief stay in Chicago are, like many areas of his personal history, spotty and contradictory. It is certain he never studied at the Art Institute; one source claims he was unable to afford the tuition. Another story asserts that McCay attended an unnamed art school, "but it closed after four days—and he did not bother again with conventional artistic education."[2]

He found employment as an apprentice at the National Printing and Engraving Company at 119 Monroe Street, a firm specializing in "Show, Commercial and Railroad Printing."[3] The circus was an especially lucrative customer for such promotional tools as the illustrated poster, which had become common as woodcut printing techniques and then stone lithography improved. Large circuses used 5,000 to 8,000 half-sheet- or one-sheet-size posters in every city they played.

The eight-page magazine-format advertisement *Avant Courier of W.W. Cole's Monster Exhibitions*, prepared by the National Printing and Engraving Company in about 1886, exemplified the type and style of material McCay would have worked on. The 9-by-13-inch booklet contained columns of shameless hyperbole ("Two Continent, World-famous, New and Massive Circus, Museum, Aquarium, Menagerie of Trained Animals, and Congress of Living Wonders. A Stupendous and Majestic Consolidation of Creation's Marvels Far Surpassing All Previous Enterprises . . . "), separated by center sections of ornate illustrations and headlines. The page space is dense with words in varied typefaces and pictures; an inconsistency in the quality of the draftsmanship suggests that a number of artists of varying abilities contributed to the illustrations. For example, the "South Sea Savages or Maori War Dancers" are clumsily executed, with torsos bent in ungraceful poses and poor foreshortening of arms and legs. A male lion is ill-proportioned, with head and mane taking up half of its form and claws too large for its limbs. Animals, especially horses, fare better than human figures; horses cavort throughout the book in a variety of graceful action poses—flying through hoops of fire, leaping over a row of fellow stallions, or circling the sawdust ring with acrobats atop them.

After a long day in a large room filled with men working with stipple gravers, chisels, gouges, and burnishers or in rooms with huge presses and drying trays and finely ground dry ink colors, McCay went home to a cheap room in a boardinghouse at 185 Dearborn Street. Living at the same address was Jules Guérin (1866–1946), who became a noted American painter, illustrator, and muralist, with work decorating the Lincoln Memorial in Washington, D.C., and

Pennsylvania Station in New York. The young men "had three things in common—they were poor, ambitious and talented. . . . In lieu of an art instructor, [they] taught each other their respective specialties . . . McCay, the master of perspective and detail; Guérin, the master of figure and color."[4]

During his time in Chicago, it seems possible that Winsor McCay joined the secret fraternal order of Freemasonry, of which he remained a lifelong member. McCay's father, Robert, was a lifelong Mason and was buried with full Masonic rites when he died in 1915, so there was precedent and familiarity with the Masonic organization within Winsor's family. A letter of sympathy containing Masonic quotations was sent to Winsor McCay's family upon his death in 1934 from Charles J. Wuest of Chicago, who claimed he and the late artist were fellow Masons whose long friendship began when they were apprentices at the National Printing and Engraving Company.

Freemasonry, which began in the Middle Ages as an early trade union for stonemasons and cathedral builders and evolved into a "system of morality veiled in allegory and illustrated by symbols,"[5] was no doubt an appealing craft-oriented organization to the two young Midwesterners. First, there was the social aspect: an exclusive club of like-minded males enjoying the camaraderie of friends who participate in secret rituals before enjoying a meal together. On a deeper level, there was the spiritual content of the society. Freemasonry is not a religion but instead embraces all forms of religious belief that include the concept of a supreme being and adheres to qualities of charity, fraternity, idealism, and humanity. The free approach to spirituality, plus the secrecy and use of symbols in Freemasonry, attracted McCay, an agnostic who believed in reincarnation. That Freemasonry had always encountered strong opposition from organized religions, especially the Roman Catholic Church, was a plus for the rebellious McCay, a young bohemian artist intent on finding his way in life outside the traditional routes of bourgeois society. (Ironically, McCay's later success in the commercial arts transformed him rapidly into the quintessential American bourgeois consumer.)

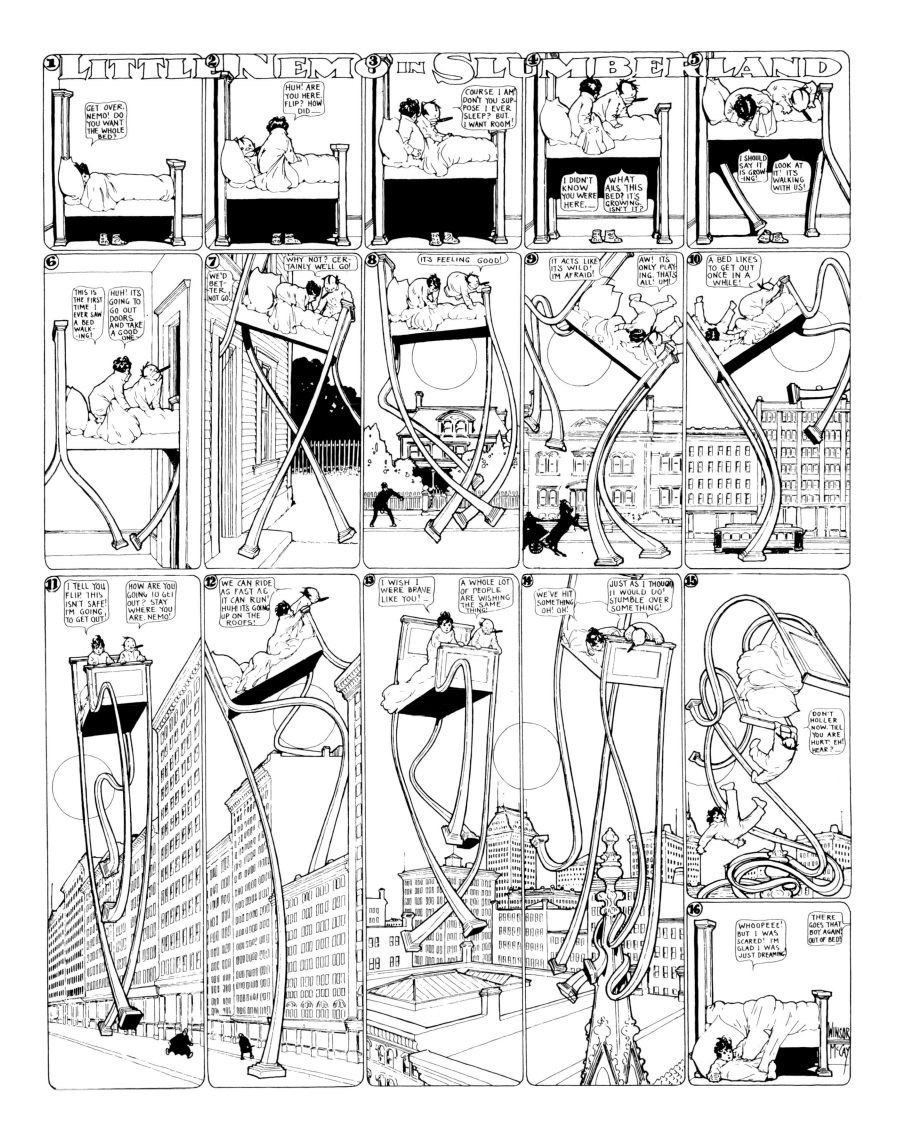

ST JOHN'S
Wed. AUG. 17

AVANT COURIER
of W. W.
COLE'S
MONSTER EXHIBITIONS

AERIAL BICYCLE RIDING

NATIONAL PRINTING COMPANY, SHOW PRINTERS AND ENGRAVERS, 119 MONROE STREET & 2, 4, 6 & 8 CUSTOM HOUSE PLACE, CHICAGO, ILL.

In his later works, McCay never lost an opportunity to use his irreverent, iconoclastic humor to twit the Pecksniffian hypocrisy of religious leaders and practitioners. For example, in the *Dream of the Rarebit Fiend* series, a parson is sent to hell to melt in a pit of hot Limburger cheese (December 2, 1904); a missionary sent to "teach the heathen" is stripped and eaten by black cannibals, who complain about the toughness of the "old hard shell skinflint" (March 11, 1905); a preacher curses vociferously (June 17, 1905). McCay even spoofed the secrecy rule of the Masons: a man confides the club secrets to his wife, who in turn reveals them to a women's club, resulting in the husband being tarred and feathered by his "brothers" (February 1, 1905). The most subtle of McCay's anticlerical jokes appeared in the famous walking bed episode of *Little Nemo in Slumberland* (July 26, 1908): the galloping bed loses its joyous power and mobility when its long legs trip over a church steeple.

McCay's attitude toward organized religion was probably passed on to him from his father; McCay enjoyed repeating an anecdote about the time his father was taken ill in Michigan: "The family thought the old man was going to pass out . . . so they got in touch with the minister [who] came over, and it was a touchy subject and he just didn't know how to broach it. Finally, he said, 'Mr. McCay, you have not been a regular member of the church. Don't you think it's about time you made your peace with God?'" To which Robert McCay answered: "Peace with God? We never had any trouble. In all my life, we're not unfriendly!"[6]

In the 1889 Chicago city directory, W. Z. McCay listed his occupation as "printer"; by 1890 he was Windsor [sic] Z. McCay, "artist." Whether or not he had left the employ of National Printing that year is unknown, but given McCay's capacity later in his career to take on several jobs at once, he may have supplemented his income by moonlighting at a dime museum. A 1909 account of McCay's early days states he was "engaged by a museum manager to paint the signs and ornamental announcements of the various freaks exhibited from week to week . . . guided by an imagination stimulated, frequently, by things stronger than water . . . [McCay] enlarge[d] upon these designs, illustrating them with semi-caricatures of the bearded lady and the dog-faced boy, together with the other profitably deformed exhibits who drew generous salaries for attempting to look like Mac's grotesque but attractive illuminations."[7]

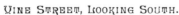

VINE STREET, LOOKING SOUTH.

After two restless years in Chicago, the footloose McCay relocated 250 miles away in Cincinnati, where he worked as an artist in a dime museum. As usual, a number of romantic stories, as doubtful as they are colorful, explain his move. One version claims his "fondness for the company of people in the show business led him sometimes to take trips with their troupes and it was one of these expeditions that finally landed him in Cincinnati."[8] Throughout McCay's career, he would unhesitatingly leave one job for a better one only when he had a definite offer; it is unlikely that McCay could have afforded to wander at will with traveling performers if his survival depended on his earnings from jobs in Chicago.

Another story contends McCay was hired by a circus as a traveling poster painter: "Arriving in Cincinnati ahead of the circus, he literally painted the town red with masterful posters depicting circus scenes. . . ."[9] The anecdote is problematic because, during the Golden Age of the American show poster

(1880–1920), advance crews handling circus promotions hung ready-made printed posters (such as those made by the National Printing and Engraving Company), not handpainted ones.

A far more likely explanation for McCay's departure is that the dime museum that employed McCay in Cincinnati belonged to Chicago entrepreneurs Charles E. Kohl and George Middleton. In 1886 they sent John Avery, a "canvasser," to Cincinnati to take over the management of the Vine Street Dime Museum. The next year the establishment was renamed Kohl & Middleton's New Dime Museum, and under Avery's management it featured hourly stage shows of "Transient and Permanent Curiosities without number . . . Freaks, fun and frolic from foreign lands for fictions fancy." Avery traveled back to Chicago on occasion to report to Kohl and Middleton and would have been exposed to McCay's colorful

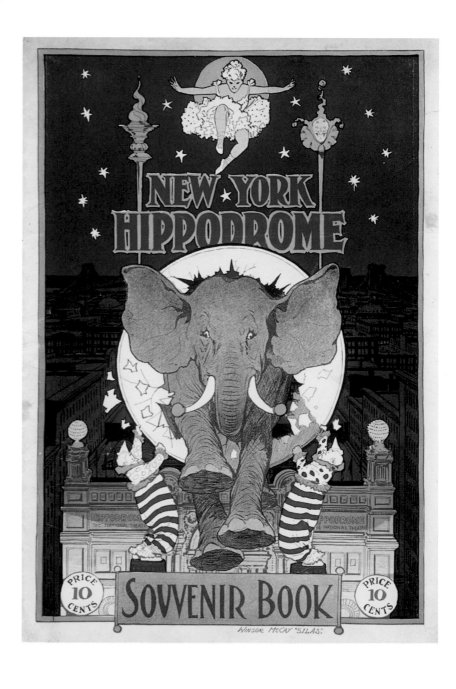

posters and signs. Realizing the skillful young artist's attention-grabbing art could be useful in promoting the new Cincinnati version of the Chicago dime museum, Avery offered McCay a job.

In an interview in 1911 in Atlanta with a fifteen-year-old aspiring cartoonist, Frank L. Stanton, Jr., McCay discussed the problem of earning a living when starting out in "this cold, cold world." He advised the boy that "determination is the main thing . . . push yourself. If you go out with the idea that you're not going to make good, you never will."[10]

Winsor McCay had few problems with self-motivation. His extraordinary energy, combined with his love of drawing, practically catapulted him into jobs. At this point in 1891, however, his work experience consisted only of brief tenures at two dime museums and a printing firm. But he had enhanced his skills and developed his graphic vocabulary enormously through determination and an openness to learning on the job.

In Ypsilanti McCay was introduced to the discipline of the laws of perspective, and he also honed his observational skills. In Detroit he learned how to please the public and make money from his artwork. Chicago tested his mettle for survival; his experience there added precision and patience to his repertoire and expanded his feeling for line, space, and color.

The world of the circus informed the imagery in McCay's art as much as freak shows and dime museums did. His work abounds with clowns, acrobats, dancers, exotic and fantastic animals, trick mirrors, and grotesque and bizarre creatures, both human and superhuman. The large-scale elaborate layouts and detailing in McCay's greatest comic strip, *Little Nemo in Slumberland*, recall the design of theatrical and circus posters. The frozen action of the characters' poses suggests the spirit of kinetic live performances by people and animals.

In addition to artistic ability, energy, and determination, another element contributed to Winsor

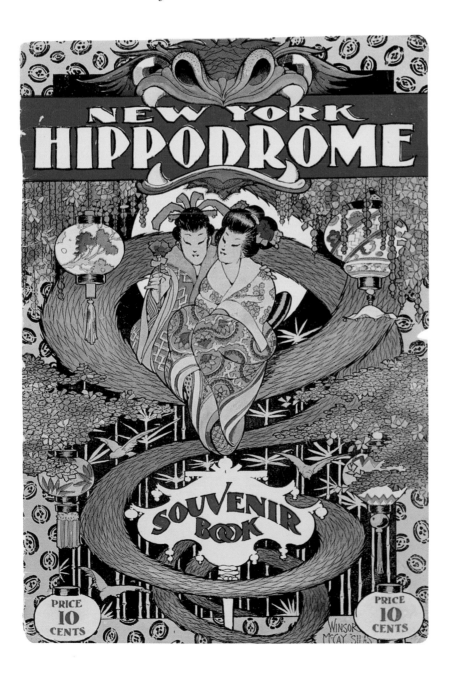

McCay's success: ambition. He was never shy about promoting himself or his work, although paradoxically he was introverted and self-effacing in his private life. McCay was evidently a man of great personal charm, in possession of a wonderfully satirical sense of humor that delighted his associates. Many of the people he met throughout his career remained lifelong friends. Whenever McCay played theaters in Detroit or Chicago, for instance, he would contact men he had first met a quarter of a century before; at his death, school friends from Ypsilanti and former printing plant apprentices from Chicago sent sorrowful letters and telegrams to McCay's family.

In Cincinnati McCay took a room at Crawford House, probably on the advice of John Avery, who also rented there when he first arrived in the city. The boardinghouse at Sixth Street and Walnut was convenient to the dime museum, located on Vine Street between Fifth and Sixth.

On the top floor of the four-story stone building that housed the museum, McCay worked in "a dingy little room . . . without adequate materials or tools."[11] In that small studio, McCay for the next nine years painted advertisements and posters ballyhooing the weekly attractions, such as the midget Jennie Quigley ("the Scottish Queen") or three albino children with pink eyes or the "Armless Wonder." Snakes were said to be a McCay specialty, and "next to these it was his joy to picture Joe-Joe, the dog-faced boy in some of his fiercest moods. . . . The 'Missing Link' and Anna Mills, the girl with the prodigious feet, were his third choice . . . or the 'What Is It' crunching a thigh bone between his saw-like teeth."[12] Soon, "the many canvasses upon the store front of the museum attracted curious and admiring crowds."

The museum was open from 1 P.M. to 10 P.M., and for the price of a dime the public could wander about the so-called Peoples' Popular Place of Pleasure, and Family Resort. In the 1924 book *Pioneers of Night Life on Vine Street*, Frank Y. Grayson recalled often putting in a day "reveling in the blood-chilling exhibits" at the "grim old" Kohl & Middleton Dime Museum. The exhibits were often tricked-up hokum, such as the "Wild Man of Afghanistan" who "in his off-hours was a good-natured and harmless colored giant who

pushed a handcart down in the West End. But when chained up and eating a raw meat, and growling maniacally, he was a fearsome-looking object and drove sleep away from the cots of many boys and grown-ups, too."

Other exhibits included "the fire eater, the glass eater, the two-headed calf, the 'savage' who walked on broken glass and upturned spikes! He also was a colored man who had spent forty years of his life barefoot. He could have walked on razor blades without causing him more than a tickle . . . all the other anatomical clowns regularly appeared at the museum, and they struck up a wide acquaintanceship in the city. They were a harmless bunch. It was a soft way and the only way they knew in which to make a living."

In the auditorium, traveling troupes of actors and musical performers amused the customers. Amateur nights featured local talents, such as James Owen O'Connor, the "only man who ever played Hamlet behind a net . . . necessary because when James Owen would meet up with the ghost the audience would relieve itself of a barrage composed of about everything from cats to onions." There was "little old" Susie Periwinkle, who did a song in which her voice cracked and a dance during which her bones creaked. Tobe Johnson danced and did acrobatic stunts with his one good leg and "one yaller crutch." Tiny Philips, a newsboy who had a stand at Sixth and Vine and liked to chase fire engines, did an imitation of the famous minstrel Billy Emerson that was letter-perfect except for a pronounced lisp.

The unwary museum visitor was advised to "pin your pocket" upon entering, for the place attracted a number of "patriarchal and benevolent con-men and shell-workers [who] were so smooth and unctuous in their work that . . . Cousin Josh from the rural districts, to whom a visit to the museum was a rare treat, was expeditiously, but soothingly, separated from his $5 bill . . . . "

The Vine Street Dime Museum would have been where Winsor McCay saw his first motion picture at a demonstration in 1896 of Edison's Vitascope projection device. As Frank Grayson remembered it:

The picture was dim and weavy, and it would have taken the entire census-taking force of the United States Government ten years to have counted the flickers in it. In the picture the train was headed directly toward the audience. On the opening night of the picture's run there was a larger audience than usual, having been attracted by the advance notices [and McCay's posters]. . . . When the picture was flashed and the monster locomotive was seen bearing down . . . there was a wild scramble to get off the track. One fat man in the middle of the house leaped to his feet and yelled "Stop her! Oh, my gosh!" When the picture flashed off it was found that a man in the front row had fainted. . . . It was two hours after leaving the museum that those who were present at this epoch-making event regained clear vision.

Vine Street was equivalent to New York's Broadway, Chicago's State Street, and San Francisco's Market Street. It was a jolly, robust thoroughfare during the 1890s, the spinal column of Cincinnati. No one ever died of thirst on Vine Street; no less than 113 drinking places thrived on Vine between McMillan Street and the Ohio River. The street was divided into two sections: from Fourth Street to lower Central Parkway the flavor was American; in the Over-the-Rhine section running north from Central Parkway to the outlying hills, German culture, cuisine, beer, and music dominated. German immigrants arrived by the thousands in the nineteenth century, seeing another valley of the Rhine in the fertile and beautiful Ohio Valley. Their mark upon Cincinnati was profound and is reflected in the city's solid conservatism, its breweries, restaurants, art, architecture, and musical traditions.

Charles Dickens called Cincinnati "beautiful," and Henry Wadsworth Longfellow immortalized it in a poem in 1854 as the "Queen City of the West." By mid-century, the Queen City was known as "Porkopolis," the focal point of corn-growing areas of Ohio and neighboring states Kentucky and Indiana for the conversion of corn into pork and whiskey. The grand and lovely Ohio River, on which Cincinnati lies, was a major channel of commerce, nurturing the nation's largest inland port and one of the leading steamboat capitals.

Late in the nineteenth century, Cincinnati was an optimistic, bustling industrial city with a variety of business enterprises contributing to its stable economy, including the candle and soap manufacturing of Procter and Gamble, watchmaking of Gruen, musical instruments of Wurlitzer and Baldwin, yeast and gin from Fleischmann, cosmetics and soap from Jergens. Skilled workers turned out brass valves, furniture, publications, shoes, paper, machine tools, and printing inks.

As was true with many growing cities, with prosperity came problems. Several Cincinnati municipal services, including street cleaning, sewers, transportation, and water supply, lagged behind the needs of the citizenry. A boss-ridden government intimidated the business community, rigged elections, and promoted a corrupt judiciary.

The city held many economic and social ties to the South, including a strong racist attitude toward blacks. The 1891 edition of *Illustrated Cincinnati* noted there were fifty-seven school buildings and thirty district schools, and of the public school scholars "about 2.7% are colored and for the most part the colored race is kept distinct having separate schools, as the prejudice here is still very strong against them, and their demeanor is generally aggressive, and unbecoming their situation among the white people."

For most white citizens, Cincinnati was an exceedingly pleasant place to live, a city that offered the opportunities of a metropolis while retaining the grace and amenities of a small town. To McCay it must have seemed to be a nice combination of Ypsilanti and Chicago. "It hasn't the hurry of New York, the anger of Chicago, or the button-down sophistication that San Francisco affects . . . ," wrote Dick Perry in his book *Vas You Ever in Zinzinnati?* What Cincinnati had, contended Perry, was "innocence," meaning a guileless naiveté, a direct and simple voice heard in "Kentucky drawls, Hoosier twangs, here and there a German gutteral, Negro laughter, and the newsboy's garbled cry."

Years later, McCay's son Robert (who was born in Cincinnati) told an interviewer that his "father's heart was always with the Queen City."[13]

chapter 3. cincinnati years

"Women are wonderful things—in their place."

—WINSOR McCAY

During the period McCay worked at the Cincinnati dime museum (1891–99), the establishment was always on shaky financial ground. It changed owners and names several times; in 1896, it became Heck and Avery's Family Theater and moved a few blocks away to 526 Vine Street. In 1898, it was called Avery's New Dime Museum; the next year Will S. Heck's Wonder World and Theater took over the space, and John Avery's name disappeared. The demolition of the building in 1957 made room for a parking lot and neatly destroyed any trace of McCay's surviving artwork.

The signs and posters McCay painted for the dime museum brought him a local reputation and led to other work, which helped to supplement his small income. Indeed, it was said that "interest was greater upon the outside than within the Heck and Avery emporium of wonders. By and by the passersby began to ask, 'Who is this fellow Mac, who pours out this seemingly inexhaustible supply of freak art?'"[1]

One person who showed a keen interest in McCay's artwork was a fellow sign painter named Philip Morton. Ph. Morton, as he preferred to be known professionally, was the same age as Winsor McCay, but he possessed business acumen and an ambition to expand in his field that McCay would never emulate or even understand. Morton began as a sign painter's apprentice, painting scenes and advertising (mostly for tobacco firms) on the sides of houses and other suitably large spaces. He soon went into business for himself, then branched out in 1888, the year of Cincinnati's centennial exposition, into constructing bulletin boards. Gradually he added surrounding towns and then Cleveland to his field of operations. At the turn of the century, Ph. Morton controlled most of the large signboards in cities and along railroad lines all over the United States and Canada, having bought out and absorbed nearly every other concern of that kind in the country. With the advent of the automobile, Morton was there with his billboards coast to coast along highways and streets. He owned an immense printing and lithography plant and employed over 200 workers in design, painting, and erection of the signs. When he died in 1941, Morton's twelve-room mansion in the fashionable Mount Airy section of Cincinnati exceeded one million dollars in value, and he was the largest individual property owner in the city.

The portly and practical Ph. Morton often hired the wiry and imaginative Winsor McCay to paint advertising assignments. Standing before a blank canvas, McCay would "do a little jig, rolling countless cigarettes to stimulate his thought. As he jigged and hummed a little tune, McCay would start to mix his pigments and begin his sketches with crayon for outlines. In a short time, the figures would appear, and then would come the vivid coloring."[2]

McCay's technique—the construction of a figure's outline in one continuous stroke—was a crowd pleaser and satisfied his need to perform before a live audience. William Apthorp ("Ap" or "Doc") Adams, onetime billboard painter with McCay and later head of the art department of the *New York American*, recalled the astonishment of McCay's fellow sign painters over "how he could draw a perfect outline without once stopping after he began, or without looking at the sketch at all until he had completed it. Unfailingly the sketch would be perfectly proportioned and exact in detail and execution. Seldom indeed was it that any part of his one-line figures had to be redrawn. The sight of him drawing an eight-foot woman—almost two and a half feet taller than himself—in a single line from a position atop a sugar barrel is one sight I'll never forget."[3]

The unforgettable performance was referred to by Damon Runyon in a 1922 newspaper column: "Whenever we went to Cincinnati with the Giants in the old days," he wrote, "there used to be a jeweler there who was fond of taking us out in the street, pointing at a store building on the corner, and announcing: 'There's where I first saw Winsor McCay. He was standing up there on a platform, drawing advertising pictures for a crowd in the street.'"[4]

Ph. Morton involved his friend McCay in a nearly disastrous three-dimensional art-and-performance piece in the summer of 1898. It was a Cincinnati celebration of the victory of the American bluejackets over Admiral Cervera's fleet off Santiago, Cuba, on July 3, among the closing events of the Spanish-American War. The battle, which resulted in Cervera's being taken prisoner and the whole Spanish fleet's destruction, was to be re-created in a floating pageant on the Ohio River. Papier-mâché model ships were designed by McCay and mounted on two separate coal barges. The plan was to tow both manned barges to the center of the river where, amid fireworks, the fleeing Spanish fleet would be "destroyed."

The banks of both sides of the Ohio River—Cincinnati on the Ohio side and Covington on the Kentucky side—were lined with spectators, all waiting expectantly. McCay, playing the part of Cervera, and Morton were manning the Spanish fleet; at McCay's signal a cannon boomed and Cervera's ships raised the Spanish flag. This was the signal to a tugboat attached to the barge to start towing it into the river.

Unfortunately, it also signaled all hell to break loose, for suddenly "hoodlums and over-zealous patriots" began throwing stones, bottles, bricks, and sundry objects at the Spanish barge as soon as the flag was raised. McCay and Morton were struck and bleeding as the bombardment intensified and they floated farther into the river. Worse, in the excitement, the tugboat retreated, leaving the barge to float uncontrolled, dangerously heading toward the piers of the giant suspension bridge.

The battered McCay told his small crew of Spanish soldiers to shoot skyrockets (for use in the mock battle) at the bridge, and, fortunately, the distress signal was seen by rivermen who dispatched tugboats to the rescue. One tug rammed into the side of the barge to deflect its disaster-bound course. A line was thrown to the hapless crew and made fast for towing back to the starting point, where the "battle" was gamely begun again.[5]

In September Morton involved McCay in another three-dimensional display project of a more benign nature. The Grand Army of the Republic was to hold its convention in Cincinnati, with a series of ceremonies and a parade. Morton was contracted by the city to supply artwork, advertising, and a group of large triumphal arches to be constructed and placed along the G.A.R.'s march route. The arches were to be over thirty feet high, sturdy enough to allow large numbers of privileged spectators to stand on top, and decorated with eagles, flags, and medallion portraits of Grant, Lee, Lincoln, and female figures representing liberty and peace. McCay designed and painted the arches and medallions; the portraits were later purchased by Democratic leader Thomas Taggart, and, as of 1936, they decorated the rotunda of a hotel he owned in French Lick, Indiana.[6]

One day in 1891, a beautiful girl with dark eyes and luxurious black hair, wearing a long dress with a tightly cinched bodice, strolled into the dime museum. Winsor McCay fell in love. He was adding finishing touches to a painted grotesque when a lively polka was heard from the orchestra playing in the auditorium. The music's rhythm got the better of him and, brush and paint can in hand, he executed a clumsy pirouette, which was interrupted by girlish laughter.

Maude Leonore Dufour was amused by the dancing young man in the paint-encrusted overalls. She had come to the museum with her older sister Josephine to view the curiosities, and she thought the silly painter was part of the show. McCay was struck by the girl's beauty—her dark good looks, her full-blown figure, her diminutive height (she was a bit smaller than he). Impulsively he decided to ingratiate himself by presenting a more attractive image to the girl.

While the sisters wandered about the place, McCay dashed upstairs to his studio to wash and change into a custom-tailored suit, a silk shirt and cuff links, a cravat with diamond stickpin, button shoes, and a fedora. One of McCay's personal trademarks throughout his life was to be impeccably overdressed. He usually worked with his hat on, and because he perspired very little, he could wear high collars, a tie, French cuffs, and a vest under his suits in even the warmest weather. Looking like a halfsized version of a model in a J. C. Leyendecker illustration, the resplendent McCay sought out his future wife in the halls of the odd museum and introduced himself.

He learned Maude was the youngest of three daughters born to a French-Canadian carriage painter, John Dufour, who had died recently. She lived on nearby Main Street with her mother, Sarah, who was a hotel pastry cook, and her middle sister, Stella. Maude's seductive speech pattern, a sort of Midwestern twang and Southern drawl (which all the Dufour women affected), enchanted McCay, as did her pouty, childlike vivacity. She acted like a child because she was fourteen years old, a decade younger than Winsor. When she first saw McCay covered in paint, he must have reminded Maude of her late father.

A whirlwind courtship ensued. Cincinnati offered a young couple many places to go on a date. In any season they could attend high-class vaudeville or the opera; they might stroll through lovely Eden Park or go bowling in Chester Park. They might view paintings at the art museum or have dinner on a riverboat moored on the Ohio River. In summer they could catch the train at the Fourth Street depot or an elec-

tric car from Fountain Square to the Latonia Race-tracks in nearby Kentucky. Or for twenty-five cents they could take a twenty-mile "palatial steamer ride on the breeze swept Ohio" and end up at Coney Island, an amusement park on the river with a mid-way and band concerts.

Soon after their first meeting, Winsor and Maude eloped. Across the suspension bridge in a horse-and-buggy they rode to Covington, Kentucky, where they were married before a justice of the peace.[7] McCay's conflicting birth dates may have stemmed from a desire to decrease the gap between his age and that of his young wife. His obituary in the *Herald Tribune* stated that "not even Mr. McCay knew his exact age." Maude had her own problems with age and aging; according to family members, she "hated to grow old and dyed her hair jet black until she died at age seventy-two . . . she hated being called 'grandma' and insisted the family call her 'Nan' instead."[8]

In one romantic gesture, McCay, the oft-described "thorough bohemian," took on bourgeois married life and its attendant financial responsibilities. Neverthe-less, throughout forty-three years of marriage to Maude, McCay was ambivalent toward the married

state. Although he loved his family dearly, he main-tained a virulent attitude toward marital hypocrisy and a rueful sorrow for his lost bachelor freedom. Some of his later comic strip titles drip with sardonic irony: *It's Great to Be a Husband, It's Nice to Be Married,* and *Ain't You Glad You're Not a Mormon?*

McCay accepted the cultural imperative that he grow up, find a mate, and settle down to married life by becoming a breadwinner. In his fantasy world, however, he was Peter Pan, angry at being tied down and expressing the then-predominant attitude of American males that women were generally super-fluous and merely to be tolerated. During the long duration of the comic strip *Little Nemo in Slumberland,* female characters were few in a male-dominated world. The bonding between Nemo and his buddies (Flip and Impie) was stronger and truer than the tepid relationship between Nemo and the pretty but vapid Princess. Nemo's most exuberant adventures occurred with his male companions, when the Princess did not intrude. The *Dream of the Rarebit Fiend* strip series provided numerous examples of antagonistic relationships between men and women;

Maude McCay in the parlor of her home in Sheepshead Bay, c. 1907. (Collection Ray Winsor Moniz)

46

arguments over money, status, sexual infidelities, and petty jealousies sometimes led to open violence.

Maude played her part in the marriage well. She enjoyed being a homemaker, was an excellent cook, and kept a spotless house. She helped her husband choose his clothes and set them out for him each morning. Winsor pampered Maude from the first, and, as his income increased, he encouraged her indulgence in luxuries. He said his wife had the "mind of a little five-year-old child,"[9] but he nurtured that part of her personality by not allowing her to grow up emotionally. Maude retained her girlish temperament even as her figure thickened, her voice deepened, and her drawl swooped to an often imperious and demanding pitch.

"Mrs. McCay was quick of thought and quick of action," according to family friend Maud H. Brown.

> She even talked with a rapid staccato voice . . . whatever she set her mind to, that is what she made happen . . . Windsor [sic] was a gentle soul, but he was no Milquetoast when it came to making decisions. I presume this came from the fact that he was a creator. Being original gives one power. Knowing that if you are copied, so what[?] [Y]ou can always think up something new or better."[10]

Five years after their wedding, a son, Robert Winsor, was born on June 21, 1896. To Maude's surprise and annoyance, she soon found herself pregnant again, and gave birth to a daughter (and final child), Marion Elizabeth, on August 22, 1897.

As McCay's family grew, so did his economic needs. In their first twelve years of marriage, the family moved (with mother-in-law Sarah Dufour) into ten different apartments in houses near to each other. Perhaps McCay was attracted each time by more space for a cheaper rent; or perhaps it was a spasm of his restless nomadism, of his desire to be carefree and footloose.

To support his family, McCay held on to the dime-museum job and took as many sign-painting assignments as Ph. Morton could throw his way. It was his poster art that led directly to work assignments on newspapers, which benefited his pocketbook and changed the direction of his career dramatically. Montgomery Phister explained how it came about in a newspaper article years later: "Occasionally pictures of the more curious of the monstrosities of the peculiar showhouse were in demand for newspaper use, and, as it was difficult to persuade the regularly employed newspaper artists to devote their attention to these nightmares, it was suggested to manager Avery that he have Mac—no one knew him as Winsor McCay in those days—make the drawings for the press."

With characteristic eagerness, McCay agreed to draw the ads and took his first lessons in "process drawing" from Joseph Alexander, the manager of the *Commercial Tribune* art room. Used to working with pencil, brush, and paint, McCay "took slowly to the pen at first, but eventually became so proficient in its use that he began dispensing small hints that he would not be averse to accepting a position on the staff of the paper."[11]

"I was a long time finding out what kind of board, ink, pens, and other utensils were needed," McCay recalled. "I did not know that one should draw his cartoons bigger than they were to be made into cuts. I did not know about the quality and quantity of lines for good clear reduction."[12]

An offer was made to McCay to join the *Tribune,* but at first he "rejected it because of his loyalty to John Avery. Eventually, [with] things growing still more discouraging at the museum, Avery advised him to look out for his own advancement."[13] In 1898 Avery left the dime museum, as well as Cincinnati, and so McCay joined the *Commercial Tribune.* Editor Charles J. Christie offered McCay "the same money you're getting at the dime museum and I'll make a newspaperman out of you. The best god damned newspaper cartoonist in the country, that's what I'll make of you!" To which Winsor McCay replied, "Where can I hang my coat?"[14]

Newspaper illustration work was an important "school" for many American artists, including Winslow Homer, John French Sloan, and William Glackens, among others. As an artist-reporter, McCay developed both a realistic and a decorative style that would coalesce later in his comic strips. The range of subjects McCay was assigned challenged his graphic virtuosity. For example, McCay's January 16, 1898, rendering of the Hamilton Law Library was photographic in its architecturally realistic drafts-manship; rows of bookshelves, desks, pillars, chairs, statuary, fans, and lights excessively fill the space from high and low angles, and complex crosshatching adds textural variety to the objects. On January 30, McCay was asked to draw a large illustration of the scene in Havana harbor the day after the arrival of the U.S. battleship *Maine*. Working from photographs and eyewitness reports, McCay showed the ships approaching in perspective, with a lighthouse and rocks on the left in a tightly realistic design; sea waves and smoke effects were slightly stylized. (Less than a month later the *Maine* was blown up, an event that led to the Spanish-American War.)

On February 13, McCay illustrated a traffic jam in midtown Cincinnati, again obsessively filling every space with detail: electric cars surrounded by crowds of citizens. A large building in the background is per-fectly rendered in perspective, and McCay experi-mented with dividing the space by providing closeups of events seen from interesting angles. For example, enclosed within a circle is the aftermath of a collision between a horse-and-buggy and a trolley, with police picking up fruit and examining the damage. In a rec-tangular space at the bottom of the drawing, a sea of heads bobs in perspective, awaiting the approach of the trolley as if it were a boat sailing through water.

In September McCay drew full-page illustrations of the Grand Army of the Republic parade and cele-brations in several editions of the *Commercial Tribune* that are spectacular in scale and detail. The perspec-tive of the buildings and memorial arches, the indi-vidualization and variety of poses of the marching men and cheering crowds demonstrate McCay's reliance on his lessons with Professor Goodison and on his memory-sketching technique. These master-ful, almost photographic sketches were also not very subtle self-promotions for the many talents of the artist who signed himself "Winsor Mc." Most of the daily drawings of the parade prominently featured the arches McCay had designed. In the September 7,

1898 sketch, he drew the side of the street containing the *Tribune* building where he worked and placed his signature at the bottom on the same side, thus con-necting his name with his place of employment.

McCay's taste for fantasy and humor was also tapped by the *Tribune;* for example, a series of simply drawn caricatures illustrating the poems of Jack Appleton, called "An International Episode," featured anthropomorphic battling vegetables reminiscent of the drawings of Grandville (Jean-Ignace-Isidore Gérard, 1803–1847).

Another profitable outlet for Winsor McCay's drawing skill was freelance work for the humor mag-azine *Life*. By the 1890s *Life, Puck,* and *Judge* were the three top humor periodicals in a format that had migrated to America from Europe in the last third of the nineteenth century. Founded in 1883 by architect and illustrator John Ames Mitchell, *Life* built its read-ership on the work of a group of fine cartoonists. The most famous of these was Charles Dana Gibson, who sold his first cartoon to the magazine in 1886. His ide-alized American woman—known internationally as the Gibson Girl—became a national symbol and obscured the artist's gifts as an extraordinarily sensi-tive master of the subtle expressions found in the human face.

McCay's favorite *Life* cartoonist was A. B. Frost (1851–1928), whom he considered "the greatest comic draftsman in the history of this country."[15] Frost achieved prominence in the humor magazines and scores of books, most notably the *Uncle Remus* series by Joel Chandler Harris. He shared with McCay a self-taught drawing ability, a satiric visual humor, and an ability to caricature action convincingly. Frost's "A Slippery Day" from an 1883 *Harper's Weekly* shows a tall, top-coated man staggering on ice in a hilarious series of extreme poses worthy of a film animator. In "The Fatal Mistake: A Tale of a Cat" from 1884, a cat eats poisoned food and runs in pain from attic to kitchen and finally outside to its doom, frightening everyone it encounters. As a continuum, the sequen-tial drawings resemble a sequence taken by a movie camera tracking backward from inside a room, then into the hallway, downstairs into the kitchen, and out to the street, reminding one of the final tracking shot in Alfred Hitchcock's *Frenzy* (1972). The expressions

The front page of the Cincinnati Commercial Tribune *of September 7, 1898, featured an illustration by thirty-one-year-old "Winsor Mc": the G.A.R. parade pass-ing under the arches McCay designed and painted, located near the* Commercial Tribune *building, where McCay worked as a staff artist/reporter. He was already able to fill a newspaper page with almost photographic detail and impressive perspective drawing. (Courtesy Rare Books Department, Cincinnati Public Library)*

A SLIPPERY DAY

"Guess if I'm careful I'll get along."

"By Jove! it is slippery."

"Oh, hang these slanting pavements!"

"A man does have to have command of his feet on these bad spots."

"Steady does it!"

"Oh dear me! I hope no one is looking!"

"Now which way is he coming, anyhow?"

"Excuse me!" "I beg your pardon!"

"Happy thought! What's the use of walking."

"————!"

"It's a mighty hard winter, anyhow."

"If ever I go out on a day like this again—"

OPPOSITE:

"A Slippery Day," by A. B. Frost, which appeared in Harper's Weekly *in 1883. Winsor McCay thought Frost "the greatest comic draftsman in the history of this country."*

BELOW LEFT AND RIGHT:

"The Fatal Mistake: A Tale of a Cat" by A. B. Frost appeared in Stuff and Nonsense *in 1884. McCay admired Frost's humorous exaggeration, his character's storytelling poses, and the drawing's vitality.*

and poses of the cat and the people it surprises are quite exaggerated and very funny. "Frost worked with the air of a man who knew what he was doing," wrote McCay, who could very well have been writing about himself and his graphic expertise. "He was careful in his backgrounds and perspective."[16]

The humor in *Life* favored the visual gag over the printed word, and tour de force draftsmanship was the rule, as seen in Hy Mayer's series of "Worm's Eye" views of the world. Jokes were simply but effectively staged; a typical example: an older woman speaking to a grocery store clerk says, "I would like some powder, please." Without looking up the clerk says, "Face, gun or bug?" a snappy rejoinder quintessentially American in its casual, economical style.

Life poked fun at a variety of subjects, including prominent people in theater, publishing, and politics, as well as current fashions and trends, such as automobiles, "scorchers" (bicyclists), antivivisectionists, and art—an April 8, 1897, cartoon showed the inside of Aubrey Beardsley's brain as paisley-patterned.

As a journalistic reflection of patriarchal American society, *Life* was filled with a large quota of sexist and ageist viewpoints. Cartoons and prose lampooned the "New Woman" and her rights; scores of drawings by Gibson and others showed how proper women were expected to behave and look: docile, languid, beautiful, very white young clotheshorses who discuss fashion and men in a passive, almost catatonic manner. Every stereotype about women was rolled out in images that include sex-starved "old maids," "battle axe" mothers-in-law, and mindless

The Fatal Mistake

A Tale of a Cat

chatterers; Willie asks of his father: "Pa, what do they make talking machines out of?" Pa replies: "The first one was made out of a rib, my son."

Life's racist broadsides are outrageously excessive and crude to a modern reader. Two cover illustrations and captions show the kind of anti-black and anti-Semitic views that were considered acceptable humor in turn-of-the-century America. The cover of *Life* on December 29, 1898, offered a triple whammy, defining three minority groups as undesirable outsiders and expressing white society's horror of mixed marriage:

A white, upper class Gibson Girl–type to her black maid: "But, Sappho, in marrying this Chinaman, have you thought of what your children will be?" Maid: "Yes'm. I know they'll be Jews but I can't help it."

The cover illustration of *Life* on October 5, 1899, featured a stout black man in a top hat speaking to a thin black woman with décolletage and necklace:

"Pardon me, Miss Saffron. But when you oberload you'se'f wif jewels you is disguising yo' nationality."
"How so, Mister Jackson?"
"You'll be took fo' a Jewess."

One of Winsor McCay's first cartoons for *Life* (February 2, 1899) was a conventionally staged drawing interesting only for its solid draftsmanship, specifically the excellent perspective used in the background. In it, two "Members of Congress" stand on the steps of the Capitol in Washington; the congressman from the Philippines is a black man in bare feet, wearing a small grass skirt. He sports a top hat and a water canteen and waist satchel labeled "U.S.," which indicates the minimal assimilation of this savage into American culture. "Whatever became of that bill to annex Mars to the United States?" asks the savage of the congressman from the North Pole, an Eskimo dressed in a hooded fur parka and mukluks. The Eskimo answers, "Oh, we defeated that at the Poles."

The static drawing was a cautious showcase of McCay's drawing skill, which proved to be the equal of *Life*'s best cartoonists and illustrators. It contained a calculated conformity with certain ideological prejudices held by the magazine's editors. This is not to

OPPOSITE:
From the November 23, 1899,
Life *magazine. (Collection Ray*
Winsor Moniz)

ABOVE:
A McCay contribution to Life
magazine on February 2, 1899.

BELOW:
Life, *March 9, 1899—"Is the*
Game Worth the Candle?"
(Collection Ray Winsor Moniz)

imply that McCay did not share white America's benighted opinions about the racial superiority of whites. His later strips contained numerous images of blacks as childlike jungle savages dressed in grass skirts, as subservient menials, and as dissatisfied Negroes who attempt to change their skin color to white.

Examples include an editorial cartoon in the December 30, 1903, *New York Evening Telegram* entitled "The Effect," in which a doctor announces to the world that X-rays will turn Negroes white; an October 23, 1904, *Little Sammy Sneeze* strip in the *New York Herald* in which Sammy sneezes white flour into the face of a black maid; a January 17, 1905, *Dream of the Rarebit Fiend,* wherein a black woman bleaches her face white in order to gain social acceptance. *Little Nemo in Slumberland* in the *New York Herald* featured a grass-skirted, black-skinned child of nature named the Jungle Imp, which was based on a character McCay drew years before at the *Cincinnati Enquirer.*

The February 2, 1899, cartoon and two subsequent *Life* contributions exploited the anti-imperialist, isolationist position strongly advocated by the magazine. In 1898 the Spanish colonial government of the Philippines had ceased to exist because of the Spanish-American War. It was succeeded by a military government under the United States (which lasted until 1901). Relations between the Americans and the Filipinos were unfriendly and grew worse, and on the night of February 4, 1899 (two days after McCay's

"Members of Congress" cartoon appeared), the inevitable conflict erupted. War was declared by President Aguinaldo against the United States; on February 6, the U.S. Senate ratified its treaty with Spain and reinforcements were immediately sent to the Philippines. Fighting continued, the Filipino government fled northward into the hills, and in November guerrilla warfare broke out with devastating results.

On March 9, 1899, *Life* published a strong McCay cartoon entitled "Is the Game Worth the Candle?" In it, a pistol-packing Uncle Sam throws doll-like American soldiers at a Filipino's head protruding through the middle of a white sheet supported by two palm trees. A box of cigars labeled Manila (im)Perfectos is the prize in this bitter take-off on a carnival midway game. McCay's visualization of *Life*'s cry against American imperialism was bold in concept, dynamic in staging, and impressive in execution.

In the November 23 *Life,* McCay again presented a vivid anti-imperialist drawing, featuring Uncle Sam entwined against a palm tree (labeled Imperialism) by a rope he is holding that is attached to a circling jackass (marked Philippines). The cartoon's ironic title reads: "Oh! He will come around pretty soon."

Not all of McCay's *Life* cartoons (for which he was paid fifty dollars upon acceptance) were tied to international politics. Sometimes he experimented with

style and different media in gag cartoons, alternating between pen-and-ink and brush-and-gouache. On January 1, 1903, there appeared a long, rectangular-shaped painting of a jungle tree holding an adult ape and three lively youngsters. At the base of the tree, among the plants, a surly ape is looking up at the family in the tree. The caption reads: "The first Janitor: Hey there, You! No children allowed in this tree!" This mild comment on one of the housing problems encountered by city apartment dwellers (perhaps by McCay himself in Cincinnati) is well drawn and moody but barely recognizable as a McCay work because the sharp pen line had been replaced by wide areas of brushed chiaroscuro.

The November 5, 1903, *Life* presented an easily recognizable McCay offering entitled "Saved," one of his most exciting early efforts to depict sequential motion. In six rectangular panels, McCay pitted nature (in the form of horse and human power) against machine (automobiles): in the first panel, six Indians on horseback hold hostage two white couples in an open car. The hostages are dressed in elaborate riding costumes; the two women are crying, and in the next panel one of them will faint. The men in the car and the Indians are distracted by noise from a second automobile appearing in the distance over a desert rise.

In the second panel, the Indians ride in dusty pursuit toward the approaching vehicle. Throughout, Indians and horses can be viewed as individual key poses of a single action or as six separate positions. One horse with rider rears back, another gains balance, a third begins to gallop, a fourth gains speed by leaning into the wind, and so on, in drawings resembling the motion studies of horses by photographer Eadweard Muybridge, first published in 1887.

McCay's panels seem like separate frames of widescreen motion-picture film and anticipate his later work in animation. But characters are not the only thing in motion here. The viewer's point of view is like that of a movie camera pulling ahead of the action. In the third panel, the "camera" moves to the left, ahead of the second car and the attacking Indians.

In the fourth panel, we are still moving forward of the car, now surrounded by Indians, two of whom attempt to reach out to stop the auto as one would a runaway stallion. In the distance are the original automobile and passengers and two riders who fell out (in the third panel) of the currently besieged car.

The fifth panel surprises the viewer as much as it does the unsuspecting Indians when the car explodes. The intense detonation is impressively rendered in fine pen work of radiating lines and crosshatched smoke effects. Pieces of the machine fly outward from the white-hot center. Indians and horses are thrown into the air, their forms outlined by delicate shading of shadows on the sides of their bodies away from the blast. Far in the background, the auto containing four riders picks up the two who have witnessed their car's self-destruction.

The final panel in this highly animated continuum features a large smoldering hole in the ground surrounded by litter and debris. Driving toward us is the remaining auto with six frightened passengers, watching the Indians (who managed to survive) ride away into the distance.

McCay's drawings for *Life* were experiments with motion, various rendering techniques and media, design, and subject matter. The *Life* political cartoons anticipate the editorial cartoons McCay created later for William Randolph Hearst. As always, McCay did his best work in this area when he was emotionally involved or deeply interested in the subject matter. Then his stimulated imagination invariably led to a striking image. He was always more comfortable with nonpolitical subject matter, gags, or flights of fancy where his mind and pen could soar unencumbered by weighty ideology.

It was during this time, as Winsor McCay was steadily progressing in his career and gaining recognition beyond Cincinnati as a cartoonist of promise, that disturbing news came from home. Robert and Janet McCay were, by 1898, living with their daughter, Mae, in the small town of Edmore, Michigan, ten miles north of Stanton. On March 7, Robert and Janet traveled with their thirty-year-old son, Arthur, over one hundred miles northwest of Edmore to Traverse City, located on the west arm of Grand Traverse Bay.

There, Arthur McCay was admitted to Traverse City State Hospital, the northern Michigan asylum for the insane, where he would remain for forty-eight years until his death on June 15, 1946.[17] Hospital records show he was admitted in a paranoid condition, meaning he was uncommunicative, antisocial, and depressed (and would remain so for the rest of his institutionalized life). A modern diagnosis of Arthur's problem might have led to a less extreme nonsolution, but nothing is known of Arthur's early life, and apparently his behavior proved to be extremely alarming and finally unmanageable for his family.

What is difficult to understand, too, is the total abandonment of Arthur McCay by his family—he received no visitors during his nearly half-century at the hospital. Because he outlived his parents, sister, and brother, when Arthur died of bronchopneumonia and arteriosclerosis at age seventy-eight, his unclaimed remains were sent (according to law) to the Demonstrator of Anatomy in Ann Arbor.

Winsor McCay never mentioned his brother publicly, and even his descendants never knew of Arthur's existence (or that of his sister, Mae) until recently. It is impossible to speculate on the relationship between Winsor and his siblings when they were growing up. One can only assume that McCay's silence on this family tragedy stemmed from an overwhelming sense of shame and embarrassment.

But in his art Winsor remembered Arthur and the terrible thing that happened to him. The *Dream of the Rarebit Fiend* comic strip often deals with paranoid behavior, delusions of persecution, hallucinations, irrationality, and insanity. *Little Nemo in Slumberland* explores the fragile state of consciousness and the instability of reality, the fine mental membrane separating the inner from the outer worlds.

Winsor McCay's finely honed sense of irony could not fail to be sensitive to the quirk of nature and circumstance that caused two brothers, whose birth dates were so near, to have such radically different fates. Arthur was Hyde to Winsor's Jekyll, a dark Gemini twin to its bright opposite. One brother became an internationally acclaimed genius who created a fantasy world to contain and control his dreams and nightmares and to share them with millions of people. The other brother was an uncommunicative prisoner whose demons were locked tightly inside his head and shared with no one.

No doubt Winsor saw much of his brother in himself and feared and hated the horrible possibility that he might suffer Arthur's unfortunate fate. His drawing ability saved him from that, and so he kept on drawing for escape, for survival, and for salvation.

A pen-and-ink wash (with white gouache for highlights) for Life *magazine, August 11, year unknown. A spot gag for a continuing series imagining famous people returning to earth, in this case Shakespeare visiting a theatrical agency. On the back of this drawing, McCay printed his return address c. 1903: 2137 Gilbert Avenue, Cincinnati. (Collection Ray Winsor Moniz)*

In 1900 Winsor McCay joined the staff of the *Cincinnati Enquirer* when the newspaper's owner, John R. McLean, "dangled the enticing bait of a larger salary before McCay's ambitious eyes and hooked him without the slightest semblance of a fight."[18] During his three-year tenure at the *Enquirer*, McCay became head of the art department and contributed hundreds of illustrations and cartoons to the daily and Sunday editions. A random sampling of his work during the first year includes a half-page on March 25, 1900, of "The Elks Circus," an extremely crowded, animated drawing featuring caricatures of local politicos cavorting as costumed clowns, aerial gymnasts, bareback riders, tumblers, con men, and animal trainers. A thick black line defines the characters, and thinner lines are used to lend distance to the background, an early manifestation of the international Art Nouveau style that McCay would continue to use in his work.

On September 18, McCay acted in the capacity of a cartoonist/reporter by drawing a tragic fire at the Salvation Army Refuge. The next day's edition contained a full-page McCay illustration for the paper's "Fall Festival Edition," which featured a Roman arch and pillar and tunic-garbed adults and children bearing flowers. Flags are draped at the bottom of the frame showing Cincinnati at night during a fireworks display, a spectacularly stylized drawing full of Art Nouveau outlines and white line drybrushing on black.

On December 25, McCay's Christmas drawing was the pictorial report "Santa Claus's Gift to the Detective." In a series of amusing drawings bordering a photo of William Smith, "the celebrated Rubber Heel Thief," McCay shows Santa informing the cops, capturing the thief (who has wings on his shoes), and putting him in a birdcage, a fanciful retelling of a true event. (On December 30, a full page of about 100 photographs of Cincinnati children "Ready for the New Century" featured a large center portrait of McCay's three-year-old daughter, Marion Elizabeth.)

Occasionally McCay's duties as the *Enquirer's* top artist/reporter took him on the road to cover a story. These brief adventures excited him, reminding him of his recent itinerant past. He once covered a lynching, and three decades later wrote a vivid account of the assignment that sheds light on the methods, spirit of competition, and excitement that surrounded news gathering and mass communication at the turn of the century.

McCay wrote of the residents of Versailles County in southern Indiana, who were plagued by a series of burglaries, highway robberies, barn burnings, and horse stealings committed by an elusive gang of five men. One evening, while attempting to crack a safe in a bakery, the incorrigible quintet's luck ran out. They were captured after a brief shootout and jailed by the county sheriff and his deputies. The next evening, a mob of the town's good citizens decided not to wait for a trial to punish the wrongdoers. They stormed the jail, removed the prisoners, and lynched all five men "on two small trees."

"Now," wrote McCay with hyperbolic relish, "here is where I burst upon the scene with about a million other newspaper men":

Cincinnati and other cities throughout the Middle West were dying of dry rot for a big story, and at 4 P.M., I, with two carloads of reporters, artists, photographers, telegraph operators and wire men, was on a special train bound to Osgood, Indiana, four miles from Versailles.

Osgood normally then contained maybe 250 inhabitants but when we arrived there were 250,000 farmers with horses, wagons, buggies and buckboards.

"Fifty cents a head," they shouted, "to Versailles to see the big lynching!"

Walter Emerson, who looked like Jack Garf, our Major Domo, packed our crowd of six into a phaeton, which got in line and away.

Special trains were arriving from Chicago, Cleveland, Columbus, and Indianapolis, and our dusty road was one long procession of every kind of vehicle. And that procession tore down the road like fire horses answering a general alarm.

I made sketches of everything Emerson asked—the jail, inside and out, the sheriff, his brother-in-law, the cornfield, the farm, the trees, the "presents" on the trees and the winding staircase [in the jail].

HOW THE GIRAFFE GOT HIS LONG NECK

A TALE OF THE JUNGLE IMPS BY FELIX FIDDLE

MOST ev'ry one's heard of that creature so tall,
The Giraffe.
Well, long, long ago he had no neck at all!
The big calf!
His head was right down on his shoulders so tight
He couldn't reach down to the grass for a bite,
And so he ate bushes from morning till night.
Poor Giraffe!

*(I wonder how a long-necked giraffe's mouth, away up there,
knows when his stomach is hungry.)*

THE bad Jungle Imps were the creature's worst foes,
For they'd tease,
The way they did that was to tickle his nose,
So he'd sneeze!
Poor Mister Giraffe couldn't jerk his stiff head;
His heels, when he sneezed, would fly upward, instead;
He'd tumble so hard that his blood always bled
From his knees!

*(Then those mean, hateful, mischievous Jungle Imps would
laugh till they got an ache, on their insides.)*

A SPUNKY GIRAFFE one day got so mad,
I declare!
He wore out the very last swear word he had,
Then and there,
Said he: "I've a plan that I think is a peach!
I'll get a long neck and a lesson I'll teach
To Imps that so carefully keep out of reach.
Hear me swear!"

(Never lose your tempers, my little dears. It's very wrong.)

HE went to a rubber shop quick as he could,
And he said:
"I want a long neck, and I want it glued good
To my head!"
The monkeys got busy and made it; you bet!
Then sawed his head off, and, while still it was wet,
So fast glued the neck he'd be wearing it yet,
But he's dead.

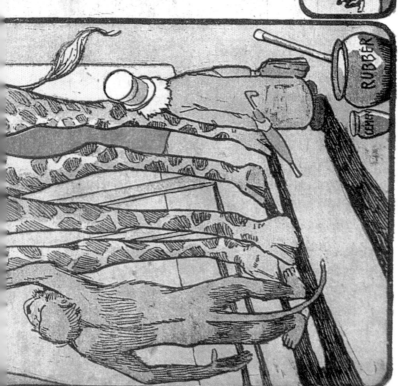

"How the Giraffe Got His Long Neck" from the February 15, 1903, A Tale of the Jungle Imps by Felix Fiddle, published in the Cincinnati Enquirer. (Collection Ray Winsor Moniz)

The cameramen were out of luck. It was dark and flashlights were not so hot in those days. So Emerson hustled me back four miles to Osgood.

While writers were working under lanterns and torches on dry goods boxes, beer kegs and barrels with operators wiring their stuff over the loops hooked by linemen up telegraph poles, young and old farmers were cleaning up with their frothing horses at 50 cents a head.

I told Emerson I was informed that I could not get my sketches to Cincinnati until 4 in the morning on a milk train! And that they had some mighty fine Lawrenceburg beer in the hotel bar of the town.

"All right," he said, "but be there when I want you. Stay there."

I stayed only long enough to start on my third mug, when he came rushing in and beckoned me away from the gang.

"Follow me and say nothing," he warned.

He led me into a lumber yard, through dark passageways, to a huge, hot, black locomotive. Emerson whispered to a brass-buttoned man with a lantern. A paper was signed and I was ordered into a way car and told to get busy when I should get back to the office.

We oozed out of the lumberyard as quietly as a cat could creep, and stopped two miles down the road to sidetrack for the Chicago Limited. Then we had the right of way for 53 miles to Cincy.

McCay admired the seven-foot driver engine and asked if he could ride in the cab instead of the way car. Permission was granted by the engineer and his crew, who "were so delighted over the lynching that I could have ridden on the smokestack, if I had chosen to do so."

The night was perfect. Almost as moonlit as day. The Chicago Limited shot by us. . . . Then we seemed to leap on to the main line. It appeared no time when we were flying through space. Objects that appeared half a mile away were on us immediately. . . . The more coal the fireman shoveled in the faster we went, and he never stopped shoveling coal. . . . Then the whistle started blowing shrilly, and never stopped. Once I did lean way back to beckon the engineer to slow down, but he had his chin on the window sill, attending to his own business. He was standing up, a little fellow. I could have licked him, but I wouldn't have dared let go my hold on the seat. . . .

In pantomime, I pleaded to the boiler, to the piston rods, to the headlights and smokestack, to those big 7-foot drivers . . . I cursed the moment I asked to sit in the cab.

. . . Suddenly I saw a river ahead. The moon was reflected in it, and our track stopped on its edge. No, I thought, it curves and there's a bridge to the right! We'll never make that curve. Never! Our speed is too great . . . we smashed into, on and across steel beams, rods, braces, cables, ties, plates and bolts, with my feet in the air and my head down among a lot of oil cans, waste and wrenches alongside a hot boiler. And I thought we'd soon be in China.

. . . We crashed into the yards at Cincinnati, tearing down freight houses, and suburban stations, ripping up switches, sidetracks, semaphores, block station. Panting, steaming, puffing, we stopped.

McCay had traveled fifty-three miles in forty-eight minutes, and after six artists hastily helped him ink in his rough pencil sketches, the *Enquirer* "scooped the country pictorially!"[19]

Of all Winsor McCay's work experiences during his five years on Cincinnati newspapers, none would prove more significant for his future than the proto-comic strip he created for the *Enquirer* entitled *A Tale of the Jungle Imps by Felix Fiddle*. This experimental series of forty-three illustrations ran from January 11 to November 9, 1903, and was based on poems written by George Randolph Chester (1869–1924). Chester, who started at the *Enquirer* in 1901 as a reporter, became Sunday editor of the paper before he left in 1908; he later achieved fame as a writer of popular short stories.

The basic theme of the *Tale of the Jungle Imps* series concerned the ways that gentle and/or beautiful creatures of the jungle adapted their physical and spiritual selves for survival in a hostile world. The weekly titles describe the basic plot: "How the Elephant Got His Trunk," "How the Quillypig Got His Quills," "How the Ostrich Got So Tall," "How the Alligator Got His Big Mouth," "How the Swordfish Got His Sword," and so on.

The series can be seen as a spoof of Darwin's theory of evolution, but it was actually closer to Rudyard Kipling's *Just So Stories*, which contained some similar tales about the physical changes animals decide to undergo or have brought upon them, e.g., "How the Whale Got His Throat," "How the Camel Got His Hump," "How the Rhinoceros Got His Skin," "How the Leopard Got His Spots."

In each episode of *A Tale of the Jungle Imps* the narrative was presented in three sequential stages. First, a defenseless animal is tormented by three aggressive Imps, who are large, seminaked black children. In the second phase, the animal decides to retaliate and consults a team of wise monkeys, headed by Doctor Monk, who performs cosmetic surgery to change the look and function of the animal. In the final phase, the "new" animal, now armed with a formidable physical appearance and a personality to match, becomes the victim victorious by attacking and driving away the Imps in fright and pain.

The role reversal of the animal is accomplished through a "mechanical" metamorphosis: the monkeys saw, hammer, cut, and sew the transformations onto the animal's body. In his later work, McCay would "organically" change a character's appearance; that is, gradually over a number of panels on a newspaper page (or, in films, over a number of frames) the physical forms would alter their shape from inside out.

Consistent characters in each strip included a trio of Imps, who represented the uncivilized, mindless forces of nature. As they sadistically play at torturing helpless creatures, they seem barely human, especially compared to the series' other team, the intelligent and industrious monkeys. These practical craftsmen would, for a fee, confidently and professionally help any animals asking to be equipped for the savage realities of life in the jungle. The third constant character in the series was Felix Fiddle, who represented both author Chester and artist McCay. He was an enigmatically silent, elderly white man with a long beard, who stood about observing passively, holding an umbrella and briefcase. He was a visitor from the civilized world of the white race, so removed and detached from the culture of the black natives and the lives of the animals that he was invisible to them. Felix Fiddle's apparently imperceptible presence lent a strange dreamlike quality to the work, similar to McCay's later dream strips *(Rarebit Fiend* and *Little Nemo)*.

McCay's jungle imagery was undoubtedly derived from his experience making circus and dime-museum posters, from reading Kipling's *Jungle Book* (1893), and from following the extended search of explorer Henry M. Stanley for the missionary David Livingstone, who was thought to be lost in Africa in 1869. The long quest, which ended on November 10, 1871, with Stanley's famous greeting "Dr. Livingstone, I presume?" was initiated and financed by McCay's future employer, James Gordon Bennett, publisher of the *New York Herald*.

A Tale of the Jungle Imps was Winsor McCay's first attempt in an extended series format to bring together all of his eclectic talents in a cohesive graphic style. On each page he found fresh ways to combine his exquisite draftsmanship, dynamic staging, sense of caricature, mastery of perspective, and feeling for motion with his version of the decorative Art Nouveau style.

The delicately sensuous line, the simplification and stylization of form, limited tonalities, and flat color patterning—all elements of the Art Nouveau look— were personified by the graceful French posters and illustrations of the Czech Alphonse Mucha (1860–1939). Mucha, who reached the height of his fame at the turn of the century and established a studio in America in 1904, repudiated any description or classification of his work as Art Nouveau, protesting that art was eternal and so could never be new. His art was "essentially concerned with the propagation of ideas that would contribute to the spiritual evolution of the human spirit."[20]

Mucha admired Puvis de Chavannes and other symbolists, and his style evolved from several contemporary trends in the art world, including Japanese graphics, Beardsley's simplified line as the essential element of composition, and the irrational color sectioning of Gauguin, with whom he briefly shared a studio in Paris. McCay was influenced by all of these visual motifs, which were not unknown in the Midwestern city where he lived and worked. As Judith O'Sullivan pointed out, the "internationally acclaimed Rookwood Pottery Company of Cincinnati, famous for its Art Nouveau ceramics, during the 1890s had hired Japanese artists as instructors. It is altogether possible that McCay passed these Oriental craftsmen on the street as he hurried to work at the Dime Museum and *Cincinnati Enquirer*."[21]

A close look at a *Jungle Imps* page from early in the series' run, "How the Giraffe Got His Long Neck," demonstrates McCay's ability to combine all of the above elements into a charming and attractive design. The short T-shaped top panel contains the title and an illustration of the animal's plight. The cramped space of the panel corresponds to the shape of the short necks of the presurgery giraffes. Chester wrote:

> His head was right down on his shoulders so tight
> He couldn't reach down to the grass for a bite,
> And so he ate bushes from morning till night.

As the ever passive Felix Fiddle watches in profile next to a pelican to the right of the frame, three monstrous Imps (arranged across the space) mercilessly and gleefully tease three cute short-necked giraffes.

> The way they did that was to tickle his nose,
> So he'd sneeze!
> Poor Mr. Giraffe couldn't jerk his stiff head;
> His heels, when he sneezed, would fly upward instead;
> He'd tumble so hard that his blood always bled
> From his knees!

Two giraffes, left and center, anticipate sneezing, while on the right, a giraffe is knocked upside down and hangs mid-air in suspended animation from the force of the nose-blow. All the characters are outlined in thick black lines, as if embedded in frames of stained glass, while the surrounding flora is drawn in thin lines and flat colors resembling a stage cyclorama or dime-museum backdrop.

The text is grouped in a long rectangular space in the center of the page, surrounded on both sides by longer rectangular panels that mirror the new long shape of the transformed giraffe's neck. In the left panel, three monkeys are putting finishing touches on the stitched and glued neck of a smiling giraffe, who suffered no pain during or after the crude operation.

> The monkeys got busy and made it, you bet!
> Then sawed his head off, and, while still
> it was wet
> So fast glued the neck . . .

Felix Fiddle stands with his back to us watching the completion of the process. His long shadow and those of the animals suggest time passing, another reference to motion and change. Extended shadows, flat colors, irrational coloring, and solitary detached observers anticipate motifs of the surrealist painters.

In the right side panel, two giraffes take sweet revenge on the Imps. One giraffe flips his elegant new neck violently backward, revealing his chin and small jowls, and in doing so has flung one Imp toward us and another, with legs akimbo, into the sky. A second giraffe pushes his neck and head toward a fleeing Imp running forward. Felix, of course, is standing to the left, mute and watching.

The feeling of animation is intense in this final panel; the backward thrust of the animal's neck and head and the Imp bodies are frozen at the height of the action. Foreshortening adds dynamism to the action; for example, the Imp on the ground headed toward us thrusts an exaggerated-sized left foot forward. The coloring throughout is subtle and lovely, featuring muted yellows for the sky, lavender and turquoise for the trees in the background, yellow-green for the plant leaves, and variations of orange for the interior of the monkey's office.

WHY THE STORK BRINGS THE BABIES

A TALE OF THE JUNGLE IMPS BY FELIX FIDDLE.

BY THE River Ooo-La-La the wee Babies grow,
    The dear little things!
Just as pink as the morning and all in a row,
    Awaiting their wings.
There's at first a green pod, with a lining of red;
And when this opens up there's a white, downy bed
That so gently enfolds them, from curled toes to head,
    Like a fond mother's arm,
    Safe from harm.

(Oh, but that's a drowsy place, with the bees droning by, and the soft wind rustling the leaves, and the birds singing the sweetest lullaby songs you ever heard.)

NOW, these wee Babies turned into fairies at last—
    The kind that do good!
When their wings sprouted out they'd break loose and fly fast
    Away through the wood.
You would scarcely believe that those Jungle Imps, sly,
Would so torment those poor helpless tots that they'd cry!
But they did, though! Each time those bad Imps passed them by,
    They would pinch them a nip,
    Then they'd skip!

(That whole row of Babies would be crying at once till the green pods closed up at night and the wind sprang up to rock them to sleep again.)

IN THE cool, rippling river the grave Storks would wade,
    Just humming a song.
They'd no wings in those days and their bills were not made
    So sharp and so long.
How they loved the pink Babies that grew on the banks!
Why, it made them heart-sick when the Imps played their pranks!
But they couldn't do much! They'd get thumped for their thanks,
    If they tried to put in:
    Sure as sin!

(As soon as the Imps were gone, though, the kind-hearted Storks would run and get oil from the Woogelly tree and rub on the pinches and talk baby talk to them.)

BUT THE cries of the Babies were too hard to bear.
    It made the Storks ill.
So they went to the Monkeys and got a strong pair
    Of wings and a bill.
To the river they flew when the Monkeys got through;
And those bad Jungle Imps they just pecked black and blue,
Then they plucked those sweet Babies, before their wings grew
    And flew off through the air
    Ev'rywhere.

(You just ought to see a great, white Stork flying through the air with a pretty little Baby on its back. You'd love the Storks forever after that.)

SO THEY left each nice Baby with folks that were kind
    To the wee little tot,
Who would love it to pieces and wouldn't much mind
    Its crying a lot,
If they'll try to be good boys and girls when they grow
That is better than growing up fairies, I know.
But it's hard to be good after Imps tease you so,
    And I guess that is why
    Babies cry.

(Sometimes when a Baby is asleep it will screw up its little face and cry. It's dreaming, then, that an imp is pinching it again. And sometimes it will smile in its sleep. It's dreaming, then, about the birds and the bees and the gentle winds along the banks of the river.)

BUT the Imps get small chance now to make Babies cry.
    Storks watch them all day,
And as soon as a dear little Babe opes its eye,
    They bring it away.
If you'd like to have one, here is what you must do:
Write a letter, addressed, "Mr. Stork. At the Zoo."
If there's any to spare he might bring one or two.
    If he's slow don't despair.
    They're not rare.

(I asked an old Stork the other day how the crop was this year, and he said there were just as many as ever! They have all kinds, pink and red and yellow and brown and black. But he says the pink ones are the most popular.)

In sum, the page is appealingly designed, a cleverly balanced space full of charming characters (even the naughty Imps have a certain appeal, especially when they are bested), action, motion, and a satisfying finish with the triumph of the underdog. In the *Jungle Imps* series, McCay introduced and experimented with character designs and themes he would reuse throughout his career. An Imp design would reappear two years later in *Little Nemo in Slumberland;* in the *Jungle Imps* episode "How the Mosquito Got His Bill" on June 14, McCay drew the prototype of the insect he later used so often in comic strips and as the star of his second animated film.

"Why the Stork Brings Babies" (April 26) includes an early fantasy image of flying—a baby rides the back of a stork through the skies; flying and falling through space are recurring themes in McCay's later work. An explicit dream setting in the lower right of the page presages all the dream worlds to come, and this particular *Jungle Imps* page includes a rare image of women: a nurturing mother and her maid intrude upon the all-male fantasy jungle world.

McCay's final *Jungle Imps* illustrations have a conformity to their layout that implies he was preoccupied or in a hurry to turn the drawings out—for example, "How the Zebra Got His Stripes" on November 1 and "How the Walrus Got His Tusks" on November 8.

In fact, when these last two panels were published, McCay was living in New York City, working full-time for the newspaper publisher James Gordon Bennett.

Events leading to McCay's quick departure from the *Enquirer* and Cincinnati began with a letter dated September 15 from Robert J. Carter, a former Cincinnati journalist, who wrote from the city department of the *New York Herald:*

> Dear Mr. McKay [sic]:
> I do not know what your attitude has been toward leaving Cincinnati since our last correspondence on the subject of coming to Baltimore. I think, however, if you care to consider it, I can find an opening for you on the *New York Herald* where you would be asked to do just the work for which you are fitted.
> If New York and the best paper in this country for your purposes have any attraction for you, please reply by return mail and send me some of your work which I will take care of and return to you. An immediate reply will oblige.
> Yours very truly,
> Robert J. Carter [22]

The formality of the letter's salutation and misspelling of McCay's name indicate that Carter was not a close friend of the artist; he was a professional acquaintance who admired the artist's skill and thought

he could thrive in a bigger marketplace than Cincinnati. McCay apparently thought so too, since he was considering a move to Baltimore, even though it was for work for which he was not "fitted." It has often been said that publisher Bennett himself was interested in hiring McCay after viewing his cartoons in *Life*, but there is no existing correspondence between the two in McCay's personal papers.

Hastily the cartoonist sent Carter examples of his artwork, perhaps originals of his strongest material from *Life* and color tearsheets of *Jungle Imps* panels. On October 14 a wire from the *Herald* signed in care of the busy art director, J. C. Baker, coolly gave McCay the good news:

> Work is satisfactory. Wire me when you can come out. Would like you to come at once so as to do election stuff. After election, you can arrange to move your family here. I'm sure we will be mutually satisfied.[23]

McCay consulted the editor of the *Enquirer* for advice: "What do you think I ought to do?" he asked. "Wire 'em and tell 'em if they'll send you a check for traveling expenses you'll take their offer," replied the editor. This McCay did.[24]

Maude McCay was less than enthusiastic about the abrupt offer and understandably concerned about the major changes it would force on their family. Theresa (Tedda) McCay, Winsor's daughter-in-law, recalled her husband describing Winsor's determination to accept the challenge despite Maude's reluctance: "He said, 'I'm taking this job and I'm going to be a very busy man. And I don't want any questions if I stay out late!' He made her do it. She never opened her mouth. He made her understand."[25]

McCay's years of experimentation in Cincinnati were over. He had become "Winsor McCay" with as sure a hand as Leonardo. He had enormous energy and supreme confidence in his ability to handle whatever lay ahead in New York. He could not know that he was to become the first master of two new art forms, but he felt fame and fortune were at the end of the path he was taking. And he knew so clearly how to achieve that goal. He merely had to "Work! Work! That's all there is to cartooning."[26]

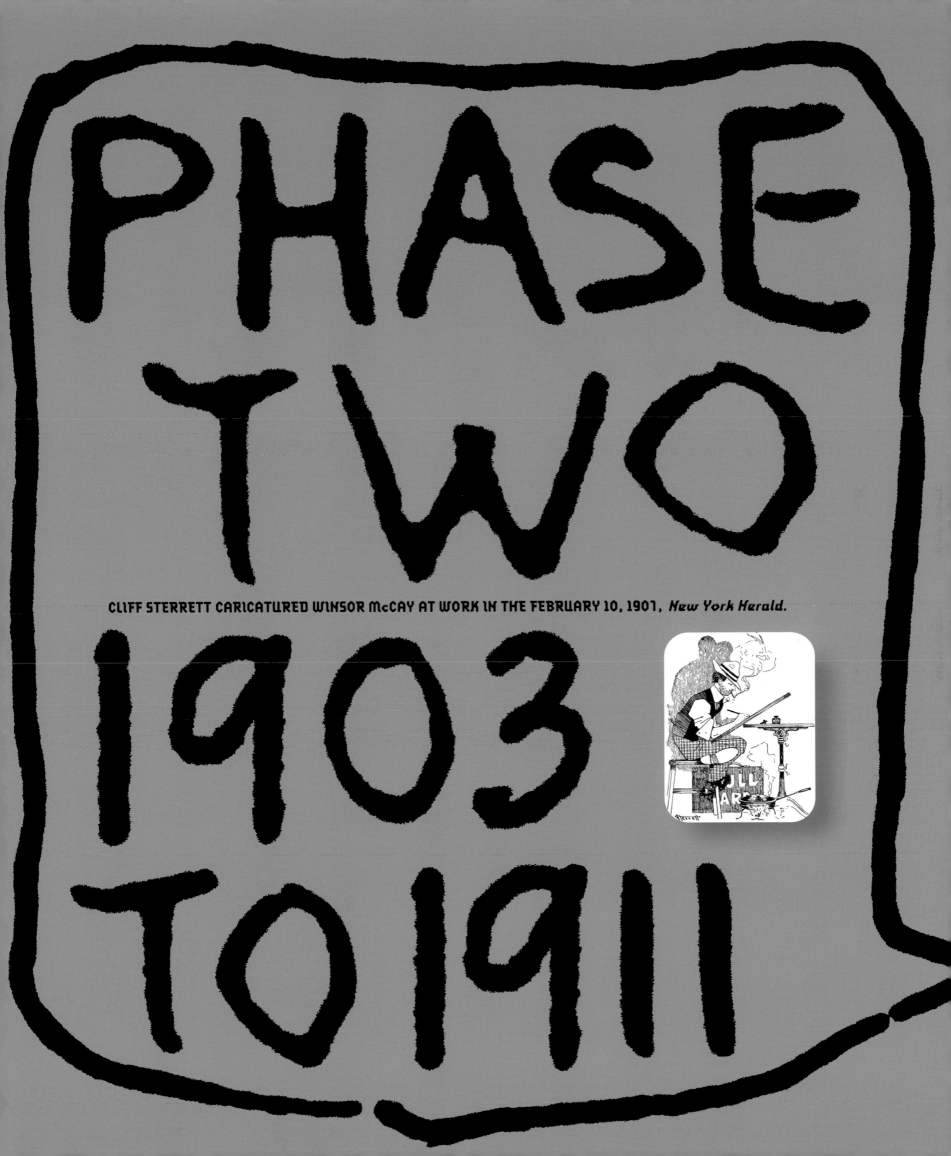

PHASE TWO 1903 TO 1911

CLIFF STERRETT CARICATURED WINSOR McCAY AT WORK IN THE FEBRUARY 10, 1907, *New York Herald.*

chapter 4. new york and the great comic strips

"I would give you 39 out of any current 40 gallery exhibitions along Madison Avenue and take Little Nemo *instead as a work of art that had a reason for being and fulfilled it."*

—JOHN CANADAY

"Herald Square has become one of the danger spots of the city," reported the *New York Herald* on the morning of October 28, 1903, which may have been near the date Winsor McCay arrived in Manhattan. The newspaper referred to the fact that the day before, three pedestrians were killed by traffic in an area where it was estimated that fifty people crossed the street every minute.

This section of New York City, known as the Tenderloin, was a constant swirl of human movement amid horses, electric trolleys, pushcarts, bicyclists, and noisy automobiles. The clattering cars on steel rails of the elevated train running the length of Sixth Avenue added to the din. Hundreds of workers poured into and out of the surrounding tall office buildings during chaotic rush hours. Shoppers dashed through the large department stores on Broadway in search of bargains, and after business hours the area remained alive with night people seeking pleasure in the flourishing dance-halls, theaters of all kinds, and nightclubs.

Sitting like a serene shrine in the middle of the bustling madness—on a trapezoidal space between 34th and 35th Streets where Broadway crosses Sixth Avenue—was the *Herald* building. It was a small structure, only two stories high in contrast to its tall neighbors, and audacious in design. Its architects were the great firm of McKim, Mead & White, who modeled the building loosely after the Palazzo del Consiglio in Verona; bronze bell ringers on the roof were inspired by Calducci's clock tower in the Piazza de San Marco in Venice.

The architects had managed to persuade the building's owner, publisher James Gordon Bennett, Jr. (1841–1918), not to duplicate the Palace of the Doges in Venice. They were unsuccessful in dissuading the

headstrong Bennett from his determination to place owls (his personal totem), their eyes wired with electric lights, as decorative touches along the eaves. "When the new Herald building was completed [in 1894] . . . no feature of its choice design attracted more attention than the owls that blinked at nightfall over its portals."[1]

There was puzzlement regarding Bennett's choice of that particular bird, for the *New York Herald* certainly "did not typify any high-brow grade of wisdom."[2] In fact, the newspaper was the "darling of the cotillion and club sets" and had achieved mass circulation "by treating gossip as news."[3] *Life* magazine once wrote a dry satiric profile of Bennett and found that "his face denotes great philanthropy, and he has done much to ameliorate the condition of the very rich . . . It is said that he reads the *Herald* every day with the aid of an interpreter, and that he has been known to faint when he was informed of an intelligent observation that had crept unawares into the editorial page."[4]

The presence of the small, elegant *Herald* building was so strong that the square on which it stood was named after the building. The press room, one level below the street and running through two floors, was visible through plate glass windows under a roofed open gallery on the Broadway side. McCay surely paused to look through the windows at the gleaming news machinery before entering the main entrance at the narrow 34th Street end.

Inside, the various departments were cramped for space and overlapped each other. "Situated on an island, so to speak, it had no room for expansion such as was soon needed. The composing room, up under a hip roof, was hot and low. The typesetting machine operators had to sit under the eaves."[5] McCay entered a small vestibule, was ushered upstairs to the executive offices, where he signed his contract, met the art room staff, and got to work.

In the two months left in 1903, Winsor McCay drew about thirty-five cartoons for both of Bennett's papers, the *Herald* and the *Evening Telegram*. Among this body of work were editorial and political cartoons and illustrations for news reports and fictional prose. On November 2 in the *Telegram*, he drew a line of people waiting to vote ("Ye Merry Citizen exer-

cises inalienable right of franchise"). The November 15 *Herald* contained a half-page McCay drawing made on location in Washington, D.C., depicting "Our Statesmen as Viewed by the Loquacious Capitol Guide."

On November 14 he drew a portrait of the mayor-elect ("Everybody likes McClellan"). McCay covered the horse show on November 17 and drew the event "as seen in a dream," featuring perspective angles of the riders and horses and silhouetting of the forms. Sometimes three of his drawings were scattered throughout the *Herald*: on November 22, McCay illustrated a whimsical article, from a series that appeared irregularly, based on Washington Irving's *Rip Van Winkle.* At the bottom of the same page, McCay sketched a "defense of the American Girl's love for titles [who] see demand for dukes in this country [a] solution of Great Britain's Financial Problem." On page six of the magazine section, McCay drew sketches for another irregularly appearing series featuring "Baron Munchausen."

McCay experimented with the comic strip form as early as December 24 in the *Telegram:* in ten sequential panels entitled "Hubby Goes Shopping with the Usual Results," a crowd of shoppers build in number until they engulf a hapless husband, who goes mad. The artist who signed his work "Winsor Mc" was working hard to prove himself to his new employer, but also ambitiously looking toward the day when he would have a successful comic strip of his own. Those cartoonists lucky enough to have their strips syndicated in newspapers across the country were assured of fame and money, and McCay was determined to be among them.

The comic strip at that time was in its earliest and most innovative stage of development in America. It derived from the illustrated narratives of nineteenth-century Europe, most significantly the work of the Swiss Rodolphe Töppfer, the German Wilhelm Busch, and the Frenchman Christophe (George Colomb). In the 1880s the American humor magazines *(Puck,*

Judge, and *Life,* among others) provided a showcase for the emerging artists who would pioneer the comic strip form, among them Richard Felton Outcault, James Swinnerton, F. B. Opper, and Winsor McCay. By 1890 the essential elements of the form were established: narrative by a sequence of pictures, a continuing cast of characters in each sequence, and the inclusion of dialogue within the picture frames.

A ruthless struggle for newspaper readers pitting Joseph Pulitzer's *New York World* against William Randolph Hearst's *New York Journal* began in 1895; illustrations and cartoons were key weapons in the war to attract a semiliterate population of immigrants and the working class. Pulitzer experimented with applying color to his paper's cartoons, most significantly in a series by Richard Outcault: the yellow on the nightshirt of a jug-eared slumbrat in *Hogan's Alley* in 1896 proved irresistible to the public. *The Yellow Kid* became popular overnight, and the color of his shirt was quickly adapted as a term to describe the increasingly sensationalistic and exploitative journalism practiced by both Hearst and Pulitzer: Yellow Journalism.[6]

Staff-stealing was part of the newspapers war, and Outcault was soon enticed by Hearst to come over to his *Journal* and join a burgeoning staff of cartoonists on "eight pages of iridescent polychromous effulgence that makes the rainbow look like a lead pipe."[7] The Hearst lineup of cartoonists and their strips included Jimmy Swinnerton's *Little Tigers,* Rudolph

Dirks's *Katzenjammer Kids* (based on Busch's *Max und Moritz*), and F. B. Opper's *Happy Hooligan.* Hearst was personally avid for cartoons, having collected German comic picture books (*Bilder Bücher*) as a child, and he oversaw the use of editorial cartoons and illustrations in his first newspaper, the *San Francisco Examiner.* Enthusiastically he sought new talents and new strips, gleefully raiding the staffs of rival newspapers. Thus did Hearst do "more than any other man to establish the comic page as the most successful circulation builder for newspapers ever invented."[8]

The ideology of the comics related to their primary purpose—to sell newspapers. No startling intellectual or social theories were embedded in the strips, no suggestions for change from the status quo. The common man, woman, and child could look at or read the comic page with confidence that their world, values, mores, and prejudices would be exactly reflected there. The comic strips validated and celebrated the average American's existence.

If the freedom to express ideas was restricted, the opposite was true when it came to style and technique. Each of the cartoonists was free to fill the allotted space on the page (often the entire page) with any graphic means at his disposal. All the "Founding Fathers" of the American comic strip, as historian Maurice Horn called Outcault, Dirks, Swinnerton, and Opper, had strong stylistic signatures. "It is undeniable," wrote Horn, "that the artists of the comics displayed a mastery, however uncouth, and a self-expression, however unformed, that one would rarely find in most of the 'art' of the turn of the century."[9]

OUR STATESMEN AS VIEWED BY THE LOQUACIOUS CAPITOL GUIDE

Pioneer Richard Outcault's work displayed a vigorous vulgarity, as seen in the crowded and busy pages he drew of *The Yellow Kid* and, later, his social antithesis, *Buster Brown*, a foppishly dressed upper-middle-class brat. Outcault and McCay moved in and out of each other's lives, starting when both lived in Cincinnati and were married at about the same time (1890–91). In New York Outcault worked for Pulitzer's *World* and Hearst's *Journal* drawing *The Yellow Kid;* ". . . there was hot rivalry among the newspapers," wrote Thomas Craven in his 1945 book *Cartoon Cavalcade*, "and artists were bought and sold like baseball players. Outcault was bought by Hearst, for whom he fathered *The Yellow Kid*, but the *World* retained the copyright to *Hogan's Alley* and continued the older strip as a parallel attraction, the drawing and coloring done to order by George Luks, the painter. The two Kids vied with each other for popular support. . . ." In 1902, Outcault joined Bennett's *Herald*, where he created the popular *Buster Brown* strip.

One year later, the ambitious and energetic Winsor McCay arrived at the *Herald* and began his extraordinary rise. Shortly thereafter, according to the *Cincinnati Enquirer*, a "rivalry sprang up between them, resulting in Outcault leaving the *Herald* and connecting himself [again] with the *Journal*."[10] McCay's creation of three strips starring child protagonists may have been partly motivated by the success of the kid strips of his rival Outcault. McCay's enormous popularity with *Little Nemo in Slumberland* (begun in 1905) could have convinced Outcault to return to the Hearst papers, where *Buster Brown* survived until 1926. McCay joined Hearst in 1911 and continued to follow Outcault's lead in other entertainment areas. In 1905 Outcault toured with a vaudeville act in which he drew his familiar characters on a large easel, and the performance was filmed by Edison. In 1906 McCay launched his own "lightning sketch" vaudeville act and eventually filmed himself in prologues to his animated cartoons, which were part of his stage act. Outcault preceded McCay's lavish Broadway musical version of *Little Nemo* in 1908 with a touring play of *Buster Brown* (which starred

actor Master Gabriel, who was later to star as Little Nemo). Both cartoonists attempted to exploit their cartoon characters in various merchandising and licensing schemes, although Outcault was the cannier businessman of the two. McCay was less organized and aggressive when it came to marketing his work, although he was Outcault's artistic superior.

On January 21, 1904, McCay began his first continuous comic strip, *Mr. Goodenough*, which ran irregularly through March 4 in the *Evening Telegram*. In five of the strip's panels, Mr. Goodenough, a millionaire, seeks a more active life. This always leads to his personal discomfort or injury, and in the sixth and final panel he gratefully resumes a contemplative, sedentary life. The first strip of the series ("Why Mr. Goodenough Took the Street Car, After All") has the distinguished older gentleman deciding to stretch his legs by taking a walk. Unfortunately, the wind makes him cold, he slips on an icy street, dust blows in his face, and he is bothered by the crowds. Back in the comfort of his richly appointed home, Mr. Goodenough announces to himself, "I think exercise is good for anybody at any time, but this is good enough for me."

An even briefer attempt to create a continuing strip may have been inspired by the marriage of McCay's sister Mae to a Stanton, Michigan, barber, Clyde Disbrow, on April 21, 1904. Three days later, *Sister's Little Sister's Beau* appeared in the *Herald* and promptly disappeared. It was, however, the first time McCay used a child as the protagonist of a strip.

The first McCay strip in color, entitled *Phurious Phinish of Phoolish Philipe's Phunny Phrolics*, appeared once in the Sunday supplement of the *Herald* on May 28, 1904. For this, McCay recalled his circus/dime-museum experiences and featured two clowns and a showgirl in a short skirt and slippers. The clown's slapstick antics anticipate similar roughhousing between Nemo's pals Flip and Impie.

LITTLE SAMMY SNEEZE

On July 24, 1904, McCay began his first sustained and popular effort in comic strips. Each week, usually within six inflexible panels, a most ordinary little boy anticipates a violent sneeze in a variety of settings. When the sneeze occurs in the fifth panel, it wreaks havoc on the surroundings and people near the blast, and in the final panel Sammy is usually rejected—most often kicked out. He is punished in spite of the disclaimer surrounding the title that "He Just Simply Couldn't Stop It" and "He Never Knew When It Was Coming."

In the first episode, Sammy—dressed as foppishly as Outcault's Buster Brown—sits watching two old men play chess. In panels one to four, Sammy sequentially opens his mouth in exaggerated anticipation of sneezing, while the chess players ignore him. Sammy's explosion occurs in the fifth panel with a loud "Chow!" that sends chess pieces flying off the table, ruining the game. Finally, Sammy is booted out the door by one of the men. This simple gag repeats itself throughout the strip's duration; it ended on December 9, 1906. Sammy appeared in a grocery

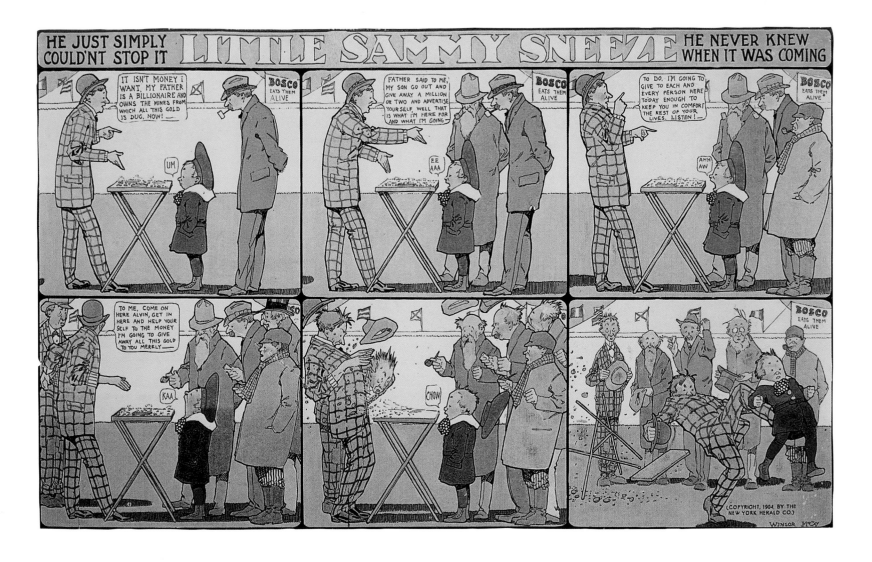

ABOVE:
On November 13, 1904, Little
Sammy Sneeze destroys a carny
pitchman's product line when
he blows away his phony gold.
McCay once again returns to
the familiar turf of the circus
midway and its denizens.
(Collection Ray Winsor Moniz)

LEFT:
On September 24, 1905,
Sammy sneezed and broke the
frame lines of his strip's panel.
(Collection Ray Winsor Moniz)

OPPOSITE:
Two more episodes starring the
hapless Sammy Sneeze.

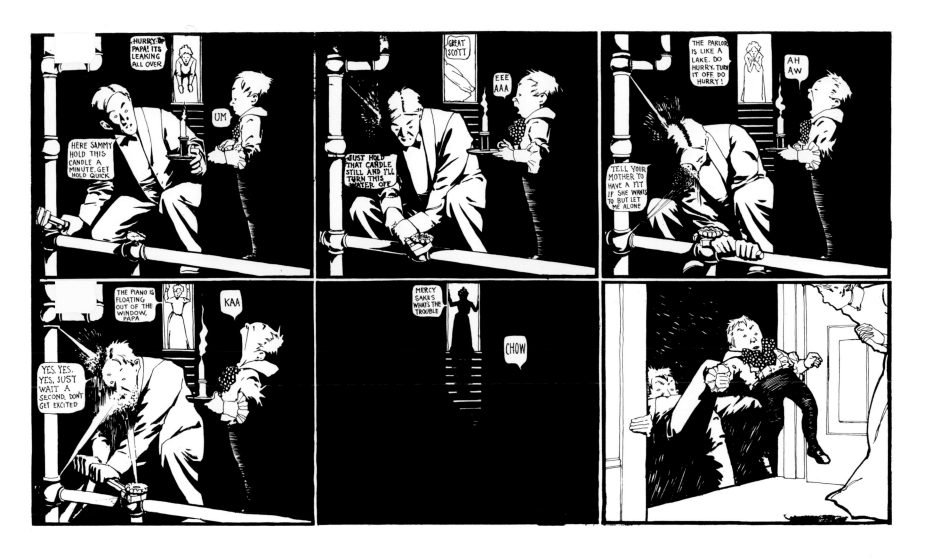

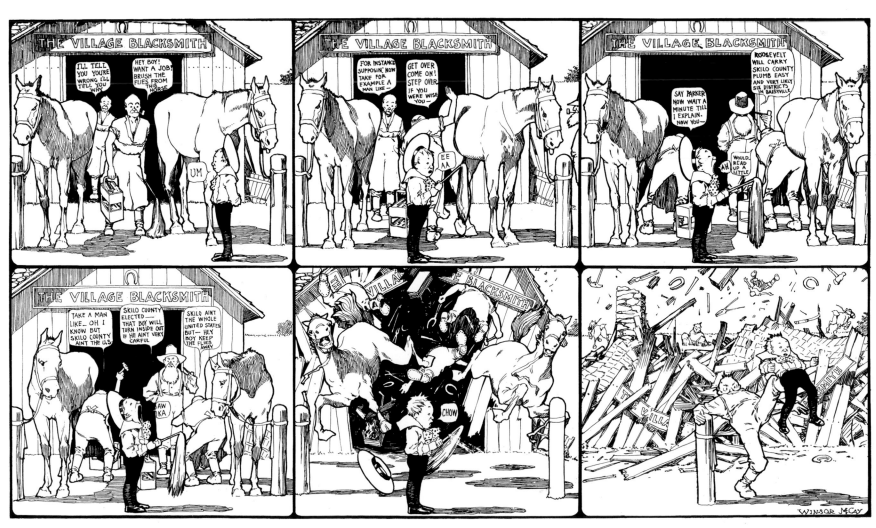

store sneezing everything off the shelves; in a watch-maker's shop; in a blacksmith's barn; at the circus frightening the lions; in a dark cellar helping his dad fix a leaky pipe by candlelight; at a high-toned parlor recital blowing the wigs off pretentious guests; and so on. At least once, McCay announced his presence when Sammy sneezed and broke the black border surrounding the strip's panels.

Sammy Sneeze was a rather unappealingly designed character. He seemed as dull-witted as he looked—gauche, rude, and insensitive to others in his continual refusal or inability to cover his nose and mouth when sneezing. He never learned anything throughout the strip's duration, never grew in knowledge or self-awareness (as Little Nemo would). Sammy was more of an object than a person, and so we feel no sorrow for him when he is kicked. The main pleasure of the strip is seeing how McCay varies the climactic moment in the explosion panel and the subtle differences in the panel's details leading to Sammy's sneeze. It appears that McCay was consciously experimenting with principles of animation and sequential changes in the character's movements and Sammy's face, while the background remained static.

DREAM OF THE RAREBIT FIEND

In contrast to *Little Sammy Sneeze*, McCay began a new strip that held a decidedly adult point of view. *Dream of the Rarebit Fiend* is one of the most sophisticated and witty comic strips ever created. It became the longest running of all of McCay's strips, starting in the *Evening Telegram* on September 10, 1904, running until June 25, 1911, and then revived in the *Herald* from January 19 to August 3, 1913.

The January 28, 1905 drawing inspired the classic 1906 live-action trick film by Edwin S. Porter, *The Dream of the Rarebit Fiend*, and the series was the basis of three of McCay's animated films released publicly in 1921: *The Pet, Bug Vaudeville,* and *The Flying House*. Frederick A. Stokes published selected *Rarebit Fiend* strips in a 1905 book.

So popular was the comic strip that McCay signed a contract agreeing "to collaborate in the production of a comic opera or musical extravaganza, to be known as 'The Dream of the Welsh Rarebit Fiend!'" with music by Max Hirschfeld, book and lyrics by George Henry Payne and Robert Gilbert Welch, and

In a self-referential Dream of the Rarebit Fiend *on April 7, 1907, McCay found release from the drudgery of drawing daily comic strips by playfully (or angrily) parodying the medium itself. He lampoons both his fastidious drawing style and his propensity for fashionable clothes by bombarding a hapless character (who resembles the artist) with a literal smear campaign using inkblots. (Collection Ray Winsor Moniz)*

"ideas and such assistance as he may be able to give" from McCay.[11] Unfortunately, no stage production was ever produced based on the *Rarebit Fiend* strip.

For this particular comic strip, Winsor McCay used the pseudonym "Silas," which he began placing on his editorial cartoons in the *Telegram* just before *Rarebit Fiend* began. Previously, his artwork was signed "Mc" or "Winsor Mc." Supposedly, James Gordon Bennett wished to separate McCay's child-oriented strips in the *Herald* from his adult-directed work in the *Telegram*.[12] "My contract," explained McCay, "would not allow me to sign my real name when I started to draw those pictures for the New York papers and I had to make up a name." In a small act of defiance and anger at not being able to use his own name on one of his most personal creations, McCay chose "Silas," the name of "an old fellow who drives a garbage cart by the *New York Herald* office every day . . . a quaint character."[13]

The *Dream of the Rarebit Fiend* series had no continuing characters; in each episode an adult man or woman (or, on rare occasions, a child) of the bourgeoisie experiences a nightmare situation, usually in a mundane urban setting. The intensity of the dream ranges from mild titillation or embarrassment (walking in public without trousers or stuttering while making a public speech) to horrific (being buried alive or watching an inanimate object become a dangerous monster). A dream atmosphere pervades each episode because of the detached calm of most of the protagonists. For example, in the October 26, 1904, strip, an elderly man is dismembered by traffic on Broadway, yet he keeps up a rambling monologue as he loses limbs, torso, and head.

The dreamer awakens in the final panel always blaming the disturbing night visions on a before-bedtime meal of Welsh rarebit, a concoction of melted seasoned cheese cooked in cream with ale added and served on toast or crackers. It is typical of McCay's sly humor to blame disturbing dreams on such an innocuous snack instead of alcohol or narcotics, although in at least two episodes, McCay does acknowledge the hallucinatory potential of booze and dope. In the October 21, 1904 strip, a man drinks wood alcohol in a bar and is joined by exotic animals wearing clothes. A giant lobster with a man's head threatens him, and a huge python wraps the man in its coils and prepares to snap his head off. On August 19, 1905, the strip featured a pompous Professor Probe intent on trying "the actual smoking of opium for educational purposes." A nattily dressed man offers to escort the academic to Chinatown. In the dialogue balloons accompanying the drawings, McCay demonstrates his familiarity with contemporary drug slang; for example, "If you want to hit the pipe . . . I know a chink who can cook all the hop you can smoke. . . . This gent wants to pull on the stem; he wants you to cook up a few pills." Again a giant serpent attacks the hapless experimenter, who wakes up screaming "The Yellow Peril. Don't please. Oh!" In both dreams, the frightening imagery is blamed (in the final panel) on a snack of Welsh rarebit. (It is unknown if McCay's knowledge of a drug lexicon was based on personal experimentation; in his middle and late years, he was known to be extremely moderate in his drinking habits.)

McCay once explained the origin of the *Rarebit Fiend* strip by using, as an example, the first episode, which set the format for the series:

> You know how a cigaret fiend is when he gets up in the morning and can't find a dope stick? Well, I drew a picture once showing a fiend at the north pole without a cigaret and about ready to die. I introduced some other characters who happened to have paper and tobacco and a match, but the only match went out before they got a light. Then I had to frame up a finish and I made it a dream. My employer suggested that I make him a series of pictures and make them as rarebit dreams and you know the result . . . .[14]

McCay's interest in animation is evident throughout the run of the strip; accelerated changes in size and age, as well as metamorphosis, are continuing themes. Examples include Santa Claus hanging from a roof and becoming an icicle; a bathtub turning into a jungle swamp; a man eating youth tablets and

On January 28, 1905 (early in the long run of the Dream of the Rarebit Fiend strip), McCay drew this nightmarish depiction of a young woman's prenuptial anxiety, complete with a phallic arrow penetrating her nightie. The episode was the basis for The Dream of the Rarebit Fiend, a famous live-action Edison film of 1906, directed by Edwin S. Porter. In the film version, made without McCay's collaboration and with every then-available special effect except animation, the protagonist was changed to a male, and a prologue showed the victim gorging himself on rarebit and ale. (Collection Ray Winsor Moniz)

regressing to infancy; a gigantic man asking his boss for a raise but decreasing in size as the boss and his desk enlarge; a furnace evolving into a horned demon who chases its owner over rooftops; a small pup changing into a horned monster impervious to dynamite; a woman's handbag evolving into a devouring alligator; a woman and her husband taking "Get-fat-quick" and "anti-fattino" pills with grotesque results; a corn on a woman's toe growing into a stalk complete with corn cobs.

In 1900 Sigmund Freud published *The Interpretation of Dreams*, a subject that had fascinated many nineteenth-century artists, among them Goya, Fuseli, Redon, and Burne-Jones. "The nineteenth century," wrote Philippe Robert-Jones, "usually regarded as the golden age of bourgeois materialism, was also the period in which Realism was called into question by its own proclamation (the most obvious image of this being caricature) and by a desire to escape into a different kind of reality."[15] Proust made the following comparison of reality and dream: "To my alarm it occurred to me that this dream had had the clarity of consciousness. Could consciousness, conversely, have the unreality of dream?"[16]

McCay was fascinated by the alternative world possible in dreams, a realm indifferent to rationality, logic, and coherence. He might have found inspiration for some of his nightmare episodes in the *Rarebit Fiend* series in Lewis Carroll's *Alice in Wonderland* (1865) and its John Tenniel illustrations. Alice, like the Rarebit eaters, was physically altered by substances she drank and ate in a dream world that was both ordinary and extraordinary. Specific Tenniel *Alice* drawings appear to have been adapted by McCay; for example, the famous image of Alice with an elongated neck reappears in a *Rarebit* of October 17, 1904, where a woman's neck is outrageously stretched by the pull of a dentist's pliers. On May 29, 1905, a man at a racetrack stretches his neck to trip the horses, strangling himself instead.

Alice's abrupt changes of size found counterparts in McCay's imagery, already discussed. Alice almost drowns in a sea of her own tears; McCay makes a tardy commuter dashing for a trolley perspire so profusely that a salty lake is formed from the sweat of his brow.

One of the most disturbing episodes of the Rarebit Fiend *series (from August 4, 1907) presented a suffocatingly real nightmare image of helplessness and vulnerability as a man's face is invaded and covered by birds, small mammals, and insects. (Collection Ray Winsor Moniz)*

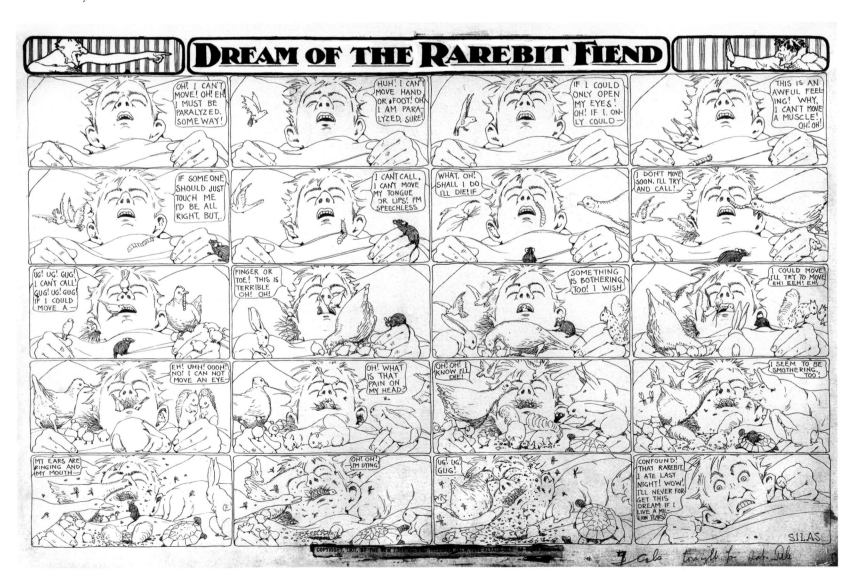

Many of McCay's ideas came from his own imagination and personal dreams and those of his readers. At the bottom of some *Rarebit* strips he solicited the public to "send in their dreams addressed to Silas the Dreamer," care of the *Herald* building. At least one episode, on February 25, 1905, may have been inspired by the writings of Edgar Allan Poe; a man is buried alive and the reader's point of view is that of the corpse. We are the deceased, overhearing two doctors admit they botched our surgery and plan to notify our widow who "won't be sorry [for he] was a high liver." In the third panel, the wife peers in at us with an anguished face and asks, "Why did you die without leaving me even five cents? I'm glad you've gone. You led me an awful life. It was coming to you." At the funeral, mourners continue to make statements that ironically contrast with their sad demeanors: one professes love to the widow, and even a Bible-toting parson has nothing positive to say about the dead man ("He was absolutely no good"). Finally, to the reader's claustrophobic horror, the seventh panel shows clods of black earth raining down from the gravedigger's shovel. Finally, the frightened dreamer wakes, vowing "I'll be good" to his annoyed wife.

Many *Rarebit* episodes reflect McCay's interest in circuses and dime museums; for example, a large elephant performs high-wire acrobatics above a man in bed before falling on him (January 14, 1905); a gentleman out for a stroll meets multiple images of himself like those in a funhouse mirror (April 15, 1905); a man attempts to buy a new suit but is afflicted with "fits" that alter his form by stretching and squashing him, again as in a trick mirror; a man rides with a female circus driver in an open auto as she performs her specialty, "a little death dipping," that is, driving through impossibly convoluted suspended circular roadways, to the great fear and anger of her passenger. (The episode reflects McCay's personal distrust of the automobile, which he refused to learn to drive.)

A number of other themes emerged during the long run of the *Rarebit Fiend* comic strip, among them, a jaundiced attitude toward romance: those who practice it are fools who do so at their own peril. A woman receiving an alligator-skin handbag from a beau named Willie gushes about how lovesick she is and "so crazy about that man." If only he were present she would "hug and kiss him, yum yum yum!" The handbag, gradually changed into a full-grown

OPPOSITE:

One of McCay's most brilliant
Rarebit Fiend episodes (from
February 25, 1905): a burial
seen from the point of view
of the still-living corpse.
(Collection Ray Winsor Moniz)

BELOW AND THE
FOLLOWING TWO
PAGES:

Three Rarebit Fiend *strips*
demonstrate McCay's fascina-
tion with metamorphosis and
extreme alterations in sizes
and shapes. On June 23, 1907
(below) a child's teddy bear grows
into a large beast that devours
the baby and attacks its parents;
on March 2, 1907 (p. 86), a
man with the gout finds his toe
swelling to a ludicrous size; on
October 14, 1908 (p. 87), a
woman, urged by her dentist,
widens her mouth to cavernous
proportions. (Collection Ray
Winsor Moniz)

toothy alligator, mocks her and her lover: "That peanut-headed Willie of yours . . . he and his frazzled face. . . ." Soon the beast is twice the woman's size and entraps her in its massive jaws.

In another episode a man and woman embrace on a settee, murmuring sweet nothings to each other ("Oh, Ducky darling!" "My little pansy blossom"). A tiger rug comes to life and, disgusted by what it hears, eats the man head-first in front of the horrified woman, who wakes in the last panel.

In the same vein, the *Rarebit* strips often depicted the state of matrimony as a minefield of hypocrisy, jealousy, and misunderstanding. In one 1904 episode, a man, one week into his honeymoon, arrives home late after being delayed in traffic. His angry wife physically attacks him, flings him about the room, and throws vases while metamorphosing into a demonic wraith. With characteristic irony, McCay has the man awake from his nightmare to stare at his lovely bride asleep beside him in a bed festooned with cupids and doves, and wonders "if Welsh rarebit dreams ever turn out true?"

In a 1905 strip, a man new to the "cursed state of Utah," has joined the Mormon Church. The dozen women he married stand waiting for him to draw his salary "with their mitts out as usual" and "all on the lookout for the mazooma." Finally, the women surround him, insist he recount the money, and refuse to allow him to buy one beer. When he decides not to release his pay to them, the wives violently beat him.

Money concerns often appeared in the series, typically involving the lack of it or the burden of responsibility that comes with it. The latter problem occurred in the April 22, 1905 strip in which a man accepts a gift of $5 million from Andrew Carnegie. He promises to "put it to good use," but both he and his wife literally go insane trying to decide what to do with the money. McCay's compelling depiction of madness progresses from infantilism (playing with dolls and riding rocking horses) through dressing outlandishly (watering cans and garbage can lids for hats, a skirt on the man, tennis rackets on the woman's feet) to a final grim scene showing the couple down on all fours, chained to posts and grimacing

DREAM OF THE RAREBIT FIEND
BY SILAS

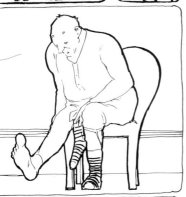

like wild animals. Perhaps the tragicomic intensity of this particular episode stemmed from McCay's contemplation of his brother Arthur's illness: he may have been trying to use the drawings as a catharsis.

Other *Rarebit* subjects consistently pricked by the sharp point of McCay's iconoclastic pen included lawyers, doctors, businessmen, and the clergy. Mothers-in-law, unmarried "old maids," and women's vanity were attacked by the artist in a chauvinistic manner typical of his era. McCay had an obsession with women's hats—the size and cost of them—that drove him to satirize ladies' chapeaux often. In one strip, a man literally burns up with anger over the price of his wife's new hat; in another episode a woman's gigantic hat topples houses.

Many *Rarebit* dreamers fall out of bed in the strip's final frame, anticipating the conclusion of McCay's future dream-strip epic, *Little Nemo in Slumberland*. On December 10, 1904, McCay closely prefigures *Little Nemo,* which would debut within a year, in an adventurous *Rarebit* episode starring a child. New York's first subway line had opened the month before, so McCay created "Flatiron Joe, the Subway Terror," a homely kid brandishing a rifle bigger than he is. A man offers Joe a million dollars to save his daughter from 10,000 Indians. Surrounded by knife-wielding Indians, Joe and the girl ride off on a horse, then fall into a ravine. While plunging through space, Joe asks the girl to marry him. The boy wakes up on the floor with one foot up on his bed, as his parents ask what the matter is—the same finale that would be used throughout the run of the *Little Nemo* strip.

Drawings for Flatiron Joe have great vigor and imaginative staging of the action in each panel. It must have been fun to draw and its success probably encouraged McCay to think of a new strip using a boy in a dream format. Years later, he recalled the origin of *Little Nemo in Slumberland* as "an idea I got from the *Rarebit Fiend* to please the little folk."

But before launching *Little Nemo* in the fall of 1905, the indefatigable McCay began two other comic strips. (Remarkably, McCay was still turning out daily and weekend editorial cartoons and other graphic assignments in addition to drawing comic strips.)

OPPOSITE TOP:

*On January 9, 1909, the flight
of a new kind of bird—the
product of genetic engineering—
is shown in a variety of cinematic angles and perspectives.
The calm attitude of the two
doomed men, who face violence
and imminent death as they
ride the bird, adds to the
dreamlike quality of the strip.
(Collection Ray Winsor Moniz)*

OPPOSITE BOTTOM:

A Rarebit Fiend *strip from
September 1, 1907, eaves-
dropped on the courtship of two
scarecrows. Here is McCay at
his most charming, investing
emotional life into anthropomorphic creatures who communicate
in very human ways with each
other and the reader. Reality
intrudes in the final panel, for
McCay was cynical about
romance. (Collection Ray
Winsor Moniz)*

ABOVE:

*An episode illustrating McCay's
unrelenting obsession with
women's hats. On May 24, 1908,
a woman's newly purchased hat
is so gigantic it must be delivered
by a platoon of men, rolled down
streets and precariously pushed
across rooftops until it finally
falls onto the woman's house.
McCay stages this farcical incident in a step-pattern of panels
that matches the shape and size
of the hat; the strip contains
highly amusing images that
anticipate surrealism: a familiar
object seen in an incongruous
context, as when the huge hat
rests atop a skyscraper like a flying saucer from a distant planet.
(Collection Ray Winsor Moniz)*

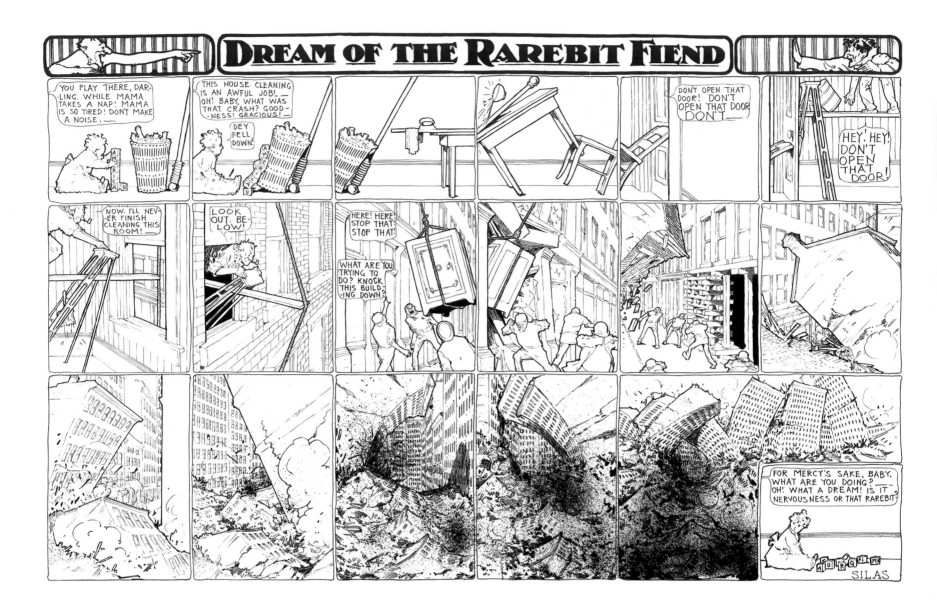

On April 17, 1908, McCay offered a spectacular display of cause and effect and his mastery of animation and perspective drawing: a baby playing with blocks that spell "America," which topple and ultimately destroy a city. (Collection Ray Winsor Moniz)

Money worries surface in a number of Rarebit Fiend episodes: On April 22, 1905, in an ironic twist, a couple who received a $5 million gift from Andrew Carnegie go literally mad because of the burden of responsibility that comes with it. McCay's depiction of madness is both funny and chilling as his characters move from melancholy and depression into a twilight world of infantilism, unconcern about their appearance, and, finally, raw animal behavior as they crawl on all fours and growl. (Collection Ray Winsor Moniz)

DREAM OF THE RAREBIT FIEND
BY SILAS

THE STORY OF HUNGRY HENRIETTA

From January 8 to July 16, 1905, McCay drew a serial comic strip that followed a little girl with a voracious appetite from infancy through early childhood. McCay used *The Story of Hungry Henrietta* as another testing ground for animation experiments: each week Henrietta aged visibly. In addition, characters within the frames changed their poses and gestures while the background remained static.

In the first episode, Henrietta is three months old, sitting nude in a small basin and about to have her photograph taken. In four of the six panels, family members and the photographer attempt to make the child smile by contorting themselves into increasingly ridiculous poses and making absurd grimaces. This silly display (including a man standing on his head) only causes the baby to cry, which the incompetent parents interpret as a sign of hunger instead of a need for comfort and reassurance ("You've got to feed her a little sumthin'!"). The final frame shows the disconsolate baby with a tear in her eye, alone, sitting in the basin sucking a nippled bottle.

Week after week, Henrietta is plied with food instead of the love and warmth she really needs and wants. Becoming a compulsive eater, she devours whole picnic lunches, the entire contents of an icebox,

(while calculatedly reciting a poem for a food reward); and in one meeting with Sammy Sneeze, she picks up and eats pieces of candy Sammy has blown off a plate.

An article in the February 10, 1907 *Herald* on McCay suggested that Henrietta was based on his daughter, Marion: " . . . and as the artist has made no denial of the charge, it may be taken for granted that there is some truth in it. And it may also be ventured that any man who can glean humor . . . from the howls and yowls of his own squalling infant has attained a height reached by few professional funny men nowadays." Donald Crafton considers the strip "a subtle but damning comment on middle-class child rearing," in which McCay showed "an extraordinary sensitivity to the delicate depths of the child's mind."[17]

McCay's approach to all of his cartoon children was quite different from that of his contemporaries. Sammy, Henrietta, and Nemo were innocents compared to the anarchic demon children of Rudolph Dirks *(Katzenjammer Kids)* and Richard Outcault *(The Yellow Kid; Buster Brown)*. On December 4, 1904, for example, Buster Brown attempted to electrocute his father in the bathtub, an act McCay's kids would never dream of.

BELOW AND OPPOSITE:
Three examples from the serial comic strip The Story of Hungry Henrietta *(pp. 92 and 93), which ran in the* New York Herald *from January 8 to July 16, 1905. Like* Little Sammy Sneeze, *the strip is another showcase of McCay's experimentation with animation: the action progresses sequentially within the strips and Henrietta ages visibly from week to week. (Collection Ray Winsor Moniz)*

A PILGRIM'S PROGRESS BY MISTER BUNION

On June 26, 1905, "Silas" created a second strip in the *Evening Telegram,* geared toward adults; *A Pilgrim's Progress by Mister Bunion.* The strip, which ran until December 18, 1910, was a cartoon allegory based on the seventeenth-century masterpiece of English religious writer John Bunyan (1628–1688).

On the reverse side of the original art of the first episode of *Pilgrim's Progress,* McCay wrote a note to his editor, a Mr. Harris, attempting to sell him on the idea of the strip:

> . . . in Mr. Bunion's progress he tries all manner of schemes to get rid of his burden "dull care" but like the cat it comes back. I can get a lot of fun out of it and think it offers as good a field as the Rarebit. He will always be looking for "Glad Avenue" and will have occasional visits to Easy Street, but his burden will stick to him and I will have him try to burn it, bury it, and throw it in the sea, blow it up, advertise it for sale or give away, get it run over by trains, hit by autos, and hundreds of things he will try to do to get rid of it but can't—I hope you will see my scheme. It's a good one.

The eight-panel strip featured a tall man named "Mr. Bunion," dressed in a black coat and high hat, who walks a desolate, minimally sketched "Rocky Road." Bunion always carries a large suitcase labeled "Dull Care," which he seeks in vain to rid himself of. In the first episode, a burly man offers to carry the suitcase; happy to be rid of Dull Care, Bunion runs away to Easy Street to wine and dine in a restaurant, observing, "Well, there's something in life after all. Life, life. I love life. We all love life." But then, the burly man enters and throws the suitcase on top of Bunion saying, "I don't want it. Give me my dime. Slick, ain't ye?"

And so it went in each episode: on July 3 while Bunion chases a "money bird," a starving man steals the suitcase, but returns it in the tall grass where Bunion trips over it. On July 10, Bunion places the suitcase on a keg of dynamite and it blows up. As Mr. Bunion heads toward Gilded Lane ("I was never intended to be poor") the suitcase falls from the sky onto his head. On July 17, Bunion leaves the suitcase in a hotel that is on fire. (McCay put special effort into

this, calling on his experience as a cartoonist/reporter to depict dramatic scenes of firemen, flames, smoke swirling, and shadowy victims crying "We have lost everything.") Unfortunately for Bunion, the Dull Care suitcase is found in the rubble. Each time the grind of daily life and the burden of its responsibilities accompany Mr. Bunion and weigh him down with worry and frustration.

"In the world of the *Rarebit Fiend,*" notes McCay scholar Judith O'Sullivan, "the monotony of daily existence is replaced by an alternate universe, which is governed by esoteric rules, in which the ordinary is that which is unexpected. In *Pilgrim's Progress,* however, daily cares press upon the protagonist with exaggerated force. The two tendencies provide a constant tension in McCay's work."[18]

During this peak creative time, as McCay continued to experiment and develop his comic strip style, he was turning out spot illustrations for the Bennett papers, sometimes from outside New York. On March 3, 1905, for example, McCay wrote his family a letter from the *Herald's* Washington, D.C., bureau, revealing his hectic schedule and exhaustion:

> My Darlings Maude Robbie & Marion
> You must excuse me this time for not writing a long letter, but it is fearce [sic] here to get anything. I am terribly rushed. I expect to come home Saturday P.M. Everything else is swell but that I don't get a chance to write you. I *"dressed"* last evening under great excitement and eat [sic] dinner with Loomis & his wife and she is a very nice little lady who says she has heard so much of *you* that she is crazy to see you. Well when I tell you all how I am fixed here and rushed you will be surprised that I wrote this much. I hope you all are nicely fixed. I wish I was with you but better more [sic] I wish you all were here. I will write you a longer letter tonight. I am going out now and hustle. I worked until 2 this morning and was almost dead for sleep. Kisses and huggs [sic] from
> Your loving Hubby & Papa
> Winsor

OPPOSITE AND THE PAGE FOLLOWING:
Mr. Bunion, the protagonist of A Pilgrim's Progress, is constantly frustrated in his attempts to improve his life by ridding himself of his burdensome valise, "Dull Care." The title of this allegorical comic strip was taken from John Bunyan's seventeenth-century masterpiece, and the series ran from 1905 through 1910. (Collection Ray Winsor Moniz)

A Pilgrim's Progress
By Mister Bunion.

SILAS

A pleasant surprise awaited readers of the *New York Herald* color comic section on Sunday, October 15, 1905. Adults and children found their familiar favorites among the seven comic strips packed into four 16-by-22½-inch pages; such as Richard Outcault's full-page *Buster Brown*. That day Buster and his dog, Tige, had their photograph taken in a crowded barnyard, and proceeds from its sale would be donated to "the home for old horses and cows."

Among the other strips was a half-page of *The Terrors of the Tiny Tads* by G. Verbeek, a charming strip of verbal and visual puns. Featuring four boy-pixies in an enchanted land of hybrid animals, the strip often mixed the natural with the mechanical; for example, a Cockatooring Car, a Camelevator, and a Hippoautomobile. Winsor McCay was represented by six panels of *Little Sammy Sneeze,* an episode in which Sammy tags along with three girls prattling on about collecting autumn leaves. In his inimitable way, Sammy blows both leaves and dust into the girls' faces.

But on the last full page of the comic section, readers discovered a second and new offering from McCay. *Little Nemo in Slumberland* was unlike any comic strip seen before or since and, for McCay, it represented a major creative leap, one far grander in scope, imagination, color, design, and motion experimentation than any previous McCay comic strip (or those of his peers). For readers, *Little Nemo* became an exhilarating weekly fantasy adventure, a cartoon epic of sustained drama, both visually beautiful and compelling, with a cast of developing personalities, chief among them the boy-dreamer Nemo. McCay's son, Robert, was the model for Nemo, a juvenile Everyman whose name is Latin for "No one."

Little Nemo in Slumberland ran in the Sunday supplement of the *Herald* until July 23, 1911. (When McCay joined the Hearst papers, the strip reappeared in the *New York American* under the title *In the Land of Wonderful Dreams* from September 3, 1911, to December 26, 1914.) Within a year of its debut, *Little Nemo* was translated into seven foreign languages; Victor Herbert composed music for a lavish operetta adaptation of the strip that opened on Broadway in the fall of 1908; and McCay's first animated cartoon, *Little Nemo,* featuring characters from the strip, was presented in his vaudeville act in 1911. The popularity of the strip led to numerous merchandising items, including articles of clothing, playing cards, and games.

Each week in the *Nemo* comic strip, Winsor McCay slowly revealed Slumberland bit by bit, as it gradually became clearer to him. This dreamlike way of unraveling a story was how Lewis Carroll revealed Wonderland and L. Frank Baum presented Oz. Like those classic works of fantasy, of which *Little Nemo in Slumberland* is the creative equal, the whole of the adventures is less satisfactory than the many memorable episodes.

In the first *Nemo* episode, in the top panel extending across the page and incorporating the title, the King of Slumberland orders a clown (called an "Oomp") in a tall hat to bring Nemo to him. In the second panel, the Oomp appears in Nemo's bedroom and presents the nightshirt-clad, tousle-haired boy with a spotted pony named Somnus.

When Nemo rides his galloping steed through the night sky, the Oomp (now changed to a bird) warns him not to race. But by the sixth panel, Nemo is challenged to a race to Moontown by various animals astride other animals. Nemo accepts the challenge and gallops through space until Somnus trips on a star. Nemo falls off the horse and, descending through the black, wonders calmly, dreamlike: "what the Oomp will say." In the last panel, awakening in his bedroom—head on the floor and his feet on top of the bed—Nemo has failed his first test. Reality intrudes upon the fragile fantasy and readers must wait another week to continue the adventure.

LITTLE NEMO IN SLUMBERLAND

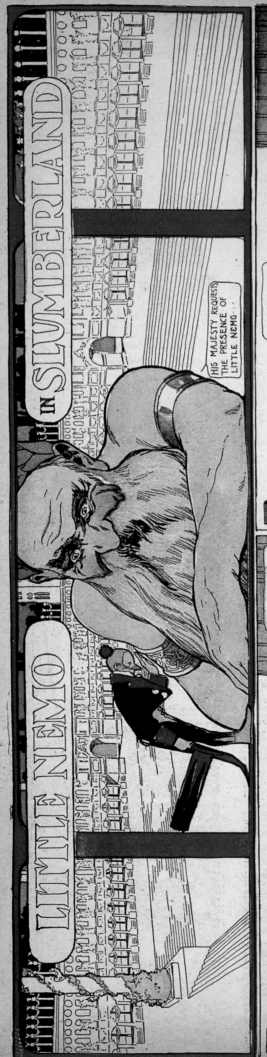

HIS MAJESTY REQUESTS THE PRESENCE OF LITTLE NEMO-

AND I'VE BROUGHT A LITTLE SPOTTED NIGHT HORSE FOR YOU TO RIDE BUT YOU MUSTN'T WHIP HIM OR DRIVE HIM FAST. DO YOU HEAR?

HIS NAME IS SOMNUS AND HE'S AS GENTLE AS CAN BE

BE KIND TO HIM, I WARN YOU.

GRACIOUS! WHAT IS THAT?

1 LITTLE NEMO HAD JUST FALLEN ASLEEP WHEN AN OOMP APPEARED WHO SAID "YOU ARE REQUESTED TO APPEAR BEFORE HIS MAJESTY, MORPHEUS OF SLUMBERLAND."

2 NEMO WAS SURPRISED AS WELL AS DELIGHTED TO RECEIVE THE KING'S INVITATION, SO HE SCRAMBLED OUT OF BED AND MOUNTED THE PRANCING PONY WHICH NOW APPEARED.

"SLUMBERLAND IS THE MOST WONDERFUL PLACE IN THE SKY. YOU MUSTN'T MISS A SINGLE THING. SEE IT ALL!

I'LL RACE YOU TO MOONTOWN WHAT DO

3 "SLUMBERLAND IS A LONG WAY OFF THROUGH MANY MILES OF WEIRD SCENES" SAID OOMP "BUT BE GOOD TO YOUR HORSE AND YOU WILL ARRIVE THERE SAFE AND SOUND."

4 AFTER TRAVELING SOME THOUSANDS OF MILES HE MET THE OOMP IN DISGUISE WHO CAUTIONED HIM AGAIN TO BE CAREFUL ABOUT SPEEDING HIS FAITHFUL MOUNT

October 15, 1905: The premiere episode of Little Nemo in Slumberland *in the New York Herald. (Collection Robert Lesser)*

This simple beginning afforded McCay an ample showcase for exciting visuals. The King, seen at the top of the page from the chest up, dwarfs the Oomp and, with furrowed brow, stern countenance, and massive size and presence, resembles Michelangelo's colossal God the Father. This patriarchal symbol of authority set the tone for the predominantly masculine world that was Slumberland. Beyond the King, we glimpse a portion of the palace grounds and buildings of Slumberland—wide spaces and long staircases leading to ornate loggias and arches. This dreamland would not be fully revealed until February 1906, when Nemo finally arrives there; and not until he meets the Princess of Slumberland in July would we leisurely tour the grounds and the buildings.

In the meantime, each week readers saw tantalizing parts of Slumberland, bits of architecture that appear to be based on McKim, Mead & White's contributions to buildings and areas at the World's Columbian Exposition in Chicago in 1893. McCay may have returned to Chicago to visit the famous "White City" or viewed stereopticon photographs of the buildings' classical and romantic eclecticism, generous scale, and placement within broad spaces. As further portions of Slumberland were revealed through the years, it appears that parts of it were inspired by the Luxembourg Palace in Paris (a photo of which McCay had among his stereopticon collection) and Luna Park and Dreamland, two amusement parks at Coney Island near McCay's home.

The character's outline was in McCay's now-familiar Art Nouveau line: thicker than that of objects (and characters) in the background, which lent a feeling of distance and perspective. McCay used color abstractly, adding to the visual intensity of the work. For example, in the premiere strip's fourth panel, Nemo's bedroom has been replaced by a lemon yellow limbo space in which Nemo sits upon his pony, Somnus. In the next five panels the background colors change to orange, green, blue, red, and violet, reflecting a psychedelic simulation of the boy's dream experience.

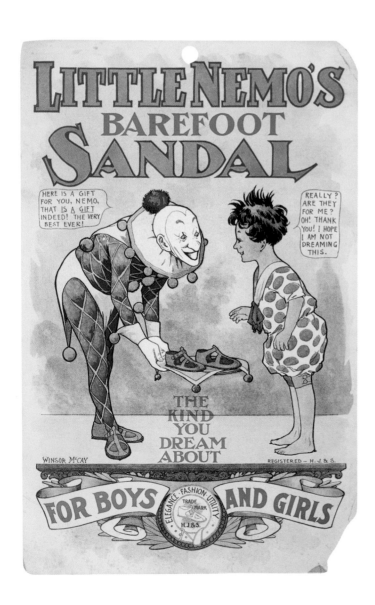

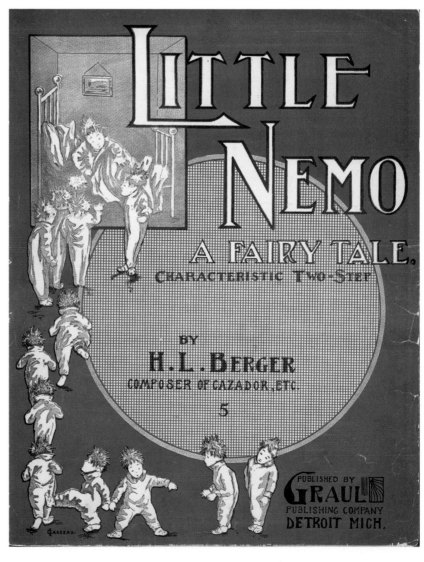

The unreal color styling extended from the backgrounds to the characters: in the sixth panel Nemo is challenged to a race by a pink monkey riding a green kangaroo; in the next two panels they are joined by a purple rabbit astride a yellow pig, an orange frog on a red lion, an orange squirrel on a blue camel, and an orange cricket on a violet goat. The addition of the multicolored animals cavorting across the sky in action poses increased the visual energy of the strip, and McCay increased the intensity even more by bringing on an array of radiating stars.

McCay as craftsman and artist was at the height of his skill in the *Little Nemo* series, as was the *Herald*'s printing staff. In fact, the *Herald*'s method of color printing was superior to that of any other newspaper of the time. In 1914 the New York Graphic Arts Exposition cited the *Herald* color plant as "representing absolute perfection of application" of the Ben Day process of shading pictures for reproduction on the press or the lithographic stone.

Court of Fountains, Luna Park, Coney Island, N.Y.

2005

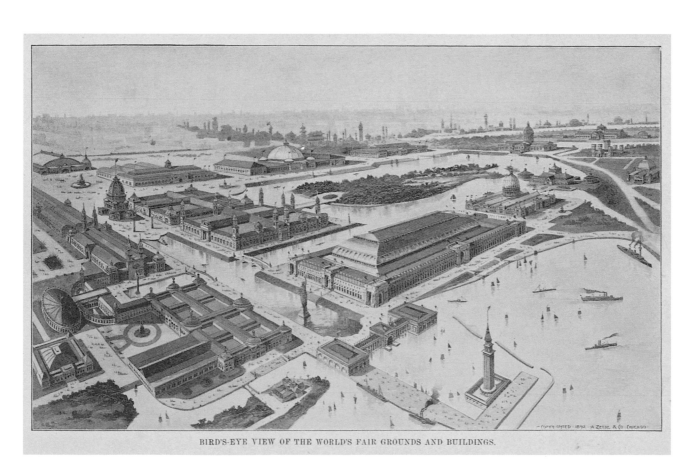

BIRD'S-EYE VIEW OF THE WORLD'S FAIR GROUNDS AND BUILDINGS.

103

In reporting this honor, the *Herald* revealed how its skillful master craftsmen achieved subtle gradations in hues:

One of the problems of etching on plates of zinc is to get gradations of light and shade or tone.

The Ben Day process consists in placing a fine meshed, inked screen over the parts of the plate to be shaded and then making dots by passing a roller over it. That portion of the plate which is not to be printed from is protected by a gamboge solution.

The screen is regulated by a delicately adjusted gauge, manipulated by a thumb screw, and the ground may be light or dark as the operator thinks best. It is in the various modifications of the process, the placing of dots and lines in greater number where deeper color is desired, and in the soft blending of tones that the artist-artisans of the *Herald* plant excel in.

Experts who have watched the application of the Ben Day process in the making of color plates for illustrating the Magazine section, the Fashion Magazine and the Comic Supplement of the *Herald,* declare that the skill and the fine perception of values there shown are marvelous. The artists in zinc, who make these etchings for the use of the *Herald,* have to foresee what the effect of the various color combinations will be when the final proof is made because often 4 or 5 different plates are used in the preparation of one color page. The harmony of colors depends much upon the ability of the makers of the plate. The slightest variation in tone may destroy the conception of the artist and produce an effect that would be harsh and coarse. The men of the *Herald* color department turn out plates of exceptional excellence, and yet rapidly enough to meet every requirement of newspaper speed.[19]

BELOW:
On October 4, 1908, McCay contrasts the mundane with the exotic when Nemo's bathtub metamorphoses into a swamp complete with reptiles, then becomes an open sea full of passing ships. Finally, the boy dreamer finds himself nude on a small ice floe in the Arctic Ocean, being chased by a hungry polar bear. (Collection Ray Winsor Moniz)

OPPOSITE:
Nemo loses Flip and a pig-Latin–speaking friend during a wild ride down a bizarre staircase that constantly changes its shape and leads to outer space. Here, McCay again proves his total mastery of alternating (even irrational) perspective and architectural points of view. (Collection Ray Winsor Moniz)

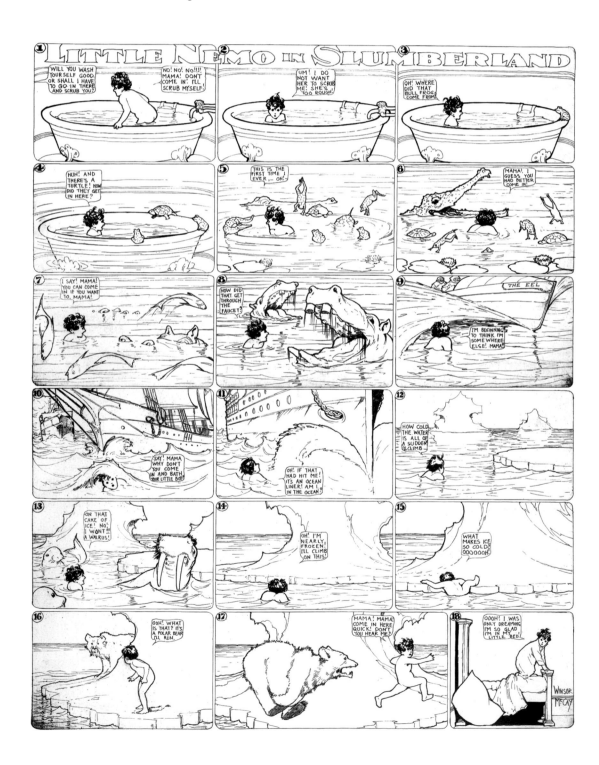

LITTLE NEMO IN SLUMBERLAND
COME ON, MAMA SAYS FOR US TO GET OUT OF HERE! WE'LL SLIDE DOWN!
CUT IT OUT! CUT IT OUT PROFESSOR! HIS MOTHER DOES NOT LIKE MUSIC! WE'LL SLIDE DOWN!
FOR MERCY'S SAKE STOP THAT NOISE! WHO IS THAT PLAYING THAT HORRIBLE MOUTH-ORGAN WHY DON'T YOU ALL COME DOWN STAIRS, AND GO OUT IN THE YARD?
ARE YOU READY? SAY THE WORD!
WAIT A MINUTE! WAIT A MINUTE!
I AM EDDY RAY!
AH! HERE WE GO! A MILE A MINUTE!
BE CARE-FUL!
GO FASTER! GO FASTER WHAT'S THE DELAY?
GOING FAST E-NOUGH TO SUIT ME!
THIS IS THE WAY TO SLIDE A BANISTER! YOU SEE? TAKE IT EASY!
THIS STAIRWAY LOOKS AWFUL BIG TO ME ALL AT ONCE!
I DON'T CARE HOW BIG IT IS! I'M COMFORT-ABLE! SEE?
I NEVER KNEW IT WAS SO LONG, HUH!
OOK LAY OU TA! IS THAY IS A ARP SHAY URVE CAY! EE BAY AREFUL CAY!
WOW! WHAT WAS THAT? OH! OH!
IT'S A SHARP CURVE! OH! FLIP! WHERE YOU GOING?
I OLD TAY OO YAY OO TA OOK LAY OUTAY IDDEN DEY I DE?
WHAT AILS THIS STAIR WAY ZOWIE!
MAMA! MAMA! SOMETHING IS THE MATTER WITH THIS STAIRWAY!
CAN'T YOU COME AND HELP YOUR LITTLE BOY?
IS THAY IS I MAY INISH FAY!
OH! THERE GOES KIDDO OH! OH!
OW NAY OR FAY A OOD GAY UMP BAY! OH!
I NEVER KNEW THIS STAIRWAY WAS SO LONG!
SURELY THERE IS AN END TO IT SOMEWHERE OH! IF I COULD ONLY STOP!
I'M GETTING DIZ-ZY! WHERE CAN THIS PLACE BE? OH! I'M SO DIZZY!
HELP! OH! OH! HELP ME! HELP ME!
OH! I'M GLAD MAMA DID NOT HEAR ME! HUH!
WINSOR McCAY.

It is true that the sensitive *Herald* color craftsmen and their technical expertise added enormously to the grand rainbow of colors that saturated *Little Nemo in Slumberland,* but the daring choice of hues came from McCay himself. On the original *Nemo* drawings, inked in black on quality white bristol board, McCay would write notes in nonphotographing blue pencil to a Mr. Hunt of the *Herald* color department, requesting specific colors for backgrounds, props, and characters.

In the margin on the right side of the original *Nemo* drawing published on January 21, 1906 (in which Nemo tunnels through snow and is chased by a polar bear), McCay penciled this message:

Mr. Hunt,
This is a snow forest. All the trees and foliage are snow. Plenty of purple and blue tones. The only bright color will be in the costume of the figures. An orange sky. The rest all pale blues, pinks and purples. Creme colored [indecipherable] with cold blue shadows.
Mc.

McCay placed dialogue in balloons within the strip's frames and added captions under the picture panels, but the latter proved superfluous and were eliminated five months later. The emphasis in the strip was on action—characters in motion in settings that alter their perspective in almost every panel. The total design of each week's page varied in order to accommodate the action within the narrative. In the first strip, the panel sizes were almost all uniformly based on the wide rectangular shape of the top panel containing the King, but the next week's episode featured a forest of giant mushrooms, and as Nemo walks downward into the forest, the shapes of the panels elongate into a step design as the length of the mushrooms is revealed. When they collapse and fall, the step shape of the panels reverses itself. A similar page design was used in the next week's strip to showcase the length of stork legs and Nemo on stilts.

For a Thanksgiving page, a giant turkey attempts to swallow Nemo's house. McCay placed this pivotal moment within a large circle in the middle of the page. He repeated the device the following week when Nemo arrives on the moon. McCay's imaginative use of the page space and his free alterations of the layouts to complement the action add to the jolts of visual pleasure one enjoys in *Little Nemo in Slumberland*.

McCay's intuitive awareness of dream psychology is apparent in the first five pages of the strip, which are based on classic dream fears everyone has experienced: falling through space, being crushed by falling objects, impalement, drowning, and the instability of the surface beneath us. Reiterated over and over in *Little Nemo* is the theme of the fragility of the dream world and the moralistic rule of obedience and respect for laws (even if one does not understand them) in order to accomplish your goals.

In the strip's second appearance (October 22), another clown—a harlequin named Pokoko—causes Nemo's bed to sink through the floor to an underground cavern and a forest of giant mushrooms. The clown warns Nemo not to touch the mushrooms ("They are so very tender") on his 777-mile trek to Slumberland. But, nervous and tired from walking, Nemo accidently stumbles against a mushroom, and the entire forest collapses on him. On October 29, the clown Chiceeko lends Nemo his stilts and advises him to "get on the royal path" and "fear no one." A flock of lovebirds—storklike creatures with unusually long, stiltlike legs—crowd Nemo, trying to kiss him, resulting in his fall into a thorny cactus bed. Judith O'Sullivan found a "reference to the world of narcotics and the theme of hallucinogens" in the use of mushrooms and cacti: "Peyote is obtained from one species, mescaline from two others."[20]

LEFT:

The marvelous dragon-chariot from Little Nemo in Slumberland, *which appeared in the* Herald *on July 29, 1906, carries Nemo and the Princess through the royal gardens to visit the talking Honey Buds, flowers that "never die"—as anthropomorphic and charming as the flower people in Grandville's illustrations for* Un Autre Monde (Another World). *(Woody Gelman Collection— Ohio State University Library for Communication and Graphic Arts)*

OPPOSITE:

The February 2, 1908, episode from an extraordinary seven-week adventure in Befuddle Hall, a dime-museum-like area of Slumberland filled with distorting mirrors, trick staircases, and spookhouse effects. Here Nemo, Flip, and Impie change shape drastically in McCay's tour de force depiction of funny and eerie funhouse-mirror shape shifting. (Collection Robert Lesser)

NEW YORK, SUNDAY, FEBRUARY 2, 1908.— BY THE NEW YORK HERALD COMPANY.   PRICE FIVE CENTS.

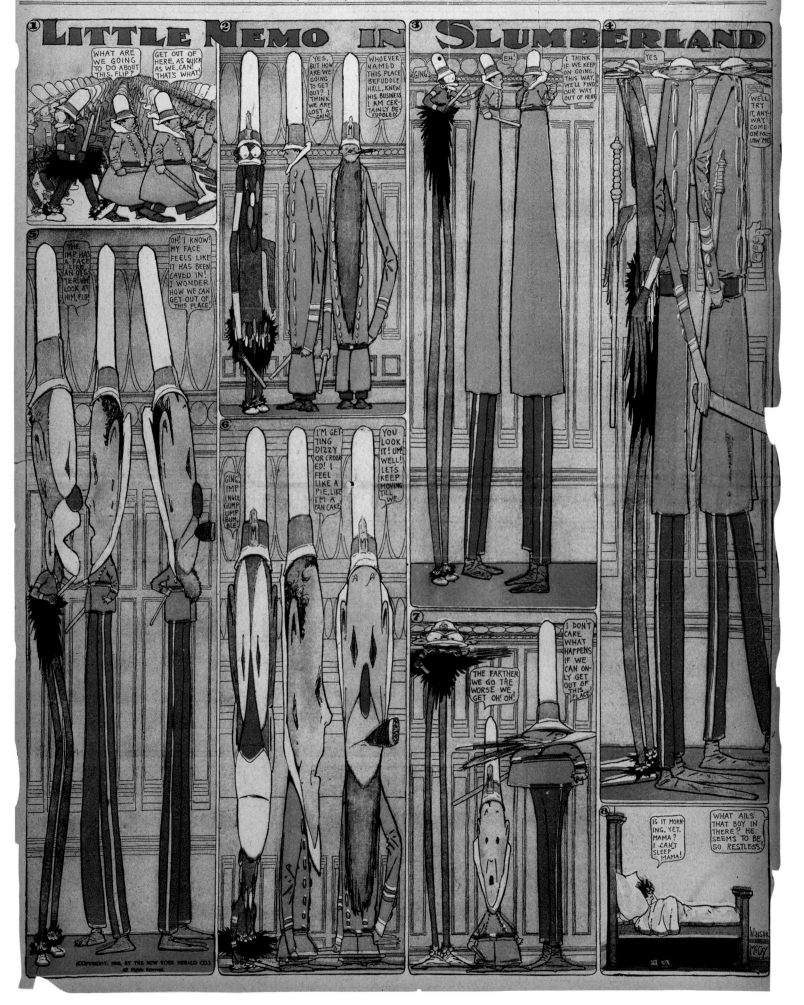

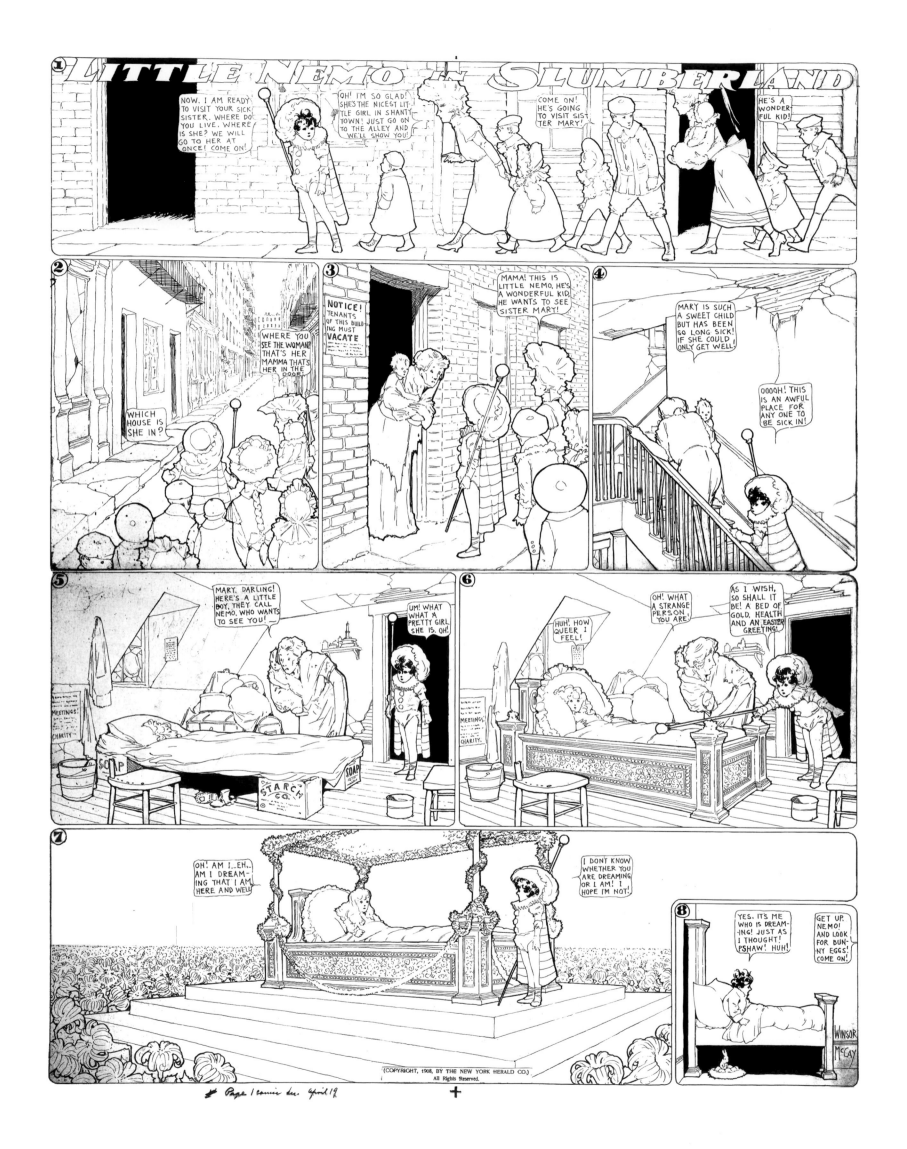

By the third episode (November 3), Nemo's bedroom is flooded with water and he floats out to sea, going underwater where the "Magoozla," an ugly aquatic monster sent by the Oomp, tries to swim with Nemo to Slumberland, but the boy kicks and screams himself awake. On November 12, Cheecaumo, a pretty fairy in a tutu, guides Nemo across "the enchanted bridge," a carpeted pathway supported by a long line of slaves. The slaves try to catch Nemo and wobble the bridge. The fairy changes Nemo into a monkey (a "chiquito") in order to speed his journey, but the road collapses beneath him.

The instability of dreams and their world is particularly poignant in the November 19 episode: Nemo gets up for a drink of water and discovers a cave of glass inhabited by glass people. Bulzubb, another clown, brings him to meet beautiful Queen Crystalette, who is made of glass and is so fragile she can barely bow. Nemo, "blind and deaf with infatuation," ignores Bulzubb's warning not to touch her. He bends the glass Queen backward in an embrace and kiss full of sexual passion that is completely out of character for the shy seven-year-old boy. Nemo's lustful impulse and disobedience are immediately regretted, for the Queen and her retinue shatter to pieces. "Heartsick and frightened," Nemo runs home and wakes up with "the groans of the dying guardsmen still ringing in his ears."

Little Nemo was based on McCay's son Robert's physical appearance, but Nemo was really Winsor McCay's alter ego, his child-double acting out the artist's fears and hopes, escaping into a world beyond drab reality.

For dramatic and romantic interest, McCay introduced the Princess of Slumberland in the second episode. Daughter of the King (named Morpheus), she is a dark-haired beauty resembling McCay's wife Maude. McCay took his time getting the Princess and Nemo together. After many delays and detours, they formally meet face-to-face on July 8, 1906, nearly nine months after the debut of the strip. Part of the reason for the delay was the introduction (on March 4) of an adversary to Nemo. This was Flip, a green-faced clown who chews a large cigar, wears a top hat labeled "Wake Up," and is a "bad and brazen brat [the opposite of Nemo], and an outcast member of the Dawn family, arch enemies to Slumberland and its people." McCay's son, Robert, once said Flip was based on Tiny Philips, a tough newsboy midget his father knew in Cincinnati, a fellow who smoked big cigars and dressed in oversized uniforms donated to him by the local firemen. Another source recalled McCay saying Flip was derived from seeing "a rotund black man with a greenish cast to his face" smoking a cigar on a Brooklyn street.[21]

The dramatic tension between Nemo and Flip led to a number of visually stunning adventures. After a visit to the Candy Islands, Flip brings away with him a grass-skirted black called Impie (or Impy), whose design was based on the *Jungle Imps* strip McCay drew in Cincinnati. Flip's attempts to teach the mischievous Imp to behave precipitated a slapstick relationship that continued for the duration of the strip.

Although a rival, Flip awakened in Nemo a generosity of spirit. First, Nemo helps Flip down from a precarious perch; eventually he stops a firing squad from shooting the fellow. Nemo's charitable qualities developed into Messianic tendencies, particularly in an unprecedented visit to Shanty Town (March 22 through April 26, 1908). Nemo already displayed Christlike abilities by walking on water (August 19 and September 2, 1906), but in run-down, poverty-stricken Shanty Town, he enables the blind to see and the lame to walk, and restores the dying to full health. With a tall staff (a magic wand?), a gift from a fairy, Nemo transforms not only people from rags to regal raiment but dilapidated buildings and streets become mini-versions of Slumberland's classical architecture.

The specific source of McCay's raised social consciousness is not known, but it was evident sporadically in his other comic strips and would reappear dramatically in *Little Nemo* between April 24 and August 14, 1910, when Nemo, Flip, and Impie visit Mars, a corporate-controlled, polluted planet of unhappy citizens.

OPPOSITE:

By November 8, 1908, Nemo and Flip are fast buddies who often participate in adventures with Impie, a black playmate who was captured by Flip from the Candy Islands. Here McCay plays with the comic strip itself as pastries become outlines before disappearing altogether. The trio is left in limbo—Flip and Impie fall away with no floor to stand on, while Nemo hangs on to the lines of the panel borders. When these collapse onto him, Nemo wonders "what is the matter with the artist . . ." (Collection Ray Winsor Moniz)

RIGHT:

This Little Nemo in Slumberland *strip from January 3, 1909 demonstrates McCay's mastery of animal anatomy and "animation."*

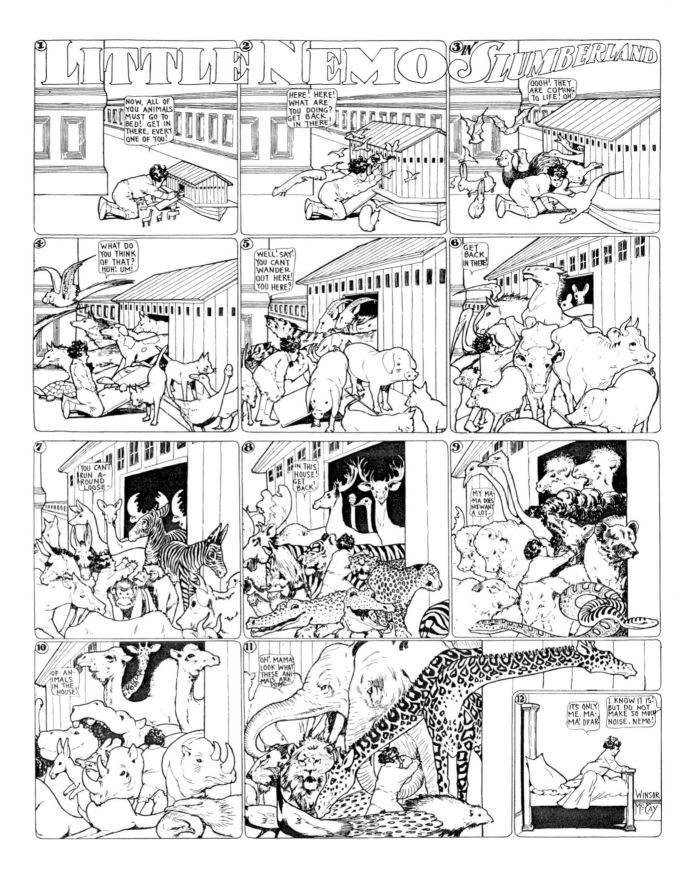

The bonding between Nemo and his buddies and the predominantly male environment of Slumberland led to an exclusion of the Princess in the series' most exuberant episodes. Maurice Sendak, who acknowledges Winsor McCay as a major artistic inspiration, has commented:

> The Princess is almost characterless, a glossy, fortyish-looking, Klimt type; and she is often very badly drawn—something so rare for McCay, it must be significant. Slumberland, like Wonderland, is a masculine-dominated society and the Princess is its token female, the only female in the regular cast. Nemo links up here with Captain Ahab and Huck Finn in the great American flight from women. Despite all talk to the contrary, he is not really satisfied with his princess; he'd much rather be out with the boys.
>
> Toward the end of 1907 the Princess is temporarily dropped, and immediately the action picks up.[22]

Some of the most visually complex episodes occur between January 19 and March 15, 1908, when Nemo, Flip, and Impie go off to explore an especially odd area of Slumberland known as Befuddle Hall. Here the trio stumble clownlike into multiples of themselves, stretch like distorted mirror images, and wander upside down and sideways over architectural sites dazzling in their detail and Renaissance perspective.

Little Nemo in Slumberland offers an extraordinary array of ravishing images that stay in the mind like remembered dreams. McCay's virtuoso draftsmanship is irresistible, as when butterflies seek shelter from the rain under an "umbrella tree," or the open mouth of a giant dragon becomes a traveling coach, or when a walking, talking icicle escorts us up the cold staircase of Jack Frost's palace.

As the strip continued, McCay moved from the fantastic inexorably toward reality, and he felt compelled to address current and future social problems. In the spring of 1910, Nemo and friends travel to Mars, which turns out to be similar to the nightmare of congested, polluted areas of overcrowding and greed on earth.

Mars is the antithesis of Slumberland—an unhappy world controlled by a selfish business magnate (Mr. B. Gosh and Company), who owns all the property and sells the inhabitants even the words they

COMIC SECTION.   THE NEW YORK HERALD.   FOUR PAGES.

NEW YORK, SUNDAY, MARCH 15, 1908.—BY THE NEW YORK HERALD COMPANY.   PRICE FIVE CENTS.

OPPOSITE:

*On March 1, 1908 an "earth-
quake" turns Slumberland and
its explorers topsy-turvy.*

BELOW:

*Neither cold rain nor scorching
sun deter Colonel Stall from
mercilessly exploiting Poor
Jake, a mute laborer in his
employ. Poor Jake, McCay's
last strip for the New York
Herald before he joined the
Hearst papers, appeared from
spring of 1909 through spring of
1911 and reflects the artist's
developing social consciousness.
(Collection Ray Winsor Moniz)*

speak and the air they breathe. Depressing as McCay's
Mars is in its prediction of Earth's current problems,
with the destruction of natural resources, selfish cor-
porate despotism, hijacking, oppressive architecture,
and all the rest, we are still impressed by his convincing drawings of the place.

Little Nemo in Slumberland won praise not only for
its technical perfectionism, but for the wholesome-
ness of the lead character and the general high moral
tone throughout. The Reverend R. J. (Bob) Burdette,
speaking at a 1909 dinner of the Associated Press and
the American Newspaper Publishers, called *Little
Nemo* "the only good comic." As reported in the April
23, 1909 *Herald,* Burdette attacked the Sunday colored comic supplements as "atrocious in drawing and
banal in humor," with *Little Nemo* the one exception.
"The morality of the comics supplement," concluded
Reverend Burdette, "is damnable when it is not
puerile, and out of all those I have seen I can find
only one that pleases me as being sweet, and clean
and beautiful and that is *Little Nemo.*"

McCay's raised social consciousness, demonstrated
in the Shanty Town and Mars sequences of *Nemo,* was
employed again in the last strip he created for the

Evening Telegram, one that appeared in 1909: *Poor Jake.*
The title character was a mute laborer, an employee
of Colonel Stall, who exploited Jake without mercy.

On two pages of his diary dated March 13 (no year
indicated), McCay wrote a draft about the origins of
Poor Jake and a summary of the series' plot:

How did I stumble onto the idea of *Poor Jake* for a
comic? said "Silas" in answer to a question put to him
by one of thousands who ask in their minds and by
mail to him. Well I didn't stumble on it—it was on the
horizon a tiny speck that grew as it came towards me to
be the big hit that it is. I have seen thousands of poor
Jakes in my life. The very reason you like the series is
because you have seen him too any time you look or
place you go. He may be disguised by a better appearance and better surroundings but underneath his hide
he is Poor Jake.

My Poor Jake is perhaps the limit of Poor Jakes or will
be before I get through with the series. He works for
Colonel and Mrs. Stall from early till late—no matter
how early one will get up one will find Jake up and
doing and no matter how late one stays out one will find
Jake has not yet returned. If you get up in the night
you will see Jake with a lantern attending to some detail
of work undone or overdone—he never says a word
and would be miserable idle. He is faithful, honest and

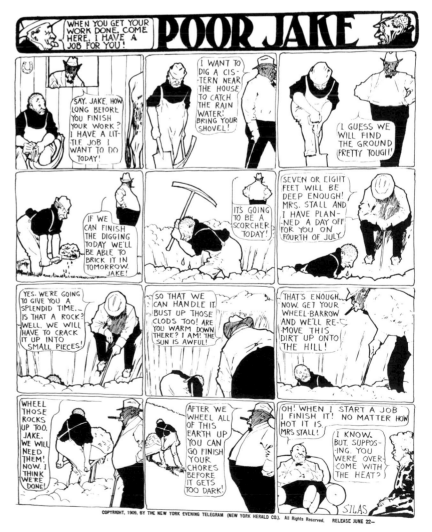

Here *Are* Men Who Make Evening Telegram Readers Laugh *Expert Artists* of Brush, Crayon, Pen and Pencil

PHOTO SCHERER

JOHN P COLLINS

S. CLIFFORD STERRETT. PHOTO STEFANO

WINSOR McCAY SILAS PHOTO SARONY

GARNET WARREN PHOTO STEFANO

HEPPNER BLACKMAN

(FROM THE EVENING TELEGRAM.)

CLEVER CARTOONISTS AND COMIC ARTISTS TO MAKE 1907 MERRY.

Staff of Experts with Brush and Crayon for Coming Year Is Presented in Formidable Array.

IN devoting ourselves to specializing a department of true wit and humor we present to our readers to-day a description and biographical sketch of our artists for 1907, who may well be called the "Kings of Fun."

Never before has this newspaper gathered together so formidable an array of humor makers, funny men and powerful cartoonists who stand at the head of their class. For 1907 special plans have been laid for the insertion every day of some special feature of humor which has been chosen because of its originality and true essence of wit. No stale, tiresome, old or worked out jokes will be presented. Nothing but fresh, crisp, snappy and side splitting humor will appear from day to day to delight the readers of this newspaper as in the past.

This newspaper has reason to congratulate itself and its readers in afford[illegible] ...y and to look forward [illegible] humorous treat of up to date fun that will [illegible]eal to young and old.

NORMAN E JENNETT

C S RIGBY.

GEO. E. WESTCOTT JR.

Winsor McCay.

HAVE you ever eaten a cheese sandwich and suffered the consequences? Or have you ever partaken of a Welsh rarebit and spent a night of mental agony with strange, imaginary beings? If so, Winsor McCay, or "Silas, the Dreamer," needs but little recommendation, as

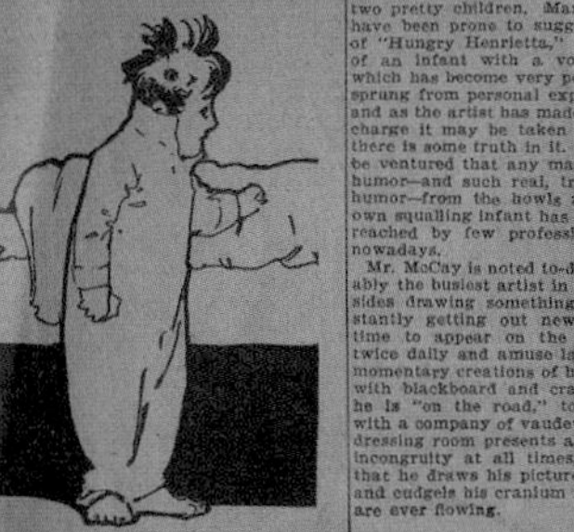

LITTLE NEMO,
One of Winsor McCay's famous characters.

his fame as an interpreter of the ravings of sleeping dyspeptics is spread broadcast.

So effective has he become in placing a humorous side on the sufferings of a disordered stomach that it is easy to imagine the victims themselves laughing at the manner in which their helpless writhings are pictured.

As one of the chief diaphragm splitters of a modern age Winsor McCay ranks among the best. His humor is always fresh, satisfying and original. His ideas seem to be legion and his pen ever ready. Not content, however, with the success brought to him by his creation of "The Rarebit Fiend," he has added to his various courses of humor with studies of Topsy Turvy Land as depicted in "Little Nemo in Slumberland," "Little Sammy Sneeze," "A Pilgrim's Progress" and other lines which for clean, wholesome satire have never been equalled in their respective lines.

Anybody who has seen his pictures of "Little Nemo" need not be reminded of the ingenious surprises every chapter of the dreaming boy's adventures bring forth. The pictures are more than literary in that they amuse both young and old, as well as furnishing them with food for thought. His imaginary lands with their startling fauna and flora and their odd inhabitants posses such a strange, logical coherence in their topsyturviness as to almost convince you that somewhere they really exist.

Mr. McCay has only himself to thank for his fecundity of ideas. They are his and his alone, and it is through his home life more than his worldly experience that he has been able to give a picture expression to the many phases of a natural existence as shown in his drawings. "Little Nemo" in real life is Mr. McCay's own son, who, when very young, was in the custom of telling his father of the queer dreams he would have at times. Oftentimes Mr. McCay will show his drawings of some resplendent dream to the boy for approval and act on the little fellow's suggestions as to the correctness of things.

His idea of founding the series of "Dreams of a Rarebit Fiend" came from outsiders, and not from personal experience. Mr. McCay, it is pleasant to relate, has what is popularly known as a "cast iron stomach," which is shown by the absence of any pessimistic strains which otherwise might have been sifted into his various studies.

Mr. McCay was born in the far Northwest, but lived most of his life in Cincinnati. His home is now in Sheepshead Bay, N. Y., where he lives with his wife and two pretty children. Many of his friends have been prone to suggest that his idea of "Hungry Henrietta," a pictorial study of an infant with a voracious appetite, which has become very popular, may have sprung from personal experience at home, and as the artist has made no denial of the charge it may be taken for granted that there is some truth in it. And it may also be ventured that any man who can glean humor—and such real, true, side splitting humor—from the howls and yowls of his own squalling infant has attained a height reached by few professional funny men nowadays.

Mr. McCay is noted to-day as being probably the busiest artist in the country. Besides drawing something funny and constantly getting out new ideas, he finds time to appear on the vaudeville stage twice daily and amuse large audiences by momentary creations of his various studies with blackboard and crayon. At present he is "on the road," touring the States with a company of vaudeville players. His dressing room presents a scene of strange incongruity at all times, for it is there that he draws his pictures for publication and cudgels his cranium for the ideas that are ever flowing.

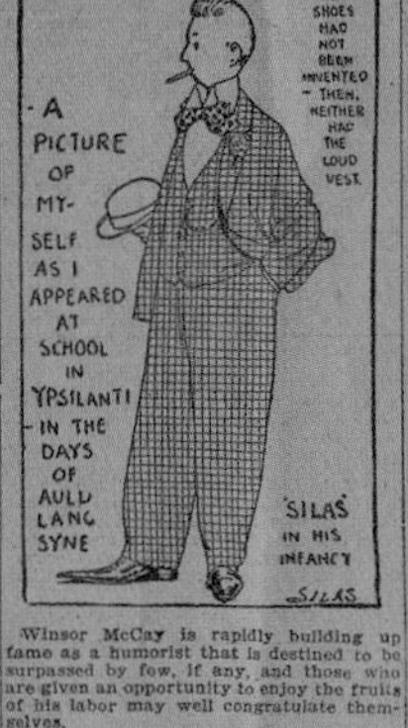

Winsor McCay is rapidly building up fame as a humorist that is destined to be surpassed by few, if any, and those who are given an opportunity to enjoy the fruits of his labor may well congratulate themselves.

Garnet Warren.

IN that true saying "The pen is mightier that the sword" might be embodied the fact that in modern times the pen would not prove half so effective were it not embellished with live, striking, up to date cartoons. Newspapers of the present day are coming to depend upon the cartoon as a weapon and instrument of power more and more as the times progress.

It is apparent, therefore, that it is no trifling commission which will be held in the little army of artists depicted on this page by Garnet Warren, known from coast to coast for his forceful cartooning of public men.

Of the few artists who make cartoons their specialty and have by reason of the effectiveness of their work become widely known, Mr. Warren stands in a class by himself. Hardly anybody could have failed to notice the sameness in style which a majority of cartoonists develop in their work, but in Mr. Warren's case this is not so. He never draws two car-

BUSY MR. WARREN.

toons that are alike in style, facial expression or caricature. In fact, apart from the subject depicted, it would seem that he develops some new characteristic in every line.

Mr. Warren has recently come from the Boston Herald, where his talent was conceded to be of a signal order. With the ability to draw a fine, strong and artistic picture he at all times possesses the imagination that is uppermost in the public mind and expresses it in such a way that it will make more impression than the labored argument of an editorial leader.

One of the chief reasons for Mr. Warren's rapid rise in his work is his ability to employ some apt quotation from Shakespeare or other well known author, or an epigrammatic phrase of his own.

Mr. Warren was born in London a little more than thirty years ago, but his early days were spent in Australia. When in boyhood he turned his talents to caricature many a "licking" was his reward from the school teacher, who discovered himself a victim of his pupil's by-work.

Mr. Warren's idea regarding cartooning as a profession was greatly stimulated by the appearance of several drawings of Phil May in a local newspaper in a little Australian town. It was then that Mr. Warren began studying hard to improve his work, and later came to the United States to complete his success.

John P. Collins.

NOT very long ago a young man was sitting in a Broadway car when a middle aged man pushed his way through the crowd and clung to a spare strap. The conductor, a big, burly man, brushed over to the spot, where the little man was vainly struggling to get his hand out of his pocket so as to pay his fare. Finally he did so, and as the conductor reached for the register handle his elbow knocked off the little man's hat, and the young man who was watching him began to foresee breakers ahead. To his surprise a look of joy spread o'er the little man's face and he made a wild rush for the door.

"That reminds me," he muttered, "my wife told me to be sure to buy a new hat."

The expression "that reminds me" remained rooted in the mind of the young man, and for the remainder of the journey he studied out a series of funny adventures which are nearly true to life, as many can testify. The young man was John P. Collins and he is the artist whose drawings of "Pa Puddin'head" proved one of the hits of the year. The forgetful old man and the manner in which he is forcibly reminded of a neglected errand have been pictured by Mr. Collins in a style peculiar to himself and exceptionally funny.

Mr. Collins is also noted for his pictures of children. Street gamin, urchins and the motley crew who yell themselves hoarse with their "wuxtries" are his special delight, and he has adopted a unique method of obtaining local color.

With a pocketful of small change Mr. Collins is wont to assemble some of the "toughest" characters he can find averaging from six to twelve years old, and while they eagerly await the bounty which is always forthcoming he makes the sketches he wishes. Some of the drawing resulting from Mr. Collins' efforts in this branch of his work have called forth unstinted praise from critics and he is fast becoming an acknowledged master in his line of "kid" pictures.

S. Clifford Sterrett.

SELDOM it is that Jack of All Trades is master of any one of them, but S. Clifford Sterrett, whose idea of "Ventriloquial Vag" is one of the hits of the year among humor artists, is the exception to the rule. Mr. Sterrett is an expert on steel manufacturing, has been a commercial traveller and is also adept in many other lines of work. But in none of these has he so excelled or met with such success as has been his since he turned his versatile mind to comic drawings.

His pictures of the funny bald headed tramp who causes all kinds of trouble by transferring his voice from one person to another have caused a hit that it is safe to say will last beyond those of many of his fellows. Mr. Sterrett has been fortunate in finding a subject which never

STERRETT AS COLLINS SEES HIM.

seems to tire and also affords seemingly never ending situations that are excruciatingly laughable.

Mr. Sterrett was destined by his parents to be a herdsman of cattle on the home farm in Minnesota, but from the first the boy longed to adapt himself to other lines of work and finally succeeded in gaining permission to journey to Cleveland.

His natural propensity for drawing did not develop itself until several years later, when he was busying himself in mechanical lines. While attempting to draw a caricature of a friend at one time he found that the task was easier than he had imagined and the result more pleasant than he had expected. It was shortly after that, or, to be exact, about two years ago, that he visit New York city to try his hand there. The suggestion was followed out and there hasn't been a day since that the artist has had to worry about the future.

Sterrett's Idea of Winsor McCay.

George E. Westcott, Jr.

"GOOD OLD ELI" is represented among the clever coterie by George E. Westcott, Jr., a cartoonist and comic sketch artist who has recently been "discovered" and who is "budding" fast. Although only twenty-one years old, Mr. Westcott has developed many new and original ideas of great promise and is a valuable addition to the staff of the artists who are pictured herewith.

Mr. Westcott has a little secret stowed away which is now made known for the first time. Some months before Charles Dana Gibson's great picture "The Eternal Question" was produced before the public Mr. Westcott drew a sketch along similar lines. It was published and brought forth great praise from all sides.

It was shortly afterward that the great Gibson picture was brought out, and, although Mr. Westcott does not claim that there was any plagiarism on Mr. Gibson's side, he points the incident out as a strange coincidence and a proof of the saying that "great minds run in the same channel."

C. S. Rigby.

KNOWN to his many friends as the "Fairyland Artist," C. S. Rigby has probably brought more delight to the hearts of children by his quaint sketches of toy life than any other artist of the day. He possesses the unique trait of animating toys with his brush in exactly the manner a child would wish to see them if it were possible to do so in reality.

Noah and Mrs. Noah and Ham and Shem, the animals and the Ark are all given a lifelike look and appearance, although retaining their wooden features. The monkey on the stick, the jumping jack, the Teddy bear and all the other animal toys can be portrayed by Mr. Rigby in comic situations just as if toys had always been able to converse and quarrel and were not inert objects.

Mr. Rigby's specialty in this line has always made him a favorite with the younger generation, while for grown folk the artist has developed other lines of humor that are leaders.

Who has not seen a real "Health Crank Hopkins" in everyday life, or a "Book Taught Bilkins" whose disappointments and struggles to learn how to do everything by the book brings to him so many calamities?

For 1907 Mr. Rigby has prepared an especially humorous line of adventures for both these characters. Their troubles seem to be unending, and, according to Mr. Rigby, so long as human beings furnish him with the material he will keep on caricaturing them in their various phases of disappointments.

For Mr. Rigby, like many other artists, gathers his ideas from what he sees going on around him every day. Nearly every series of comical happenings which are pictured in Mr. Rigby's drawings are taken from real life, so that there is more truth than fiction in what he draws.

Mr. Rigby is one of the most experienced artists in this country. He has drawn his funny toy pictures for nearly every prominent publication in the United States, but "Book Taught Bilkins" and "Health Crank Hopkins" are specialties reserved for exclusive use in these columns and will be seen nowhere else during the present year.

Heppner Blackman.

HEPPNER BLACKMAN, the originator of "Epitaphs for Live Ones," a series of caricatures on noted men of the present day, is another of the funmakers who deserve special mention.

A man with a new idea in any line of business is quickly appreciated in the present times, and Mr. Blackman has sprung into fame as a comic artist at short notice. In addition to the series mentioned Mr. Blackman has developed a penchant for making up jokes on current topics, accompanied by sketches, grotesque and possessing an original style with a peculiarly humorous flavor.

Unlike his fellows, Mr. Blackman is of grave demeanor and looks anything but the part of a comic artist. In fact, until two years ago he had little idea of ever turning his talents in drawing to business.

Mr. Blackman possesses a unique history. He was born in Heppner, Ore., in 1882 and was named after the town, which had been founded by his uncle. He also bears the distinction of being the first white child to be born in the town.

His ambition as a young man was to become an expert stenographer, and in this he succeeded to the extent that he secured, after hard study, a position as private secretary to Judge Campbell, of San Francisco. It was while holding this position that he discovered that he had a natural talent for drawing, and was surprised after submitting some sketches to the San Francisco Call to have them accepted and a request made for more.

So successful did he finally become that he gave up his position with Judge Camp-

BLACKMAN, BY HIMSELF.

bell and devoted himself entirely to his drawings. It was shortly before the earthquake in San Francisco that he conceived the idea of drawing a series of "Epitaphs," and so good did he consider it that he came East, where he found little difficulty in securing high remuneration for his ideas.

Norman E. Jennett.

NO matter what may or may not have been said of his artist associates, Norman E. Jennett, who is responsible for the laughable "Monkeyshines of Marseleen," is the real "Huckleberry." His friends from his home town, Wayne, N. C., have called him that ever since he drew his first picture, and as such he has been known elsewhere.

His drawings are as satisfactory as a huckleberry. He makes poor Marseleen as blue as a huckleberry and then fills him with joy such as fresh huckleberry pie would give. So Mr. Jennett has come to be known as the "Huckleberry Boy," and the nick name will probably stick.

Few artists can make their hearers smile as quickly as "Huckleberry" Jen-

JENNETT, BY WARREN.

nett. His face, in fa[illegible] is generally one big smile. A long tim[illegible]o, when he first appeared at a New Yo[illegible] newspaper office to submit sketches for p[illegible]lication, he was smiling broadly, althou[illegible] the refusal of the drawings would ha[illegible] meant going supperless.

And from that time he [illegible] been one of the funniest funny men [illegible] New Yo[illegible] city, which is saying a gre[illegible] man. Mr. Jennett probab[illegible] career as an artist at an ea[illegible] any of his confreres. He [illegible] years old when he came to w[illegible] son county, North Carolina[illegible] and Observer. In a fe[illegible] worked himself to the t[illegible] toons were the talk of th[illegible]

Mr. Jennett, however, [illegible] much for cartooning as [illegible] which, it has proved, was [illegible]

[illegible] ot at [illegible] owing. [illegible] for nightfall, [illegible] begagoing. [illegible] mber you lie, [illegible] blisses, [illegible] lingering by, [illegible] with kisses. [illegible] ou be near, [illegible] above you; [illegible] don to me the most [illegible] —I love you! [illegible] VE FARNELL.

willing—strong, healthy and cheerful. He will drop his work to run an errand or hoist a safe and return to his own work again without a murmur. He suffers no heat cold or pain and laughs only when alone. If by chance you should ask where does he sleep? We just role [sic] our eyes toward the barn or garret and forget it. He eats little quickly and alone. In fact eating and sleeping are only trifling incidents of the day and the least hindrence [sic] to his duties. He does not have to be asked. He sees work everywhere he goes and at all times.

McCay's contract as an employee of James Gordon Bennett was coming to an end. By June 1911 William Randolph Hearst was already crowing proudly in a quarter-page announcement in his papers that Winsor McCay and his "funny folk" had joined the *New York American* "family." An illustration by McCay, spread across the top of the Hearst newspapers, featured all his characters, most of them dancing for joy. Mr. Bunion, for instance, doffs his hat as he dances a jig, saying "At last I'll get rid of this valise!" Little Nemo proclaims, "Now we can do and go where we please!" A man and woman in bed complain about an "awful dream . . . that Silas had quit working!"

McCay left Bennett's papers for a number of reasons, chief among them money and the need for artistic and personal freedom. It is sad and ironic to see McCay's joyful cartoon characters looking toward the Hearst organization as a panacea. Unfortunately, the opposite would prove true, for gradually his new employer would lock McCay into a financial dependency that limited his artistic outlets severely.

Before leaving the *Herald,* McCay completed one last extended adventure in *Little Nemo*: an airship tour to a number of American and Canadian cities. Between January 8 and March 19, 1911, Nemo, Flip, and Impie visited Boston, Montreal, Quebec, Ottawa, Toronto, Buffalo, Pittsburgh, Wheeling, Cleveland, Toledo, and Detroit. McCay served up a number of lavishly detailed city and country panoramas for the tour, which in reality was a means of maximizing McCay's name and characters throughout the country before making the switch to the Hearst papers. (The chosen city usually featured the *Nemo* strip on the front page of the local paper.)

During his eight years on Bennett's newspapers, McCay drew hundreds of editorial cartoons and spot illustrations, and he created seven comic strips that explored the creative possibilities of the form. *Little Nemo in Slumberland* was Winsor McCay's masterpiece, a personal and original work of art whose impact and success would never be duplicated, not even by Winsor McCay.

chapter 5. sheepshead bay

"I've just had the worst dream I ever experienced. I dreamed we lived in Brooklyn."

—DREAM OF THE RAREBIT FIEND, JANUARY 7, 1905

Winsor McCay's wife and two children joined him in New York City in the fall of 1903. At first, the family lived at the Hotel Audubon, an apartment hotel. Such dwellings provided hotel services to longterm or permanent residents  and were popular with single men and young families unable to afford a house or a staff of their own.

The Audubon offered moderately priced "nicely furnished" apartments, consisting of parlor and bedroom, with or without a private bath, hotel service, and a "restaurant à la carte." The Audubon was also convenient to McCay's office building, for it was located at 39th Street, just up Broadway from the *Herald* building.

But for all its advantages, an apartment hotel was not a real home in a house, like the McCays had known in Cincinnati. Sometime before 1905, the family rented a cottage in Sheepshead Bay, Brooklyn. In a *Rarebit Fiend* episode on January 10, 1905, McCay parodied the plight of his wife and himself attempting to find a suitable home in New York City.

In the cartoon's first frame, the wife, with head buried in her husband's chest, sobs, "Oh! I don't know what to do. I can't find a house anywhere fit to live in. I've searched the city from end to end all day long." In succeeding panels the husband offers words of encouragement, but by the fifth panel the wife is "desperate." She begs her husband not to be angry with her, but claims she "must give up unless we move to Brooklyn. What else can we do?" The husband declares that would be "torture," but is resigned to their fate.

In the sixth panel, a horse-drawn van is shown very small on the Brooklyn Bridge, and a balloon holds the wife's dialogue: "Cheer up, dear. Remember the worst is still to come." In the seventh panel, the wife is seen watering a plant as she says, "We are settled at last." Her husband, wearing a smoking jacket and puffing on a long pipe, sits in a fat armchair reading a newspaper with the headline "Froze to death in street-car—Sixty-five passengers on bridge," a comment on the cold reality of traveling across the Brooklyn

Bridge in the winter of 1905. The husband ruefully mutters, "Yes, we're settled, all righty, all right—to a dead moral certainty, beyond all doubt, 'tis true—." In the final frame, the man, now awake and sitting on the edge of his bed, tells his wife he just had "the worst dream."

The McCays chose to live in Sheepshead Bay, which was over an hour away from midtown Manhattan by train, for a number of reasons. They were looking for a suburban environment in which to raise their children, away from the hectic city that Maude found "overwhelming." Sheepshead Bay was a well-known seaside resort on Long Island, and after visiting it (perhaps in the summer of 1904), the McCays found much about that section of Brooklyn that reminded them of Cincinnati.

The Brooklyn Bridge, for example, looked like the Cincinnati–Covington Suspension Bridge, for both were designed and built by John A. Roebling. The Queen City bridge was completed in 1867, sixteen years before the Brooklyn version, but both structures have a similar elegance because Roebling was an advocate of innovative steel-cable suspension and cross stays on the steel ropes.

The three racetracks of Sheepshead Bay were considered to be the finest in the country, with the biggest purses, and were a major attraction for the posh set from Manhattan. For the McCays, the racetracks recalled exciting times at the Latonia Racetrack back in Kentucky, across the river from Cincinnati. It was the opening of the racetrack in Sheepshead Bay in 1880 and the Brooklyn Bridge in 1883 that encouraged people to settle in the sleepy fishing village and afforded access to visitors, particularly in the summer.

The increase in tourists attracted by the bay's racetracks and the ocean precipitated the building of boardinghouses, hotels, and cottages. Local residents rented out rooms, restaurants prospered, and fishing and boating grew. The affluent and middle-class came to the bay by horse-and-carriage, bicycle, or horse-trolley over the bridge, or they caught the Long Island Railroad, which ran a spur down from the elevated track near Avenue M.

Along the bay side of Emmons Avenue, from Ocean Avenue eastward, there were numerous seafood restaurants, such as Lundy's, where sports figures mingled with vaudeville and Broadway performers. People well-known in the worlds of industry and finance drank toasts and dined at Villepigue's with film actors from the nearby Vitagraph Studios. Villepigue's restaurant was located on the southwest corner of Ocean Avenue and Voorhies Avenue, the street the McCays lived on—a wide avenue of large homes and leafy trees set well back from the sidewalks.

Near to Sheepshead Bay were the amusement parks of Coney Island, which reminded the McCays of happy times in a similar area with the same name in Cincinnati. Steeplechase Park, on the eastern end of Coney Island, attracted a middle-class family crowd and led to the construction of two more entertainment enclosures: Luna Park and Dreamland. Both parks used design elements from the Chicago Exposition, and both were strong stylistic influences on the dream architecture in *Little Nemo in Slumberland*.

Luna Park, which opened in 1903, was "a fantastic *mélange* of plaster and lath towers, by day somewhat seedy, but by night dazzlingly outlined in electric light."[1] The architecture of the park reflected the belief in eclecticism espoused by its owner, Frederick Thompson, who advocated a mix of decorating styles and periods; for example, "a minaret with Renaissance detail or Romanesque with l'Art Nouveau. . . ."[2]

If Luna Park recalled the raucous midway of the Chicago Exposition, Dreamland "harkened back to its formal Court of Honor, organized around a central lagoon and a sunken plaza where chariot races were staged."[3]

After first renting a cottage, the McCay family moved to a house at 2675 East 18th Street. In May 1906 the family was listed in the Sheepshead Bay phone book. By 1910 the McCays had moved to the three-story house they eventually bought at 1901 Voorhies Avenue, which would be Winsor McCay's main residence for the rest of his life.

In the Voorhies Avenue house, McCay's studio away from the *Herald* was a study off the front porch and a third-floor study, where he would work into the night after dinner and on weekends, in order to meet his many newspaper deadlines. As his fame increased, McCay was allowed to work at home as often as he liked. Messengers carried his artwork to and from the newspaper office, or McCay might have his chauffeur drive him in with it.

John A. Fitzsimmons (1893–1984) was a young neighbor of the McCays. He was the son of famed horse-trainer "Sunny Jim" Fitzsimmons and a friend of McCay's son, Robert. As an aspiring artist, Fitzsimmons was privileged to spend hours talking with Winsor McCay as he worked over his drawings, and eventually he assisted McCay on two of his animated films. Years later, when he was in his eighties, Fitzsimmons wrote an articulate and detailed remem-

brance of his hero, "Mr. Mac." The following is an excerpt of Fitzsimmons's keen observations of McCay's drawing technique:

> In a matter of minutes, I got the feeling that due to his deep concentration my presence had been completely dismissed from his mind. . . . From the magnificent quality of McCay's work, one would naturally assume that in order to produce such elaborate material, the finest array of drawing equipment and mechanical instruments were needed. Such was not the case. I was astonished to notice his working tools consisted only of a bottle of Higgins black drawing ink, a few Gilliot #290 pens in holders, a large lump of art gum, a T-square and angle, plus an assortment of sharpened Venus lead pencils and, of course, his always conspicuous ashtray.

No inspirational copy was required for detail and authenticity in creating his fabulous and intricate architectural and scenic backgrounds and marvelous perspective handlings, of which he was a master, such as the average artist would need for that type of work. McCay had only to call upon his remarkable memory and creative genius in order to produce his fantastic drawings.

. . . usually McCay would be found thoroughly relaxed, seated on a high-back, plain wooden chair with a tufted corduroy cushion on the seat for comfort. His most characteristic working position was one that I had seen him assume so often: one end of his drawing board resting on his lap, the other on the edge of the desk. At times he would lean forward with his bent left arm or just the elbow resting on the board, his chin in the palm of that hand, while between two extended nicotine-stained fingers would be burning away his favorite "little cheroots" [little cigars called "Between the Acts"] from which the smoke softly ascended discoloring the underside of his hat brim. His working right hand, drawing away in lightning fashion, never seeming to make a false move.[4]

Fitzsimmons was amazed at "how little preliminary outlining work McCay needed to do before starting on the finishing stage of inking in even on the elaborate technical drawings for which he was so justly famous. The directness with which he could finish a complicated piece of art work was simply fantastic."[5]

When McCay first went to work at the *New York Herald,* his salary was sixty dollars a week, more than he was earning in Cincinnati and certainly more than the average workman's gross weekly wages in 1903, which were about nine dollars a week for fifty hours of labor. By 1905 McCay took stock of the amount of work he was contributing weekly to the Bennett papers, the success of his comic strips, and his family responsibilities. He decided to ask for a raise, and in a straightforward letter to *Herald* art director J. C. Baker, McCay made plain his discontent while confidently outlining suggestions for change:

Dear Sir,
As I can not find time to talk to you I will write. Don't you think *The Herald* can afford to commence the New Year by paying me $15.00 more per week?

I have been in your employ 14 months and have worked very hard to please.

The great quantity of work I do in the short time allowed me forces me to sacrifice the quality of it. I can do better work than I am doing.

Eight hours is what is expected of a man. I wish I could do my work in eight hours a day.

Here is my work for the week
Sammy Sneeze 1/2 page . . . . one day
Hungry Henrietta 1/2 page . . . . one day
John Kendrick Bangs 1/2" . . . . . almost one day
Brooklyn cartoon 5 col[umn]s . . one day
Comic 5 cols . . . . one day
4 or 5 one cols and 9 out of 10 weeks on a local assignment or special job for Sunday.

Robert Winsor McCay, the model for Little Nemo, *with his bicycle, c.1908. (Collection Janet Trinker)*

I can't do this amount of work *good* in the *short* time allowed me especially for such a small salary and feel interested.

If I worked on space I could earn $175.00 per week. Surly [sic] if I am willing to do it for $75.00 per week you ought to snap me up.

Comic artists that are doing better work than I am able to do—are not "knocking it out" as I am and are getting twice my salary.

I do not care to discuss my chances on some other paper for I *prefer* the *Herald* at a lower price than elsewhere for a higher one and if I can have the opportunity will make it as well as my self *the best* for clean humor.

I make two comics for the *Telegram* a week which I do on my own time (Sundays) which is the only chance I have to do any outside work for myself although I have been *asked* by two periodicals to contribute something each week.

I like you very much and like to work for you and will willingly at any time do anything for you. *But* your interpretation of "The Simple Life" in Art Room C is so vastly different to mine that I am compelled to set up this whine for a "raise."

I hope you will arrange this matter for me at once. I know I am worth what I ask for. If the *Herald* thinks differently I will understand that it is the quality of the work and not quantity they refuse to pay for and then I shall insist on doing space work when I can do my work better. You know what to do to a thrashing machine to make it run better? Grease it.

Yours respectfully,
Winsor McCay
I hope this is no *Rarebit Fiend*. I don't want to wake up!⁶

McCay got his raise: in the top right corner of his letter, art director Baker wrote "OK," initialed it, and drew a simple cartoon of a circle-faced man with a wide smile, dressed in a high-collared coat with two buttons. Whether this is a caricature of Baker or McCay is impossible to tell.

Three years later, when McCay renewed his contract with the *Herald* on December 24, 1908, he was in a much stronger negotiating position and was able to win better terms for what would be his final three years with the *Herald* and *Telegram.* As one of America's most celebrated cartoonists, the creator of the phenomenally successful *Little Nemo in Slumberland,* whose stage version opened in the fall of 1908 to rave

reviews, McCay let his attorney work out the multi-paged contract.

The terms included a weekly salary of $175 paid every week in advance for one full-page cartoon and one half-page cartoon. In addition, McCay was at last allowed to "work on space"; that is, for each additional full page, McCay would receive $100; for an additional half-page, $50; for an extra quarter-page, $25; and so on for a smaller fractional part of a page.

McCay's comic strips and miscellaneous editorial cartoon work, plus a percentage of monies he received from the Broadway version of *Little Nemo* and various merchandising items based on the *Nemo* characters, brought McCay's weekly earnings in early 1909 to around $1,000. And that amount does not include the salary McCay commanded by touring regularly all around the country as a top vaudeville performer.

McCay's appearances in vaudeville, which began in 1906, not only added extra disposable income to McCay's already considerable salary, but were an important extension of McCay's creative life. The ritual of performing was a necessary and healthy respite from the daily grind of turning out newspaper cartoons. It stimulated and encouraged him, and his times on stage were among the happiest and most satisfying of his life. Most important, McCay's success in vaudeville eventually provided the impetus and showcase for his innovative development of the animated film.

chapter 6. vaudeville

"A man's best friend is himself—in vaudeville."
—BUD FISHER

"What a piece of chalk in the hands of Winsor McCay can do!"
—VARIETY

In mid-April 1906, a representative of F. F. Proctor, famous vaudeville producer and theater owner, approached Winsor McCay with an offer to appear at Proctor's 23rd Street Theater, a top vaudeville house, twice a day for two weeks in June. "Mr. Proctor felt that so many admirers of my newspaper comics would stampede the box office," wrote McCay in his diary, "that he could afford to pay me several hundreds of dollars. I sighed deeply and shuddered faintly."

Ten days later, on May 3, McCay signed a contract "like a real theatrical star," and agreed to make quick sketches of his famous characters on a blackboard during the weeks of June 11 and 18. Chalk-talk artists, "lightning sketchers," were popular Victorian parlor entertainers who made the transition to the vaudeville stage in the late nineteenth century. Several of McCay's cartoonist peers, including James Stuart Blackton and Bud Fisher (*Mutt and Jeff*), found lightning sketching not only an easy way to make extra money, but a means of advertising their strips and other salable projects.

Proctor was using McCay to compete with the Keith circuit of vaudeville houses, whose management had signed Richard Outcault (*Buster Brown*) to appear in his own quick-sketch act. "The two circuits have long been fierce rivals, and the management of each is determined to make a strong feature of each artist," reported the May 11, 1906 *Cincinnati Enquirer.* This same article claimed McCay and Outcault had a professional rivalry but hastened to add that "strange to say, [it] has not entered into personal relationships, as they are warm friends." The paper outlined a difference between the two cartoonists' acts: "McCay . . . will not give much attention to dialogue. He will devote himself almost entirely to 'free hand' work on a blackboard, while Outcault will . . . give more time to telling of his experiences."

The Proctor office began planting numerous publicity items about McCay in the newspapers, particularly the show biz and racetrack daily, the *New York Telegraph*. "If the artist draws audiences with half the ability and ease that he draws cartoons," read one puff piece, "Mr. Proctor says he will have to increase the size of his theaters." The article emphasized that "Mr. McCay is going to do no talking whatever. He will appear like an ordinary human being— a clerk, a cashier, or a mere gentleman—but he will make his pencil speak for him." Within fifteen minutes, McCay would draw a series of twenty-five pictures "in his well-known manner," as a two-step by composer Fred Day called "Dream of the Rarebit Fiend" would be played by the pit band, a tune "full of queer, unexpected musical phrases of an amusing nature. . . ."

McCay eagerly cooperated with the advance publicity. Speaking to reporters about his nervousness, he said, "Hitherto, I've always stood in awe of one man who passes the decisive verdict on my work—the editor. And now it makes me feel pretty shaky to go out and present my work to thousands of people who will compose my audience, and each one of whom will be practically my editor. Think of that! It's a Welsh rabbit [sic] dream all by itself."[1]

Of course, McCay, an intuitive showman, knew that the public would find appealing the image of himself as a "fish out of water," and so he stressed how worrisome the whole idea of appearing on a stage was to a shy, desk-bound cartoonist. In truth McCay was delighted with the prospect of appearing before a live audience, which was not an alien experience to him. In a way, he would be performing the same mute "act" he had given for years, drawing caricatures at dime museums or showing off before the public while painting posters in Michigan, Illinois, and Ohio. Vaudeville was familiar turf to McCay; it was an eclectic American entertainment medium that developed from dime museums and the circus, as well as minstrel and medicine shows, the legit stage, grand opera, musical comedy, and pantomimes.

Another incentive to help McCay overcome any nervousness was the salary he would earn: $500 per week, the same as Outcault.[2] Vaudeville salaries ranged from $150 to $200 a week for an opening act, such as acrobats, jugglers, or knockabout comics; warm-up acts, such as singer/dancers with "patter" (talk) were paid $225 to $250; stars could command $750 to $1,500 and up. McCay and Outcault were "featured novelty acts," that is, performers well known to the public, but not superstars like Harry Houdini, Sarah Bernhardt, George M. Cohan, or Harry Lauder.

For most vaudeville troupers, the chance to play an important New York house like Proctor's meant that their acts had to have been sharpened to perfection traveling the lesser circuits across the country for years. McCay was starting at the top; his reputation as a popular newspaper cartoonist preceded him and paved the way.

A faithful diarist, McCay wrote down his thoughts and activities each day in dozens of notebooks and pocket calendars. Unfortunately, only three of these valuable documents are known to have survived, and those are in fragmentary form. One diary, however, contains McCay's writing about the day he opened in vaudeville, which began the morning of June 11, 1906, at an orchestra rehearsal:

> I walked quietly into the theater and onto the stage. I was as usual late. The rehearsal was over with and the orchestra was just finishing a rehearsal of my overture. . . . I was very sorry that I had not come earlier so that I might have heard it. I was then presented to the stage manager, Mr. Frank Caps, a very clever gentleman who made me feel at home immediately I saw him. We had a small confab about when and where I was to do my act and I felt as easy as a general would who's [sic] army was completely surrounded by the enemy.
>
> A suitcase that weighed 850# accompanied me through a steel doorway and up a flight of iron stairs to cell no. 7. Brick walls, steel shelves and door, several mirrors, electric bulbs, chairs and two big trunks

A self-parody by McCay of his lightning-sketch act and the precarious life of a vaudevillian appeared in a Rarebit Fiend strip on March 18, 1906. Where McCay quickly drew familiar characters on a blackboard, the hapless performer in the strip sculpts them out of cheese to the vigorous disapproval of the audience. (Collection Ray Winsor Moniz)

greeted me in silence three solid hours before I was to go on the stage. I hung my hat up and gazed into the mirror just as I did once in a big hotel when a boy after leaving home for the first time. The awful silence, the tomb-like painted walls, the clanging of iron in everything I touched suggested the condemned criminal soon to be led out before the gaze of the multitude and executed. Ah! I would smoke. That's one thing I can do under any pressure, but . . . perceived through the mist [of smoke were] the words POSITIVELY NO SMOKING IN THESE DRESSING ROOMS. . . . I then sat down and wondered what I should do until 3.10 my scheduled finish. I was too nervous to go out and eat, to walk or stay or lie down. . . . I managed to occupy a half hours time in unpacking my suitcase and arranging my toilet outfit along the shelf, and in another half hour I was dressed, talk about the hands on a clock moving slow when waiting for a train . . . I still had an hour and a half. I would go down on the stage and size up my accessories, yes, and familiarize myself with them and the stage in general. So I stepped out into the corridor, a dream of beauty, a perfect fashion plate only to see a sign: PERFORMERS WILL KEEP OFF OF THE STAGE UNTIL CALLED FOR THEIR ACT. THIS RULE IS PREIMPTORY [sic]. Back, back to my cage. . . .

[A few minutes before the start of the matinee, in walked] the gentleman who was to dress with me: Mr. W. C. Fields and his brother, both smoking big fine fat cigars . . . they were pleased to meet me but rather shocked to see me dressed up for the stage so early and I felt the shock also. It was advertised, broadcast that this was my first appearance on any stage. . . .

Bill [Fields] reached into his bag and took out a bottle . . . "Here you are," he said offering me a haymaker. "A little scotch for my little Scotch friend. . . ."

The three of us walked down to the stage together. And they kept up a running fire of conversation to keep my mind from weighing my fate. But I was no longer scared—I laughed and talked with them as though I were an old friend and an old hand at this vaudeville business. The dance act which preceded my act finished. The orchestra was playing my introductory music and I faintly heard the stage manager say, "You're on!"

Bill clapped me on the back as I started for the entrance. "Lay 'em in the aisles, my little Scotch friend," he shouted after me. On the other side of the stage I could see a crowd of the performers on the bill standing in the wings waiting to catch my act. I learned afterwards that it's an old custom among vaudevillians to watch all the other acts on the bill perform during the first show on opening day.

A portrait of Winsor McCay
used in advertisements for
his vaudeville act, c. 1906.
(Collection Ray Winsor Moniz)

I trembled a little as the footlights blinded me, but the sound of applause that went up as I made my entrance reassured me. I made my way to the blackboard, which the stagehands had shoved out on the stage directly the preceding act finished and the stage was blacked out. Once I felt the chalk in my hand the tension eased, and after I had made the first mark upon the blackboard, I was well at ease.[3]

Newspaper reviews of the evening performance reveal how McCay looked and acted from the other side of the footlights. "It was a great success," according to the *Cincinnati Enquirer,* whose reviewer was among the many friends from Ohio who attended the opening to give McCay "a royal greeting."[4] *Variety* found McCay's act "a solid hit," not only because of the quality of the performance, but "because of the favorable regard in which certain of his creations are held."

Variety described the act in some detail, noting that the "artist made his entrance in an ordinary business suit, the only stage preparation evident being an apparently new hair cut. He was very much at home and gaily waved his hand at some friends in a box." McCay opened with his "Seven Ages of Man" bit, in which he drew on a blackboard facing portraits of two infants, a boy and a girl. "By skillful strokes and changes in headgear," said *Variety,* "he took his two creations through life to old age in a succession of some eight or ten persons. Beyond the hair or hat, not more than a line or two was required for each change, and the idea was clever enough to have commanded attention without his reputation."[5]

Next, McCay changed to paper on which he "drew the characters he has made famous, and which in turn have brought him fame." When the act finished, "a large floral horseshoe was dumped on the stage" and "seemed to embarrass the artist more than anything else. As a last resort he kissed his hand to the audience, and made an exit and a hit that brought him back to do it over again." *Variety* found McCay preferable to "other [unnamed] full chested cartoonists" because he is "refreshingly human. It is a pity that his stay in vaudeville is so limited. The *Herald* would profit by letting him keep on."

Variety need not have worried; McCay was back playing Proctor's Fifth Avenue Theater and the 125th Street Theater in October. The *Telegram* observed McCay's act "must have been good, for the Proctor circuit has since offered him a tour of thirty weeks. Mr. McKay [sic] says he wants only two. . . . That's all he can spare just now."[6] McCay was already tinkering with the act by adding an encore in which he drew a man, dressed to attend the opera, who waits with increasing agitation for his wife to get herself ready. "While the wife proceeds serenely," wrote the *Telegram,* "the husband gradually loses both his temper and his patience."

McCay continued to receive very good notices ("His act is one of the most interesting and novel seen in vaudeville in some time," said the *Telegram),* and he began accepting bookings on the road. In March 1907 he played Toledo's Valentine Theater and brought along Maude and the kids. The *Toledo Blade* found McCay "a fine cartoonist, not so rapid as some others seen on the stage, but he produces results that mean a great deal, while not forgetting to add a touch of humor."[7]

In April McCay played Pittsburgh's Grand Theater, and the *Post* called his entry into vaudeville "somewhat spectacular": "It was during the time Keith and Proctor were at war in New York. Keith had secured Richard Outcault, the creator of *Buster Brown*, and Proctor, to offset Outcault's drawing powers, engaged McCay to appear concurrently in his house. So friend and friend were pitted, and now that Keith and Proctor are together [the former rivals had become partners], Outcault and McCay are playing the same circuit."[8]

McCay allowed his bookings to increase. In the back of a 1908 pocket diary/calendar, McCay listed all the cities he had played in the fall of 1907. Beginning on September 2 in Rochester, New York, McCay made a continuous run of one-week engagements in Philadelphia, New York (the 23rd Street Theater),

Brooklyn (the Orpheum), back to Manhattan to the Alhambra Theater (7th Avenue and 126th Street), out to Newark, New Jersey, then a week's rest starting October 14. On the 21st, he was playing Washington, then up to Boston on the 28th.

In Boston McCay stayed at Adams House on Washington Street and wrote a letter to his family back in Brooklyn full of information about the life of a vaudevillian on the road:

Monday 6:30 P.M.

My own darling sweetheart and little sweethearts

Well! I am here and have had my first spasm this matinee. The house is beautiful and packed. I didn't think I went very well but Gosh! a dozen people swamped me when I was through and said I floored the bunch—The blackboard had castors [sic] on it (the new frame they gave me) and every stroke I made the Easle [sic] would roll around the stage.

Also the management of the house sent word down to the orchestra just when I was sailing at the start to play my music piano, that is low and soft and it almost made me collapse—I like lots of noise when I'm at work but when they played so soft it queered me. I made a big kick about it and am having the castors [sic] ripped off. When they saw I was mad they couldn't do enough for me.

Oh! I wish I was in Sheepshead Bay this minute—I am one of the headliners and everybody said I was the cream of refined vaudeville as usual but I did miserable.

Maybe tonight I will do better.

This is the queerest town you ever saw, every street is like Wall Street. Well! There is [sic] no streets. They are all alleys and run in every direction. They have some fine big depart. stores though. I just came from one where I bought some ink etc. Its [sic] a big city but a queer one. I'm not going to write until tomorrow as I'm tired out. I didn't sleep good on the sleeper at all and have been (as you always say) "on my feet all day." This show business is hell.

The Davis Tragedions [sic] are here and the show is a corker. I'll send you the billing. Have not a program handy. This is a hotel similar to the Gibson House in Cincinnati.

You and the babes better come up—Friday or Thursday. I think I'll close Sat. night. . . .

Regards to all and love and a million kisses to you and Marion and Bobbie.
Winsor[9]

After Boston McCay traveled back to Paterson, New Jersey, on November 4, then to Hoboken on the 18th, followed by two weeks off. December 9 he was playing a week at the Colonial Theater on Manhattan's Upper West Side, followed by another week off before a Christmas week appearance at Hammerstein's and the 125th Street Theater. A sure sign that McCay had arrived as a vaudeville attraction was his booking at Hammerstein's Victoria, a layer cake of a theater in the heart of Times Square. Hammerstein's was, before the Palace was built, the country's major vaudeville house. In the summer, when most theaters closed because of the stifling heat, the shows continued at the Victoria in the Roof Garden atop the theater on a stage large enough for light opera and comedy acts, and a movable glass roof in case of rain.

Willie Hammerstein ran the place with a canny instinct for what audiences would like and a philosophy that "no one, however good an act, was important enough to play the Victoria unless he had a tremendous reputation. Drawing power was more important than talent."[10]

During an increasingly hectic travel schedule, McCay was turning out three separate comic strips *(Nemo, Rarebit Fiend, Pilgrim),* as well as extra page-fillers and spot illustrations. Some of his finest works of this period were created in dressing rooms backstage at theaters or in hotel rooms in the various cities where he toured. The artwork was always produced on time and of a consistently high technical and imaginative quality, a testament to McCay's incredible powers of concentration, organization, and artistic skill.

Winsor McCay was now a full-fledged celebrity less than three years after his arrival in New York. His financial situation had improved as quickly as his rise from obscurity as a "page-filler" to his preeminence as a popular comic strip cartoonist and vaudeville headliner. But a loss of privacy accompanies celebrity, as McCay found out in January 1908, when a private family tiff developed into something that attracted newspaper headlines.

Signs of domestic tension between McCay and his wife are evident throughout the artist's 1908 pocket calendar/diary.[11] The little book contains McCay's daily activities, written in a code to conserve space. For example, "A" means "went to city," "B" means "Stayed home," and so on, through fifteen letters of the alphabet and other symbols outlined in the code's key in the front of the booklet.

The diary shows that on January 9, a Thursday evening, a Mr. and Mrs. Muir "came to dinner." Muir was a Sheepshead Bay horseman who ran a boardinghouse with his wife on Shore Road near Emmons Avenue, close by the McCay residence. The Muirs and the McCays had known each other for three years, and "the two women attended all the social affairs in Sheepshead Bay and were seemingly the best of friends," according to the *Brooklyn Eagle,* which published reports about subsequent events.

The day of the dinner, McCay's diary records that he "stayed home till evening," but when the Muirs arrived, he "stayed away." Wherever he went, either to his private study or to a bar, he writes he "teaded well," a code word for imbibing; then he "retired early" and "hungry."

On Saturday, January 11, McCay's children went to see a show at the Hippodrome in Manhattan, and his wife "went out, too," with the Muirs. McCay again "had no supper," "retired early," and was "sore," meaning angry. The next day McCay stayed home and Maude went out. At 3 P.M. the Muirs and their relatives, the Kuykendahls, "came over," so McCay "sneaked" over to a friend's house.

On Monday, McCay "got up early," and "sent job to city" *(Nemo* and *Rarebit Fiend* strips were sent by messenger to the *Herald),* then stayed home. Again, Maude "went out" to "visit with [the] Muirs." On Tuesday, January 14, McCay's diary reports a "big blow off—success." But for the next three days, McCay writes that he is "feeling bad," "awful blue," and "blue all day." By Sunday, again feeling "terrible blue," he has taken his son with him to Manhattan to stay at the Hermitage Hotel, a "bachelor hotel" on Seventh Avenue, south of 42nd Street.

Rumors about the "big blow off" at the McCays flew around the small town on the bay and eventually were published in the widely read *Brooklyn Eagle.*[12] "When it became noised about," reported the newspaper "that Mr. McCay came home one evening recently and found William Muir there, the gossips were more than interested." McCay, it was said, slapped Muir's face and ordered him to leave, although Maude McCay "did not recall having seen any blows struck at her house when her husband returned and found the horseman there. She said she saw her husband put his hand to the other man's face and that he pushed him, but all was done playfully, she thought."

Maude protested, "I cannot see why the gossips should single me out. There is no truth whatever in the story that my husband struck Muir. Everything has been stretched considerably and you can say for me that there are no family differences, nor is there any divorce or separation proceedings contemplated, as some of the rumors have it."

During McCay's week-long self-imposed exile at the Hermitage, he was visited by Maude, her sister Stella (who was living with the McCays), and his daughter. In fact, despite blizzard weather conditions, McCay's whole brood was in and out of Manhattan nearly every day visiting him, dining at restaurants, seeing shows at the Colonial and Hammerstein's, and buying clothes. By Sunday the 26th, McCay wrote he was "home at last," and the next morning, according to his diary, he and Maude made love.

Although McCay and his wife worked through the incident and wished to forget it, the press dragged it to the fore on January 30 when William Muir placed an advertisement in the morning *World* offering a reward of $500 for "information that will lead to the identification of two thugs who slugged him on the night he was leaving the home of Winsor McCay . . . ." Now Muir alleged that upon leaving McCay's home, "after an altercation with the cartoonist," two men in blackface, one wearing a policeman's uniform, tackled him.

"As I went out of the house McCay said something to them," claimed Muir. "Right after that they attacked me." He denied that McCay had slapped

him: "It would take about six McCays to do that." The reason Muir went to McCay's house that fateful night was "because I received an anonymous letter the day before," which was said to contain "some scandalous statements." Mrs. McCay, her sister, her two children, and a maid were present when Muir arrived with his wife.

"I hear," Muir told reporters, "that McCay told a friend over the telephone that the affair at his house was just for the purpose of breaking up an acquaintance. It strikes me as a funny way to go about it." For his part, McCay admitted he had slapped Muir and ordered him out of the house, "but I didn't arrange to have any black-faced man attack him on the street. I don't believe he was attacked."

The altercation blew over and at least Mrs. McCay and Mrs. Muir began speaking to each other again. However, another disagreeable and silly incident occurred in March, which landed the whole cast of characters in court and (once again) in the newspapers.[13] It seems a Mrs. William Kuykendahl brought Mrs. William Muir to court on charges of disorderly conduct. "The genesis of the affair," reported the vulturelike *Eagle,* "is a kiss (now generally denied)

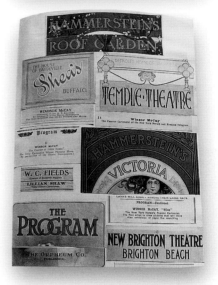

that [William] Muir, who is a horseman, was said to have given to Mrs. Windsor [sic] McCay, the wife of the artist, while the McCays and Muirs were stopping at the Hotel Gladstone, Atlantic City last summer."

According to Mrs. Muir, her brother, William Kuykendahl, came to her house to tell her "he had heard that Muir kissed Mrs. McCay at Atlantic City. Mrs. Muir denounced her brother for saying such things. Then she hit him. Later that same night she met Mrs. Kuykendahl on the street and called her an 'old hypocrite' and other uncomplimeritary things."

After this exchange Mrs. Kuykendahl brought Mrs. Muir to court in Coney Island, where Winsor McCay was summoned to the stand to testify that he was "satisfied that there had never been a kiss delivered or received between his wife and Muir." Maude McCay testified "stoutly that Muir had never kissed her, nor had she ever been made love to by any other man than her husband. Asked if Muir ever tried to make love to her, she said pointedly, 'No gentleman ever has.'" The puzzled magistrate reserved decision on the case, and everyone went home.

Winsor McCay was a paradox; he was an intensely shy and private man who also enjoyed publicly pro-moting himself and his art and loved to appear on the stage. The absurd episode involving the Muirs and Maude attracted unwanted attention he could not control and manipulate. It surprised and humiliated McCay and was especially embarrassing for someone proud of the "clean humor" of his cartoon creations.

McCay was grateful when public interest in the smarmy incident blew over before spring, for he was about to start a major new project. He wanted nothing scandalous to detract from a lavish musical production on Broadway of his wholesome *Little Nemo*.

chapter 7. *little nemo* on broadway

"Little Nemo . . . *marked an innovation in [Victor] Herbert's approach to the musical stage. More than that, it was a landmark of America's musical theater . . .*"

—EDWARD WATERS, *A LIFE IN MUSIC*

David Belasco was the first producer to see theatrical possibilities in the sumptuous dream adventures of Winsor McCay's *Little Nemo in Slumberland*. He took an option on the dramatic rights to the comic strip and its characters soon after its first appearance in the *Herald* in 1905. Four playwrights, including Belasco himself, attempted to produce a script worthy of the McCay fantasy and failed. The option next went to playwright Edgar Temple and composer Manuel Klein, who also failed to create a musical spectacle from the property worthy of Belasco's Hippodrome, then the world's largest theater.

In the summer of 1907, Marcus Klaw and A. L. Erlanger, partners in the most powerful theatrical syndicate of the era, announced that they would stage *Little Nemo* in the coming year at the unheard-of cost of $100,000. "It will be a series of monstrous tableaux," said Klaw, "designed by Mr. McCay himself. The settings will be so exquisitely splendid, so artistically lit, that the sound of the audible 'Ahs' and 'Ohs' will resound through the auditorium as each curtain is lifted."[1]

Klaw felt *Little Nemo* was "unquestionably the best vehicle for a spectacle of this kind that has ever been conceived. *Alice in Wonderland* was a wonderful, popular creation. But I consider *Little Nemo* a better one in its elements of popularity and stage possibilities." The optimistic producer predicted he and his partner would "realize five times our investment of $100,000."

Victor Herbert was engaged to compose the ambitious project's operetta score. "The idea appeals to me tremendously," said Herbert. "It gives opportunities for fanciful incidents and for 'color.' It's all in Dreamland, you know, and that gives great scope for effects, the writing of which appeals to me immensely." Two playwrights, George V. Hobart and Henry Blossom, were originally hired to write the

book to which Herbert's music would be set, but they were replaced by Harry B. Smith, who explained his approach would "get cross the footlights some of the charm of child life which we all love, no matter how old we are."[2]

Work began in earnest on the script and music in the spring of 1908 and continued through the summer in a hunting lodge on Lake Placid in the cool Adirondacks. Meanwhile, back in New York, Klaw and Erlanger put their organization to the task of casting actors to fill 22 principal roles and over 150 chorus parts.

Three top comedians, all stars of their own touring companies, were hired to play Dr. Pill, Flip, and the Dancing Missionary; respectively, they were Joseph Cawthorn, Billy B. Van, and Harry Kelly. Cawthorn was a type of comedian known by rivals as a "fly catcher," that is, a performer whose subtle expressions and movements could steal any scene in which he appeared. It was this talent that drove W. C. Fields to knock Cawthorn cold on a stage they shared once in vaudeville. During the run of *Little Nemo,* Cawthorn improvised a tale about a mythical creature he named a "Wiffenpoof." The name caught the public's fancy, entered the English language, and became a famous song and the name of a Yale singing group. But there was never a Wiffenpoof song in *Little Nemo,* as has often been erroneously reported.

The key role of Little Nemo was won by Master Gabriel, a vaudeville favorite who starred two years earlier in *Buster Brown,* a stage version of Richard Outcault's comic strip. Master Gabriel, whose real name was Gabriel Weigel, was not a child actor; he was a thirty-three-inch midget, of an age "32-past." So convincingly childlike was the tiny comedian that the Gerry Society, protectors of young stage performers, was about to descend on the show until they saw Master Gabriel backstage "scraping off a beard that would have done credit to the Cardiff Giant."[3]

In addition to the casting of the show, over 1,000 costumes had to be designed by F. Richard Anderson for such diverse characters as Attendants to the Princess, Guards of Slumberland, Teddy Bears, Toy Soldiers, Jungle Animals, Cannibals, and Sailors. Scenery was based loosely on McCay's drawings but was built by T. B. Macdonald and John Corrigan.

There were many special electrical effects designed, including a "fireworks display" made of lights and compressed-air devices, by Hugh Thomas and the Globe Electric Company. Herbert Gresham was the stage director, and Max Hirschfeld directed the music.[4]

Plot was minimized in favor of spectacle. The following synopsis from the detailed program indicates what the show was like:

ACT I, Scene 1. The playroom of the Little Princess of Slumberland, in which the chorus sings "Slumberland." Another song, "The Happy Land of Once-Upon-a-Time" introduces storybook characters such as Cinderella, Bo-Peep, and Aladdin, and a trio of comedians (Cawthorn, Kelly, and Black) sing "There's Nothing the Matter with Me."
Scene 2. A playground in a city park, where the chorus sings "Blow upon Your Bugles," Nemo and Princess sing "Won't You Be My Playmate?" and the trio of comics sing "Read the Papers Ev'ry Day."
Scene 3 takes place in Nemo's bedroom—a pantomime to music with the Candy Kid enticing Nemo to Slumberland.
Scene 4 is a stop in the Land of St. Valentine. Songs include "When Cupid is the Postman," "Won't You Be My Valentine," and the finale of ACT I: "March of the Valentines." No intermission between ACTS I and II.
ACT II, Scene 1. At the Weather Factory in Cloudland, where kinds of weather describe themselves in song, e.g., "Sunbeams," "Snowflakes," "Raindrops," and a trio titled "Weather Vane."
Scene 2. The Wreck of the Ship of Dreams and the Isle of Table D'hote. Songs include "Will o' the Wisp" and the ensemble singing "The Barbecue."
Scene 3. At the Amusement Park in the Jungle, with songs "If I Could Teach My Teddy Bear to Dance" and "The Olympian Games."
Scene 4. Back in Nemo's bedroom where he sings "I Guess I Talk Too Much" and Dr. Pill sings "I Wouldn't Take a Case Like That."
Scene 5 is A Dream of the Fourth of July, a patriotic appeal with songs titled "Remember the Old Continentals" and "The Chime of the Liberty Bell." After a ten minute intermission:
ACT III, Scene 1 opens on the deck of a battleship. Chorus sings "Give Us a Fleet," Nemo and the Candy

Kid sing "Happy Slumberland," and the comedy trio sing "Is My Face On Straight?"

Scene 2. Slumberland at last, and the King sings "The Subterranean Dream." Other songs include "The Dream of Love," "The Nightmare," and "The Celestial Dream." The entire company assembles for the Grand Finale.[5]

"Herbert was confronted by a real problem in composing music for a hodgepodge like *Little Nemo*," wrote his biographer, Edward Waters. There was no passionate love song in the show, for the two protagonists were children, and "being childlike, careless, and fanciful, the songs were too much alike." But in scenes requiring instrumental music and no text, Herbert could "let his fancy soar. The first long pantomime was the park scene, for which Herbert provided some delicious musical phrases. Extremely skillful and effective was the use of an underlying musical figure to which new and characteristic motives were added (and continued) as park visitors enjoyed the grounds . . . . The music for the dance of the Valentines is both spritely [sic] and graceful, with instrumental effects which are masterfully accomplished. Finally, the incidental music for the cannibal island scene and the Fourth of July celebration are likewise highly effective."[6]

For the fall opening of *Little Nemo* in New York, Klaw and Erlanger booked the New Amsterdam Theater on the south side of 42nd Street near Seventh Avenue. The inventive architects Henry B. Herts and Hugh Tallant, who were responsible for transforming Times Square "into a glittering and festive world of theaters, an urban Coney Island,"[7] created the New Amsterdam, inside and out, as a synthesis of sensual Art Nouveau and modern French decorative styles. It was the perfect setting for the play with which it opened in 1903, *A Midsummer Night's Dream,* and perfect five years later for another dream play, *Little Nemo.* (A more recent fantasy/animation occupant of the theater is Disney's *The Lion King.*)

Throughout the musical's preparation and rehearsal period, the production's creative team consulted McCay. He was, in fact, given an office in the New Amsterdam Theater building, where he could draw his newspaper assignments and be readily available to the *Little Nemo* crew.

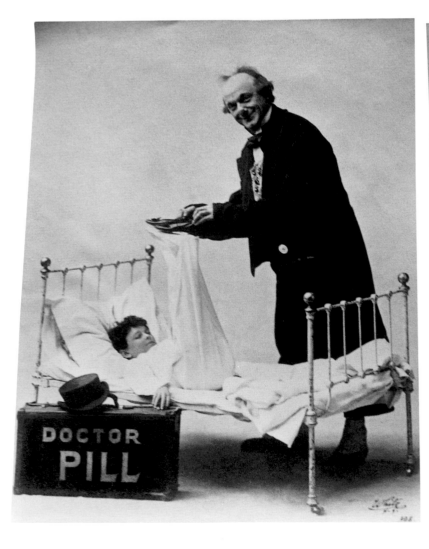

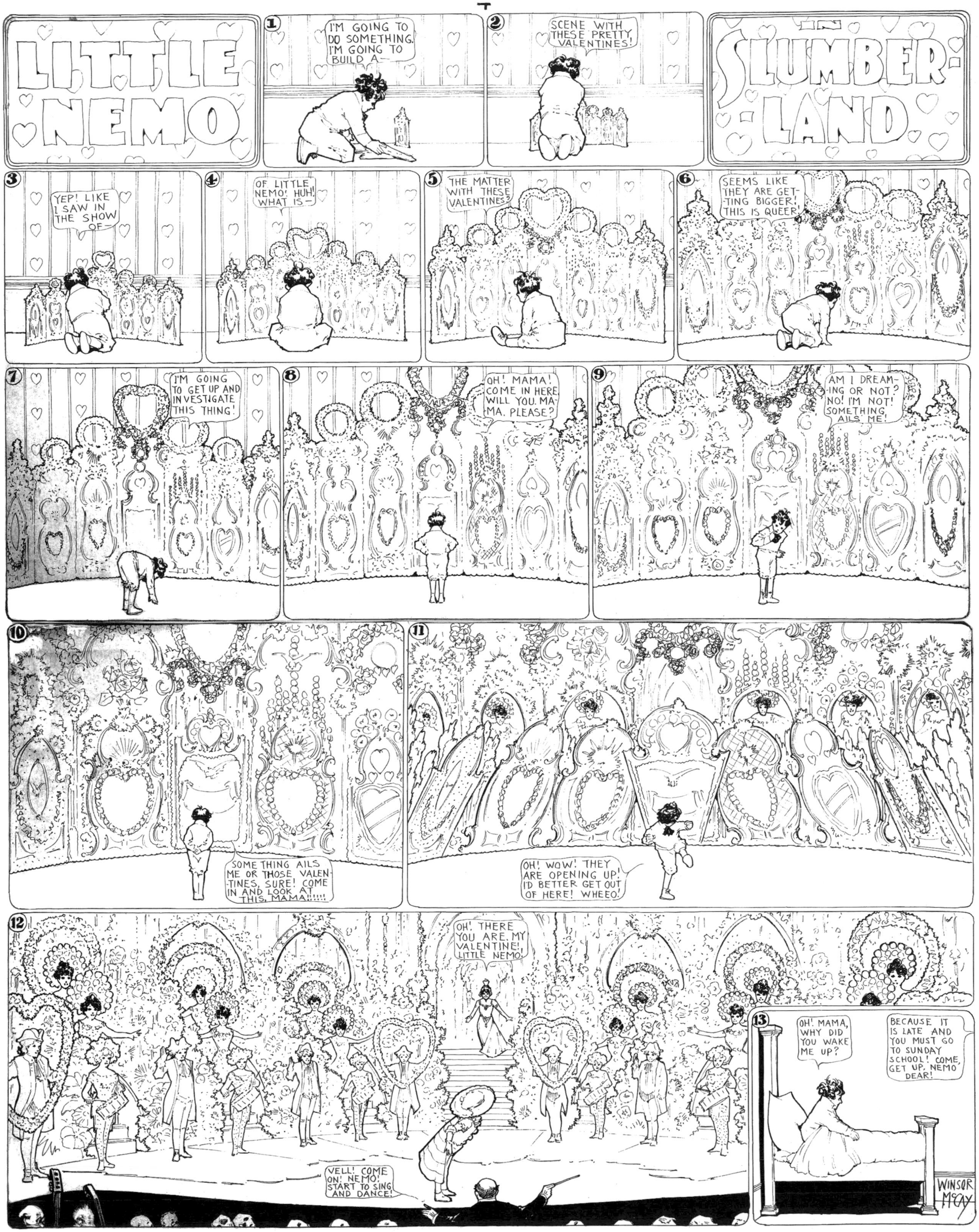
LITTLE NEMO
IN SLUMBER-LAND
I'M GOING TO DO SOMETHING. I'M GOING TO BUILD A—
SCENE WITH THESE PRETTY VALENTINES!
YEP! LIKE I SAW IN THE SHOW OF—
OF LITTLE NEMO! HUH! WHAT IS—
THE MATTER WITH THESE VALENTINES?
SEEMS LIKE THEY ARE GET-TING BIGGER! THIS IS QUEER!
I'M GOING TO GET UP AND INVESTIGATE THIS THING!
OH! MAMA! COME IN HERE, WILL YOU, MA-MA, PLEASE?
AM I DREAM-ING OR NOT? NO! I'M NOT! SOMETHING AILS ME!
SOME THING AILS ME OR THOSE VALEN-TINES, SURE! COME IN AND LOOK AT THIS, MAMA!!!!!!
OH! WOW! THEY ARE OPENING UP! I'D BETTER GET OUT OF HERE! WHEEO!
OH! THERE YOU ARE, MY VALENTINE! LITTLE NEMO!
VELL! COME ON! NEMO! START TO SING AND DANCE!
OH! MAMA, WHY DID YOU WAKE ME UP?
BECAUSE IT IS LATE AND YOU MUST GO TO SUNDAY SCHOOL! COME, GET UP, NEMO DEAR!
WINSOR McCAY

As usual, McCay carried a full load of drawing duties, as well as appearances on the vaudeville circuit. June 21 saw him open across the street from the New Amsterdam at Hammerstein's Roof on top of the Victoria Theater. The *New York Mirror* reviewer said, "His turn is quiet, but extremely effective, and even the rather *blasé* audiences that gather on the roof were intensely interested in watching his deft fingers as they moved the chalk swiftly over the blackboard, creating quaint and pleasing pictures."[8]

After performing a week each at the Fifth Avenue Theater and the 125th Street Theater, McCay returned to Hammerstein's Roof on August 3 for a full month's booking. During the four weeks, according to the *New York Telegraph*, McCay performed two shows a day, and while off-stage he drew "four full pages of *Little Nemo,* four one-half pages of *Rarebit Dreams* [sic], four three-column *Rarebit Dreams,* four three-column *Dull Cares,* drew a twenty-four sheet design, an eight-sheet design and a three-sheet design for the Klaw & Erlanger production of *Little Nemo,* also designed a scene for that big spectacle, and in his odd moments while going to and from meals dashed off a souvenir cover and a programme cover for a theater."[9]

The Roof Garden was kept open an extra week, and Willie Hammerstein brought back the popular McCay. "Talking acts are impossible in the open air for knock-about purposes," explained the *Telegraph.* "An act that does not appeal essentially to the eye cannot hope for great success. That is what had William Hammerstein busy. He took no chances on the programme, but engaged acts that have already shown themselves winners both to the farm following and the patrons of the Victoria Matinees."[10]

The clever Hammerstein then contracted the equally clever McCay to an engagement at the Victoria for the weeks of October 12 and 19. This would occur at the same time as the New York opening of the musical *Little Nemo* and assured maximum reciprocal publicity for Willie's theater and Winsor's Broadway show. The Victoria stage manager, Mike Simons, sweetened the pot even more by assuring McCay that he would have a dressing room to him-

WINSOR McCAY
(Silas)

Souvenir

...of the...

Welsh Rarebit Fest

Given to

Winsor McCay

by the

Cartoonists and Newspaper Men of Philadelphia

at the

Pen and Pencil Club

Wednesday, September 23, 1908

FIEND'S WELSH RAREBIT
(A LA CHAFING DISH)

BOSTON BAKED BEANS AND BROWN BREAD

DRAUGHT BEER   INDIA PALE ALE (On Draught)

LITTLE NEMO CIGARETTES

COFFEE

self, complete with a desk and a student lamp for drawing his newspaper assignments.

As a seventeenth-anniversary gift, Winsor offered Maude a summer house in Sea Gate on the western tip of Coney Island. He ordered "complete furnishings for the new house and also consulted numerous automobile firms, for an auto necessarily goes with a Sea Gate residence."[11]

In mid-September, the *Little Nemo* cast and crew moved to Philadelphia to rehearse at the Forrest Theater prior to opening there on September 28. McCay joined them on the 21st, not only to watch over his fantasy land come to life, but to perform his vaudeville act at Keith's Theater. The day before *Little Nemo*'s opening, the *Telegraph* reported, "'Silas' has been cartooning at Keith's in the Quaker City for a week and continues through *Little Nemo*'s run there. Mrs. McCay is also there and their two children, Bobbie McCay, who is Little Nemo in real life, and Marion McCay (so pretty her father is unable to do justice to her in his drawings of the Princess). Mr. McCay's mother also will be in the *Little Nemo* box tomorrow, having come from Michigan to be present."[12]

The reviews in Philadelphia proclaimed *Little Nemo* a "tremendous hit" and a "gorgeous production" that was a "marvel of scenic investiture." An ecstatic McCay wired the *Telegraph:* "Abraham Erlanger [*Little Nemo*'s producer who also supervised the show's direction] is a wizard . . . Wow! Wait until it hits the little village on the Hudson."

McCay's home newspaper, the *New York Herald,* was trumpeting the good news about the show, in whose success it had a vested interest. Within a week of the Philadelphia opening, three articles appeared describing the praise of the press reviews, how "society" was flocking to see the show, and how it had "three different styles of comedy." Three days before the New York premiere, the *Herald* gave *Little Nemo* a full-page article with photographs and drawings.

McCay opened his act at Hammerstein's Victoria on October 19; the next evening, *Little Nemo* premiered on Broadway at 8:10 sharp. In the dark at the end of Act I, an usher from the Victoria rushed down the aisle of the New Amsterdam to summon McCay. "You're on," whispered the usher to the artist

seated on the aisle. McCay dashed out of the theater, ran across 42nd Street, up Broadway into the stage entrance of the Victoria, and out onto the stage as the orchestra began playing his introductory music.[13]

"*Little Nemo* scores a triumph," blared the *Herald* in a full-page review the next day. The *Telegraph* agreed, calling the show an "All-American Hit!" In fact, all of the New York papers raved about McCay's musical: the *Daily Tribune* found it "a delightful spectacle; the *New York Commercial* saw it as "a very glittering bit of gorgeousness"; the *New York Times* said it was "a great big frolic" and "New York has seen nothing bigger or better in extravaganzas than *Little Nemo.*"

Ashton Stevens of the *Evening Journal,* who was the only by-lined critic, felt that "it is an unruly parent or a querulous child that will not be happy in the good old-fashioned joys of *Little Nemo,* which is a large extravaganza staged with truly Klaw and Erlanger extravagance." The *World* called *Little Nemo* "fancy in iridescent riot."

Despite excellent reviews and sold-out houses, *Little Nemo* lasted only fifteen weeks in New York before going on the road for two seasons. A quarter of a million people saw 123 performances, and promotional plugs continued in the *Herald* throughout the show's run. For example, on December 13, 1908, the *Herald* interviewed "the elongated comedian" De Wolf Hopper, who was appearing at the Majestic in *The Pied Piper,* and quoted him as saying, "Vulgarity spoils the average musical comedy and the stage needs more plays like *Little Nemo.*" McCay himself plugged the musical in his *Nemo* comic strip on November 15, 1908, and January 17, 1909.

Unfortunately, the ambitious production simply cost too much. $86,000 was spent before it opened and for its New York run the show cost in excess of $300,000 (this in a time when the average production was budgeted between $20,000 and $30,000). "It was staggeringly expensive for its time," wrote Edward Waters, "because of the number of scenes, the weird

lighting, manifestations through trapdoors, and a vast array of exotic costumes. Up to 1910 it was supposed to be the most expensive production ever placed before the public, and after two years of performances [including the post-Broadway tour] the original investment had not been returned."[14]

A special seventeen-car train, called the "Little Nemo Special," transported the show's stars, chorus members, stagehands, wardrobe handlers, musicians, treasurers, press agents, enormous sets, and hundreds of costumes. The train first went to Boston for a five-week engagement starting January 25, 1909, then to Pittsburgh for one week, and on to Chicago for two months, where the show closed for the season at the end of April.

McCay wanted to appear with his act in each city on the *Little Nemo* tour to maximize publicity for himself and the show. He met with resistance, however, from the Boston booking agent for the Keith Circuit, Carl D. Lathrop. McCay must have a new act, said Lathrop, who also wanted to see it before he would give McCay time on a Boston stage.

This was certainly odd treatment of a top vaudeville attraction, who had received consistently fine reviews and attracted appreciative audiences for two years. McCay rightfully felt insulted and angry. "I have not played Boston this season," he said, "and last summer when Mr. Hammerstein booked me to play the Victoria when *Little Nemo* opened at the New Amsterdam I asked if I should get up a new act, as I had been playing with him all summer. He told me to stick to the act I was doing and not to change . . . . I felt sure the manager of Hammerstein's knew more than a booking agent from New England on a question of vaudeville policy."[15]

McCay acted quickly. He switched to the William Morris circuit, which gladly and promptly booked him in Boston and nine more weeks elsewhere at $100 more per week than he had received on the Keith circuit. "Only a week ago I played both Keith & Proctor houses in New York," explained McCay. "Nothing was said about changing my act then. I played on Sunday because I was asked to help them out. When I asked a favor Mr. Lothrop [sic] made so many con-

"LITTLE NEMO" AND OTHER ENTERTAINMENTS AT THE THEATRES

MR. JOSEPH CAWTHORN AS DR. PILL IN "LITTLE NEMO"

MR. BILLY VAN AS FLIP IN "LITTLE NEMO"

MR. HARRY KELLY AS THE DANCING MISSIONARY IN "LITTLE NEMO"

NURSERY TALE CHARACTERS IN SCENE FROM THE FIRST ACT OF "LITTLE NEMO" AT THE NEW AMSTERDAM THEATRE

MISS MARY McEVILLY ON CONCERT TOUR

MASTER GABRIEL AS "LITTLE NEMO"

MR. WILLIAM GILLETTE "SAMSON" AT THE CRITERION THEATRE

On Sunday, October 18, 1908, the New York Herald *announced the Broadway premiere of* Little Nemo *in two days (October 20).*

ditions that I went where I was wanted. Should that week in Boston be the last I ever play in vaudeville as a result of my action, I shall feel I did exactly right notwithstanding."[16]

McCay, at the behest of the Klaw and Erlanger publicists, took his son along with him on the Boston, Pittsburgh, and Chicago tour. In the lobbies of each theater where *Little Nemo* played, Bobbie McCay, dressed in clothes resembling the cartoon character he inspired, sat on a small throne on exhibition as audiences filed into the auditorium.

In September the *Little Nemo* tour began again, starting in Syracuse and traveling to half-a-dozen Midwestern cities through December 1909. In November, when the show played in Cincinnati, Winsor and Maude McCay returned to their former hometown for the opening.

Montgomery Phister, a Cincinnati *Commercial Tribune* writer, observed McCay on that occasion and described the artist as "a small bundle of humanity pacing nervously up and down the main entrance" to the theater, dressed in "a Michael Strogoff top coat that threatened every moment to crush him with its weight. He was munching Dr. Cook gumdrops and muttering something about 'Little Nemo' long before the ticket box was set out."[17]

The artist, "his patient wife by his side," greeted many old friends and watched as a huge floral horseshoe, his gift for the show's company ("with none of whom has he any personal acquaintance"), was brought through the lobby. "'Tain't half big enough,' he said as he contemplated the gigantic horseshoe, at the same time rubbing his hands in an excess of glee. . . . 'I'm plumb nutty about the show!'"

McCay selected and paid for a lower proscenium box, where he "applauded everything in the first act from the entrance of the Fairy Princess to the final march of the Valentines." While Winsor "twisted and squirmed, his rather sedate better half smil[ed] occasionally at his delirium of joy, while the ponderous form of his old college [sic] chum, Ph. Morton, for whom he used to paint signs, lolled at ease in the shadow of the draperies."

McCay had good reason for his high spirits on this special occasion. He had returned in triumph as a famous and popular artist, with a glamorous theatrical production based on one of his own creations. It was a far cry from his beginnings, painting posters of freaks on Vine Street. To share his success with old friends and professional colleagues in the Queen City made it, as McCay said at the time, "one of the happiest nights of my life."[18]

After filling a number of bookings in the South, including New Orleans and Atlanta, the *Little Nemo* tour finally came to an end in the winter of 1910. McCay had continued to accompany the show at least during its first week in a new location, where he would play the local vaudeville theater.

The demise of the lavish musical play left a void in McCay's professional life, and he immediately looked for a way to fill it with a new project. He decided to explore one of several inquiries he had received regarding the performance of his quick-sketch act in Europe. A representative from H. B. Marinelli, an international theatrical agency with offices in Paris, London, Berlin, and New York, met with McCay and in a letter dated April 6, 1910, offered a first engagement of four weeks in London at fifty pounds per week.

This initial foray into European music halls was, the letter continued, to convince the cautious British theater managers of McCay's unique talents as a stage cartoonist and his attractiveness to audiences. If all went well with what was essentially an audition, Marinelli promised more bookings at a higher salary, and cited four American entertainers—Walter C. Kelly, Houdini, Horace Goldin, and Clarence Vance—who first "went over" for only forty pounds weekly (about $200).

McCay, wanting to make sure the *Herald* had no problem with one of their artists traveling across the ocean, sent a letter to his employers, a copy of which exists in rough draft form in one of his diaries. In it,

McCay explained that because of his "great popularity," which resulted from his comic strips, he had "become quite valuable to vaudeville managers." He recalled his competition with Outcault's act (though not naming him): "My highly refined and excellent performance not only put all previous stage cartoonists in the shade but made me so valuable that I was offered a thirty week tour of the country."

McCay claimed he could not accept that offer "on account of my *Herald* work," but, managing to "dip in occasionally," he had an "excellent record [of] 67 weeks as far west as Saint Louis [refusing to go farther west] in only the best theaters of our largest cities." Here McCay totted up some of his bookings: "29 weeks in New York City, 5 weeks in Boston, 5 in Philadelphia, 4 in Chicago. Just finishing a 10 weeks tour—always featured and billed as America's Most Famous Cartoonist of the *N.Y. Herald.* . . ."

After writing this opening, which established his popularity and value to the *Herald,* McCay got to the point:

> All this is to inform you so that you may decide on an answer to the question to come. For 2 years Rudolph Aronson and other European agents have made me offers—recently they are quite enticing—I have just received from the Marinela [sic] Limited of London and Paris an offer of 50 pounds per week for 4 weeks in London & Alhambra Theaters to play as America's Most Popular Cartoonist of the *New York Herald.*
>
> This is quite an honor for it is considered a very high price for a stranger in the field—Houdini, Walter C. Kelly and other big stars receiving the limit 40 on their opening in London. If I thought it necessary I would enclose their letter to me. I do all my newspaper work on the road as good if not better than at my desk at home. I conduct myself at all times on and off the stage in a manner befitting the Great Journal I work for and all predict great success in London, Paris and Berlin. In fact the whole affair looks glorious until I wonder what you should think of it all. Would you feel proud or ashamed of me? If you gave me your sanctum [sic] I am sure you would have not [sic] regret and I would be quite happy. If you think it out of order I shall gladly drop it and continue my work as in the past.
>
> I would be the first American cartoonist to cross the water and I have such a peculiar act (no speaking) that I pugilistly [sic] speaking, challenge all comers to duplicate it.[19]

McCay closed with information about a London newspaperman who wrote "tributes" to McCay and "promises his papers will treat me royally when in London." He apologized for "this long talk about myself" and asked the unnamed *Herald* boss to let him "know your feeling in regard to this affair for they always have and will come first."

In a postscript, McCay warned of his ambitions to play beyond London: "Of course, if I 'create a furor' in those four weeks I shall go to Paris and Berlin at a high figure and headline."

It must be assumed that the *Herald* disapproved of McCay's request to perform in Europe. He never appeared there, and though he toured in vaudeville on a regular basis until 1917, he never ventured west of the Mississippi with his act.

Robert McCay, Winsor's son, strikes a "Little Nemo" pose in a formal studio portrait, c. 1906. Three years later, during the road tour of the musical Little Nemo, *Robert made appearances in theater lobbies, posing in a similar way, to the delight of audiences. (Collection Ray Winsor Moniz)*

At least the *Herald*'s refusal was consistent: four years earlier, when McCay began in vaudeville, "he did not receive the slightest encouragement from the *Herald* executives," according to the *Telegram*. *Herald* president William C. Reich told McCay, "Nay, nay, Silas, do not go on the vaudeville stage. Let others do it, but not you. You are far too young and unsophisticated. It's a rocky old road, is vaudeville, and you may stumble." McCay persisted, "But I'm getting large rouleaus of glittering samoleans, and I'm at Sea Gate, where I need the money." Because of a loophole in McCay's contract, "it did not specify that 'Silas' must keep away from vaudeville."[20]

McCay's frustration over not being allowed to appear in Europe was expressed that spring of 1910 in an extraordinary adventure in *Little Nemo in Slumberland: The Trip to Mars*. This episode, which lasted from April 24 through August 14, 1910, represents McCay at his most cynical and angry. On Mars the inhabitants' lives are controlled by a monstrous businessman, a magnate who makes the Martians pay for the words they speak and the very air they breathe. Images abound of Nemo and friends gasping for air, losing their individuality in a sea of Martians, suffering the loss of free speech and freedom of movement because of one powerful individual who uses his power selfishly. Further, Mars is polluted, overcrowded, and filled with oppressive architecture, a result of the greed of the business magnate.

Standards of behavior and beauty are perverted. In a Martian zoo, grotesque animals are "humiliated" and "subdued." In this disturbing *Nemo* episode, McCay predicted the problems afflicting late-twentieth-century urban America. McCay was clearly in a black mood, and the death in 1910 of his sister, Mae Disbrow, added to it.

The *Herald* made a serious mistake in not allowing McCay to perform in Europe. True to form, the artist would go "where I was wanted," and within a year he left the Bennett papers for the Hearst organization. McCay was what behaviorists describe as a high achiever; that is, a person who desires to perform according to a standard of excellence and to be successful in competitive situations. Money is not a major motivation for such a person, but it is important as a measurement of performance and worth. For a high achiever, there must be continuous opportunities for achievement, recognition, advancement, and growth.

McCay needed new worlds to conquer, and by the fall of 1910, he had found them. The *Little Nemo in Slumberland* strip can often be seen as an emotional barometer for McCay, and by September his mood had lifted. Nemo began a free-floating airship exploration of several American cities, a last grand adventure in the *Herald,* full of images of freedom, spatial expansiveness, and release. He had already decided to join the Hearst papers when his *Herald* contract terminated the next year.

There was another reason for McCay's lightened mood: he had decided to change his vaudeville act. This was partly a reaction to the Boston booking agent's insolent demand the year before, but more important, it was a way of challenging himself with a new means of self-actualization. For years McCay had experimented in his comic strips with sequential motion, and since 1909 he had attempted to bring his art to life in a more direct way by privately drawing a number of "flipbooks"—sequential drawings on small pads of paper that, when flipped rapidly, created an illusion of motion.

Now he began working toward committing his experiments to film. He planned to present the films in his vaudeville act, which would outdistance him from his competitors by light years. As it happened, his impact on the history of the animated film would be as spectacular and inspiring as was his effect on comic strips. For McCay, his work in animated films would always remain "the part of my life of which I am proudest."[21]

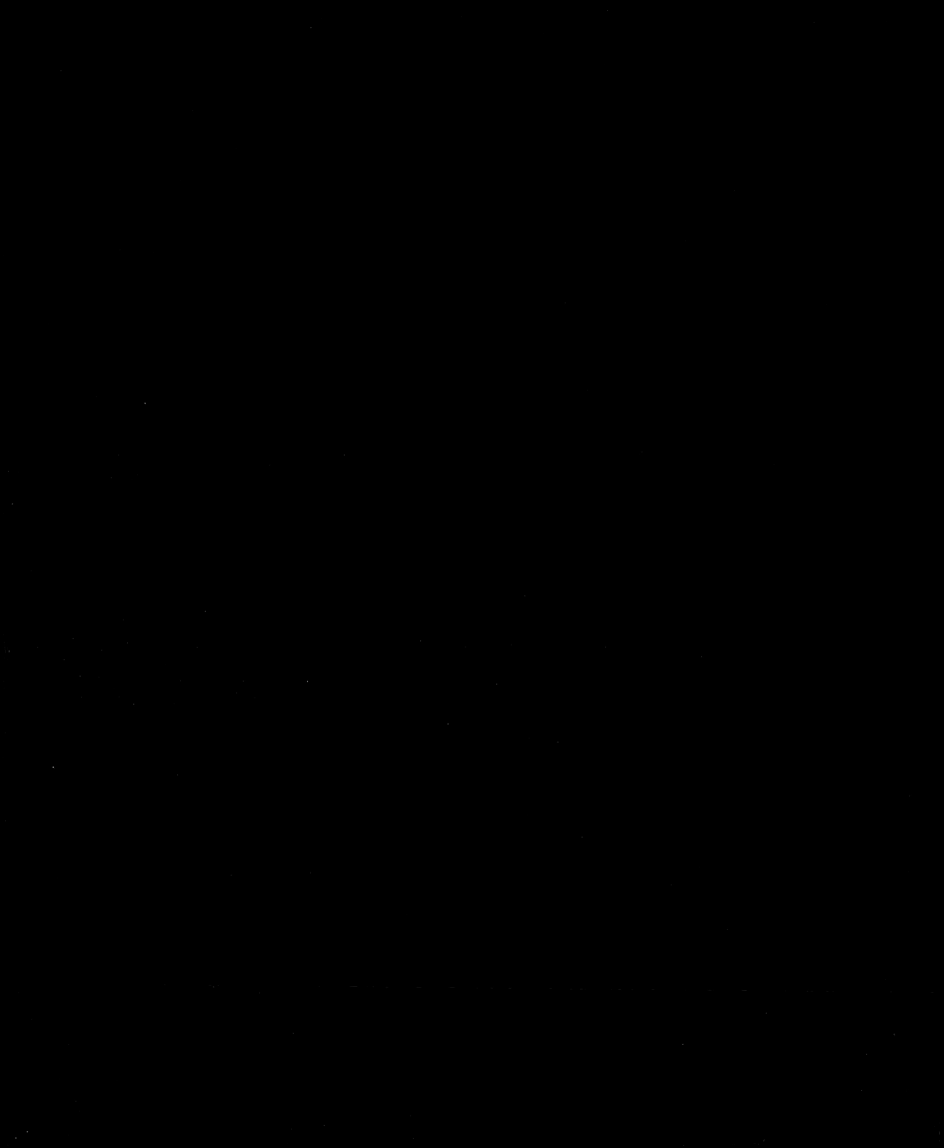

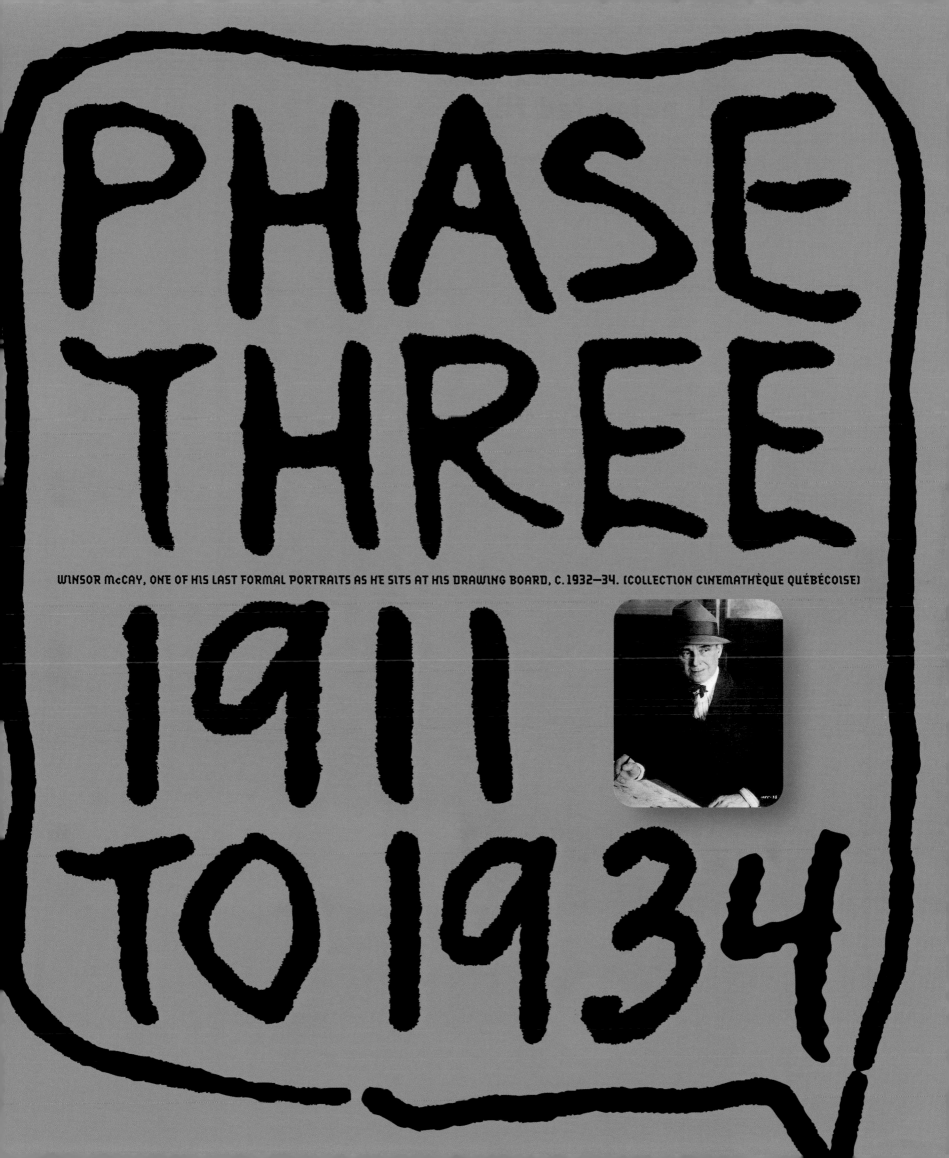

PHASE THREE 1911 TO 1934

WINSOR McCAY, ONE OF HIS LAST FORMAL PORTRAITS AS HE SITS AT HIS DRAWING BOARD, C. 1932—34. (COLLECTION CINEMATHÈQUE QUÉBÉCOISE)

chapter 8. animated films

"Artists haven't yet taken animation seriously enough. When they do, they will make some marvelous pictures."

— WINSOR McCAY

Winsor McCay often credited his son, Robert, with introducing him to animation. In 1909, he explained, the child brought home several flipbooks, and McCay "came to see the possibility of making moving pictures for entertaining an audience by observing one of the little flipper advertising pads, where a man in a mackintosh was made to raise his right hand, unfasten a flap at his throat and drop his hand to his side again."[1]

As we have seen, McCay's avid interest in motion and sequential action preceded 1909. It was, in fact, evident throughout his newspaper comic strips and in his vaudeville act. McCay seemingly had a natural affinity for animation, an extra visual sensitivity that accounted for his ability to draw highly detailed "memory sketches."

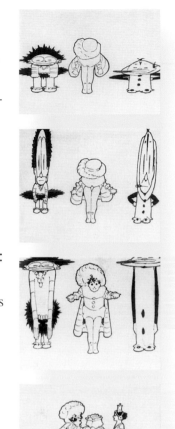

In his talent for vividly capturing motion in his drawings, McCay may have been gifted similarly to Leonardo da Vinci. Kenneth Clark's description of Leonardo's gift of sight and his ability to analyze what he saw also could be applied to Winsor McCay:

> . . . his studies of flight have a bearing on his art because they prove the extraordinary quickness of his eye. There is no doubt that the nerves of his eyes and his brain . . . were really super-normal, and in consequence he was able to draw and describe the movements of a bird which were not seen again until the invention of the slow-motion cinema.[2]

McCay's initial interest in the animated film must also have sprung from viewing the films of two contemporaries: James Stuart Blackton (1895–1941) and Emile Cohl (1857–1938). McCay liked to say that he was "the first man in the world to make animated cartoons," but that statement is not historically accurate. What he probably meant to suggest was that he was the first to make animated cartoons *his* way, which was to transfer his beautifully drawn, lavishly detailed drawings to the screen with little compromise in their design. McCay's work set a high standard for character animation, not to be surpassed until the Golden Era of the Walt Disney studio in the mid-1930s.

James Stuart Blackton, a former newspaper reporter/cartoonist and theatrical lightning sketcher, was a partner in Vitagraph, one of the most important of the early live-action studios. Blackton used his animated "trick-films" to attract audiences to Vitagraph's live-action features; his frame-by-frame animation of objects in the 1907 trick film *The Haunted Hotel* was state-of-the-art special effects in its day.

THE VITAGRAPH COMPANY'S STUDIOS

R. Hemba

ABOVE:
A June 1911 advertisement to announce Vitagraph's release of the film Little Nemo *in France. (Collection Maurice Sendak)*

PREVIOUS PAGE:
Frame blowups from Little Nemo *of Nemo in grand costume causing Flip and Impie to squash and stretch magically, and of Nemo presenting a flower to the Princess. (Collection La Cinémathèque québécoise)*

Blackton's *Humorous Phases of Funny Faces* (1906) is generally considered to be the first film to use frame-by-frame animation of drawings. In the film, faces of a man and a woman drawn on a blackboard undergo progressive changes—the man flirts with the woman, she smiles, he blows smoke in her face, and so forth. The animation was accomplished by turning the camera crank once, erasing part of the artwork on the blackboard, redrawing the art in a new position, then turning the crank again, and so on.

McCay must have been impressed with the animated shorts of the French caricaturist Emile Cohl, whom his biographer Donald Crafton acknowledges as the filmmaker primarily responsible for disassociating animation from the trick-film genre.[3] In 1909 Cohl's films reached the height of their popularity, imported from Gaumont in France and released in the United States by distributor George B. Kleine. (McCay pinpointed 1909 as the year he became actively involved with animation experimentation.) Cohl's primary graphic signature in most of his films (such as *Fantasmagorie* in 1908) was a magical metamorphosis of simply drawn characters in a nonnarrative dreamlike situation.

McCay borrowed from both of these pioneer animators in his first film, adding his own innovations as well. From Blackton he adapted the inconographic motif of a live artist drawing characters that come to life. From Cohl he used the free-flowing abstract metamorphosis of pencil lines that become recognizable characters.

Where McCay differed from his predecessors was in his ability to animate his drawings with no sacrifice of linear detail; the fluid motion, naturalistic timing, feeling of weight, and, eventually, the attempts to inject individualistic personality traits into his characters are qualities that McCay first brought to the animated film medium.

For his first film, McCay chose three characters from his comic strip *Little Nemo in Slumberland*. Thus, McCay was the first artist to bring comic strip cartoons to the screen as animation. McCay compiled about 4,000 animation drawings on rice paper by late 1910. John A. Fitzsimmons, who assisted the artist on two later films, recalled some of McCay's technical procedures:

After each drawing was completed and a serial number assigned to it, marks for keeping it in register with the other drawings were placed on the upper right and left corners. To facilitate handling and photographing of the drawings, mounting them on slightly larger pieces of light cardboard became the next step.

. . . the purpose of being so critical regarding this phase of the operation was the urgency of eliminating all unnecessary vibration in the picture on the screen. If this explanation on the first part of the operation sounds technical, that's because it was, and handling of each unit of the entire process many times was a long, tedious piece of work for McCay.[4]

In order to test the smoothness of the animated actions, the drawings (mounted on cardboard) were placed on a device similar to a Mutoscope, a nineteenth-century viewing machine used in penny arcade peep shows. It was a box 24 by 12 by 20 inches, open at the top, with a shaft running through it on which a hub containing slits held the drawings. A crank revolved the hub and the drawings while a brass rod running across the top caught the cards momentarily, simulating the interruption provided by the shutter of a movie projector.

In early 1911, under the supervision of Blackton, both the drawings and a live-action prologue and epilogue for the film called *Little Nemo* were shot at the Vitagraph studio on Avenue M, two miles from Sheepshead Bay. Vitagraph released the short in movie theaters on April 8, and McCay used it in his vaudeville act (with the live-action sections included) beginning on April 12 at New York's Colonial Theater.

The prologue was supposedly based on a real wager made between McCay and some newspaper cronies regarding his ability to make drawings move. In the film, the scene takes place at a restaurant where tuxedoed gentlemen (including Hearst cartoonist George McManus and Vitagraph star John Bunny) laugh continuously as McCay claims he can complete in one month 4,000 drawings that move.

McCay, who resembled actor James Cagney with a forelock, displays elfin charm and a naturalness in front of the camera. The bet is made, after much pointing to McCay's head and to a wine bottle, indicating (in the broad pantomime of the silent-film era) that the artist is either crazy or drunk to consider such a foolish project.

The scene shifts to a hallway outside a door labeled "Studio." McCay, now dressed in a natty vest and fedora, directs burly workmen delivering barrels of ink and huge cartons of paper. "One month later" (reads a title card), McCay gathers the betting gentlemen around a movie projector; the film within a film begins with a close-up of McCay's hand drawing Nemo, Flip, and Impie on one sheet of paper, a rare glimpse of McCay's legendary ability to draw rapidly in one continuous line.

McCay's hand-drawn portraits of characters he is about to bring to life reinforces the artist's relationship to his creation. A single drawing of Flip is inserted by McCay's hand into an open-ended wooden slot in front of the camera, which tracks in for a close-up of the drawing. The words "Watch me move" appear above Flip's head, and at last the animation begins.

Flip comes to life by rolling his eyes, tipping his cigar, blowing smoke, and waving it away in a grand gesture. The smooth naturalism of the animation is startling in this opening and throughout the film's four-minute duration. Next, Impie is formed in sections like building blocks falling from the sky. But there is no sky or land—Flip and Impie bounce, tumble, disappear, and reappear in limbo. Perspective is indicated by the characters moving toward and away from the viewer. McCay was obviously experiment-

ing in this opening segment, contrasting the realistic motion of the characters with an exploration of the magical possibilities of the medium.

Nemo enters as tiny lines resembling steel filings attracted to an invisible magnet; soon the lines form the famed boy dreamer, grandly resplendent in plumed hat, cape, and tights, standing between Impie and Flip like a benevolent visitor from a more peaceful planet.

Nemo separates the fighting twosome, demonstrating his total control over the situation and the world of lines he inhabits. By raising and lowering his arms, Nemo causes Impie and Flip to stretch and squash repeatedly like distorted images in a dime museum mirror. Nemo is McCay's self-figuration, his alter ego, proving his mastery over the actions of his creations. This becomes most obvious in the next charming scene: Nemo imitates McCay's lightning-sketch act by drawing the Princess, who then comes to life (a cartoon version of the myth of Pygmalion and Galatea).

A rose grows just in time to be plucked by Nemo, who presents it to the Princess. Then a dragon's head enters the frame and opens its huge mouth, which contains two thrones. Nemo and his lady fair sit in the mouth of the monster, waving gaily to us as the dragon turns and slithers into the distance, a breathtaking moment thanks to McCay's flawless perspective animation.

Flip and Impie drive off in a jalopy, a typical McCay contrast of the fabulous with the mundane. The car explodes, as Dr. Pill enters. Flip and Impie fall from the top of the frame onto the good doctor. The two float down softly, rather than fall hard, a rare miscalculation of the timing of an action by McCay

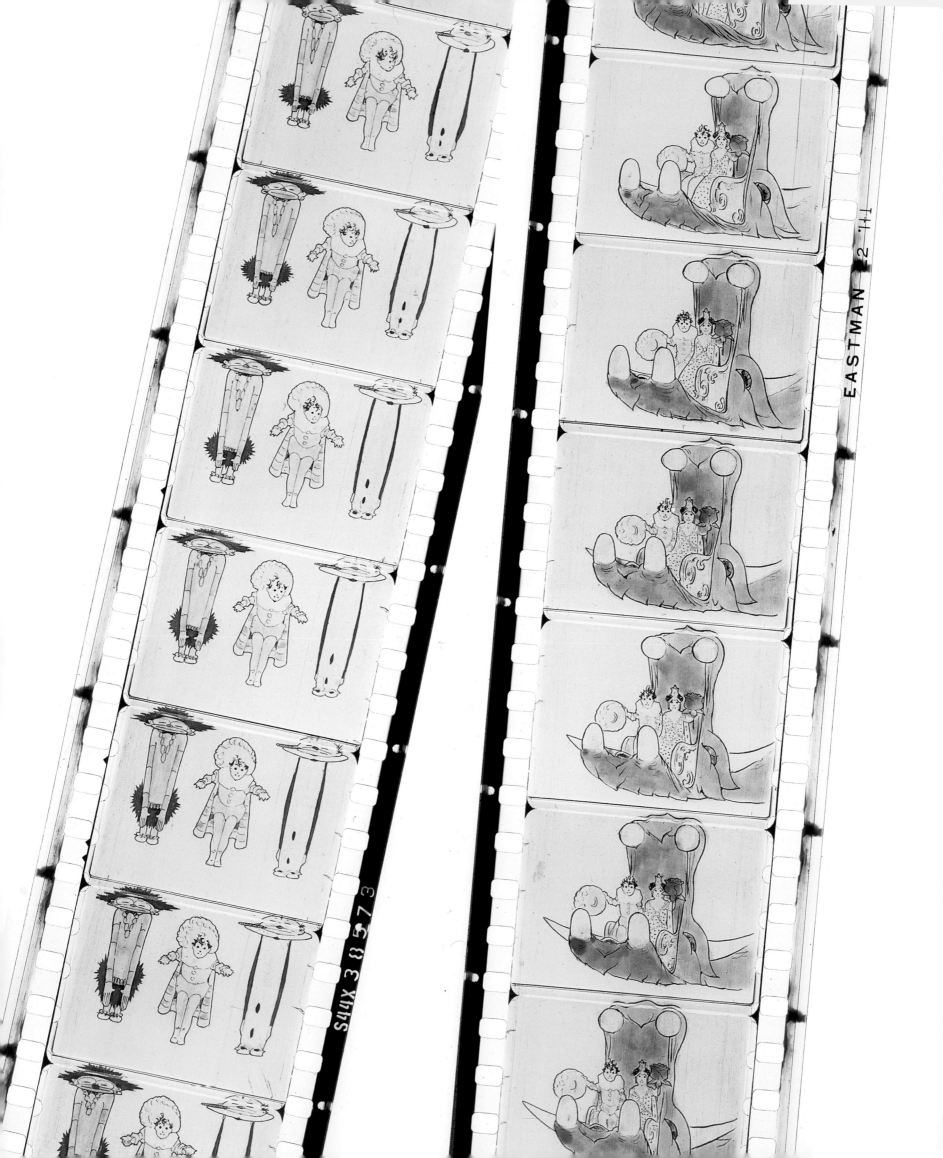

and an example of how experimental this amazingly self-assured animation really was.

Claude Bragdon, in his book *More Lives Than One* (1938), wrote: "I shall never forget [McCay's] first animated picture: in pure line, on a white background, a plant grows up and unfolds into a flower; a young man turns and plucks it and hands it to the girl beside him. That is all there was to it, but it excited me greatly, and no wonder! I had witnessed the birth of a new art."[5]

McCay had shown the way to all the possibilities in this new medium, both artistically and commercially, as a review from *Moving Picture World* on April 22, 1911, indicates:

Here Little Nemo and his friends are made to do amusing and surprising stunts. Indeed, after watching these pictures for awhile one is almost ready to believe that he has been transported to Dreamland along with Nemo and is sharing his remarkable adventures. . . .
. . . it is an admirable piece of work. It should be popular everywhere. It is one of those films which have a natural advertising heritage in the great and wide popularity of its subject—Little Nemo is known everywhere.

McCay started the symbiotic relationship between comic strips and film animation, soon to be fully exploited by Bud Fisher *(Mutt and Jeff),* George McManus *(The Newlyweds,* animated by Emile Cohl), Rudolph Dirks *(Katzenjammer Kids),* among many others, and continued into modern times by Charles Schulz *(Peanuts),* Garry Trudeau *(Doonesbury),* R. Crumb *(Fritz the Cat),* and so on.

Winsor McCay, however, never fully explored all the commercial possibilities of animation. He never headed a large factory-studio with a staff to turn out series of cartoon shorts, as did others who soon followed after. McCay found joy in working by himself slowly on each film, testing, finding his way in his own good time, and contemplating the artistic possibilities in the medium.

McCay held a dream of what animation could be and feared (correctly as it turned out) that the technical limitations of the medium would not be overcome in his lifetime. He often spoke of his visionary hopes for the young art:

The future successful artist will be one whose pictures move. By that I mean a creator of subjects who first paints his pictures which are later photographed and then thrown upon the screen by means of the moving picture machine. . . . I believe the public is becoming a little weary of going to art museums where they can only see some unanimated object, at the most, and I can safely predict that these so-called revolutions in art that I have originated will within the next generation achieve great popularity. Nor is this a radical statement, quite the reverse, for just see the furor my *Little Nemo* drawings, the first of these paintings shown via the moving picture route, made in artistic circles both here and abroad.[6]

Take, for instance, that wonderful painting which everyone is familiar with, entitled *The Angelus.* . . . There will be a time when people will gaze at it and ask why the objects remain rigid and stiff. They will demand action. And to meet this demand the artists of that time will look to the motion picture people for help and the artist, working hand in hand with science, will evolve a new school of art that will revolutionize the entire field.[7] It was too bad that Michael J. Angelo [sic] didn't draw for the movies . . . The coming artist will make his reputation, not by pictures in still life, but by drawings that are animated.[8]

McCay's "new act" was really his old quick-sketch act with the addition of the *Little Nemo* film, but it won him renewed attention plus a slew of fine reviews, and it kept his name before the public as an innovative artist and celebrity. The *Morning Telegraph* listed McCay among its "Blue List" of vaudeville artists, that is, "Actors and Acts of the Highest Rating," and stated that "Winsor McCay's new act has proven even a greater go than his previous one."

Delighted by the public's acceptance of the new act, McCay had each of the individual 35mm film frames of *Little Nemo* hand-colored. The characters were rendered in vibrant primary hues, another subtle advertisement for McCay's comic strip in the color pages of the Sunday *Herald.*

The *Herald,* however, lost McCay to William Randolph Hearst's *American* that spring. "Hearst never makes a star. He buys them!" was the word among newspaper people about Hearst's policy of raiding rivals' staffs. This angered publishers "to the vast joy of innocent bystanders and to the financial advantage of reporters, cartoonists, editors, advertising men and others."[9] To Hearst, the policy was merely a good business practice. "A ready-made journalistic star has a large reader-following," explained reporter Padraic O'Glasain. "Readers mean circulation; circulation means advertising; advertising means revenue; and revenue, if there's enough of it, means profit . . . newspaper publishing is a business and there's no justification for the existence of any business save profit. It was the profit motive, call it greed if you like, that made America . . . ."[10]

As we have seen, McCay was more than ready to leave the *Herald* when the offer from Hearst came. The last dozen episodes of the *Nemo* comic strip, after the grand airship tour of America, involve a flower that allowed Nemo to talk to animals. The drawings are so spare and unimaginative that they may reflect McCay's cynical disgust with the *Herald* and his eagerness to be done with his work there. Or they may have been drawn by another cartoonist, as one source claims:

> Brought into the Hearst organization to create further adventures in the life of "Little Nemo," McCay was promptly enjoined from doing so by the *Herald,* the copyright owner. The *Herald* couldn't restrain him from using the characters, however, and he likewise couldn't stop the *Herald* from enlisting the services of other artists to continue the comic in newspapers that had contracted it. As a consequence, McCay drew *Little Nemo* for Hearst under the title of *In the Land of Wonderful Dreams* [which began in the *American* on September 3, 1911] and six artists in turn made abortive attempts to create it under its original title for the Herald Syndicate.
>
> Eventually the *Herald* discontinued running *Little Nemo* [the final one appeared July 23, 1911] for none of the artists on its staff was capable of imitating McCay's style with a reasonable degree of accuracy."[11]

McCay and his career were on a high roll: he was a star cartoonist with a star publisher, as well as a top vaudevillian who "clearly shows he is in a class by himself in this line of work."[12] He had begun his love affair with animation, and from May until January 1912, McCay devoted the maximum of his creative energies to completing his second film. *Variety* of July 22, 1911—the day before the last appearance of *Little Nemo in Slumberland* in the *Herald*—contained a final tiny slap in the *Herald's* face: a small notice announcing a "moving picture, containing six thousand sketches, all drawn by Winsor McCay, [that] will be a 'release' for vaudeville next season by Mr. McCay. The film will be named *How a Mosquito Operates.*" (The film is also known as *The Story of a Mosquito.*)

The film's original drawings were almost lost before they were filmed at Vitagraph. A blizzard raged the day of the photographing and McCay "hired a cabman to haul them to the city because he had a closed carriage." The cabman stopped for a few drinks en route, and the "police found the cab several days later in a shanty 'way down on what they call the flatlands, and the horse was two or three miles away. The pictures were all right, fortunately. . . . "[13] When the drawings were shot at Vitagraph, the alternating intensity of the arc lights used to illuminate the artwork caused annoying flickers when the finished film was projected, and so it had to be reshot.

In *How a Mosquito Operates,* McCay once again borrowed imagery from one of his comic strips. In this case, a June 5, 1909 *Rarebit Fiend* provided the basic premise and even the layout of the film's major scene. A live-action prologue (now lost) featured McCay and his daughter at their "summer home in New Jersey [where] they are pestered to death by mosquitoes."

McCay never had a New Jersey home, but the "Jersey Skeeter," its size and viciousness, was a common joke in vaudeville and humor magazines. McCay was obsessed with "skeeters," going back to his Cincinnati years where he drew them in the *Commercial Tribune* (on April 3, 1898) and the *Enquirer* (in *A Tale of the Jungle Imps* on June 14, 1903—"How the Mosquito Got His Bill"). In the *Little Nemo in Slumberland* strip of October 23, 1910, Nemo returns from a trip to Mars and passes in an airship over New Jersey, where he is attacked by a cloud of giant mosquitoes. While making the animated drawings for the *Mosquito* film, McCay drew a similar plot in his strip

A Midsummer Day Dream (July 25, 1911). Fourteen years later, on June 14, 1925, McCay again used mosquitoes in a disturbing episode of the revised *Nemo* strip in the *Herald Tribune*.

In the film's live-action prologue, McCay consults a professor who can speak the mosquito's language. He suggests the artist "make a series of drawings to illustrate just how the insect does its deadly work." After several months of toil, McCay joins the professor in a movie studio projection room, where they view his animation.

In *How a Mosquito Operates,* it was McCay's intention to reach beyond the magical motion-for-motion's-sake action (inspired by Emile Cohl's films) that he explored in his first film. In *Little Nemo,* he established believability through naturalistic movements, realistic timing, and a feeling of weight in the line drawings that validated the most outlandish actions. Now McCay wanted to use these discoveries to develop a story and a character.

The metamorphosis used in *Mosquito* was rational, not magical: the insect's abdomen swells each time it quaffs more of its victim's blood. Over a number of scenes in the beginning of the film, the mosquito's size changes for expressionistic reasons. The animation begins with a man in a nightshirt looking fearfully about before opening a door and entering his bedroom. (The diminutive McCay amusingly chose a large man to be afraid of a tiny insect.) After the door closes, the mosquito flies into the scene, where, too large to squeeze through a keyhole, it enters the sleeping chamber through the door's transom.

Once in the bedroom, the mosquito is about the same size as the sleeping man's head, considerably smaller than when he went over the transom but still a formidable monster. The insect's unnaturally large size is McCay's symbolic visualization of how the mind of the victim perceives its tormentor. (In a darkened room, the whine of tiny mosquitoes can seem like that of giant dive-bombers.)

EDITORIAL PAGE OF THE **BOSTON AMERICAN** BOSTON JUNE 28, 1911

Just Arrived! Winsor McCay's Funny Folk Join the American's Family

No wonder the figures are expressing their joy. Henceforth they will appear exclusively in these pages. Jake is abandoning his grindstone for a moment, Colonel Stall having grown tenderhearted for the time. Mr. Bunion is ready to abandon Dull Care and Sammy Sneeze is trying to smile under difficulties. Impie, Flip, Nemo, the Princess, the Candy Kid and Dr. Pill prepare for new adventures in fairyland, and Hungry Henrietta forgets to eat her pie. The Rarebit Fiends are waking up from the worst dream they ever had, but they can't resist their favorite dish and will have another dream to-night. In to-morrow's paper we shall see what it was all about, and every day afterward there will be pictures of one of their dream-adventures.

Of Course You Know Winsor McCay, the Author of "Little Nemo."

And of Course You're Going to Follow His Charmingly Fantastic Characters Through the Most Wonderful of All Fairy Lands. Young or Old, You'll Enjoy Every One of Their Extraordinary Adventures as Told in Mr. McCay's Inimitable Series of Delightful Pictures

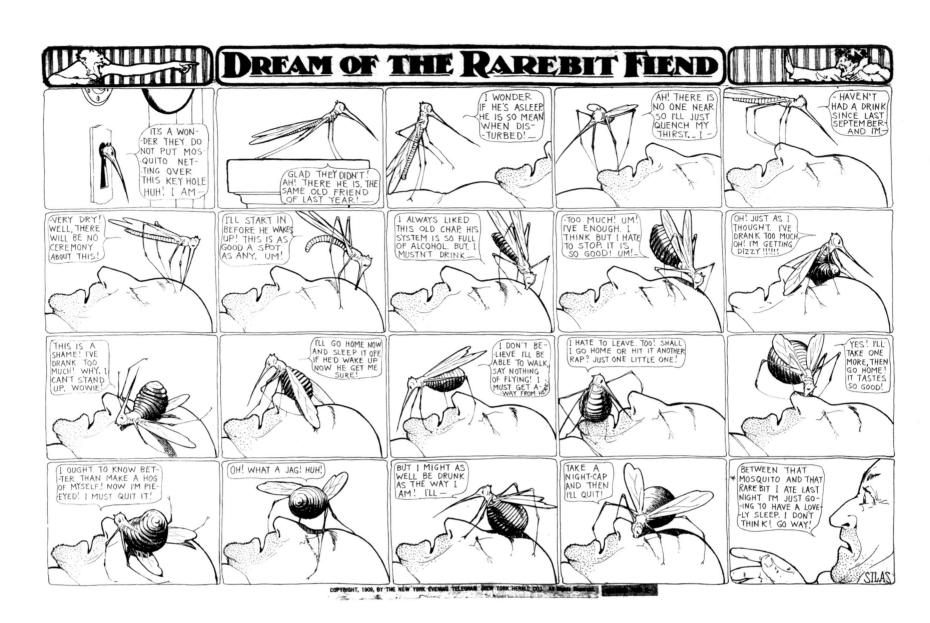

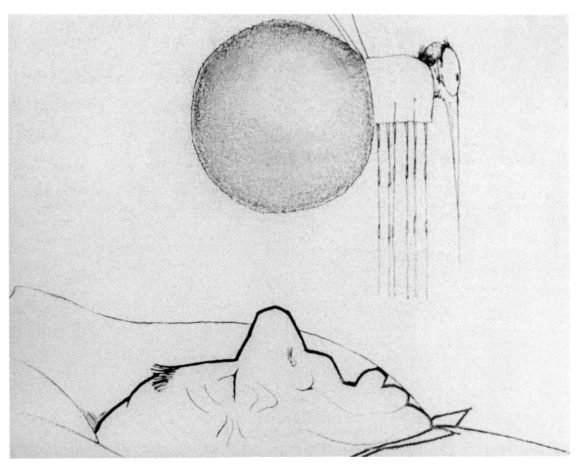

McCay's line and accuracy in drawing delight the eye. A thick Art Nouveau line surrounds the man in close-up, and his horrified, wide-eyed expression makes us feel his fear and pain as the mosquito pricks him repeatedly. The mosquito is delicately drawn in a design that disturbingly combines human and insect elements. There is no doubt that this is an anatomically correct bug with six spindly legs, two slender wings, and oversized eyes. But it also possesses small pointed ears, eyebrows, a receding hairline, and short-legged trousers. And carries a valise.

McCay's innate feeling for timing and weight is uncanny (particularly when the mosquito's weight increases by degrees and affects its balance). It lent great verity to the cartoon, and the small actions and mannerisms that individualized the character gave him the beginnings of a personality.

When a cartoon character has personality, audiences identify with its actions, and it becomes more than a mere drawing—something truly alive. The mosquito constantly establishes eye contact with us as he waves his hat, sharpens his bill on a portable stone wheel kept in his valise, and shows off by balancing himself on the bridge of the man's nose. He is an intelligent creature who can think and consider solutions to problems. McCay wished not only to amuse us by making lines move; he wanted us to feel close to the character made of those lines and involve us emotionally.

"In our animation," wrote Walt Disney in a studio memo in 1935, "we must not only show the actions or reactions of a character, we must picture also with the action the feelings of those characters." Here, in Winsor McCay's earliest experimental films, we see the beginnings of a type of character animation that reached its apex in Disney's *Snow White and the Seven Dwarfs* (1937).

McCay's mosquito contains hints of a real personality whose thinking processes produce actions that in turn strongly affect audiences. The mosquito seems to be egotistical, with a fondness for showing off; he is calculating (when he prepares his proboscis on the stone wheel), gluttonous, and doggedly persistent.

McCay's tour de force animation is all the more impressive when one considers the rather frightening face of the mosquito, the repulsive, almost sexual action of repeatedly penetrating his host's face with his long beak, and the bloody finale in which parts of the mosquito wash over the screen. That McCay's weird bug holds us fascinated through all of the above is impressive; it is attributable to the creature's recognizable personality traits but also to McCay's dexterity in alternating ugly or disturbing images with those that make us laugh or impress with their beauty. One such intriguing vision occurs after the mosquito quaffs so much blood his abdomen becomes a fat round circle and he must lie down. The rear-view image becomes abstract—a delicately shaded circle with two oblong projections (wings)—and strangely lovely.

Audiences and critics were enthralled by McCay's film: "It is a marvelous arrangement of colored drawings," said the *Detroit Times* of the *Mosquito* animation, whose final film frames McCay hand-colored blood red. "The Jersey product takes on a big cargo of blood and finally explodes much to the relief, one would imagine, of the victim of the attack . . . . The big audience at the opening of the bill Monday afternoon laughed until the tears ran down its face, and went home feeling that it had seen one of the best programs in the history of the Temple theater." In August when McCay returned to Hammerstein's, the *Morning Telegraph* said, "His moving pictures of his drawings have caused even film magnates to marvel at their cleverness and humor."

McCay sold the film's theatrical distribution rights again to Vitagraph, but with the stipulation that it show theatrically only outside the United States. He wanted to avoid competing with himself as he did when *Little Nemo* was simultaneously in his vaudeville act and on movie theater screens.

McCay toured through the spring and summer of 1912 with his new film, and in a number of interviews he primed audiences for his next animated cartoon. "What interests me the most," he told *Motography,* a film trade weekly, "is the possibilities of serious and educational work with this method of producing moving pictures. I have already had a conference with the American Historical Society looking to the presentation of pictures showing the great monsters that used to inhabit the earth. There are skeletons of them on exhibition and I expect to draw pictures of these animals as they appeared in real life thousands of years ago and show them as they trampled their way through dense jungles, ate a stump or pulled down a tree or had a battle with others of their kind. There is almost no end to what an artist might do with such an idea."[14]

But it would be nearly two years before McCay's dinosaur film appeared; the film known as *Gertie the Dinosaur* would be the first McCay animated cartoon containing a detailed background tediously retraced onto each of the thousands of drawings. Also, McCay was extremely busy juggling vaudeville appearances and fulfilling work assignments for his new boss, William Randolph Hearst. From July 18, 1911, until August 29, 1913, McCay drew the comic strip *In the Land of Wonderful Dreams,* starring Little Nemo and friends, for the Sunday *American.* (A successful lawsuit against the *Herald* allowed him to use his Slumberland characters and plot device in a retitled series.)

McCay drew daily editorial cartoons, and within two years he created a total of twenty-seven short-lived weekday comic strips. Their titles included: *A Midsummer Day Dream; Autumn Daydreams; It Was Only a Dream; The Fall Guy; Will It Ever Come to This?; As Our Ancestors Played It; Fairy Tales; The Making of the Christmas Cigar; Humpty Dumpty; Not Seen at the Garden Show; Everyone Has Met That Well-Known Character, Mr. Duck; Telephone Friends; The Faithful Employee; And Then—Kerchoo!—He Sneezed; Dream of the Lobster Fiend; The Man from Montclair; Ain't You Glad You're Not a Mormon?; Nobody Cares for Father; Little Sweetheart—Ain't He Cute?; Mr. Bosh; According to Webster; Everybody's Got an Axe to Grind; It's Great to Be a Husband; I Should Worry; A Perfect Gentleman; Dear Dad and His Daughter.*

In addition, from January 19 through August 3, 1913, McCay drew a weekly *Dream of the Rarebit Fiend* for his former employer, the *New York Herald.* How and why this contractual concession was allowed by Hearst is not known.

McCay's workload was exhausting, mentally as well as physically. Something had to give; what suffered most was the quality of his work. None of the new strips contain much imagination or creative thrust, and none endured beyond 1913. Even his retitled version of the *Little Nemo* strip became an empty parade of gaudy sets inhabited by a passive Nemo dominated by a super aggressive Flip, who by default became the strip's protagonist. This disappointing output was certainly counter to McCay's intentions, for, as usual, he took on a superhuman workload in order to impress his new employer and prove his worth.

But McCay's mind and heart were all too clearly somewhere else. He was churning out his newspaper duties, working automatically by relying on technique alone (which was often dazzling) to carry him through, hoping to find time and space in his life to work on his new film. Sometimes McCay revealed within his assigned work where his true interest lay; for example, in the May 25, 1913, *Rarebit Fiend* strip, a hunter shoots at a scaly male dinosaur in surroundings that later reappeared in McCay's film. There are the same barren rocks behind which the shy creature peeks, the foreground tree, and the stones the dinosaur eats. Although the strip's dinosaur was male, it foreshadowed the design of the film's female star.

Another example is found in *In the Land of Wonderful Dreams* on December 21, 1913, in an adventure called "In the Land of the Antediluvians," where Nemo meets Bessie the blue dinosaur. By that time the gender of the dinosaur and its design match exactly that of the cinematic *Gertie,* whose drawings were at last ready to be photographed at Vitagraph. Disney director Paul Satterfield was an art student in Atlanta when he met Winsor McCay, who was playing a theater there around 1915. "He told us how he happened to get the name Gertie," recalled Satterfield. "He heard a couple of 'sweet boys' [gay men] out in the hall talking to each other, and one of them said, 'Oh, Bertie, wait a minute!' in a very sweet voice. He thought it was a good name, but wanted it to be a girl's name instead of a boy's, so he called it 'Gertie.'"[15] Another name considered and abandoned was "Jessie the Dinosaurus" [sic], which appears on the cover of a McCay notebook listing the shooting continuity of several of his films.

A photo lineup in the December 18, 1915, New York American of Hearst cartoonists includes (top, left to right): James Swinnerton, R. F. Outcault, Frederick Burr Opper, T. E. Powers, Winsor McCay; (bottom, left to right): Cliff Sterrett, Thomas A. ("Tad") Dorgan, Tom McNamara, Harry Hershfield, George McManus.

Production for *Gertie* had begun in earnest during the summer of 1913. McCay hired twenty-year-old art student John A. Fitzsimmons, a neighbor and friend of the family, as his assistant. McCay sketched the animated actions of the dinosaur on separate sheets of 6 ½-by-8 ½-inch rice paper, then handed them over to Fitzsimmons, who had the unenviable task of delicately retracing the background (rocks, trees, and water) from a master drawing onto thousands of drawings. Later he helped McCay mount the finished sketches, complete with dinosaur and background, onto larger pieces of cardboard containing registration crosses in the corners that perfectly matched crosses on the rice paper. This minimized "jitters" on the screen: unwanted movement caused by poor registration of one drawing to the next. McCay was not, however, averse to such "life" in his drawings: "I animated even the 'still' figures," he once said, "which some movie cartoonists don't do. Unless all the live figures vibrate, the picture really isn't animated."[16] Even though Fitzsimmons's youthful hand was amazingly steady, his backgrounds vibrate slightly, making a breeze seem to touch a tree's leaves, the sun's heat bounce off rocks, and light glimmer playfully on the lake's water.

Fitzsimmons once corroborated the erratic quality of McCay's work schedule: "He was doing so damn many things at one time. He sometimes would sit up all night doing a batch of drawings and then give them to me to put on the background. Then he might not be able to get at it again for a week. He might go off on a vaudeville tour, then come back. He never worked steady on these things."[17]

McCay was determined to make *Gertie the Dinosaur* his finest animated cartoon to date. He put painstaking research into the timing of particular actions to make them appear superrealistic. Years later he explained some of his experiments: "When [Gertie] was lying on her side I wanted her to breathe and I tried my watch, and also stopwatch, to judge how long she was inhaling and how long it took her to exhale. I could come to no exact time until one day I happened to be working where a large clock with a big second dial accurately marked the intervals of time. I stood in front of this clock and inhaled and exhaled and found that, imitating the great dinosaur, I inhaled in four seconds and exhaled in two."[18] In the silent-film era, film generally ran through the projector at sixteen frames per second, so McCay knew that he must draw sixty-four drawings of Gertie for her to inhale and thirty-two drawings for her to exhale once.

McCay also pondered several problems dealing with the processes of drawing animation. He differentiated between "progressive" animation and "stationary local" animation; the former might be a bird flying through space with simultaneous secondary action occurring, i.e., the bird's wings flapping up

and down. The latter was "merely a modification of the position of a hand or foot or tail, or the lines denoting expression while the main figure remains located in a stationary position."[19]

McCay advocated the repetition of drawings "for getting a lot of work on your film without making the drawings over and over." This method, later termed "cycling," was used by McCay when Flip and Impie stretched and squashed in *Little Nemo,* in several places in *How a Mosquito Operates* (rather excessively when the frightened man turns to look behind him), and in *Gertie* in a scene where the dinosaur rests on her side and breathes deeply. "I only drew her breathing once," said McCay, "but I photographed that set of drawings over fifteen times."

The artist was particularly proud of a method of animating he called the "McCay Split System." This involved dividing an action into sections: instead of animating straight ahead from position A through to position Z, McCay broke an action into main (or extreme) poses or positions, say A, E, J, P, T, and Z. He would then sketch drawings between A and E, then between E and J, and so on. Not only did this method lessen the tedium of the work, but it was an important reason why McCay's animation was so well timed and contained such strong storytelling poses.

McCay knew where his characters were headed because he established solid action drawings like goalposts. This allowed control of the action; characters' movements did not float aimlessly but were dynamically directed from beginning to end. Eventually, animation studios termed this sensible method "inbetweening." It proved especially useful during the sound era when actions had to conform to a particular beat, word, or music. Formerly, "straight-ahead animation" was the prevailing method used in animation studios. Walt Disney favored the inbetweening system starting in 1928 with his first sound cartoon, *Steamboat Willie,* starring Mickey Mouse.

In *Gertie,* the dinosaur tosses a rock at a mastodon swimming in the lake. McCay told Paul Satterfield he was thinking that "he had to have mathematical precision in the trajectory of that [rock] going over there, as well as the perspective of it, you see, and the elephant [sic] swimming out the same. He wanted to know how fast that [rock] would have to go from the

ground up to the apex, where it would slow up and stop and start again. Of course, nobody would ever know that anything was done like that. He laughed about it. He said, 'I drew the [rock] hitting the elephant on the head out in the lake first, and I knew it was going to hit him because I had it doing it.' Then all he did was cut his inbetweens in there, and he had it. The same thing we would do today, exactly."[20]

Satterfield affirmed McCay's desire to create an extraordinary film:

Mr. McCay said he haunted the museums of New York trying to figure out what breed of animal or classification of animals the dinosaurs belonged in. He had [Gertie] laying down one time and wanted to get it up. He was trying to figure out how to make this thing get up correctly. Well, the people in the museum didn't know how, and what would the public care. But when he had his dinosaur get up, he brought a flying lizard up through the sky—he told us this there in Atlanta—and he had a pointer, and he said, "Oh, look at the flying lizard," to distract the audience from seeing his dinosaur get up. He was that sincere in what he was trying to do. I think that was just the nature of Mr. McCay. He was such a conscientious and thorough worker.

McCay said the split system "is my own invention, but I desire no patent or copyright on it, as I believe that such a process should be open to universal use, just as the discoveries in medicine are made known."[21] McCay's openness regarding the "mysteries" of animation processes was in direct contrast to the behavior of the earlier animators, Blackton and Cohl, who were like magicians guarding a secret conjuring trick. When McCay previewed his first animated cartoon for *Herald* art director George W. Bonty, Bonty pleaded with McCay to copyright or patent his techniques. McCay blithely replied, "Any idiot that wants to make a couple of thousand drawings for a hundred feet of film is welcome to join the club."[22]

McCay's carefree attitude toward protecting himself and his filmmaking methods backfired on him. Fitzsimmons recalled that during the production of

Gertie, McCay was visited by a young man supposedly writing a magazine article about animation. McCay welcomed the man into his home and "wishing to aid the writer in every way possible, McCay showed the young man every detail of the process he had developed, including a complete explanation of the purpose and workings of his testing machine."[23]

Time passed, and McCay was shocked one day to be served with a citation of infringement "by an entirely new studio entering the animation field. McCay, along with every other artist and business concern engaged in producing animated motion pictures, was notified that henceforth all would be required to pay royalties on all future productions of animated cartoons to the holder of the patent rights, who as it turned out was the young gentleman to whom McCay had so graciously described his art."[24]

Fitzsimmons identified the young man as John Randolph Bray (1879–1978), a man a dozen years McCay's junior, who would within five years establish the largest and most efficient cartoon film factory of its time. Bray, who became known as "the Henry Ford of animation," industrialized film cartoons; he streamlined all of the tasks by hiring a staff to divide the workload into numerous specialized jobs, such as animation, inbetweening, cleaning up (conforming the drawings), inking, painting, and photography. In the same amount of time it took McCay to laboriously produce one film, Bray could turn out dozens.

Bray patented many animation processes, but his most important patent (which he shared with animator Earl Hurd) covered the use of clear celluloid sheets, or "cels," on which the characters were traced in ink and (on the reverse side) colored with opaque paint. The individual cels could be placed over one background, which eliminated the necessity of retracing the background on each character drawing, as John Fitzsimmons did for *Gertie.*

The first of Bray's patent applications, filed January 9, 1914, contained a number of methods developed and touted by Winsor McCay, including the use of cross marks to facilitate registration of the drawings; McCay's "stationary local animation"— the sequential changes of a main action, while non-moving elements are traced by an assistant; use of thin tracing paper; the Mutoscope action viewer; the reuse (cycling) of drawings to increase screen time and lessen the number of drawings. Where Bray's methods differed from McCay's was in the "printing of a portion of the picture and the drawing in by hand of the remainder" and the "printing of a background and the drawing in of a movable object."

Bray contended that "the time, labor and costs involved in the production of [thousands of separately drawn pictures] has caused the commercial failure of all attempts to secure animated cartoons prior to my invention. In carrying out my process, I am able to eliminate a large amount of work, and reduce the time by printing a portion of each picture. . . ."

Further, Bray claimed that the novel features of his process enabled him "to place this type of pictures before patrons of the ordinary moving picture theaters, at which a small price of admission is charged, as distinguished from an interesting curiosity exhibited and lectured about in high-priced vaudeville houses. . . . " Bray's process "with its possibilities of producing better pictures at an extremely small fraction of the cost of production of the 'Little Nemo' pictures [sic] . . . tends to conclusively show that applicant's process was not obvious to the skilled and clever artist who produced the 'Little Nemo' pictures at such an enormous expense of time, labor and capital, as to absolutely preclude their commercial use in moving picture theaters having the usual low price of admission."[25]

Labeling McCay as a high-priced elitist was unfair. *Little Nemo,* as we have seen, played in regular movie theaters even before it appeared in McCay's vaudeville act, and continued to do so after. The *Mosquito* film did not play outside of McCay's act in the United States because McCay decided not to compete with himself. In any case, Bray's patent application points out the sharp differences between a commercially minded businessman's practical approach to making a new art profitable and the attitude of an artist whose concerns were purely aesthetic and "impractically" experimental.

A precursor of the design of Gertie the Dinosaur and her setting appeared in a May 25, 1913, Dream of the Rarebit Fiend. *(Collection Ray Winsor Moniz)*

DREAM OF THE RAREBIT FIEND

BY SILAS

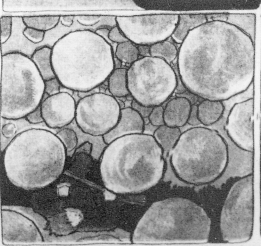

As for the infringement citation, McCay easily proved that *Little Nemo* had been shown years before Bray's patents, in a theater in New Jersey, which "brought it under interstate commerce, so that Bray couldn't stop McCay." There are indications that McCay may have countersued Bray. According to animator I. Klein, McCay "blew his top. He felt he was high-jacked and double-crossed. He sued and judging from the length of the newspaper clippings it must have been a lengthy trial."[26] No newspaper articles or court papers have yet been found to support the above story. In McCay's private papers, however, letters from Bray's attorneys prove that McCay did participate in the profits Bray derived from licensing producers for the use of his patented processes. As late as October 1932, McCay received from the Bray Hurd Process Company a check for $65.71 covering royalties for the quarter ending in September. By that time

the Bray patents had run out, but for seventeen years McCay did make some money from methods he developed but failed to protect. Or, as I. Klein said, "McCay won a moral victory but about eighteen cents in cash."

A recently discovered, undated draft of a letter (perhaps unsent) to a fan by McCay, while containing errors regarding dates, spelling of names, and techniques, nevertheless communicates his side of the Bray rivalry as well as McCay's pride as the self-proclaimed "originator and inventor of animated cartoons."

I hasten to reply to your kind letter regarding Vol. 15 Encyclopedia Britannica's statement.

It was wonderful of you to name me The inventor of Animated Cartoons and I should have thanked you long ago but I am, oh, I don't know, just careless.

The above Vol. 15 E. B. is terribly wrong and you are absolutely right.

John A. Fitzsimmons in 1975 at the age of eighty-two, holding a gift drawing of Nemo and the Princess from his neighbor and friend Winsor McCay. Fitzsimmons was McCay's assistant on two of the artist's animated films, Gertie the Dinosaur *(1914) and* The Sinking of the Lusitania *(1918). (Collection John Canemaker)*

Bray did get a patent in Aug. 1913 [sic] which never stood the test as per old clipping enclosed . . . and I have so much other data that I cannot put my hands on at this moment.

Three years before Bray got his patent I had shown my 1st & 2nd movies in every big city east of the Mississippi.

These pictures were photographed in the Vitagraph Studios by Stewart [sic] Blackton believing at the time I would fail as an animator.

But they made a 1000 footer [film] and released it all over the world—making such a hit in France that they used a 4 colored 3 sheet [poster] to advertise it.

Mr. Blackton was a willing witness against Bray in Bray's threatened suit.

Mr. Otis Wood of the McClure syndicate was another willing witness against Bray whom [sic] made an affidavit that he and Bray sat in the audience at Hammerstein's Theater and saw my exhibition 6 months before Bray got his patent out.

No animator today recognizes Bray as the inventor and all ignore his patents. I announced from the stage that I thought I had invented a new art. That it was not patented and that I hoped other artists would take it up.

My Dear Good Friend you have no fear of being wrong and I am going to take it up with the publishers of the E. B. I am quite sure Bray himself will confess that I am The Originator & Inventor of Animated Cartoons.

Why Jessie Lasky himself will tell you that he and Cecil De Mil [sic] visited my home and watched me working on cells in 1911 [sic]. I hope you are not annoyed by this E.B. incident.

I am more than yours respectfully.[27]

About a year or two after McCay's *Gertie the Dinosaur*, a bogus *Gertie* cartoon film made the rounds; to this day, it is still marketed to unwary viewers as McCay's work. The fake *Gertie*, attributed to the Bray studio, features a dinosaur performing most of the actions of McCay's creature, but without charm or convincing motion; moreover, it is poorly drawn. It was also animated completely on cels with a stationary background, as opposed to McCay's work which was animated (background and all) on rice paper. The phony *Gertie* is a brash, artistically pathetic showcase of the Bray-Hurd technical process.

Pressure increased on McCay to complete the drawings for *Gertie* when he received a letter from James Stuart Blackton of the Vitagraph Company (located near McCay's home in Brooklyn). Blackton was about to lease the Criterion Theater at Broadway and 44th Street, thus making Vitagraph the first film studio to also become an exhibitor.

The letter, dated October 10, 1913, invites the animator to show his new film ("with yourself to lecture on same") at the "Vitagraph Theater" opening the next month in Times Square. "This does not allow any too much time to get the film finished," Blackton wrote. "If this interests you and the drawings are finished, drop in to see me."

As it turned out, the Vitagraph Theater did not open until February 7, 1914. With all his distractions, McCay was not able to get *Gertie*'s drawings before a Vitagraph camera until January 1914. In a small notebook he prepared meticulous, detailed shooting instructions—a veritable frame-by-frame "exposure sheet" for the camera operator—using numbers that match the numbers in the corner of each drawing.

For example, for Gertie's repetitious dance, McCay wrote:

The Dance. Start 41 A to 51 A. Up and down 3 times. Back to 41 A . . . then jump to 52 B to 63 B & back & forth twice. The third time jump from 63 to H 65 & up and down twice . . .

He premiered the film in his vaudeville act at the Palace Theater in Chicago the next month. He began as usual with lightning sketches on a blackboard, followed by a screening of *How a Mosquito Operates*. After that, McCay returned to the stage brandishing a bullwhip and stood on the right side of the movie screen. For the first time in his act, he explained to the audience how animated films were made, photographed, and projected. Then he introduced Gertie, "the only dinosaur in captivity," cracked his whip, and the animated film flashed onto the screen.

At first, Gertie shyly pokes her head out from behind some rocks in the distance. Because her body is hidden, there is no indication of her height and girth and she resembles an anthropomorphic snake or a large worm. But with McCay's onstage encouragement and several more whip cracks, the live artist convinces the cartoon diplodocus to reveal herself in all her gigantic glory.

Gertie hops from behind the rocks with agility, like an eager child, and begins a lumbering stroll from the distance to the foreground, swallowing part of a tree and a boulder along the way. McCay's animation is, once again, incredibly realistic and convincing in the natural smoothness and masterful perspective of the dinosaur's walk. McCay continued to crack his whip with each order to the creature on the movie screen, who obeyed in her own good time.

For Gertie is a reluctant dragon with a mind of her own and a temper to back it up. At one point, pushed a bit too far by the tiny human ringmaster insisting she "raise her foot," "bow to the audience," and so on, Gertie lunges forward and snaps with her huge jaws. McCay's drawings exaggerate the fore-shortening when the dinosaur's head comes close to the screen for the attempted nip at McCay. When admonished for her fit of pique, Gertie cries, and this becomes the film's most endearing moment. Big tears fall from Gertie's eyes, like Lewis Carroll's Alice.

The personality traits McCay invested in his cartoon character make Gertie truly unique; they give her a soul and a familiar temperament, not unlike that of a child. McCay distracts Gertie from her crying as one would a little girl: he offers and appears to toss to her an apple. (Actually McCay turned away from the audience when he "tossed" the apple, putting the red cardboard prop inside his coat pocket while a cartoon apple on the screen plopped into Gertie's large mouth.)

According to McCay's shooting notebook, he originally considered placating the weeping dinosaur with an orange. In the margins of an otherwise tightly-written shooting script, he wrote in large, sponta-neous, bold strokes (as if the idea had just occurred): "After orange, work mouth & lick chops & rock [back and forth]." McCay's creative process was open to spontaneity and developing new ideas.

Sizewise, an orange pumpkin would have been the proper choice for an object large enough to read within Gertie's huge mouth; but McCay chose a smaller object easily hidden within his coat. Since red "reads" clearly to a theater audience, the prop became an apple. McCay's granddaughter Janet remembered visiting McCay backstage and seeing the red card-board "apple" in his dressing room.

A frame blowup from Gertie the Dinosaur: *the live-action prologue in which McCay, at a large drawing board, brags that he can bring a cartoon dinosaur to life. Seated at the far left is cartoonist George McManus* (Bringing Up Father).

This was one of two instances during the performance when McCay brilliantly reinforced the illusion of interaction between himself in the flesh and his cartoon creation on the screen. As the act proceeds, Gertie continues to be distracted from obeying McCay: a four-winged lizard flies by, then a woolly mammoth unluckily wanders past the mischievous dinosaur. Gertie grabs "Jumbo" by the tail and tosses him with ease into the nearby lake. In triumph, Gertie dances an absurd tango, in which McCay took considerable advantage of reusing drawings; Gertie wriggles and strikes funny poses over and over. Jumbo, watching the ridiculous display from the lake, eventually sprays Gertie with water. She retaliates by picking up a rock in her mouth and throwing it at the mammoth as it swims away.

McCay's uncanny ability to imply weight in his animation is showcased throughout the film. This is seen in Gertie's heavy movements, the way she picks up the mammoth, and (more subtly) when she loses her grip on the rock she is about to toss. It falls to the ground, and she must retrieve it with a surer bite. Finally, when thirsty from her activities, Gertie extends her neck and slowly drains the lake dry! As Gertie fills with water, she exhibits no cartoon-y exaggeration in her body. (McCay had totally abandoned magical animation for a pragmatic approach to fantasy by this time.) Her belly remains the same size, while the water line slowly descends and soon part of the cliff on which Gertie stands gives way and crumbles under her increased weight.

For the film's finale, McCay made his personal connection with the image on the screen most vivid. Earlier in the act, he had tossed a "real" apple to the beast, and it became part of the drawn imagery on the screen. Now McCay does the same with himself: he transfers his live physical presence to the movie's graphics by walking offstage in person and returning on-screen as a cartoon version of himself. Still bearing a whip, cartoon McCay gingerly steps into Gertie's open mouth; she swiftly but gently lifts her head and sets him down on her back. McCay finally bows as his docile creation carries him off-screen to immortality.

The reviews in the Chicago papers were excellent; for example, Ashton Stevens in the *Examiner* raved: "Thus the camera, that George Washington of mechanisms, at last is proved a liar . . . . You are flabbergasted to see the way the reel minds its master." A happy and triumphant McCay returned to New York to play two weeks at Hammerstein's twice a day during a winter blizzard. The bill featured seventeen acts, including former boxer John L. Sullivan, comedians Joe Cook, Ed Wynn, and Victor Moore, and a mixed bag of dancers, singers, reciters, contortionists, and a ventriloquist. Vernon and Irene Castle danced, not in person but in motion pictures, portending the demise of vaudeville, as did McCay's use of animated movies in his act. "Also in league with the cameraman," reported the *Telegraph*, "was Winsor McCay, the cartoonist and one of America's greatest draftsmen. Mr. McCay, who is in his second week, again displayed his remarkable 'movie' drawings of a mosquito and of the ancient dinosaur."

McCay's total control over his fantasy world on stage did not extend to his life at the Hearst office or in his own home. Harsh reality on both fronts dimmed McCay's newest triumph, causing him severe stress and embarrassment. Ultimately, these events proved to be the beginning of a profound alteration in the direction of his fabulous career and his life.

The trouble began almost imperceptibly. On February 22, the day before McCay's opening at Hammerstein's, Victor Watson, the *American's* "Vaudeville Chatter" columnist, wrote about McCay in two small blurbs. One mentioned McCay's turn as a "brand-new comic movie act," proclaiming that "those who have seen private views of the specialty say it is a laugh from start to finish . . . far funnier than his noted mosquito drawings."

A second mention in the same column compared McCay with yet another newspaper cartoonist who had recently entered vaudeville with a quick-sketch act, one H. B. "DickeyBird" Martin, who was playing at the Palace, a few blocks up from Hammerstein's. "Martin and Winsor McCay used to work side by side and chatter away about nothing while they made their drawings," wrote Watson. "This week they are counter-attractions . . . Their styles are so different, however, that they are really not rivals."

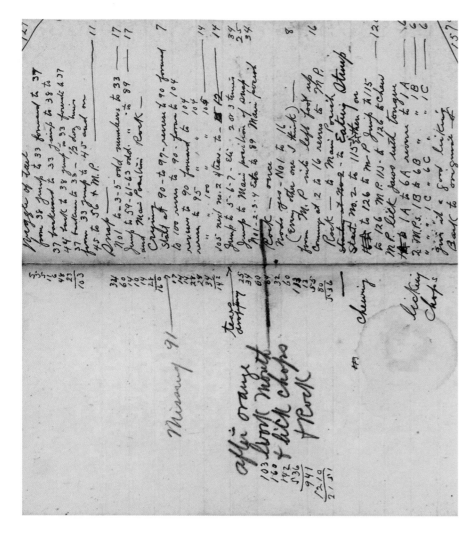

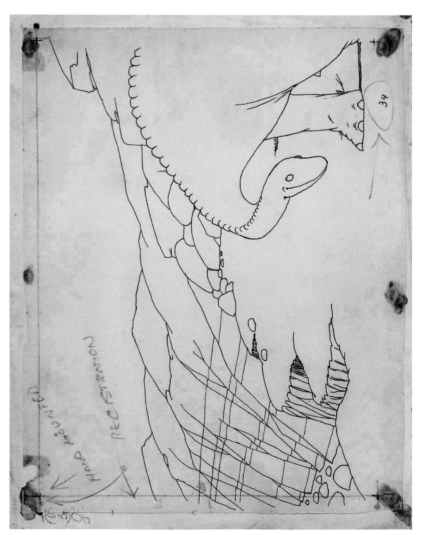

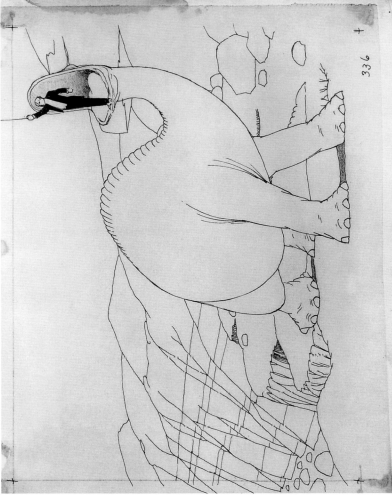

336

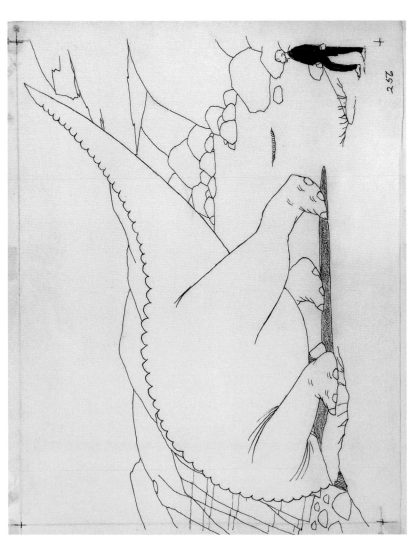

257

FROM UPPER LEFT
TO LOWER RIGHT:
*The cover of a McCay film
production notebook c. 1914–
1921, in which he wrote continuity and ideas for timings for
his animated films including
Gertie, here tagged with an
early appellation: "Jessie the
Dinosaurus." (Courtesy La
Cinémathèque québécoise)*

*Two pages in McCay's pro-
duction book. The numbers
refer to numbers or the animation drawings of Gertie the
Dinosaur, and may also be
plans for instructing the cameraman regarding the sequence
of each action. Today's animators
would write such information
on a chart called at "exposure*

*sheet." The left page contains
what appears to be a burst of
inspiration regarding Gertie's
eating of a fruit (here an orange;
later, an apple): "Work mouth
& lick chops & rock," McCay
tells himself. (Courtesy La
Cinémathèque québécoise)*

*An original 1914 drawing shows
Gertie taking a bow. (This final
section of the film is missing in
most prints today.) On the
drawing, McCay wrote indications regarding the registration
marks on his drawings meaning
where the delicate rice paper
drawings matched cross marks
printed on stiff cardboard.
Perhaps this was an instruc-
tional sample for his assistant
John A. Fitzsimmons to follow.*

*(Courtesy La Cinémathèque
québécoise)*

*Jumbo, the vengeful mammoth,
waits for his chance to squirt
water on Gertie while she
executes a clumsy gavotte.*

*Gertie quenches her thirst by
draining a lake, as a cartoon version of McCay enters the scene.*

*In the final moments of the film
Gertie the Dinosaur (1914),
a cartoon version of Winsor
McCay rides in his gigantic creation's mouth as they take their
bows and walk off to immortality. (Collection John Canemaker)*

179

The July 13, 1913, revised
Nemo strip in Hearst's New
York American.

Outside of paid advertisements, this was to be the
only article, review, or mention in the *American,* the
artist's home newspaper, about McCay's spectacular
new act. Instead, five days later, Watson wrote a rave
review of H. B. Martin's act: "I saw him at the Palace
Theater the other day, and liked it so well I've been
going every day since. 'Dickey' Martin has one of the
most progressive cartoon acts of this kind. . . ."
Martin's "progressive" act consisted of drawing a
series of caricatures of musical celebrities on two
large easels. He drew such stars as George M. Cohan,
Eva Tanguay, Eddie Foy, and others as their theme
songs were played. It was an act obviously not in the
same league with McCay's gloriously creative multimedia combination of film and live performance, or
even his lightning-sketch demonstration. Yet *American*
reviewer Watson felt Martin "deserves credit for
originality [for he] has ventured into a new field of
endeavor, and has dared to try an act that was entirely
away from any other cartoon act in the business."

One can only wonder what McCay thought of
this curious review. He must have been puzzled that
his obviously superior work was ignored by his own
newspaper and angry that the *American* reviewer was
so stupidly enamored of his rival's mediocre presentation that he never found time to attend McCay's
show. And although not mentioned by name, McCay
must have been insulted not to have his act considered "progressive" and possessing "originality."

The neglect of McCay is especially suspicious
when one reads the review by Zit in the *Evening
Journal* of the acts at Hammerstein's for the week ending February 28: "Winsor McCay offered the greatest act in the history of moving picture cartoonists."

Then, on March 7, a Saturday during the second
week of McCay's run, Willie Hammerstein noticed
that the advertisements for his theater, the Victoria,
and the vaudeville acts on the bill did not appear in
either the *American* or the *Journal,* both Hearst newspapers. After a series of persistent inquiries, the mystery was cleared up: the *American* admitted that the
ads were omitted at William Randolph Hearst's personal request, in order to express his displeasure that
a certain performer was appearing at the Victoria,
namely Winsor McCay.

It seems that Hearst made an attempt to phone
McCay backstage to confer with the artist about an
editorial he was illustrating. The minion who took
the call casually told the powerful press lord that
McCay "can't come now. He's busy."[28] Hearst flew
into a rage and canceled the Victoria's advertisements;
on the next day the *Morning Telegraph* stated, "Hearst
to Stop Vaudeville Engagements of Cartoonists."[29]

In the article, Hearst expressed his belief that
artists in his employ, such as Bud Fisher and Winsor
McCay, "should devote all their time to newspaper
work [because] their dalliance with the stage interferes with their regular newspaper work." The
Telegraph wondered if Hearst felt "that their stage
exhibitions depreciate their newspaper value." No
conclusion was forthcoming, but "whatever his
reasoning, he had made plain his opposition."

Hearst's seemingly odd outburst was to him solid
business reasoning: he wanted the most out of his
investment in Winsor McCay, and for almost three
years he felt he had gotten very little. All of the comic
strips McCay created for Hearst were either tired
rehashes of his great work at the *Herald* or new strips
unexciting conceptually and graphically. Further,
Hearst suspected McCay was not vitally interested in
his newspaper work, that he took for granted a job
for which he was being highly paid. Instead, he was
off on vaudeville tours or tinkering with his animated
films, his mind clearly not fully on his editorial cartoon work.

At the suggestion of Arthur Brisbane, Hearst's
chief editor and trusted advisor, McCay was ordered
to cease drawing his comic strips, including *In the
Land of Wonderful Dreams* with his beloved Little
Nemo. That particular series came to an end on
December 12, 1913, and even in this episode McCay
was thinking about his newest animated film: Dr. Pill,
dressed as Santa, rides a sleigh pulled by one Tessie
the Dinosaur.

Brisbane called McCay into his office and
announced, "Mr. McCay, you're a serious artist,
not a comic cartoonist. I want you to give up *In the
Land of Wonderful Dreams* and draw serious cartoon-

pictures around my editorials."[30] This was a blow to McCay; although his interest in animation was very strong, he also enjoyed the creative challenge and freedom offered by the comic-strip form. Now he would be forced to conform his creative ideas and images to the demands of two martinets—Brisbane and Hearst—a prospect deeply upsetting to McCay.

Hearst was determined not to allow what had happened to McCay's comic strips to happen to his editorial cartoons. The cartoonist was to be kept on a short leash and on constant call—ready to do his job at any time, like any good Hearst reporter. Hearst's inability to reach McCay on the telephone backstage at the Victoria convinced him that vaudeville was a major distraction for the artist, the root of the problems he was having with his newspaper work; strong measures would have to be taken.

"McCay is booked to appear at the Grand Opera House, Pittsburgh this week," said the *Telegraph*. "It may or may not have been chance that caused his employers to arrange an extraordinary amount of newspaper work for him during that period." In addition, S. S. Carvalho, one of Hearst's right-hand men, phoned McCay's theatrical agency, United Booking, to express Mr. Hearst's "disapproval" of the Pittsburgh engagement. "His representative stated further that Mr. Hearst would take it as a special favor if his views were respected."

McCay held a long conference with his agents. United Booking was torn between courting the favor of the Hearst papers for the sake of all their clients and doing right by Winsor McCay. He was an esteemed client with a contract with Hearst that did not prohibit him from accepting vaudeville engagements. Then there was the problem facing the Pittsburgh theater, which would have "the difficulty of substituting an act of equal brilliance" on short notice.

In the end, McCay canceled his Pittsburgh engagement. The following week he backed out of a booking at New York's Colonial Theater, "although he was booked there at a large salary." The *Telegraph* further stated that McCay, "it is said in vaudeville circles, does not accept the loss of his vaudeville salary with complete equanimity."[31]

Finally, in 1914, McCay was "induced by William Randolph Hearst to sign a contract not to accept vaudeville engagements outside greater New York,"[32] although exceptions were made on occasion after due consideration. McCay played New York's Orpheum in September in an understandably distracted mood, which was reflected in a review in *Variety:* "Winsor McKay [sic] did his allotted time after intermission with the moving cartoon *Gertie*. McKay [sic] does little in the act but snap a long whip, but his pen has furnished him with material which makes them laugh."[33]

On September 15, 1914, *Gertie the Dinosaur* was copyrighted, and in November McCay received "spot cash and highest prices" from William Fox's Box Office Attractions for the distribution of the film, now with a live-action prologue and epilogue attached. The prologue featured another wager between McCay and his cronies who challenge him to bring an extinct dinosaur to life. McCay's son, Robert, had a small role in the film, playing an assistant in the camera room.

McCay's stage dialogue with Gertie was replaced with intertitles, and the film held up perfectly well without McCay in person. The artist must have reasoned that if he could not travel outside New York, at least his films would keep his name and reputation alive in the hinterlands. By December *Gertie* was playing as far west as Seattle.

Although McCay's nonappearance in Pittsburgh in March was attributed to Hearst's demands, there was another reason, a secret one that would be revealed in embarrassing headlines and a trial in late December. During his March run at Hammerstein's, McCay was approached at the stage door by two strangers: an unidentified man and a woman named Mrs. Lambkin. The man told McCay that if he did not give money to Mrs. Lambkin, she would sue McCay's wife, Maude, for "breaking up her home." The woman told McCay that he would not be able to "stand the disgrace of such a suit because it would come out in the papers." McCay said he "had no money, and she replied that [he] made $50,000 a year."[34]

McCay first heard of the Lambkins one evening when Maude tearfully told him that a man she knew from Cincinnati "but had not seen for twelve years was annoying her. She said the man was calling her four and five times a day, and was evidently infatuated. The children answered the phone sometimes and it looked bad." McCay admitted at a court hearing months later that his handsome wife "had been followed home before, so I told her to forget it."[35]

Then the Lambkins made their bold blackmail pitch directly to McCay. Combined with his problems dealing with Hearst, Brisbane, his booking agents, and the quality of his vaudeville performances and newspaper work, this new problem threw the artist into an emotional turmoil. It seemed as if his carefully constructed world was caving in on top of him. The cancellation of his Pittsburgh shows *was* a desperate attempt to placate Hearst, but it also provided a chance to negotiate with the Lambkins.

On March 11, McCay met to discuss the situation with Irene Watkins Lambkin at the Hotel Hermitage, his refuge six years before when the altercation involving his wife and the Muirs proved volatile. Mrs. Lambkin accused Maude McCay and Mr. Lambkin of being "in each other's company" on a number of occasions in various locations in Philadelphia, Coney Island, and Manhattan. Then she abruptly said to McCay, "They go out together, doggone it, so why can't we go out together?"

The startled artist took Mrs. Lambkin to a restaurant, where she "drank and smoked cigarettes with him to the tune of $28." Next, they went to Shapley's, a bar where Mrs. Lambkin "did not behave like a lady," as McCay stated in court months later.

The cartoonist tried to reason with Mrs. Lambkin, asking, "why she picked me out, a married man with two children to disgrace, and she replied that she would drive my wife out of New York if I did not give her money. Then she told me she knew I would take care of her."[36]

The quality of McCay's drawing during this tense period was the worst of his career. Part of the problem was his assignments: day after day during March 1914 he was told to illustrate Brisbane's crude and simplistic prose bludgeonings of President Woodrow Wilson and his allegedly pro-England sentiments. As Brisbane's biographer Oliver Carlson put it:

> The Anglophobia of Brisbane and Hearst had been obvious for many years. It was good business, for the Hearst readers were made up largely of those whose elementary education in American schools had been colored by the red-coat theory of British aggression. The Irish, German, and Italian populations in New York, Boston, and San Francisco who composed a large sector of Brisbane's readers likewise gloried in attacks upon John Bull.
>
> Winsor McKay [sic], star cartoonist for the *New York Journal* and the special cartoonist for Brisbane's Sunday editorials, would depict Wilson as a graceless school master misrepresenting to his pupils the patriotic events of American history.

McCay was never comfortable making drawings dealing with purely political ideology. He preferred grand concepts with an emotional underpinning that would spur his imagination and provide a compelling visual hook. But over and over, each day, the anti-Wilson diatribes were spewed by the Anglophobic Hearst and Brisbane, and McCay was forced to draw the president as a perverse revisionist of American history; for example, as "Admiral" Wilson, who "introduced a new word in American diplomacy: '*Always* give up the ship!'" The series obviously did not inspire McCay, who, at this point in his life, was confused, exhausted, and emotionally drained, both personally and professionally. This upheaval was reflected in his artwork.

WINSOR McCAY
CARTOONIST, NEW YORK AMERICAN

McCay agreed to meet with Mrs. Lambkin and her husband at her apartment on June 10. There, the couple agreed to leave the McCays alone for $500; when McCay was about to comply, the Lambkins greedily raised the ante to $1,000. In disgust, McCay left, vowing to stand by his wife, who he claimed "was never away from home at night without me during all the years we have been married."

McCay hired a private detective, John Stetzle, who followed the Lambkins while their divorce suit was pending, photographing them together at Coney Island and as they entered Mrs. Lambkin's apartment. Under the law, a divorce could not be granted if husband and wife lived together after the action had begun.

During the month of December, McCay drew twenty-two editorial cartoons, almost one per day. He missed three days—December 22, 23, and 24—when he was in court attending the Lambkin trial. The quality of McCay's work was much improved since March, but it varied depending on the complexity of the design, on whether the idea inspired McCay or left him indifferent, and on whether McCay had adequate time to prepare the drawing.

Hearst biographer John K. Winkler wrote that "Clinical examination of the Hearst publications during the years 1914–18 would puzzle a pathologist . . . so weirdly fluctuating was the seeming Hearst attitude toward the war before and even after our entrance." While the publisher continually insisted on a self-serving isolationism that he labeled "America First," occasionally in his press there would appear a viewpoint that seemed to lean toward an awareness of the inevitability of war and the need for what would be termed by 1915 "preparedness." On December 4, for example, McCay drew a strongly designed, emotional cartoon entitled "Defenseless!" in which a distraught giant Uncle Sam is under attack from distant enemy guns, while New York City lies destroyed, burning in the background. Sam asks of the tiny soldiers swarming around a huge single can-

non, "Why don't you silence those guns?" To which the Lilliputian U.S. Army candidly replies, "I regret to report, sir, that we have no ammunition."

An editorial cartoon of December 16 displays McCay's superb ability to draw animals: "The Lion and the Lamb" deals with a social issue—the corruption of big business and the courts and how it harms the common man, or in this case, woman. In the top panel, a lawyer and his portly client, backs toward us, face a small lamb standing on a judge's bench. The lamb suspends sentence of the defendant, who "wrecked a bank and brought people to the brink of starvation." In the bottom panel, the defendant is a poverty-stricken woman in a tattered shawl, holding an infant, with two other children near her. She "lost her money in a bank wreck and cannot pay her rent." A magnificently drawn ferocious lion on the bench roars, "into the street with her!"

The Lambkins' divorce trial lasted only two days: December 23 and 24. Mr. and Mrs. Winsor McCay testified, as did detective Stetzle, who presented his evidence. There was damaging testimony by a building superintendent who swore Mrs. Lambkin and her husband occupied an apartment after the suit was brought. The court was convinced to dismiss the case on the grounds that "there was too much evidence of collusion to warrant granting a divorce to Mrs. Lambkin." Elliot Norton, counsel for Mrs. McCay who was named as co-respondent in the suit, told the press, "At the opening of the case I said the whole thing was a frame-up between Lambkin and his wife to blackmail Mr. McCay because it was assumed that he was earning a great deal of money by his drawings for the newspapers and his work on the stage."[37]

On Christmas Day, the day after the successful outcome of the Lambkin court decision, McCay drew a joyful cartoon of Santa Claus and a grand lady representing the *American*'s Christmas Fund. The two figures greet hundreds of tiny children, whose outstretched hands receive many presents from Santa's sleigh. In the background are icicle cave walls and detailed sun rays reminiscent of McCay's early *Little Nemo in Slumberland* adventures in Jack Frost's Ice Palace (February 24, 1907). The artist must have recalled those simpler, less complicated times, so removed from the recent emotional roller coaster of events now happily about to pass into history.

On March 21, 1915, Robert McCay, Winsor's father, died in Edmore, Michigan, at the approximate age of seventy-five. Winsor's relationship with his father remains vague. It is assumed that he respected his father but felt closer to his mother, Janet, who attended the opening night of *Little Nemo* in Philadelphia and New York and often visited Winsor in Brooklyn, staying in a suite he secured for her at the Hotel St. George.

However, an obituary in Canada's *Sentinel Review* indicates that Winsor was equally devoted to his father, for he was "almost constantly at his father's bedside since his condition became serious." Robert and Janet had moved back to Woodstock, Canada, (near their original homes of East and West Zorra) in 1913 when Robert suffered a "stroke of paralysis" that "compelled his retirement from active work."

Robert's illness extended over the next two years, "although the trouble that caused the final dissolution was only of about three weeks' duration."[38] His remains were taken to Edmore, Michigan, for burial in the family plot (which already contained Winsor's sister, Mae); local Masonic orders in Woodstock and

Edmore arranged for funerals in both towns. Mrs. McCay was said to be planning on making her home "at the old homestead in Zorra," but she later moved back to Edmore and lived there until she died in 1927.

Not until the fall of 1915 was McCay allowed to perform outside New York. Hearst gave permission for him to appear at Atlanta's fall festival on November 15, 1915. Paul Satterfield met McCay at this time in the offices of the *Atlanta Constitution:* "I had seen a lot of the animated cartoons and loved them," said Satterfield, "but I had no idea that Mr. McCay was in any way connected with them. So I asked him, 'Mr. McCay, what do you know about this new form of cartooning, the animated cartoon?' He looked up at me—I was a tall hillbilly kid and he was a little bit of a man—and said, 'Why, son, I invented it!'"[39]

In December McCay was back in the New York area, playing with *Gertie* at Brooklyn's Flatbush Theater. In July 1916, he was permitted to perform in Detroit at the Temple Theater, where cartoonist Bud Fisher had recently appeared.

Fisher, who resigned from the Hearst papers in 1915, had sued and won the rights to his own charac-

CHAPTER IN AUTHOR'S WORK.—Writers, publishers and newspapermen, clos-
nal friends of George Randolph Chester, the novelist, who died Tuesday, headed f
ocession from Church of the Transfiguration yesterday. Among them were Fr
William H. Briggs, Robert Davis, Winsor M
e Gordon and Michael Keefe.

ters. Fisher was also a silent partner in a studio that was turning out animated films based on his *Mutt and Jeff* strip every week. By summer 1916, seventeen films were completed.

In December 1915, Hearst started his own animation studio called the International Film Service, featuring shorts based on the characters of comic strip cartoonists under contract to him, such as Tom Powers and George Herriman. In 1916 Winsor McCay was listed among the lineup of cartoonist star contributors to the studio's product, but this never happened. McCay was not temperamentally suited to working in a film factory or even having his work adapted by other hands. John Fitzsimmons felt that his friend "essentially was an artist who derived a considerable pleasure watching his ideas and the creatures of his fancy come to life on his drawing board and was not a businessman with visions of great financial success." Further, Fitzsimmons "could not imagine a man of McCay's leanings being content relegated to a managerial post watching a crew of artists performing the pleasurable task he enjoyed so much doing himself."

Moreover, by the time Hearst began his studio, McCay was already committed to producing a new animated film, more ambitious and unlike anything he (or anyone) had done before. It was to be an accurate depiction of a real event, not a fantasy: the sinking of the British luxury liner *Lusitania,* torpedoed by a German submarine on May 7, 1915, while en route from New York to Liverpool. In a press interview during his vaudeville run in Detroit in the summer of 1916, McCay never mentioned his editorial cartoon work for Hearst. Instead, he plunged into a familiar monologue about the future greatness of the art of animation. "Imagine," he said, "how effective would be cherubs that actually fly and Bonheur horses that gallop and Whistler rivers that flow!"[40]

Obviously, McCay's keenest artistic zeal was for animation, and he chose that interview to reveal that he was "now working on a film which will show the sinking of the *Lusitania*." He also explained that he would use a new technique: instead of rice paper for the character drawings, which required that backgrounds be drawn on each sheet, McCay would be "drawing on celluloid and predict[ed] that the film will revolutionize cartoon movies."[41]

McCay, along with most Americans, was outraged at the supposedly random and callous act of violence on the sea that killed 1,200 defenseless civilians, including 128 Americans. The sinking of the *Lusitania* became one of the stepping-stones that led the United States into World War I two years later, a war in which McCay's son, Robert, and his son-in-law, Raymond T. Moniz, would serve.

A New York American illustration from April 26, 1936 offers an example of the artistic abilities of cartoonist Apthorp "Ap" Adams, Winsor McCay's best buddy. (Courtesy G. Preston Brown and Larry Ruppel)

Recently, long-concealed facts about the famed sea disaster have come to light. For one, the construction of the ship in 1904 was financed by the British Admiralty on the condition that Cunard build giant engines for reserve horsepower, in case conversion to naval service was necessary. Also, in 1913 the *Lusitania* was fitted with deck rings for later emplacement of twelve naval guns. After the war began more modifications were made, and the ship was listed on the Admiralty Fleet Register as an "armed auxiliary cruiser." On the fateful day of its encounter with a torpedo from a German submarine, the *Lusitania* was carrying in the hold (unbeknownst to its passengers) 4,200 crates of American-made rifle ammunition weighing 173 tons and 51 tons of shrapnel shells. It was reported at the time that two torpedoes were successfully launched, but in reality a single torpedo touched off the cargo of weapons in the ship's belly and caused the second explosion, which sank the great vessel in just eighteen minutes.

Winsor McCay and the general public were not privy to such information, but even if they had been, it probably would not have significantly altered their opinion about the tragedy. To them it was another example of the vile treachery of "the Hun," as the German army was labeled during that time. McCay's decision to make an animated film of the event, which was not recorded by any camera, was primarily fired by patriotic zeal. But he also may have wished to impress Hearst with a serious-minded film closely resembling the thought-provoking editorial cartoons he produced daily for the *American*. It must have seemed a good way to ingratiate himself with Hearst, who in turn might then encourage him to make more films that he could showcase in vaudeville, a vital outlet for McCay's restless creative energy.

If that was his plan, it was nipped in the bud. Hearst was still suspicious of McCay's loyalty to his newspaper work and increasingly critical of McCay's editorial cartoons' conception and execution. One memo bluntly stated that Hearst felt there was definitely something the matter with McCay's recent cartoons and suggested they meet at once to figure out the problem.

In February 1917, Hearst forced McCay to quit the vaudeville stage entirely, to "abandon everything but incidental pleasure for his newspaper work." McCay attempted to argue: "I know you pay me well," he said, "but candidly, Mr. Hearst, I need the money I can pick up in vaudeville." This was the wrong tactic to use on a man for whom money had never been a barricade to achievement. "Suppose," replied Hearst, "I add whatever you earn in vaudeville to your salary. How much is it?"

McCay "could not refuse to submit the figures," but he hoped to make them prohibitive. Hearst quietly accepted them without a word of protest, and a new clause was added to McCay's contract.[42] Gone were two creative outlets that gave McCay joy and fulfillment: comic strips and live audiences. The editorial cartoons restricted his artistic freedom; all he had left that sparked his creative imagination were animated films, but even his interest in them would suffer because of the limitations placed on their exhibition.

Stung by the realization of what he had lost, McCay told the press he was determined to somehow hold on to animation and the theater. He announced he was "planning novelty productions for vaudeville in which others shall appear." This, of course, never happened, for McCay truly wanted to see only himself on stage, starring and presenting his own films. The first three McCay films had been almost physical extensions of himself, made to be shown in his vaudeville act. His anticipation of exhibiting this aspect of his talents in front of a live audience provided an incentive to make the films, for his ego was excited and gratified by this direct appreciation of his moving art.

McCay won permission to appear on stage with his films at the Palace in 1922, in Milwaukee for a week in May 1923, at Keith's in Washington, D.C. in April that same year, at the Paramount in New York in July 1927, and in a few other cities. (Three months before his death in 1934, he appeared before the Society of Illustrators in New York.) Ironically, by 1917 vaudeville was dying because of the encroachment of the movies, so McCay would have lost the stage as a regular showcase and creative outlet regardless of Hearst's interference, albeit in a less abrupt way.

McCay threw himself into the work of producing *The Sinking of the Lusitania,* assisted again by John Fitzsimmons and a cartoonist pal from Cincinnati named Apthorp "Ap" Adams. Fitzsimmons recalled that Adams, who "liked to hit it up" [drink], came for a visit, and McCay "talked him into staying on and helping."[43]

A descendant of President John Adams, William Apthorp Adams (1871–1952) was born in Cincinnati, where he studied at the Academy of Fine Arts. His lifelong friendship with Winsor McCay, who was four years older, began when they painted billboard posters for Ph. Morton.

They also worked together at the *Cincinnati Enquirer* and, later in New York, both were employed by the Hearst syndicate. For the *American,* Adams became manager of the art department and later served as art director of the *New York Mirror,* where he also drew half-page editorial cartoons. Later in his life, he studied art for two years abroad at Antwerp and Brussels, Belgium; and Paris. After retiring in 1942, his final decade was spent with his second wife fishing and painting in the Kettle Creek region near Renovo, Pennsylvania.

As a teenager, Jean Adams Robinson (1903–1988), Ap's daughter, often silently observed her father working on the *Lusitania* animation cels with McCay and Fitzsimmons. Separated from his first wife at the time, Ap was in fact living with the McCay family on Voorhies Avenue in Sheepshead Bay, while Jean and her brother, William "Thorp" Adams (1896?–1961), lived with their mother nearby. "I watched them draw that [film]," she said. "My father said I could stay in the room if I kept my mouth shut. [He] did everything that Winsor did . . . my father worked as hard on these animates [sic] as Winsor did."

She recalled years later how her father explained that the drawings were made on celluloid acetate with both a shiny and a matte side. "And they would do all the artwork on the matte-finish with white and black India ink. Then they'd get on the old BMT elevated [subway] and go from Sheepshead Bay to the Vitagraph [Studio] station. Wasn't far. Fifteen, twenty minutes on the 'El' and take all these celluloid things inside [to be photographed]."

The New York American *headlines the sinking of the Lusitania on May 7, 1915. Three years later, Winsor McCay's animated film of the tragic event was completed.*

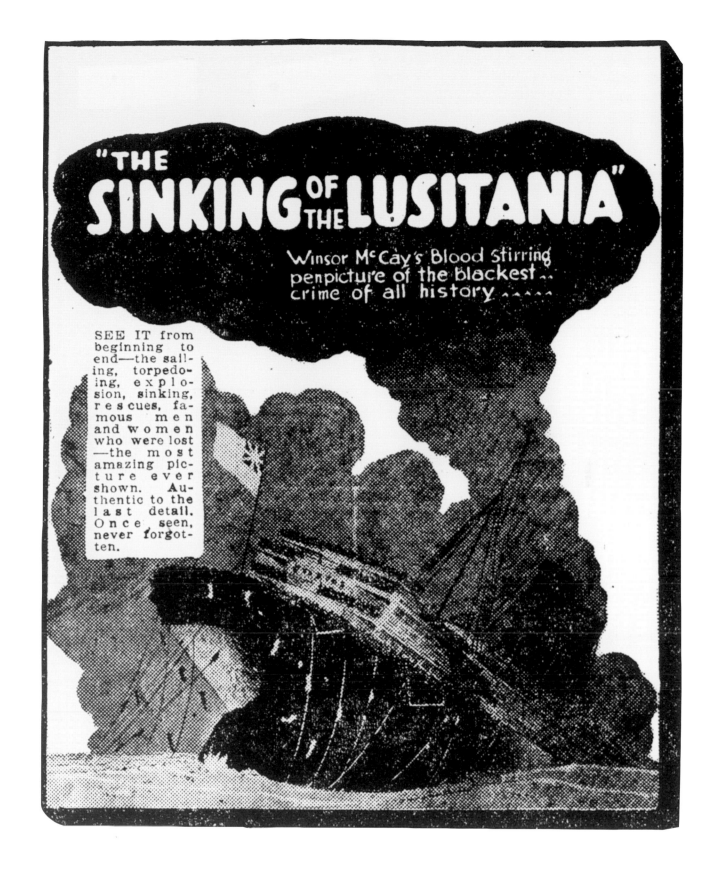

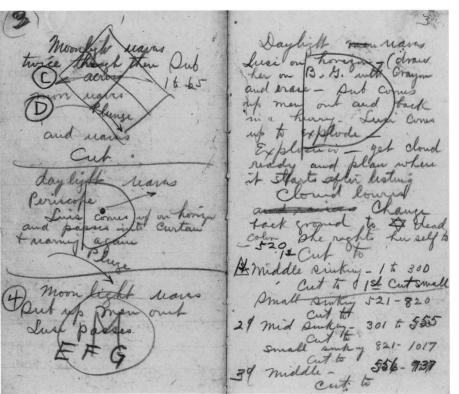

ABOVE:
A cel from The Sinking of the
Lusitania *(1918) shows the
great ship listing to one side
after a torpedo has ripped
through its underbelly.
(Collection Ray Winsor Moniz)*

LEFT:
*Two pages from McCay's pro-
duction notebook. Notes to
himself concern the visual continuity of* The Sinking of the
Lusitania. *(Courtesy La
Cinémathèque québécoise)*

A cel from The Sinking of the
Lusitania *showing passengers
bobbing in the ocean in an
attempt to stay afloat.*
(Collection Janet Trinker)

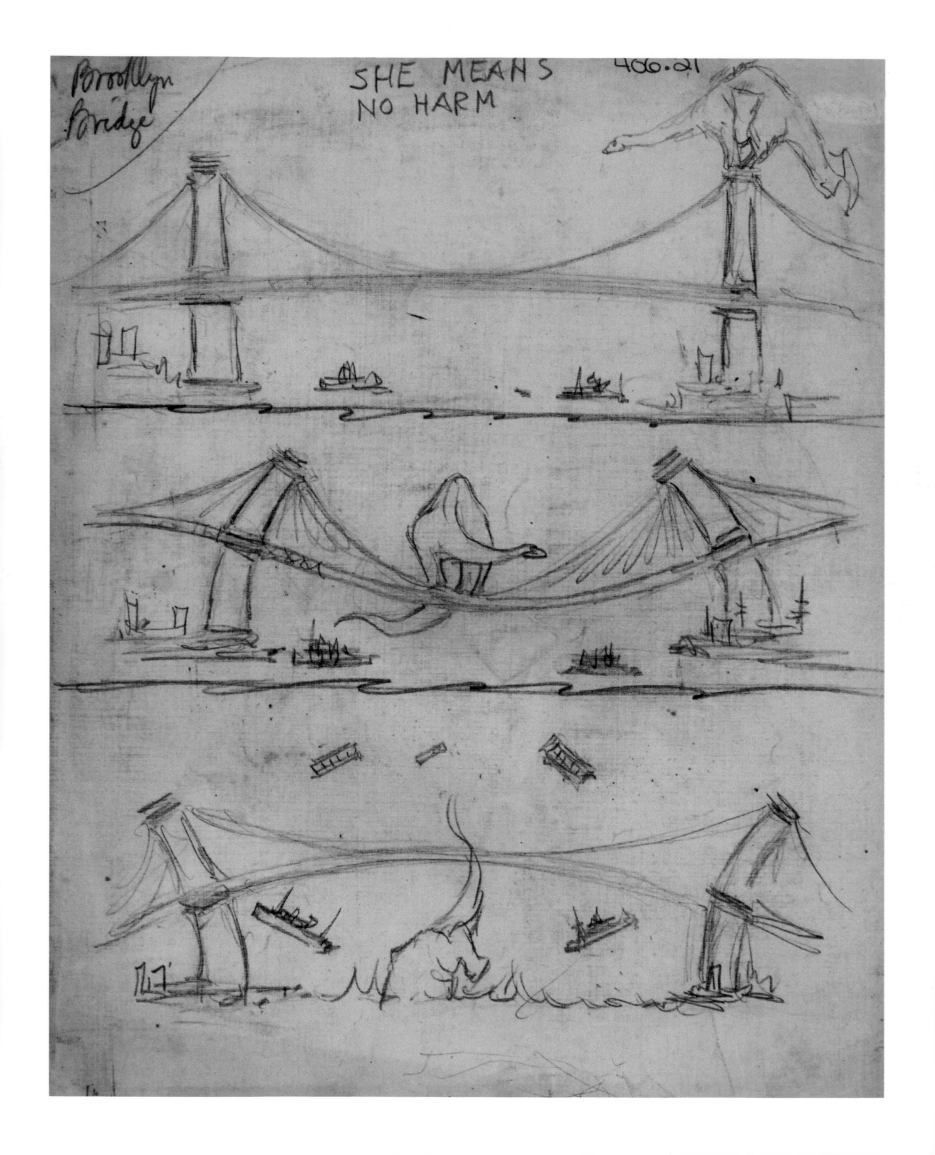

"My father was sort of a comedian," Jean Adams Robinson remembered. When McCay's chauffeur William drove the artist's new open National car [a motor vehicle manufactured between 1904 and 1924] too fast, Ap Adams wouldn't say a word. Instead, "he'd just take his Panama hat off his head and throw it out the window. William would say, 'Your hat, Mr. Adams! Your hat!' So they'd have to stop the car and pick it up. Nobody would say a word, but it always happened. I thought it was so funny."[44]

The Sinking of the Lusitania was almost two years in production, partly because of McCay's erratic schedule, but also because of technical problems, which were formidable. "In this presentation," wrote McCay years later, "I used wash and crayon, as well as pen and ink. When we came to photograph these drawings the operator commented on the fact that he worked an hour photographing one hundred and twenty-nine drawings that go through the machine in eight seconds. These drawings cost me eight weeks of hard labor. In animated drawing, as in everything else, perfection comes by working slowly to definite results."[45]

To facilitate the drawing stage, McCay decided to use transparent celluloid for the action drawings, as mentioned. This technique (covered by John Randolph Bray and Earl Hurd's patent) allowed the use of a single background per scene that did not have to be retraced on each drawing. "The advantage of this new medium," recalled John Fitzsimmons, "far exceeded any consideration of its additional cost."[46]

The problem of keeping the cels registered was solved by punching two holes in each; the holes matched pegs beneath the animation camera. The cels were thick (compared to modern cels) and had a "tooth" that allowed them to hold not only ink lines, but pencil shading and wash. The heavily rendered *Lusitania* cels tended to buckle, and so Fitzsimmons suggested using a loose-leaf binder with the center cut out to hold the drawings while filming them. "I mentioned this to Mr. Mac," said Fitzsimmons, "and he agreed that the idea held great possibilities and the plan was immediately taken advantage of. Binding posts were attached to drawing boards and the sheets of celluloid were punched to fit snugly to them. Thus the annoying problem of movement or shifting of drawings while being traced was reduced to a minimum . . . . [it] also facilitated the photographing of the drawings immeasurably and proved well-worth all additional expense."[47]

McCay was, as usual, pouring his own money into the film. He had financed all of his films himself, mostly at a loss. *Lusitania* was to be no exception; it netted McCay only $80,000 after a number of years in theaters, approximately $3.20 per drawing. He spoke the truth when he once said, "I went into this business and spent thousands of dollars developing this new art."

McCay, according to his assistant Fitzsimmons, "reserved the direction and animation work for himself because he often would innovate or improvise as he went along, leaving the purely technical and less important matters to others." But McCay enjoyed the loyalty and dedication of young Fitzsimmons and the wildly humorous antics of Ap Adams. Tall, skinny Adams was "Jeff" to McCay's "Mutt," the two often behaving like mischievous boys, to the exasperated annoyance of Maude McCay, who thought Adams unfunny and "fresh!"

Ap's humor was often fueled by alcohol and his personality held a dark side. Estranged from his wife and two children, he was fond of saying, "You should drown kids, cause kids'll kill you!" McCay and Adams loved practical jokes—walking up to a man loaded down with packages and asking, "Got a match?" The two would clip items out of newspapers they thought were funny. "Ap keeps me vibrated," said McCay of Adams's sense of humor and practical jokes. One practical joke, however, backfired on McCay and his film.

"One of the principal scenes of the picture," remembered John Fitzsimmons, "was a shot consisting of 750 drawings depicting the liner sailing serenely along the horizon in the moonlight." The foreground of rolling waves was a series of sixteen drawings recycled repeatedly throughout the scene.

As with *Gertie*, McCay again made specific notes regarding *Lusitania*'s continuity and camera exposures for the drawings. His small notebook is a sort of script, with notes to himself and specific instructions for the camera operator:

> Daylight waves. Lusi [sic] on horizon. draw her on B.G. [background] with crayon and erase   sub comes up [.] men out and back in a hurry. Lusi comes up to explode—
>   Explosion—get cloud ready and plan where it starts after listing. Cloud lowers. Change background to [symbol] dead color [,] she rights herself to 520. Cut to Middle sinking – 1 to 30 D. . . Cut to small sinking 521–820 . . . cut to to Big Sinking 1 to 129.

Fitzsimmons recalled that for the repeating wave cycle, "it was Ap Adams's chore to indicate by number which of the sixteen waves I was to draw on that

piece of celluloid." Weeks later, McCay placed a large number of the completed 750 cels into the testing machine. "The result was a catastrophe!" Fitzsimmons said. "Instead of the waves flowing smoothly as designed, the foreground resembled nothing so much as a drunken sea with ink lines shooting every which way." All the drawings were washed off the cels, and the tedious process began again from scratch. "I had not been fed the wave numbers in the proper sequence," recalled Fitzsimmons with the same embarrassment and resentment toward madcap Ap Adams that he had felt nearly sixty years earlier.

The Sinking of the Lusitania was copyrighted on July 19, 1918, and released the next day by Jewel Productions. It was advertised as "the picture that will *never* have a competitor—will burn in your heart forever! Winsor McCay's Blood Stirring Pen Picture—the World's Only Record of the Crime that Shocked Humanity!" The film opens with a live-action prologue that is a mini-documentary about why and how it was made. McCay is seen receiving details about the sinking of the ship from a "Mr. Beach," as well as studying a large painting of the ship and supervising a crew of five "assistants." (Neither Fitzsimmons nor Adams is among them.) According to a McCay production notebook, "Mr. Beach" is August F. Beach, Hearst's Berlin correspondent, who happened to be in London on May 7 and was the first newsman at the scene of the disaster. It was from Beach that McCay "got the details of the sinking necessary for the work to follow."

We are told, by intercut title cards, that the film required 25,000 drawings and that the first work done was on the moving sea; a brief glimpse of rolling waves follows. By explaining some of the inner workings of animation, McCay is again closely identifying himself with his creation. He informs us that he was able to go where no live-action camera ever could, and a card erroneously identifies McCay again as "the originator and inventor of Animated Cartoons."

"From here on you are looking at the first record of the sinking of the *Lusitania*," reads a card after the prologue. The huge liner moves grandly past the Statue of Liberty on its way out of New York harbor. A stage curtain is drawn on this scene, symbolizing the passage of time. Next seen is a German submarine cutting speedily through the waters.

McCay uses a variety of dramatic "cinematic" angles and compelling perspective and subjective shots throughout, thus dramatizing the action in a way no live-action documentary could. When the sub fires a first torpedo, the point of view is underwater, where two fish turn and flee from the path of the fast-approaching projectile. The animation of the fish is superbly timed and amazingly naturalistic.

The first explosion occurs in a long shot, and the animation of the smoke takes on a life of its own, appearing as serpentine Art Nouveau entrails from the ship's gut. The smoke billows larger in a variety of black-and-white shades, until a white haze covers the action (a clever cinematic "wipe" leading to the next scene). There are close-ups and medium shots of lifeboats being hastily lowered into the water, as seen from sea level. In the haste and confusion, some capsize and spill their human cargo into the waves.

Spectacular views show the giant ship listing on its side, smoke pouring upward, and tiny human figures falling as if in slow motion into the sea. A second explosion is a radiating abstract form in colors ranging from black through shades of gray to pure white (for the most intense searing heat), which covers the screen.

In the final scenes, McCay alternates views of the ship slowly (and almost painfully) disappearing beneath the turbulent sea with shots of helpless victims continuing to fall into the water or floating on its surface. The film's last image is the most horrific: a mother and her infant underwater—she holding the baby at arm's length trying to push it toward the surface, as both sink lower in the ocean depths while bubbles rise rapidly past them. McCay may have based this emotionally wrenching image on one of the first American posters of World War I, which depicted two of the more than 200 bodies that washed ashore on the southwest coast of Ireland. Drawn in Boston in 1915 by Fred Spear, the poster simply featured the word "Enlist" over a picture illustrating a well-known news report datelined "Cork, Ireland": "On the Cunard wharf lies a mother with a three-month-old child clasped tightly in her arms. Her face wears a half-smile. Her baby's head rests against her breast. No one has tried to separate them. . . ." A final title card in the film expresses America's anti-German sentiments: "The man who fired the shots was decorated by the Kaiser. And they tell us not to hate the Hun."

The Pet *(c. 1918–21) roams among the tall buildings of the city, about to be destroyed by the air force. (Collection La Cinémathèque québécoise)*

The Sinking of the Lusitania is a monumental work in the history of the animated film. While it did not revolutionize the film cartoons of its time, it is a milestone in the demonstration of alternatives available to the creative animation filmmaker. The dark somber mood, the superb draftsmanship, the timing of the actions, the excellent dramatic directorial choices of "camera" angles and editing—all these qualities would reappear only with Disney's mature work in certain sequences of his feature-length cartoons and some of his World War II propaganda cartoon shorts, such as *Education for Death* (1943).

The Sinking of the Lusitania was widely admired not only by the movie-going public but by McCay's contemporaries in the busy animation studios. But McCay's magnificent achievement could inspire only awe in his peers, for it was far ahead of its time and far beyond the sensibilities and capabilities of the men turning out simple gag cartoons starring clowns, cats, dogs, and kids.

McCay made six more films in the next three years, all using cels. Three survive as fragments and were presumably never distributed commercially, including: *The Centaurs*, in which a family of the

mythical beasts wanders about a sylvan landscape in desultory fashion; *Flip's Circus*, which contains fragments of scenes of bad-boy Flip in vaudeville attempting to juggle, dance, and train a Gertie-like beast, who eats part of a car; *Gertie on Tour*, a comeback film for the irrepressible diplodocus seen grabbing a trolley with her mouth and dancing for other dinosaurs. Recently discovered sketches offer amusing concepts for the film: the playful traveling dinosaur gnaws on the Washington Monument, wades in the Atlantic City surf, and uses the Brooklyn Bridge as a trampoline.

All three films are plagued by technical problems. Cel buckling causes reflections. Multiple cel levels, when used to lessen the number of drawings required, deaden the action. The "alive" quality of the films drawn on paper is missing. And there are narrative problems—the films meander weakly. One gets the feeling that McCay was wandering, too, not knowing what to do with or where to take his formidable knowledge of animation and its potential.

For his last three short films, all released in 1921, McCay decided to cling to familiar formats used in the *Dream of the Rarebit Fiend* comic strip. *Bug Vaudeville* parodies the world of circus and vaudeville performers, familiar turf for McCay, whose droll wit

makes grasshoppers juggle, cockroaches ride unicycles, and an old daddy-long-legs spider do an eccentric dance. *Bug Vaudeville* is film critic Andrew Sarris's favorite McCay cartoon:

> As we watch roaches and grasshoppers and ants on bicycles and doing flip-flops, we are struck both by the linear expressiveness of the drawings and the intuitive rhythm of the acts. The bug on the bicycle is particularly indefatigable as he runs through his whole bag of tricks in athletically professional progression. Only a man who knew showbiz to his bone marrow could conceive of such measured gallantry under stress. Even more striking are the two bugs who pass back and forth a handkerchief with which to dry their sweaty palms before doing their hand-flips. A Fellini would be honored by such insight into the ritual of performance.[48]

The Pet tells an apocalyptic tale of a man who eats rarebit and dreams that his wife's adorable new puppylike pet grows into a beast of monstrous proportions, roams through skyscrapers King Kong–like and eventually requires a platoon of airplanes to bomb and destroy it. McCay's fascination with dynamic size changes lends the film many funny scenes and a quite impressive one: the now-gigantic pet roaming the city against an extended panorama background as zeppelins and aircraft hover and finally blow him to bits. Overall, *The Pet* is a cold dark vision of despair and foreboding; the last film McCay completed over which he had total creative control.

The Flying House, the last of the *Rarebit Fiend* film series, credits Robert McCay, Winsor's son, as the sole artist, but it is highly unlikely that Winsor did not participate. It is too accomplished a work to be a first film, and too full of Winsor's imagery and sensibilities to be the exclusive creation of Robert. In the film, a man and his wife attempt to escape creditors by equipping their house with wings and a propeller. They fly to the moon and outer space before finally getting shot down to earth by a rocket. "This is not the wild but innocuous plunge that is a staple of cartooning," wrote Richard Eder of the dark tale. "It is a real, nightmare fall by real, desperate people."[49]

In its September 26, 1921 review, the *New York Times* found an unnamed McCay film (perhaps *The Flying House)* "not as brightly humorous as . . . might

be [but] interesting because of its excellent workmanship and fantastic character."

Among the films McCay considered making was *The Barnyard Band,* a project for vaudeville in which McCay (in person) would conduct a cartoon orchestra made up of animals; a live pit band would have played music in synchronization with the animals' actions.[50]

McCay also discussed collaborating again with his old friend George Randolph Chester, coauthor of the *Tales of the Jungle Imps.* This time they would work on an ambitious animated film about the history of the world according to the Bible. McCay asked Hearst for a two-year leave of absence to tackle the project, but his request was denied. Chester died in 1924, the year McCay's contract with Hearst expired. McCay abandoned the film, refusing, he said, to work with another writer on what he considered half Chester's property.[51]

There was a third possible project, which Robert McCay described in a letter in the mid-1950s:

> My father had an idea he would like to show what America did in the war (First). There were hundreds of drawings made, of all departments, etc. There [sic] efforts, it was terrific. These few at hand show one, Battleships being produced and sent out—
> Transports loaded with troop provisions, etc. on there [sic] way—
> The different institutions—Red Cross, K of C, Y.M.C.—
> This is the Salvation Army gals shooting doughnuts to Yanks, etc.
> Look at this careful pen line and detail for one mans [sic] efforts in those days . . .
> Although there were hundreds of drawings made he never had the time to really finish this big job and it remained dormant. His newspaper work kept his nose on the so called "Grind stone."[52]

McCay's heavy workload for the Hearst papers was certainly a major reason why he never made more animated films during the last thirteen years of his life. Another factor might have been his age: McCay was in his mid-fifties when *The Flying House* was exhibited; that it was a collaborative effort with his son indicates that McCay's phenomenal energy and drive were beginning to wear down. To create a complex animated film with no staff, no financial backing, and no real network for distribution or even a sustained showcase, such as he had enjoyed in vaudeville, required a commitment McCay thought he could not make anymore.

He may have felt out of step with the times. He always insisted he had "invented" the animated film, and in a way he did—by solving the technical problems, establishing the iconography of modern animation graphics, and creating films so innovative that they could not help but be inspirational goalposts pointing to future achievements.

But by the mid-1920s, McCay's contributions to the field had been forgotten by most audiences. To animators in the film industry, Winsor McCay was a great name, but his difficult and solitary style was considered impractical in a modern studio. At that time, *Felix the Cat* was state-of-the-art animation, and by the end of the decade a mouse named Mickey would lead Walt Disney to domination of movie cartoons.

"For a time, McCay had the field to himself," wrote Claude Bragdon. "[He] carried on single-handed the enormous labor of making thousands of drawings for a few brief moments of entertainment . . . . it seems a pity that McCay, with his delightful fancy, should not have continued in this field which he had made his own."[53]

Perhaps McCay stopped making animated films because of his deep disappointment over what they had become and where they were headed. As far as he could see in 1921, his beautiful dream of animation as moving art had not been realized. He always felt his own films were merely beacons shining light on a path leading to something never seen before. He was distressed that he had not achieved his impossible dream, and he was afraid that from the look of things no one else was even attempting it.

"In a sense," wrote Richard Eder, "McCay was an incipient artist who never developed fully the suggestions in his work. Partly it was because he was a pioneer. His cartoons are primitive; not in the sense of crudeness but, like the Italian primitives, in the limited techniques they could command."[54]

Animator I. Klein attended a dinner in honor of Winsor McCay in the fall of 1927, "a gathering of the animators of New York." At Roth's, a restaurant in the forties just off Broadway, about thirty men came to honor "the originator and founder of animation." Both McCay and his son attended the rowdy celebration, and after "a considerable amount of bootleg liquor" had been consumed by everyone, producer Max Fleischer introduced the guest of honor.

"McCay created the miracle of animation," Fleischer said, "and another miracle was getting all the animators into one big friendly gathering." McCay approached the podium and began his speech. Klein recalled that first he "gave some technical suggestions which I don't think his professional audience took much stock in." Another attendee, animator Richard Huemer, said McCay rambled on about his "split system," which the studio animators "had figured out long ago."

Sensing he was losing his audience, McCay quickly got to the point. "He wound up with a statement," said Klein, "which has remained in my mind. 'Animation should be an art. That is how I conceived it. But as I see, what you fellows have done with it, is making it into a trade. Not an art, but a trade. *Bad Luck!*'"

He sat down to scattered applause.[55]

chapter 9. a hearst man

"The funnies occupy four pages of the paper and the editorials two columns. That proves that merit will tell."

—WILL ROGERS

The sound of the milkman's bottles rattling in their steel carriers was Winsor McCay's alarm clock. At 1901 Voorhies Avenue, the "showplace house of Sheepshead Bay," as neighbors called it, McCay slept in the second-floor bedroom over the front porch with its green-and-white striped awnings. He may have had only four hours of sleep after a late-night drawing session in his third-floor studio, but when the milk bottles began clinking McCay started his lengthy morning ablutions.

Maude McCay slept in one of the two quiet back bedrooms. As her husband filled the tub with hot water, Maude arose and began selecting and laying out his clothes for the day: silk tie, high-collar shirt, vest, cuff links, coat, and so on. She could see Winsor in her dresser mirror and sometimes would consult him about his preference for a certain item of clothing or accessory.

McCay enjoyed a long bath each morning, and he shaved in the tub without using a mirror. To rinse his thinning hair, he placed two fingers against his nostrils, put his thumbs in his ears and plunged his head backward into the water. After drying, he would dress fully, including his hat (which he wore constantly, often during meals), dab on Pinaud aftershave lotion, and descend the stairs to the kitchen.[1]

With the help of a maid to prepare the ingredients, recalled McCay's grandchildren, Maude cooked breakfast for her husband and children, often patting perspiration from her brow with a hanky she kept in her blouse. The morning menus were large: one day it might be lamb chops and stewed fruit, another it was steak, eggs, and potatoes, or perhaps Maude's favorite meal, chicken fricassee with biscuits.

Upon entering the room, Winsor danced a little jig, greeted whoever was there with a nervous giggle and an offhanded "How are ya', kids?" and sat in a rocking chair at a table covered with a white lace cloth. He read the morning edition of the *American* slowly and spent a considerable amount of time doing the crossword puzzle with a small green pencil.[2]

This cozy morning ritual was a reassuring, nurturing part of a symbiotic marital relationship that had had its share of difficulties. In the McCay marriage, like most long-term unions formed at the turn of the century, the partners' roles were tightly defined in a traditional way: Winsor went out to work to make money to support the family, and Maude took care of Winsor, their kids, and their home.

Maude was as proficient in her role as Winsor was in his. Her clean, well-run home was a tribute to her organizational skills, as well as her ornate taste. Along the street around the house grew a row of maples with trunks stylishly whitewashed four feet above the ground. She planted a large variety of flowers, especially peonies, and filled every room of the house with fragrant blossoms from her garden, supplemented with blooms from local florists. She supervised a gardener, maids, handymen, decorators, and various food merchants who brought their wares to the house for selection, and she cooked the family's meals.

Winsor never finished the large breakfasts Maude set before him. He nibbled at the food and then smoked Between the Acts, little cigars that came wrapped in pink paper in a tin box. Maude hated cigars and cigarettes. Winsor smoked them anyway. There were a number of little differences of opinion like that, which created a palpable tension between the couple.

For instance, Maude hated Winsor's self-taught piano playing, but he loved to bang away at "Kitten on the Keys" till hell-wouldn't-have-it, or at least until Maude yelled "Stop that confound noise!" There were arguments about in-laws, especially Winsor's mother, Janet, who arrived annually from Michigan to stay in the family's winter suite at the Hotel St. George in Brooklyn Heights. According to one family member, Janet was short, tough, "straight as a die, never carried a cane, needed no help getting around," and had "a face that looked like a coconut it was so wrinkled."[3]

Janet demanded attention from her son. She was adamantly against alcohol, or so she said, but when Winsor and Maude planted a bottle of liquor in a closet for her, she sneaked a sip from it occasionally. Most of the time, Maude was "crazy" with annoyance over Janet's presence. "It bothered her," recalled Tedda McCay, "that Winsor wanted to help his mother."

For his part, Winsor had never gotten along with *his* mother-in-law, Sarah Dufour, when they all lived together in Cincinnati. Maude's mother later married William Johns, a farmer from Maryland who had read the Bible six times; when he died, she moved to Brooklyn to stay with her daughter Josephine, who had married three times and rented rooms in a house on Classon Avenue. Josephine and her sister Estelle once had a singing-sister act that played small-time vaudeville in the Ohio and New York hinterlands. Estelle was living with Winsor and Maude in 1910, when she listed her occupation as "actress" in the census; later, she married and worked as a telephone operator at St. John's hospital.

To Winsor's annoyance, the Dufour women lived with him and Maude at various times when they were between husbands or jobs. Ironically, all four Dufours—Maude, Sarah, Estelle, and Josephine— are still with Winsor: buried in the McCay family plot in the Cemetery of the Evergreens in Brooklyn.

When it came to raising their children, Robert and Marion, the McCays had differing approaches. Winsor preferred to "be a pal instead of a stern parent"[4] and left the strict disciplining of the kids to his wife. Maude had a temper and a dominating personality and took no "sass" or "fresh" behavior. She was "the boss," and the children got quick back-of-the-hand punishment for any insubordination. She once almost broke an umbrella over Robert's back when he was late coming home.

As a result, the children loved Maude but feared her, while they did not fear mild-mannered Winsor, whose humor and outlook on things often made him seem like a child himself. Robert and Marion McCay were very attractive children, and though privileged and pampered, contemporaries always describe them as "down-to-earth" and "well-liked." Sibling rivalry and resultant squabbles between the two children often turned violent, which continued into their adult years. Marion, a high-strung child given to crying spells, felt her brother was her mother's favorite child. Maude was continually correcting her daughter in public, "trying to boss her." Marion adored her father, who affectionately called her "Moonface." They were constantly together, and as she grew older, Marion accompanied Winsor to social functions that Maude steadfastly refused to attend. He would introduce her, adding, "This is my daughter, not my girlfriend."[5]

Inevitably, Maude would increase tensions around the breakfast table by bringing up the subject of money. She might complain about a special job Winsor was "doing for free" as a favor to Brisbane or Hearst, who "doesn't pay you enough." Maude was "constantly at him about money."[6] He was not making enough, he was giving it all away, and how were they going to pay the bills? And there were always bills for Winsor to pay. Not just for running the house, but for the little and big luxuries to which the whole family had grown accustomed: a car and chauffeur (because Winsor hated cars and refused to learn to drive), expensive wardrobes for the whole family, Miami winter vacations for Maude and the kids (paid for by but rarely including Winsor, who pre-

ferred to work in Brooklyn), private piano lessons for Marion, a horse and then a car and eventually a house or two for Robert, and then a house for Marion too.

Winsor paid extremely high premiums on his life insurance policy, and he also carried expensive insurance on his eyes and his hands. There were expenses in running the house, and there were Maude's daily personal expenses: visits from a masseuse named Mrs. Yard, plus a hairdresser, a beautician, a manicurist, and a dressfitter. Every day Maude would take the limo or call a cab to go shopping on Fulton Street in downtown Brooklyn department stores like Namm's, Martin's, Loeser's, Abraham and Straus, and Arnold Constable. The limousine drivers parked the cars in a line around the corner, while Maude and other well-to-do wives would buy Chinese rugs, lamps, shoes, hats, furniture (Maude's antimacassars bore the monogram "Mc"), draperies, and dresses. Then she

and her friends would go for a nice, long midafternoon luncheon, heavy on liquid refreshment and gossip.

Winsor refused to argue about money with Maude. He would pay the bills, but he did not wish to discuss them. "Often he would leave a group of people, excuse himself, and go upstairs to work," recalled McCay's grandson Ray Winsor Moniz. "He avoided arguments that way with Maude. His concentration and losing himself in his drawing was almost weird. It was an obsession. Used it to get away from the family or a problem. He used it as a retreat as well as a love."

During the week, McCay was required to report daily to the Hearst office building in downtown Manhattan, so he usually rode in the beige Packard across the Brooklyn Bridge to South Street. His driver, John, "as Irish as Paddy's pig,"[7] acted in a dual capacity as McCay's chauffeur and bodyguard. A bodyguard was considered necessary because some of McCay's drawings illustrating Hearst editorials resulted in threatening letters mailed to his home. "I have to be careful," he said.

McCay shared an office on the ninth floor of the *American* building with humorist Bugs Baer and sports page cartoonist Joe McGurk. Damon Runyon once wrote: "Personally, Winsor McCay is not one-half of one percent as serious as his cartoons might indicate. He is a jovial soul, and a man of hardy constitution, which is shown by the fact that he has survived a year of working in the same room with Bugs Baer and Joe McGurk, a true test."

The sign on the door announcing "Artist Service Department" was erased so as to read "Vice Department," and a cardboard silhouette of a man and a woman kissing behind the door's translucent glass partition startled many visitors. The room itself faced a brick wall and might have resembled a roomy prison cell but for the frivolous decorative touches supplied by the three iconoclastic inhabitants. A cowbell clanged whenever the door opened, and inside one was greeted by paper dogs, lobsters, giraffes, and snakes guarding the fire escape and crawling through windows. A clothesline carried cardboard underwear and longjohns; a paper beer barrel, tap and all, was

pinned between two desks, and Robinson Crusoe's
footprints "walked" up a wall and across the ceiling.
"Fatuoni," a five-foot-high paper dancing-girl tacked
on the wall near a window shook with the slightest
breeze, agitating her to perform her "famous oopla
dance."[8]

It was in that ersatz dime museum, known by
fellow workers as "The Chamber of Horrors," that
Winsor McCay created many of his most serious editorial cartoons. And it was there that he laughed at
and complained about his immediate boss, Arthur
Brisbane, irreverently dubbed "Big George" by
cartoonist Thomas A. "Tad" Dorgan.

Arthur Brisbane (1864–1936) was William
Randolph Hearst's "most valuable viceroy, most popular writer, trouble shooter for ailing newspapers,
partner in innumerable business ventures and save for
certain periods of estrangement, an intimate friend
and confidant."[9] He had worked his way through
Charles Anderson Dana's *Sun* and Joseph Pulitzer's
World to Hearst's *Journal* and *American*, where by 1910
he was America's highest-salaried editor. Eventually
Brisbane was earning $260,000 a year plus perks
during the Depression.

From Dana, Brisbane learned the basic principles
of editorial writing: "Iteration and reiteration, inces-
sant drumfire." His other mentor, Pulitzer, could not
improve Brisbane's writing style, which had a "terse,
cutting quality [and] avoidance of all but the simplest
words."[10]

To the masses of average Americans, particularly
large numbers of German, Irish, and Italian immigrants who were avid readers of the Hearst papers,
Hearst's opinions, communicated through his and
Brisbane's editorials, were gospel. His Anglophobia,
his isolationist "America First" attitude, his moralistic
(often maudlin) "concern" for the Common or Little
Man struggling against the selfish interests of Big
Business and Big Government, all were translated by
Brisbane for Hearst paper readers in the most simple,
direct ways. Coupled with the sugar coating of a
dynamic cartoon by Winsor McCay, the editorials
proved to be good business. Readers bought newspapers and ate it up, regarding Brisbane as a Great
Thinker.

Others not under the spell of Hearst's brand of
jaundiced journalism thought Arthur Brisbane to be
the possessor of a cluttered eighteenth-century mind,
full of "half-baked theories" and "half-remembered
fact and fiction." His amazing success "may have
been due to the fact that his mind mirrored so completely the mind of the average man."[11]

If simplicity and directness were keys to Brisbane's
success in communicating ideas to the masses, so it
had to be with McCay's drawings. If a particular
sketch proved not pleasing to Brisbane, a lengthy
memo would set the erring artist on the right path.
Sometimes the offending drawing would be thrown
back across Brisbane's desk "with a disapproving
growl, to be followed almost immediately by his
barking into his dictaphone the latest inspirational
message on the value of Courtesy and the Humane
Heart."[12]

Brisbane was both specific and maddeningly vague
in his orders to McCay for imagery. In one undated
memo for the Sunday edition, he wrote:

> Try to make the figures striking. They are looking away
> into space, or perhaps looking down at the hurdle or
> anything you like. There ought to be a big difference
> between enthusiasm of youth, which takes a man to
> the first hurdle, courage, which helps him along to the
> second, and then noble endurance, that makes possible
> the jumping of the third.

Brisbane accompanied his instructions with four
stick figure examples. Brisbane often scribbled suggestions on McCay's artwork. In a memo dated
January 9, no year, Brisbane wrote:

> My dear Mr. McCay
> I am sending this down to you with some marks on
> your cartoon, which I think will be good. As I suggest
> I think it would be better if you put the devil on the
> other side of Uncle Sam's shoulder, letting him stand
> up, a small devil
>   . . . quite far from his ear and yelling at the top of his
> voice into his ear "You're discouraged, why don't you
> quit?" and let that be coming out of the devil's mouth
> in a bladder. Uncle Sam turning away from him and
> smiling saying as you have it "You are mistaken. Just
> watch me." This will make a good cartoon.

In the first three months of 1914, after McCay ceased drawing comic strips in order to concentrate on editorials, his assignments numbered twenty-nine; all were either simplistic moral lessons or overbearing attacks on elected officials. The editorial for February 16, 1914, is typical Brisbane: finger-wagging, appearing to take on and expose evil, pitting the rich and powerful against the poor and helpless. Brisbane swaggers toward a Big Subject but offers no solution. Indeed, he appears to want it both ways by wavering in the last sentence, lest he seem to be criticizing the American way of life:

> It doesn't mean much to the rich man, or to the man with a job, but to the poor, the weak, the sick Winter means distress, and disease and death.
>
> A civilization which will permit people to freeze or suffer or die in a city where there is coal enough and food enough and doctors enough for all is a queer civilization, isn't it?
>
> And yet it is the best civilization that the human race has developed in many thousands of years.

McCay's accompanying cartoon has more feeling and dynamism than Brisbane's limp lecture. He shows a man, a woman, and two children dressed in tattered clothes standing in the middle of a snow-covered city street, unable to cross. Their way is blocked by traffic on both sides—an automobile on the left, a sleigh on the right, both filled with well-dressed, carefree people laden with gifts. It is a well-drawn, emotionally evocative illustration, perfectly laid out, with McCay's keen perspective shown to advantage in the distant grand buildings that line the avenue.

McCay's compassionate drawings of the downtrodden middle and lower classes have the timeless morality of a work by Daumier, who also detested political, religious, and judicial corruption. Like Daumier's, McCay's humanistic ideals are expressed in eloquent, emotional drawings containing lines that caricature with confident directness and sensitivity.

On February 28 and March 5, 1914, McCay drew cartoons to match Brisbane prose that blamed President Woodrow Wilson and his policies for the deaths of American citizens visiting Mexico. They were the beginning of what would become incessantly vicious attacks on Wilson, which Brisbane "gloried in."[13] Starting March 7, no less than eight cartoons that month depicted Wilson as anti-American, pro-English, and a perverter of American history.

The *New York World,* a chief supporter of Wilson and his administration, wrote an editorial on April 7, 1914, condemning the Hearstian mudslinging:

> Day after day Mr. Hearst, in word and caricature, is picturing the President of the United States as a traitor to the United States . . . . Mr. Hearst apparently has learned nothing from the assassination of William McKinley. . . . Indeed, his attacks upon President Wilson are even more malicious, mendacious and incendiary than were his attacks upon President McKinley.

McCay's draftsmanship fluctuated wildly during this period because of his disinterest in the subject matter and the emotional turmoil in his life—Hearst's crude attempts to kill his vaudeville career and the Lambkins' scheme to blackmail his wife. With the war raging in Europe, Brisbane and Hearst focused their editorials on isolationism, pacifism, and, less often, preparedness. Even the sinking of the *Lusitania* on May 7, 1915, an event that roused the fury of the country, was excused in the press of Hearst and Brisbane: "Whether the *Lusitania* was armed or not, it was properly a spoil of war, subject to attack and destruction under the accepted rules of civilized

warfare. . . . The *Lusitania* incident is, of course, no cause for a declaration of war." In another editorial Brisbane wrote that the United States had "no right to insist Germany refrain from submarine warfare."

"The policy of the Hearst press at this time," wrote Oliver Carlson, "as formulated by Brisbane was, first, to clamor for peace at all costs; second, to adopt a generally anti-British attitude with reference to war news and aspirations; third, to print fake interviews, stories, pictures and the like; and fourth, to use one type of appeal for its German-reading audiences and another for the English-reading section. A final point was to develop anew the Japanese war scare."

These editorial opinions were for once out of touch with the sentiments of Hearst's readership, but the Great Thinkers continued to express them, which led to an inevitable backlash. McCay was in a strange position—drawing cartoons for points of view he often did not share, particularly with regard to the *Lusitania* incident. He was, after all, preparing a motion picture of the sea tragedy that was intended to inflame further the anti-German, pro-war feelings of the audience he shared with Hearst. Seen in this light, McCay's film production of *The Sinking of the Lusitania* appears to have been an act of defiance against Hearst and Brisbane as well as a patriotic call to arms.

While his animated films allowed McCay complete control over their content and graphics, the opposite was true of the editorial cartoons, which had to be approved by Arthur Brisbane before and after rendering and, less frequently, by William Randolph Hearst. A half-page cartoon appearing on March 13, 1917, was exactly as Hearst (also known as The Chief) described it in a memo to his general manager S.S. Carvalho:

> McKay [sic] could make strong eight-column cartoon, occupying depth two-thirds editorial page, showing smaller figures Uncle Sam and Germany shaking their fists at each other on left side page and on right side big head and shoulders of Japan, with knife in hand, leaning over into picture and evidently watching chance to strike Uncle in back. Title of picture to be: "Watchful waiting—Look Out, Uncle Sam, Your Neighbor Japan is Eagerly Awaiting an Opportunity to Strike You in the Back."[14]

Two days after the appearance of the above cartoon, McCay received a blunt letter from Hearst on *American* stationery (dated March 15, 1917) complaining about the quality of his work. Hearst mocked the dullness of recent drawings in which characters, with labels to explain who they are, stand in static poses and unimaginative layouts.

> My dear Mr. McCay:
> There is something the matter with the cartoons. I would like to see you and find out what it is. Perhaps you don't have the right ideas given you for cartoons. Certainly there is not much real cartoon effect in two or three well dressed figures not doing anything in particular, but labeled as various characters, as they were this (Thursday) morning.
> I am not trying to be critical. I am trying to find out what is the matter and why the cartoons are not the fine pieces of work that you are capable of doing. I liked the Jap cartoon immensely. Possibly I liked it because of the idea. But I rather think I liked it because of the bold execution and the powerful effect.
>
> Since you can do such fine cartoons, let us find the way to have them always.
> Sincerely,
> W. R. Hearst

Hearst had a point. The cartoons prior to March 13 were often uninspired, with lots of standing about and little action or dynamism. The previous month Hearst forced McCay to quit touring in vaudeville altogether, and so the only thing distracting the artist's concentration was his animation work. Since McCay did that in his spare time, there was nothing Hearst could do to prevent it.

McCay appears to have tried hard the rest of the month; he came up with a number of strong illustrations, ending with a haunting image on March 31, 1917: a lean figure of death strolling across a globe featuring a devastated Europe. So many of McCay's best works have a dark Gothic quality that deeply moves the viewer while at the same time repelling him with its directness. It is one of the qualities that McCay shares with Dürer, along with his absolute precision of line. (McCay's line in action also reminds

one of the tight lines in the buoyant drawings of Gustave Doré, as seen in the ebullient *The Adventures of Baron Munchausen* [1862].) McCay's eerie cartoon of death wandering in Europe preceded President Wilson's decision six days later to bring America into the war against Germany.

McCay would have a personal stake in the United States involvement in World War I, for both his son and son-in-law were to serve as soldiers in combat in Europe. In the summer of 1917, Captain Raymond T. Moniz arrived in uniform one evening at the McCay house to ask Maude and Winsor for their daughter's hand in marriage.

Moniz was one of thirteen children born to Roman Catholic parents, an Irish mother and a Portuguese father. He was a tall, muscularly handsome man who had only recently met Marion McCay, who was twenty-one. Moniz was eighteen years her senior. With America's entry into the war making the future uncertain, the passionate couple wanted to marry as soon as possible. When Marion first saw Moniz dressed in his military uniform, Jean Adams Robinson recalled, "it was all over!"[15]

Moniz sat at a table and talked quietly with Marion's parents while she remained in another part of the house. On the front porch enjoying the cool breeze and full moon were Robert McCay and his fiancée, Theresa (Tedda) Munchausen. Robert attended Erasmus High School and art classes at Pratt Institute after graduating from public school, but neither he nor his sister were graduated from high school. He ran away from home at seventeen and within two years had forged his father's signature so he could join the First New York Cavalry, in which he served for nine months on the Texas border with Troop E. Three weeks after his discharge, war was declared, and he was recalled for overseas duty.

Robert and Tedda crouched on their knees beneath the open window to the living room and listened to Moniz talk with the McCays. Years later, Tedda remembered Maude's "shocked look" and Winsor's stoic silence. Moniz was respectful but firm, and, as he turned to leave, he said, "Well, you know, Winsor, whether you give your consent or not, we are going to be married."

There was little the McCays could object to. Moniz's Catholic religion was not a problem, given that the McCays were rare churchgoers and Maude's Methodism had nothing to do with Winsor's agnosticism and Masonic membership. As for the couple's age difference, Marion was following an example set by her own parents. Besides, Moniz was a National Guardsman about to be sent off for advanced training and then on to Europe to fight. Their daughter was almost hysterical with love and determination to marry the man, and the McCays never denied their children anything. Ray Moniz and Marion McCay were married at St. Theresa's Church in Brooklyn on October 3, 1917.

Ray Moniz trained with his brother-in-law, Robert McCay, along with William Apthorp ("Thorp") Adams III, the son of "Ap" Adams, at Camp Wadsworth, South Carolina.[16] In May 1918, Robert McCay and Raymond Moniz sailed from Norfolk with the 27th Division for France, where both men distinguished themselves in combat.

"Marion told me how she and her father saw her husband off for France," recalled friend and neighbor Maud H. Brown. "A sad day for her, especially since she had only recently learned that she was to become a mother, a new experience for her." And not a pleasant one, according to Mrs. Brown. As her pregnancy began to show, Marion "withdrew more and more. In those days, having a baby was hush-hush. All kinds of wearing apparel were worn to disguise it. A young girl with a beautiful figure was not too keen in seeing it change into a plump and perhaps cumbersome shape. Marion's new figure was hard for her to cope with."

Winsor was troubled by his daughter's attitude. "Marion," he said, "You should be proud that you are creating a real live human being. You have the sole responsibility of caring for it and nurturing it until it becomes strong enough and large enough to enter our world and into your arms. Be proud!" Marion told Mrs. Brown her whole attitude changed after that.[17]

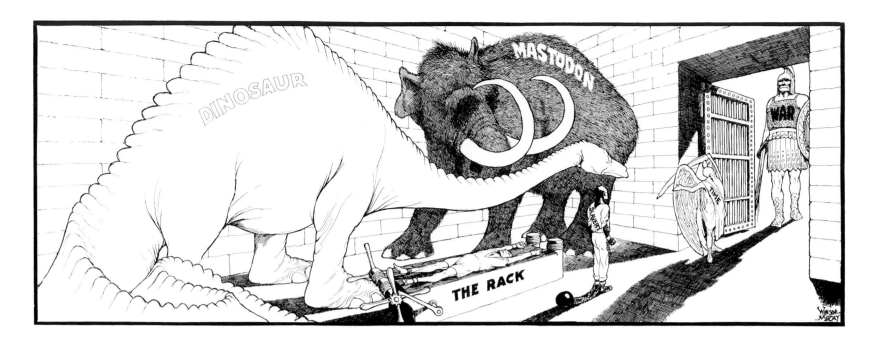

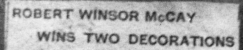

ROBERT WINSOR McCAY
WINS TWO DECORATIONS

ROBERT WINSOR McCAY

Corp'l ROBERT W. McCAY

WILLIAM A. ADAMS Jr.

SGT ROBERT WINSOR McCAY, 22, son of Mr. and Mrs. Winsor McCay of Sheepshead Bay, attended Erasmus and Pratt Institute after graduating from public school. He joined Troop C, New York cavalry, at the age of 19, and served nine months on the Texas border with Troop E. He trained with the 27th Division at Camp Wadsworth, S. C., where he was transferred to the Division Headquarters Troop. Being a remarkable horseman, he served as orderly for nearly every officer who visited Camp Wadsworth. McCay sailed with the 27th Division for France in May. When that division broke the Hindenburg line, McCay so distinguished himself that he has been decorated by the British with the British Military Medal and by the United States with the Distinguished Service Cross.

Men o

Gallant

Earn

Med

Private WILLIAM ANT...
No. 1216528; Corporal...
CAY, Jr., No. 123...
JACK MARQUSEE. 1...
Infantry—During the...
Ronssy, France, Sep...
October 1, while ...
messengers, carried...
divisional and brigade...
der a heavy shell fi...
volley which had be...
They also assisted...
stragglers and took in...
comrades under shell...
try.

Corporals McCay a...
Private Adams were ...
Military Medals in ...
United States Distin...
oss.

Served on the Border.

Corpl. Robert Winsor McCay, son of Mr. and Mrs. Winsor McCoy of No. 1901 Voorhees Avenue, was studying art at Pratt Institute when he enlisted in 1916 in Troop C, 1st New York Cavalry. He served nine months on the Mexican border. He is a despatch rider with the Headquarters Troop, 27th Division, American Expeditionary Forces. His father is wide-

ly known as a cartoonist. His sister, Marion, recently became the wife of Capt. R. T. Moniz of Gen. O'Ryan's staff.

William Apthorp Adams jr., son of William A. Adams sr., who lived with the McCays, is in young McCay's troop. He also served on the Mexican border.

NEWS FOR WAR DEPARTME

WASHINGTON, Feb. 28.—The transport Leviathan sailed from France the 26th of this month for New Yo... carrying a large consignment of 27th Division, New York troops, cording to a War Department nouncement to-day.

The Evening World in a special ... despatch from Martin Green, a S...

CORP. R. McCOY (69)
Corporal Robert McCay, ... Headquarter...

CORP.
McCOY

MOM - POP - MARION -

In Europe, Robert McCay was wounded, gassed, and suffered from shell shock when his division broke the Hindenburg line. He was decorated with the British Imperial Military Medal and the Distinguished Service Cross, and Ray Moniz was promoted to the rank of major for his service in the American Expeditionary Forces.

On July 16, 1918, Marion gave birth to her only child, Ray Winsor Moniz. She dubbed him her "little boon companion" and "Boon" became Ray Jr.'s childhood nickname.[18] Winsor and Maude sent a cable to their son-in-law overseas: "Raymond Winsor Moniz arrived safely tonight. Mother Marion is doing well. You're a papa, and we are now Grandma and Grandpa." Brooklyn newspapers announced the event, with one article describing Maude as "the youthful happy grandma [who] hasn't left her daughter's side, nor can she be induced to relinquish her embrace of the precious arrival." The baby's father cabled to say the birth had been celebrated by him and his fellow soldiers in the trenches.

Grandfather Winsor failed to draw a likeness of the child. "I try," he said, "but I cannot sketch his beautiful little face. Its expression is too wonderful. But this is the shape of his head." Mrs. John Gust, great-grandmother of the baby, presented the child with a set of captain's bars, which were placed on the shoulders of the boy just after the christening ceremony in September. The baby's lusty cries inspired

speculation about the infant eventually becoming a soldier like his father and uncle. Patriotic Winsor drew two service stars as talismans for Robert and Ray next to his signature on all of his illustrations while America was at war. "Well," he said of the baby growing up to fight for his country, "I would even add this one service star more with the signature to my drawings if need be."

The ardent isolationism of Brisbane and Hearst clashed with the mood of the country, now aflame with "militant patriotism." Pacifists were denounced as cowards and pro-Germans. Brisbane biographer Oliver Carlson assessed the situation this way:

> For once, the wily editor failed to sense the changing drift of public opinion. Even after he and Hearst did recognize it, they still believed themselves sufficiently strong to stem the tide. Again they were mistaken. For this double blunder, they were soon to become the victims of the mob spirit, and the emotional hysteria which they had so frequently whipped up against others. Their papers were boycotted. Copies were destroyed and burned in public. Newsdealers refused to handle them. These two "friends of the common people," were denounced in the press, the pulpit, and the street as traitors to their country . . . . Circulation fell. Both Brisbane and Hearst were hanged in effigy. . . .[19]

In desperation, Hearst ordered red, white, and blue titles run in all editions and little American flags on inside pages to "meet popular sentiment" during "these troublous times." Winsor McCay was dragged

BELOW LEFT:
Marion McCay Moniz and her only child, Ray Winsor, c. 1928. (Collection Ray Winsor Moniz)

BELOW RIGHT:
Robert McCay stands next to his father's rolltop desk during a visit to Winsor's office in the American building in 1919. Robert wears the British Imperial Medal he won for bravery during combat when the 27th Division broke the Hindenburg line. (Collection Ray Winsor Moniz)

into the fray to his great annoyance and embarrassment. He attempted to clarify his position and that of his employers in a defensive editorial, "Winsor McCay Writes About His *American* Cartoons and Mr. Hearst":

To the Public:
Because my name and cartoons are being dragged into the silly mess that is being stirred up by privileged interests and featherbed patriots, trying to prove that Mr. Hearst is pro-German, I make this statement in defense of myself only.

. . . If I had ever thought Mr. Hearst was pro-German I would have quit him two minutes after finding out, and I know that the hundreds of patriotic and loyal men and women in this great establishment would have done likewise. When these moneyed Hearst haters say Mr. Hearst is pro-German, they insult every one of his employes [sic]; I have been insulted a FEW times of late, always, of course, by people who say they never read the Hearst papers; therefore, they ARE few.

"Hearst pays you a very big salary that you don't like to give up!" they will say to all of this. Anyone who knows me personally will tell you that I can make more money than he is paying me. While I am working for him I will have no German taint about me. My son Robert returns soon from France with my daughter's husband, both of the 27th Division, both volunteers; both were nine months on the Texas Border. I don't want them to think I would even speak to a pro-German, let alone putting forth his miserable propaganda.

Mr. Hearst has been buncoed and tricked by believing all men are honest. Perhaps, if such a thing could be,

he is too pro-American. But the hatred of the privileged interests helped by envious newspapers will not injure him; he will come out O.K. and all of us who work for him know it.

Mr. Hearst is ONE HUNDRED PER CENT AMERICAN! I know! I have never made a pro-German cartoon. Winsor McCay[20]

A letter dated August 22, 1918, was dictated to a stenographer ("as I can talk so much faster than I can write") from Winsor to his "darling son" overseas. In it, he seeks to encourage Robert by telling him he is "planning a business that will rouse your interest as quick as you come back. I am sorry that I cannot dwell more upon the importance of the scheme but it is the biggest affair I ever heard of and I expect to go out of the newspaper business soon and go into this business. I will not do that, however, until I am assured of its success. You know me, Bob, I never move until I know, but this really is the biggest affair yet and I want you to know that when you come back you will have a dandy place to hop into. I am working night and day at it and that is why you are not hearing from me as often as you should."

McCay never specified what his grand scheme was. Perhaps it was an ambitious animated film; years later, after Winsor's death, Robert told of a long film about World War I that his father hoped to make, one he drew hundreds of sketches for but never produced because of his newspaper commitments.

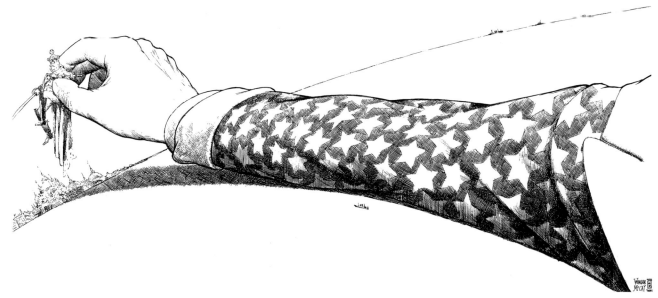

The 1918 letter contains words from a sensitive, worried father:

The city is dull, the Bay is dead and the sky is full of airplanes. I do not know what to write about because I cannot adjust my mind to your condition. I do not like to start any kidding because when you read this you may not be in the mood to read a lot of foolishness. I really feel that you are the same laughing Kiddo there in France that you were on the hot sands of Texas and yet you may not be. You may be where any ridiculous things that I could tell you about would read idiotic. Mr. Adams and I never kid about you and Thorp [Ap Adams's son] any more like we did when you were in Texas.

We are all fine here. Our car is laid up for the reason that our Chauffeur got a job for $10.00 more a week and quit but in such a nasty way that we let him go but would have been willing to pay him $10.00 more at this time, so we sit on the porch and look at Ray Jr. He is a dandy kid, looks like you, especially when he laughs. He sleeps all the time and eats all the time. I suppose Ray is wild by this time to see him.

Your mother waits on Marion continually like a nurse. We snap-shot him every day and are mailing you photographs.

In the bottom margin of two pages, McCay added the following handwritten remarks about baby Ray:

He's got Ray's eyes and your mouth—and maybe he can't cut cheeses [fart]—loud as a man can—But quietly and confidentially he certainly does shoot in the morning and plays a tune—Never has the colic—never sick—never cross—always hungry—and always sleepy—growing a mile a minute.

Let Ray see this letter. I am going to write him. Oh if he could see his heir! and his Wifie is a swell mother looks grand Better than she ever looked. Today is her birthday and each mail today brought letters from Ray and she is so happy—but drops a tear occasionally when Ray writes lovingly . . . Tedda just came in and is awful blue she says you do not get her letters, and she writes 3 & 4 times a week—long letters too!

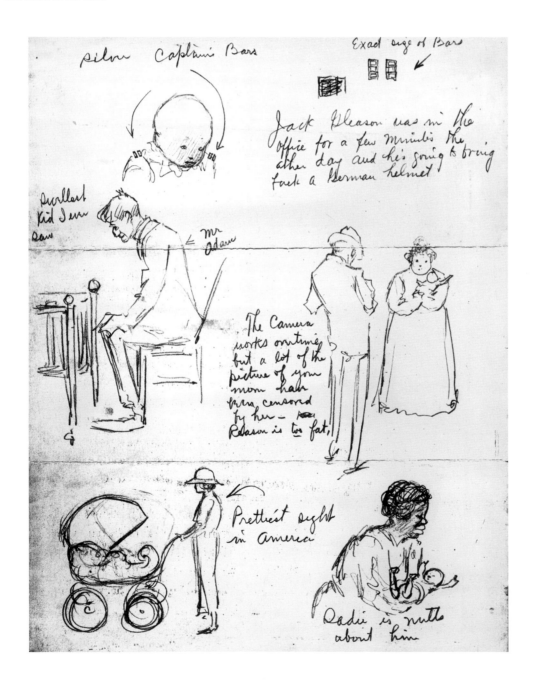

218

oke isn't he a darling—

Looks like his father.

looks likes is mother

Looks like his grandfather

looks like his grandmother

Looks like his uncle Bob

He's a tear cat

look his laughing isn't he fat

Do you nurse him

Does he have the colic

Does he sleep good

what does he weight

Expression of a Judge or Statesman

Neck like Tom Sharkey

Big Deep Chest

Me Every morning in my Pajamas I have to go get him he looks so fresh when he wakes up

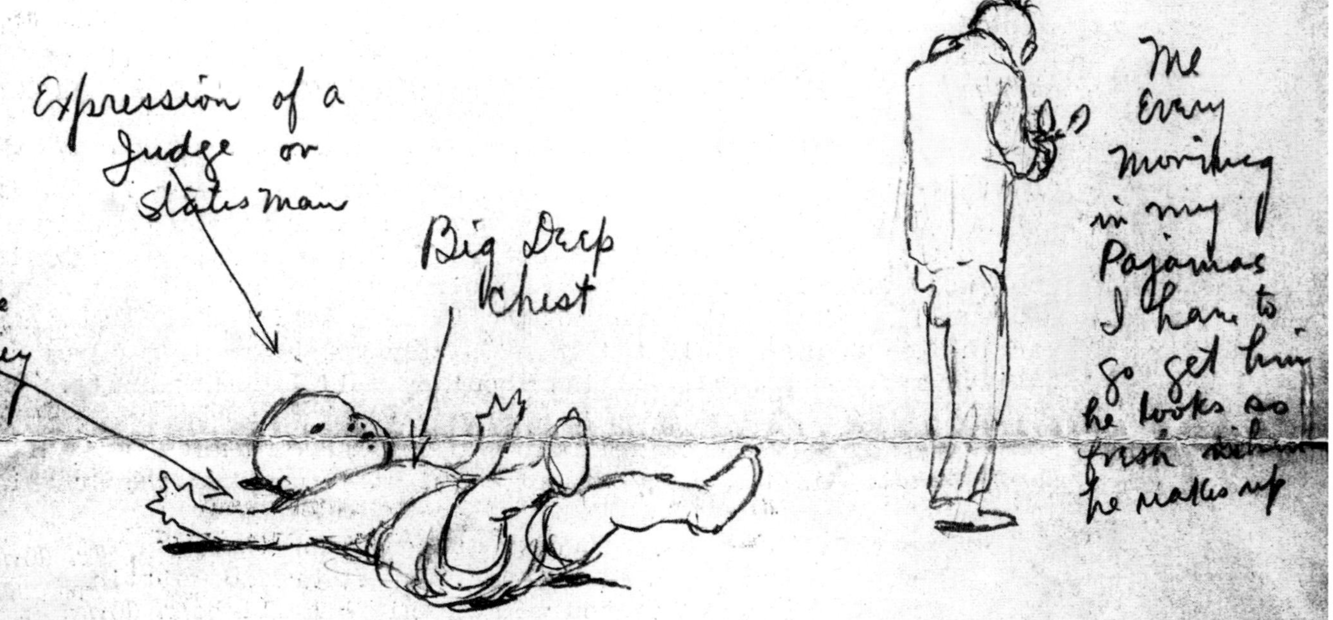

But quietly and confidentially he certainly does shoot in the morning a plays a tune — never has the colic never sick — never cross — always hungry — and always sleepy — growing a mile a minute. Your loving Pop ——— Take care of yourself.

A World War I poster designed by McCay. (Courtesy Guernsey's)

A McCay doodle on the back of a sheet of his personal stationery. A waiter at a posh restaurant (probably in Sheepshead Bay) refuses the McCays entry because of Maude's large dog. The choice of a back view personalizes for the viewer the waiter's rejection. Standing a small distance from his wife, Winsor looks on as passively as Felix Fiddle observing a torturous Jungle Imps ritual. (Collection Ray Winsor Moniz)

The rest of the letter is covered with funny and charming caricatures of the family and friends, all cooing over the newborn Ray Moniz. McCay continues his message of hope:

I really believe by the time you get this letter tremendous efforts for peace will be made by the Germans. Each day we are getting better news and I have a map of the district I think you are in and I know every move. . . .

Once again, let me say that you are going into business with your pop when you return. Tedda is most loyal and true to you. She is one dandy girl and crazy about Ray Jr. She visits us twice a week and her whole heart is set on you. Don't worry about her. . . .

Do not worry about what you saw in the *Tribune* about Mr. Hearst being pro-German. It is all newspaper bunk and only a few boneheads fall for a newspaper fight. Our circulation has jumped 25% and the *Tribune* has lost 33%. The *Tribune* has benefited us and injured themselves. Mr. Hearst is most patriotic,—always was and always will be so don't worry about that fake *Tribune*. In fact, do not worry about one single thing. You have known the Old Chief for a long time and he is always on deck. Stick by the Old Scout for "HE IS THERE." Little Old Me. [The last three words were hand-written by McCay, indicating he is the Old Chief and Scout.]

Tell Ray that he has one of the grandest sons that was ever born, and that Marion is the grandest little mother that ever lived. It is really wonderful in this house. We only have one thought and that is of you and Ray, but we are game and look forward to all being together again soon. It does not sound like I am very game since you do not get many letters from me but really, Bob, if you knew what a big scheme I have and how hard I am working on it, you would not care whether you heard it from me or not, but believe me, you are all I think about even if I do not write.

I do not know what else to say except that we are all well and happy, living in the prospects of a bright future and the crushing of The Huns.

Now that I have found a stenographer that can write my letters for me you will hear from me oftener. I just dreaded sitting down and scribbling for a couple of hours when this has all been done in ten minutes.

When the war ended, McCay's son and son-in-law returned to New York with the 27th Division in February 1919 aboard the transport *Leviathan*. Winsor pulled strings so that he and his daughter could greet the men from a tugboat escorting the troop ship into New York harbor.

THE REAL M'CAY AND THE FABLED
The famous cartoonist whose sermons in line are printed on the editorial page, and some sketches he made in "The Examiner" office last night illustrating how most people expect him to look.

Draughtsman Makes First Trip to Coast Especially to See San Francisco; Would Rather Entertain Than Be Serious, He Declares

Winsor McCay, famous cartoonist for the Hearst newspapers, paid a fleeting visit to San Francisco yesterday. He came to California especially to see the city. He said there were so many big buildings and houses that he couldn't see it and went on for a rest at the Hearst ranch in San Luis Obispo county.

He will return later to look up the fabled city of the Golden Gate which he suspects is hidden away somewhere beneath the chimney tops and among the brick walls.

McCay is the man who uses his pen to make men think. He also likes to make them smile. Among his famous characters of the comic page are Little Nemo in Slumberland, the Rarebit Fiend, Sammy Sneeze, Dull Care, Poor Jake, Hungry Henrietta and the Jungle Imps.

McCay is serious for a purpose in his powerful cartoons. "There are some things men have to be serious about if the world is going ahead," he says. If it were not for that, he would be entertaining them all the time.

Professionally, McCay frequently thunders, but personally and socially he always smiles.

People sometimes are a little afraid of McCay's cartoons—they hit home so close and so hard. A puppy dog wouldn't be afraid of McCay himself. He is one hundred per cent human. That is why San Francisco will be sure to like him.

McCay did not set out to become a preacher, although his cartoons are the strongest kind of sermons. He made a number of sketches last night to illustrate the impressions some people get of his probable personal appearance. He says he never claimed that he was handsome, but considers himself better looking than any one expects him to be.

Sarah Bernhardt Ill, Cancels Engagements
LONDON, Aug. 29.—A message from the manager of Sarah Bernhart, French actress, says she is too ill to leave Paris to keep a London engagement which was to begin next week.

$1 WEEK WATCHES AND DIAMONDS
No red tape. 703 Market st., Claus Spreckels Bldg., rm. 203. B. T. BRILLIANT.—Advertisement.

After the war, McCay's public loyalty to Hearst was rewarded by The Chief in the grandiose and mysterious manner for which he was famous. In August 1920, McCay received a letter from Hearst containing two round-trip railroad tickets from New York to California and a note that said "Come at once." Maude refused to make the long trip, so Winsor went alone. He arrived in San Francisco for a "fleeting visit" on August 29, claiming in an interview with the *Examiner* that he "came to California especially to see the city," and promised to return on his way back from "a rest at the Hearst ranch in San Luis Obispo county." The newspaper article included a photograph of McCay, at age fifty-three, looking elderly and jowly, dressed in a dark suit and bow tie, without his fedora, so that his hairline is shown hopelessly retreating despite futile attempts at a coverup with a single forelock. McCay is wearing a pince-nez and is, as usual, drawing intently. Surrounding the photo are five drawings he made "illustrating how most people expect him to look." The caricatures are amusing in that they do not resemble each other nor McCay in the least.

"Professionally," the article stated, "McCay frequently thunders, but personally and socially he always smiles. People are sometimes a little afraid of McCay's cartoons—they hit home so close and so hard. A puppy dog wouldn't be afraid of McCay himself. He is one hundred percent human. That is why San Francisco will be sure to like him. . . . He says he never claimed that he was handsome, but considers himself better looking than anyone expects him to be."

When McCay arrived at San Simeon, Hearst's Olympian abode, he learned there was no urgent reason for the trip west. The Chief merely thought McCay should have a vacation, even a forced one. At first McCay tried to do Hearst's bidding; one can imagine the tiny artist wandering through the cavernous halls and gardens of Hearst's monstrous "ranch," lonely and bewildered by the jumble of good and bad art and architecture. Soon McCay became anxious to return to his family and his work, and so Hearst allowed him to leave.[21]

On April 9, 1921, Robert McCay married his faithful Tedda, and the next year a daughter, Janet (named after Winsor's mother), was born, followed in 1928 by a son, Robert. As a wedding present, Winsor bought the couple a house at 2557 East 19th Street, a few blocks from his Voorhies Avenue residence.

Winsor and His Playmates

SPRING IS HERE! THE CIRCUS IS IN TOWN!— A FEW ANTIDELUVIAN SPECIMENS NOT SEEN IN THE ROCK CREEK ZOO.—

CHARLIE JOHN EDDIE GEORGE BILLIE ME. FRANK ANDY.

WINSOR McCAY at KEITH'S THEATRE WASHINGTON, D.C.

LEFT:
Robert McCay and his future wife Theresa (Tedda) Munchausen, c. 1917. (Collection Janet Trinker)

BELOW:
The close bonding between Winsor and his son Robert is seen in this glossy glamour photo, c. late 1920s. McCay attempted to boost his son's career as a cartoonist by posing for photos as a "team," giving him editorial cartoons to complete, and collaborating on an animated film (The Flying House). (Collection Janet Trinker)

Raymond and Marion Moniz and baby Ray lived for a time in the Voorhies Avenue house with Maude and Winsor, until an altercation with Maude about one of her maids cut short the stay. They moved to a house Winsor bought for them in Peekskill in upstate New York. Marion found adjusting to country life difficult, and so visits to her parents became a weekend ritual until Winsor died.

Twenty-four-year-old Maud H. Brown and her husband lived a block away from the Moniz family in Peekskill and she and Marion became good friends. "Our husbands hit it off well together," Mrs. Brown remembered in a 1987 letter.

> They were both good conversationalists. Full of wit and humor. The Moniz family called on us often of an evening and often with Winsor McCay in tow whenever he was visiting. McCay would regale the two families with personal anecdotes, such as his youth in rural Michigan, how he met his wife, or how he made his animated films. Winsor loved to tell stories. I expect it was sort of a relaxation for him.
>
> Maude McCay never came to the Browns' house.
>
> Marion always said that her mother could hardly wait until she could get her girdle off and relax. She was a beautiful woman even then. Her main interest, I gathered, to be clothes and the like, finery. She never wore casual clothes, like the rest of us. She was not an outgoing person, like the rest of the family, but she seemed to get along well with everyone.

McCay continued to meet his deadlines by drawing wherever he happened to be. One spring Sunday morning, he dropped by Mrs. Brown's to chat.

> In the midst of his call and conversation, he remarked casually: "You know, I have to get Brisbane's illustration in tomorrow for next Sunday's edition." With that he asked if I could give him a wooden match. "Kitchen matches," he called them because we used them to light the gas burners in the stove. No pilot lights then. . . .

He took one, went out of doors, picked up a large stone, put the match on it and with another stone hammered the end of the match, until he transformed it into frays of wooden fiber. At that, he said, "Now I'll get to work. This will serve as a paintbrush. I left mine home."

I got the biggest kick out of this. Imagine making an important illustration for which he would be paid a handsome sum, with a match brush. Such was his creativity and faith in his own ability.[22]

McCay must have come to an understanding with Hearst about his theatrical appearances, perhaps during the visit to San Simeon. In 1922 McCay arranged for the B. F. Keith circuit to "cover" his act in order to provide him with bookings. Keith president Edward F. Albee wrote McCay that he need not have an agent but could do business directly with Albee's office. Over the next three years, McCay played New York's Palace Theater, plus occasional dates in Chicago, Washington, D.C., Wisconsin, and Boston, a city from which he sent an exuberant letter full of snappy show biz slang to Robert, Tedda, and his granddaughter Janet:

> Well I am just doing grand. Got your fine letter . . . . Bought 2 dandy snake whips today—Mine went fluey at yesterday's matinee. Lash went clear out in the audience 4th row. Never saw it since. Someone took it home with them I guess for it could not be found. Big show & fine—packed houses etc. What more could you want. Just wrote Grandma & Mom so am tired of writing—don't know what to say anyway. Did you see [Apthorp] Adams—I'll bet he wishes he was up here. He flew high when he was here last with me—How is jano [Janet]? She's a wonder—Have to make a great star out of her—. . . . I am knocking them dead here—and getting great publicity but would get more if they knew last week I was coming— . . .

. . . Just mailed 2 cartoons and must now go in a[nd]
knock 'em dizzy with my new whip—
Sit tight kiddo and we'll get there—Be good.
Love to Tedda and Janet from old Doc.
(Will get at some strips tomorrow and mail 'em to you.)

The postscript to the letter may have referred to McCay's attempt to bolster his son's confidence by finding work for him as a cartoonist. Robert's wartime experiences left him "for many years too nervous to hold a pen and too jittery to sit still long enough to complete a drawing."[23] Some of McCay's editorial cartoons (October 26 and December 28, 1924, and March 1 and March 8, 1925) were signed "Robert Winsor McCay, Jr.," suggesting a collaboration between father and son. Winsor most likely supplied the concept and layout, and Robert filled in the drawing's details. Robert McCay was a talented draftsman, but, of course, not in his father's league, as indeed few artists ever have been.

Winsor was seen on movie screens briefly in 1924 as "one of the luminaries" in *The Great White Way,* a feature film about boxing with Anita Stewart and T. Roy Barnes, plus the entire Ziegfeld Follies chorus. "One of the interesting sequences is that in which the making of a newspaper is shown," noted the *New York Times* reviewer (January 4, 1924). McCay is glimpsed, as is George McManus, Bugs Baer, Harry Hershfield, Damon Runyon, Florenz Ziegfeld, Jr., and Arthur Brisbane, who "seemed to be at home in a role he has enacted for many a year."

The film was six months in production and said to cost almost one million dollars; the newspaper office and pressroom scenes were touted as "the most remarkable of their kind ever filmed."

McCay "reviewed" his performance in an advertisement for the film: Within a small circle, Flip says to Nemo, "I dreamed last night that Winsor McCay was an actor." Nemo replies, "He is an actor! He may be a bad one, but he is an actor, Flip!" This expensive piece of Hearstian cinematic self-promotion created little stir and soon disappeared.

While his occasional return to the stage gave McCay a boost, the daily pressures at the *American* never ceased. There he was obliged to conjure up a pleasing illustration daily for "The Old Man" (as

Brisbane was referred to behind his back by the cartoonists) no matter how uninspiring the copy might be. Typical titles for 1924 editorials included: "One Curse of Life: Noise," "Where Do Souls Go?" and "The Toad under the Harrow." Brisbane often relied upon McCay to contribute subject matter and even copy for the editorials, but he was a demanding martinet who lacked a sense of humor.

One afternoon, Joe McGurk painted a voluptuous female nude on one of the long shades in the room he shared with Winsor McCay and Bugs Baer. As a final touch, he printed the words "The Vestal Virgin" above the nude and rolled the shade up. Some time after, McCay was working alone in the office and, without looking up, he drew the shade to change the lighting in the room. At that moment, Brisbane came unannounced into McCay's office. (Usually, when Brisbane was sighted exiting the elevator, headed toward his office, a secretary would open the door to McCay's room and let out a low and juicy "razzberry" as a warning.)

Now Brisbane saw the nude painting, of which McCay was oblivious, and walked over for a close inspection. "Mr. McCay," said Big George with distaste, "as a grandfather you should know better." McCay looked up and for the first time saw the shade and the painted lady upon it. For a long moment, there was silence as McCay tried hard not to laugh; he was bursting with anticipation over what he would tell McGurk and Baer. Presently, Brisbane took a blue pencil from his vest pocket, drew a circle around each of the nude's ample breasts (as if he were editing overblown prose by one of the staff writers), and said, "That young woman is no virgin!"[24]

"During my ten years or so with the Hearst organization," recalled a veteran worker on the *American,* "I frequently heard men talk affectionately about Mr. Hearst, but I fail to recall a single instance where anyone used affectionate terms about Brisbane."[25] The Old Man has been described as niggardly, ruthless, and disloyal to long-time employees, a boss who thought it necessary to rule by fear. The anxiety and trepidation Brisbane encouraged permeated his staff, leading to Byzantine office politics. For instance, at night his "spies" inspected the contents of desks and wastebaskets for evidence of insubordination or disloyalty.

The Most Brilliant Cartoon Pen on the Whole American Scene

Upon the expiration of his contract with Hearst in 1924, Winsor McCay turned in his resignation and left the *American*. Office pressures and anxiety were certainly contributing factors to McCay's leaving. In fact, there had been a recent stressful crackdown on drinking on the job. When a full bottle of liquor was found in McCay's desk, he received a stern letter from the managing editor demanding an explanation and an accounting. The tone of the letter was that of a schoolmaster chastising a wayward student; it was insulting to a great artist who never missed a deadline and deserved more respect than was shown by rifling his desk and making unfounded accusations.

What directly occasioned McCay's resignation, however, was the refusal of the *American*'s business manager, known as the "Silver Fox," to pay the artist a promised bonus of $5,000 upon expiration of his contract. "Do you think you're entitled to a bonus?" said the Fox. "You haven't lived up to your contract."

McCay asked what he had done to nullify it and was rudely dismissed. "You *know* you haven't lived up to the agreement, McCay. Don't bother asking me what you did. You know very well yourself. I'm busy now. Talk to me later about it."[26]

Later never came. An undated rough draft of McCay's resignation note exists, written with bitterness and a barely contained anger:

On May 17th my contract with you expires. On that date I expect to make a change & I have a very favorable offer from people friendly to you where I can make myself more valuable than I can on your great newspapers.

There is nothing unpleasant about my leaving. Except I may be disappointed in not having my daily cartoons featured instead of down to postage stamp size and during recent campaigns having them take second place to Comic Dept stars uptown—

I have been told recently and firmly where I stand as a value to you but I refuse to believe him.

I also deny that I am trying to hold some one up or that I am swell headed. I will leave with my very pleasant memories of your many kindnesses to me and will ever hold you in the highest regard and esteem.

Please acknowledge receipt of this within ten days so that I will know that I have been fair to you and so that I may arrange my plans—

McCay had already arranged his plans before he quit, for as usual, he never jumped to something new without knowing where he was going to land. He returned to the *Herald Tribune,* and, miracle of miracles, revived his beloved comic strip *Little Nemo in Slumberland* starting August 3, 1924.

The impossible had occurred: Winsor McCay was again drawing a comic strip, and not just any strip, but a new version of the greatest strip of all time! He felt as free as a kid when school lets out for the summer. No more Brisbane or his memos—threatening, suggesting, demanding. McCay's imagination and creativity would no longer be held back by another's vision. He and his alter ego Nemo were back together, on the road again to the land of dreams.

Hoping to reassert his supremacy in the comic strip area, McCay indulged himself in the revised *Nemo,* intent on making it a lavish showcase of his ability to create a stunningly designed page. This he did—the new strip contains marvelous virtuoso draftsmanship. But gone was narrative thrust, plot structure, and continuity. Gone too was Nemo as protagonist; the questing boy who evolved as a character throughout the first version of the strip was now dull and passive. Boisterous Flip and his slapstick antics filled the gap left by Little Nemo. The debut page of the revised strip demonstrates the virtues and faults of the entire series, which ran until December 26, 1926: Nemo is awakened by water flooding his room, and the major characters of the strip float in on a grand gondola— Flip, Impie, the Princess, Dr. Pill, and Professor Figures. "Come with us," says the Princess. "We're going to Slumberland."

Before Nemo can respond, Impie jumps on the bed, catapulting Nemo onto the boat, knocking the Prof and the Doc into the water with the Imp. Flip immediately takes charge and brays into a microphone, "Hey! Marconi. Broadcast Mike in the pump room to draw the water out of this lake."

Immediately, the tops of trees appear at water level as the boat descends. At the bottom of the now empty lake, two distressed mermaids ask that the water be returned. Before Nemo can respond, Flip orders the boy below deck to "dress up." Nemo obeys and returns *sans* pajamas, but in the plumed hat, tights, and cape costume recognizable from the earlier strip and animated film.

The Professor and the Doctor are caught in the treetops and Impie is chased by a giant lobster. Flip to the rescue again: he prepares a large lasso and is swinging it widely as, in the tenth and final panel, Nemo wakes up screaming, "Run Impie!"

Water in this first episode is symbolic of McCay's career cleansing: a veritable flushing away of the troubled waters of his recent past and a new beginning surrounded by old friends. The initiative for action is taken throughout by Flip, while Nemo observes or obeys orders. The drawing is lovely, and the variety of action poses and feel for animation is fine. But there is more dialogue than necessary and certainly more characters involved than necessary (the Princess, Professor, and Doctor Pill have nothing to do). The size and shape of the panels remain basically the same; they do not elongate or otherwise

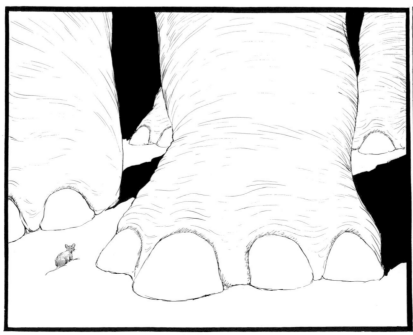
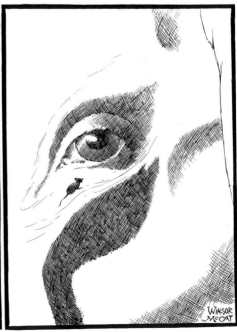

3—29—3 "Make Your Dream Garden A Reality."—Farm and Garden Tools.

WINCHESTER
FARM AND GARDEN TOOLS
STAND THE TEST OF
CULTIVATION

WINSOR McCAY

LITHOGRAPHED IN U.S.A.

An example of the fame and
wide appeal of McCay's Nemo
and friends is this large, three-
panel (undated) poster, in which
the artist uses his familiar cast
and Slumberland setting to sell
farm and garden tools.
(Collection Maurice Sendak)

adapt to the visual changes of the action within the frames as the more flexible earlier strip did.

McCay seemed intent on diminishing the magic and mystery of Slumberland. In the strip's first version, we discover new aspects about the land of dreams each week, which enhances its grandeur and otherworldliness. Now we find that the magically appearing lake is merely a plumber's invention, altered by levers and switches in a control room. The encroachment of modern inventions that began in the earlier version of *Little Nemo in Slumberland* clutters almost every episode of the new version's two-year run, from Flip's wireless mike and chrome-plated sports cars and airplanes, to ambulances, clowns with electric noses, and a chewing gum factory filled with giant cogs and wheels. The mythical Slumberland had become too much like real America circa mid-1920s.

By revealing pipes and plumbing, using telecommunications to send messages, and showing the mechanical guts of dream factories, McCay once again announced his presence as the master manipulator behind the fantasy, as he did in his animated film prologues. He was impressing upon his audiences that magic does not just happen; it exists because of a greater force, whose godlike power ultimately belongs to Winsor McCay.

ALLAY-OOP!

CARTOONS

YOU are invited to attend a Private Exhibition of Mr. Winsor McCay's serious and comic cartoons moving.

At the Criterion Theatre, Tuesday evening, 8.30 o'clock, July 19, 1927.

Winsor McCay, the originator of Animated Cartoons is to appear at the Paramount Theatre during the week of July 23d with some of the remarkable films to be shown for the first time at this Private Exhibition.

Present This Invitation

McCay was observed during this period by a young aspiring cartoonist, Gregory D'Alessio, who became a painter and teacher of anatomy at New York's Art Students League. A friend took D'Alessio to the *Herald Tribune* building in midtown to meet cartoonist Bill Holman, who at that time was drawing a "kid strip" called *G-Whizz, Junior* and years later became known for the zany strip *Smokey Stover*. "So there," recalled D'Alessio, "I met my first professional cartoonist. But what commanded my attention more was the figure of a middle-aged, if not old, man, sitting on a high stool at a drawing table, drawing slowly but surely at one of his imaginative cartoons."

It was Winsor McCay, who was "small, bespectacled and behatted; he was wearing a large, heavy fedora as it would look after having just been blocked. . . . he had an enormously high forehead, so much so, that his head actually filled the crown of the hat clear to the top. I was not surprised. So enormous a head must have been the secret of McCay's great gift of imagination and magical style of drawing, I was sure. An inexhaustible repository of ideas, so to speak."[27]

The *Herald* Sunday comics were colored at Powers Photo Engraving Company, which had contracts with newspapers in New York and other cities. The plant was originally located in a dark, old factory-like building on Manhattan's Nassau Street, and later in cleaner, more open spaces at the new *Herald Tribune* building on 41st Street. Powers's color artist in charge was diminutive August "Gus" L. Bornkessel, who looked to be McCay's twin.

The two men, according to Bornkessel's son, Lew Haskins, "had a working relationship." Gus was a perfectionist who "recognized the superior skills of Winsor McCay so that each time he colored one of his *Nemo* strips, he would run a color proof of his efforts on heavy glossy paper to take home along with Thursday's or Friday's evening *World Telegram.*" Haskins recalled with pleasure that "rainy-day entertainment was often led by the ritual of relooking at the well-preserved *Nemo* comics, and as their numbers grew, so did, too, the hours that we spent reabsorbing the magic of McCay's wonderful storytelling skills."[28]

An invitation to a "Private Exhibition of Mr. Winsor McCay's serious and comic cartoons moving" at the Criterion Theater, July 19, 1927. McCay depicts "Cartoons" as a ferocious beast needing to be tamed— as was Gertie the Dinosaur— by a fearless, bullwhip-cracking cartoonist in a tux. (Collection Ray Winsor Moniz)

Hair Rats Are Gone!
AN ANCIENT PREJUDICE HAS BEEN REMOVED

Modern woman, freed of the restraint of long tresses, realizes the comfort and sanitation of the bobbed head. The shears in the hands of AMERICAN INTELLIGENCE have severed the bonds of another archaic dogma.

"toasting did it"—

Gone is that ancient prejudice against cigarettes—Progress has been made. We removed the prejudice against cigarettes when we removed harmful corrosive ACRIDS (pungent irritants) from the tobaccos.

YEARS ago, when cigarettes were made without the aid of modern science, there originated that ancient prejudice against all cigarettes. That criticism is no longer justified. LUCKY STRIKE, the finest cigarette you ever smoked, made of the choicest tobacco, properly aged and skillfully blended—"It's Toasted."

"TOASTING," the most modern step in cigarette manufacture, removes from LUCKY STRIKE harmful irritants which are present in cigarettes manufactured in the old-fashioned way.

Everyone knows that heat purifies, and so "TOASTING"— LUCKY STRIKE'S *extra* secret process—removes harmful corrosive ACRIDS (pungent irritants) from LUCKIES which in the old-fashioned manufacture of cigarettes cause throat irritation and coughing. Thus "TOASTING" has destroyed that ancient prejudice against cigarette smoking by men and by women.

"**It's toasted**"
No Throat Irritation-No Cough.

TUNE IN—The Lucky Strike Dance Orchestra, every Saturday night, over a coast-to-coast network of the N. B. C.

© 1929, The American Tobacco Co., Mfrs.

"It's Toasted"—the phrase that describes the extra "toasting" process applied in the manufacture of Lucky Strike Cigarettes. The finest tobaccos—the Cream of the Crop—are scientifically subjected to penetrating heat at minimum, 260°—maximum, 300°, Fahrenheit. The exact, expert regulation of such high temperatures removes impurities. More than a slogan, "It's Toasted" is recognized by millions as the most modern step in cigarette manufacture.

Winsor McCay's name on the marquee of the Paramount Theater, New York City, during the week of July 23, 1927. This was McCay's last appearance in what was left of vaudeville; he performed four shows a day, alternating his act with the motion picture Man Power, *starring Richard Dix. McCay is seen standing in a white hat with his hands folded. (Collection Ray Winsor Moniz)*

While McCay happily pored over his born-again comic strip, layering detail upon detail, Hearst executives continually attempted to woo back the rebellious artist. Hearst was reportedly wild with rage because his prize cartoonist had gotten away. Arthur Brisbane found a cartoonist with a style similar to McCay's named Mel Cummin, whom he hired in 1925 to originate ideas and draw eight-column Sunday editorial cartoons. Brisbane informed Cummin that he was using him to fill the vacancy left by McCay, and if McCay should decide to return, Cummin's job would be terminated.

Cummin made himself useful drawing the daily and Sunday *American* editorial cartoons and spot sketches for the Automobile and Real Estate pages of the *Evening Journal,* as well as drawings of local happenings, sports, and politics. McCay finally did return to the Hearst papers in 1927, and Cummin was let go, only to be brought back seven years later to fill the vacancy left by McCay's death.

McCay's return was no doubt sweetened by a salary boost, but he claimed more important considerations were his personal admiration for Hearst as a "great American" and a "great newspaperman" and the fact that McCay always thought of himself proudly as "a Hearst man." But another, less pleasant reason was behind McCay's abandoning his job at the *Herald Tribune* and, for the second time, ceasing work on *Little Nemo in Slumberland*. The truth was that the revised version of the *Nemo* strip was not successful enough with the public to justify the *Herald Tribune*'s continuance of it.

Bill Holman sat to the right of McCay in the three-man office they shared at the *Herald Tribune* with editorial cartoonist Ted Brown. He claims that McCay's strip "was too far between its first popularity [1905 to 1911] and it didn't sell [to enough newspapers between 1924 and 1926]. The newspaper syndicate couldn't fool with it any longer. They had to drop it. They weren't getting Winsor cheap."

Holman recalled that McCay ("one of the nicest guys I've ever known") came to the office in the morning and was gone by one o'clock P.M., often accompanied by his son, who would "hang around with his father." Holman noticed something odd in the way McCay approached the drawing of the *Little Nemo* strip: "He would sit there with the smoke from his little cigars curling under his hat brim sketching quietly. He didn't have any idea of where he was going in the strip. He would just start drawing and see what would happen."[29]

This improvisational approach accounts for the lack of continuity and narrative structure in the revised strip. The thirteen-year gap between McCay strips left the artist out of touch, not only with his muse but also the modern tastes of the public and changes in the comic strip marketplace in postwar America. McCay's contemporaries, who stayed with the comic strip form through the years he was absent, were able to refine and adapt their work to the changing times and to keep abreast of the needs of their audience, as demonstrated by George McManus's *Bringing Up Father* and Cliff Sterrett's *Polly and Her Pals.* These widely popular and graphically inventive strips and

others were domestic comedies that dealt in humorous ways with ordinary people and their ordinary lives. *Nemo* was too child-oriented and held a quaint "innocence," out of step and remote from the Jazz Age. The boy dreamer's adventures lacked the suspense and threat of death that war-sobered American readers found in new comic strips such as *Little Orphan Annie* and *Wash Tubbs,* both of which had strong stories and characters. Elaborate graphics were not enough; comic strips had to relate to the newspaper-buying public or they died. The exception was the brilliant *Krazy Kat* by George Herriman, which mass America did not understand and therefore did not like. But William Randolph Hearst adored the strip, and that is the main reason *Krazy Kat* ran from its birth in 1913 to the cartoonist's death in 1944.

Unfortunately, Hearst had other plans for the prodigious gifts of Winsor McCay, and they did not include comic strips. For this reason and because of McCay's own need to explore other art forms—animation—McCay's time as a comic-strip artist passed. It was an incredibly glorious time at the beginning. Ironically, however, in the end McCay was estranged from an art he was primarily responsible for creating, just as he was finally estranged from animation.

The *Herald Tribune* was so convinced that *Little Nemo in Slumberland* was commercially moribund that on February 23, 1927, a letter was drawn up separately from McCay's discharge papers of the same date. The letter, signed by *Tribune* Second Vice President Howard Davis, stated that "In consideration of One Dollar . . . we herewith transfer to you all copyright privileges which we may own in connection with the color comic page which you have been drawing for New York Tribune, Inc., entitled "Little Nemo in Slumberland."

Almost two years later, McCay wrote in a letter to Howard Morton, a friend in the Hearst building on South Street, that he was "looking through some papers, and finding several of great importance, I think it right, you, as a friend should know what is on my mind this moment." McCay had come upon the letter turning over to him all rights to "my once famous fantasy," and he was concerned about the future of those rights:

If anything should happen to me, some day my wife Maude L. will become owner of the 'Rights.' She must never allow anyone to take these said 'Rights.' They can be loaned but at her death all 'rights' immediately return to my direct family, namely, my daughter Marion Moniz and my son Robert Winsor Jr. my model and creation for 'Nemo.' They then will do as they see fit. there [sic] children should hold my 'possession.'

What Art material pertaining to said named page is there [sic] property. This is a thought and I demand it always be acted upon 'just in case.'

You as a dear friend should know this as I want you to someday, tell this to Bob or will it to him, as the original Nemo, he maybe draw the page or go to Hollywood, who can tell . . . .

McCay returned to his old desk at the *American* and began again to illustrate the editorials of Arthur Brisbane, the "sage of the crossroads store and the Demosthenes of American barber shops."[30] The dour editor treated the artist with the usual polite distance, never missing an opportunity to assert his control over McCay. Usually this took the form of detailed memos suggesting images for his prose. A note from April 25, 1930, begins with an offhand request for McCay to think over two or three separate cartoons, including one for Sunday, all to be ready in one week. One important subject was the accidental burning of convicts in an Ohio prison, but Brisbane cautioned McCay not to make the scene too grisly, just mildly unpleasant.

In a memo dated December 19, 1930, addressed to McCay at his winter residence at the Hotel St. George, Brisbane gave McCay's "strings" a stronger jerk than usual in order to ensure his continued loyalty to the Hearst papers. He wrote that he had learned McCay approached the Sunday comics editor of the *American* with a suggestion for a *Little Nemo* comic strip but was turned down because the color pages were oversupplied. And Brisbane asked about a plan McCay allegedly had to work on the radio. (No doubt McCay was exploring several ways to exploit his newly acquired copyrights on *Little Nemo,* including a radio serial.)

In the memo Brisbane slyly wished McCay well with his plans but pointedly asked if McCay were truly interested in continuing to draw Sunday editorial cartoons. For if he were not, Brisbane claimed to have lined up a new cartoonist, who, he hastened to add, was not as accomplished as McCay at his best but would be satisfactory should McCay decide to announce a sudden need for a prolonged vacation. Brisbane asked for an answer within three weeks, then ended with a classic back-down-turn-around in a postscript: he claimed the memo was sent because he had in mind an idea for a Sunday cartoon that only McCay could do justice to.

Notes and memos, sometimes six pages or more in length, flowed from the verbose Brisbane right up to the time of McCay's death. The messages they contained were invariably manipulative, humorless, imperious, and calculated to make McCay "a nervous wreck," as his family has attested. It was during this period that McCay sadly wrote to his friend, Howard Morton, "My one and only wish is to draw Nemo again, but it's impossible, as A. B. wants me."

Brisbane's attempts to control McCay once backfired when the president of the American Tobacco Company, George Washington Hill, offered McCay a "sum in excess of his annual salary" to draw a series of advertisements for his company. McCay was obliged to ask management to waive the exclusivity clause in his Hearst contract. Permission must come from Hearst personally, Brisbane told McCay, which was his way of saying McCay could freeze in hell before he'd obtain a waiver.

A week passed, and Hill again approached McCay, who said he had not heard from Mr. Hearst on the West Coast. Another week went by, and an impatient Hill came to see McCay at the *American*.

"I want you to illustrate this campaign, McCay," Hill declared, "and I want you to begin right away. Who's holding up the permission?"

"I don't know, Mr. Hill," replied McCay politely. "All I know is that Mr. Brisbane has not received a word from the coast as yet."

OPPOSITE:

A mock battle for the photographers between Winsor McCay and his friend boxer Tom Sharkey. Robert McCay is at the far right. (Collection Walt Disney Archives)

BELOW:

McCay (seated far right) gazes at two showgirls backstage at a theater, c. late 1920s or early 1930s. (Collection Janet Trinker)

With that, the tobacco tycoon strode into the Old Man's office hollering, "Look here, Brisbane. I want McCay's illustrations for my campaign. Do I get them or don't I?"

"It's contrary to our policies," replied the startled Brisbane, "to allow our men to do outside work."

"Policies be damned!" boomed Hill. "If I don't get McCay, the Hearst papers don't get another cent of advertising from the American Tobacco Company!"

Having brought this excellent point to Brisbane's attention, Hill was immediately rewarded with access to McCay's talents. But McCay used this rare opportunity to turn the screws on Brisbane a little: he demanded a letter from Brisbane to protect himself and seal the bargain. A memo dated June 14, 1929, arrived addressed as usual to "My dear McCay." In it, Brisbane says how glad he is that McCay will make some nice drawings for Mr. Hill, a good and personal friend to Brisbane and the Hearst organization, and that such work will, of course, not jeopardize McCay's position with said organization."[31]

A private invitational screening of McCay's "serious and comic cartoons moving" [sic] took place at the Criterion Theater on the evening of July 19, 1927. McCay was to return to vaudeville the week of July 23 "with some of the remarkable films to be shown for the first time at this Private Exhibition." Vaudeville was almost dead when McCay did four shows a day

during his brief run at the Paramount Theater on a bill with the movie *Man Power* starring Richard Dix.

In September, McCay was on the radio saying "some startling things, many probably presumptuous things in his microphone address during the metropolitan broadcast, WNAC." It was McCay and his familiar litany of complaints about the state of film animation, offered with a decidedly bitter and nagging edge to its tone:

> Since I originated animated drawings the art has deteriorated.
>
> I hope and dream the time will come when serious artists will make marvelous pictures that will love and live in life-like manner and be far more interesting and wonderful than pictures you now see on canvas. I think if Michelangelo was alive today he would immediately see the wonders of moving drawings. The artist can make his scenes and characters live instead of having them stand still on canvas in art museums. The time will come when people will not be "little children come unto me" as Michelangelo might have done in moving drawings had he known this art.

On November 2, 1927, he was back on the radio interviewed by Frank Craven on the *Evening Journal's Woman's Hour*. The next day McCay drew a cartoon in the *Journal* showing himself in twenty-seven panels having an attack of nervousness before going on the air, then enjoying the experience so much he must be forcibly removed from the radio studio.[32]

On November 22, 1927, McCay's mother, Janet, died in her home at Edmore, Michigan, at the approximate age of eighty-six. The *Sentinel Review* newspaper of Canada noted the "late Mrs. McCay was a native of the township of East Zorra where she resided for many years. She made frequent visits to Tavistock [Canada] where she had many friends who will deeply regret to learn of her passing. She was an aunt of Miss Helen S. Murray, D. S. Murray and R. R. Murray. Burial will take place at Edmore. . . . She is survived by one son, Winsor McCay, the famous cartoonist of New York." The obituary made no mention of Janet's other surviving son, Arthur.[33]

I. Klein, animator and freelance contributor of cartoons to *The New Yorker*, met McCay a number of times during the early 1930s at the *American*. An editor introduced Klein "with the explanation that I had animated on the *Mutt and Jeff* animated cartoons [produced by Bud Fisher]. McCay nodded in acknowledgment without looking up from his work. He was drawing a large editorial cartoon that seemed to have hundreds of people in active movement. I stayed for a moment then turned to walk away, when he asked me how long I had worked at animation. My reply was 1918 to 1925. And that I then changed over to do magazine cartoons. He also inquired if I had seen

Gertie. My answer was in the affirmative and that I had seen him with *Gertie* on the stage of the Palace."

At each of their subsequent meetings, McCay talked with Klein but continued to address his drawing board ("He never looked up or stopped working on his complicated drawings.")

On one visit, Winsor McCay said: "I sure got a laugh on Brisbane" . . . there was a large storeroom where [quality tearsheets of] McCay's published cartoons were kept. [McCay kept the original artwork after publication in his home.] Every once in a while Brisbane would dig up an old McCay cartoon and reprint it with a line "REPRINTED BY REQUEST." This made McCay sore. . . . He received no extra pay for the reprint. Well, one night there was a fire . . . everything was destroyed by the fire or by water . . . McCay . . . went to Brisbane's office, stuck his head in the doorway and said: "I see where there will be no more REPRINTS BY REQUEST for a while, ha-ha-ha!"[34]

McCay was to experience one last fling as a cartoonist-reporter when the Lindbergh baby was kidnapped in 1932. "Young Bill" Hearst, the Chief's son who was learning the newspaper business, phoned McCay at home to tell him the news. McCay wanted to get to the Lindbergh house near Hopewell, New Jersey, as soon as possible. Bill Hearst agreed to drive him, and in what McCay recalled as "the wildest ride" he had in his life, the two raced across the Jersey meadows to the scene of the crime at 85 miles per hour. They arrived about two hours after the kidnapping was reported to the police, and McCay immediately started working.[35]

William Randolph Hearst, Jr., was interviewed at age 80 by this author in 1988. The then editor in chief of Hearst newspapers recalled that after verifying the kidnapping "it came to me as a newspaper editor, as a man, that I'd want to go out and . . . visit this scene for myself and see what was going on . . . So I called Winsor, who lived at the St. George Hotel in Brooklyn [during the winter months]."

It was the next morning, Hearst said, that he drove McCay and an *American* writer to the scene of the crime in Hopewell, New Jersey. "We were still allowed to go up into the garage, the grounds," Hearst remembered more than half a century later. "They closed it off the next day . . . talked to all the cops assembled.

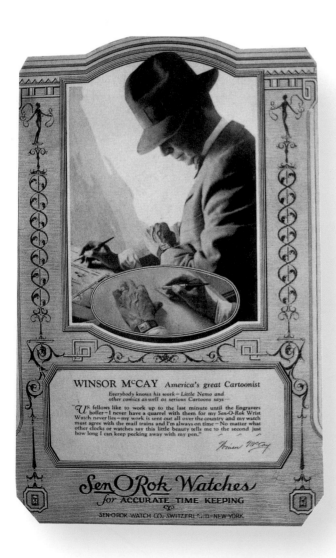

WINSOR MCCAY *America's great Cartoonist*
Everybody knows his work—Little Nemo and other comics as well as serious Cartoons says—

"Us fellows like to work up to the last minute until the Engravers holler—I never have a quarrel with them for my Sen-O-Rok Wrist Watch never lies—my work is sent out all over the country and my watch must agree with the mail trains and I'm always on time—No matter what other clocks or watches say this little beauty tells me to the second just how long I can keep pecking away with my pen."

Winsor McCay

Sen O Rok Watches
for ACCURATE TIME KEEPING

SEN-O-ROK WATCH CO., SWITZERLAND-NEW YORK.

In the 1920s, McCay appeared in an advertisement endorsing Sen-O-Rok wristwatches, billed as "America's Great Cartoonist." The copy is supposed to be a McCay quote: "Us fellows like to work up to the last minute until the Engravers holler—I never have a quarrel with them for my Sen-O-Rok Wrist Watch never lies—my work is sent out all over the country and my watch must agree with the mail trains and I'm always on time—No matter what other clocks or watches say this little beauty tells me to the second just how long I can keep pecking away with my pen." (Collection Janet Trinker)

RIGHT:

McCay, third from left, and others pose (c.1932) in front of an 1872 statue of Benjamin Franklin holding a copy of his Pennsylvania Gazette *at Printing House Square in lower Manhattan. The area (the intersection of Park Row, Nassau, and Spruce Streets) was where several newspapers were published, including the* Times, Sun, Herald, Tribune *and* World.

BELOW:

Winsor McCay (far right) looks on at a ceremony involving New York Mayor Jimmy Walker (third from right), c. late 1920s or early 1930s. (Collection Janet Trinker)

Top left spread

MR. BING

Where its always Winter and Snow,
Balls grow on Trees and Icicles hang from Noses!

Good Skating and ~~Coasting~~ Coasting in the Parks — Nice cold ICE on the Sea shores.

Hotel St. George

Dearest Ray, Marion and Boon,

This place shook like the proverbial dog last night from an earthquake — There was lots of Excite — Helen phoned for Mom and was greatly frightened — on

Top right spread

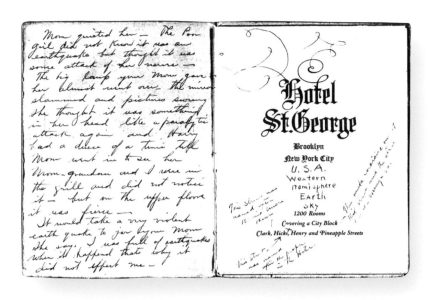

Mom quieted her — The Poor girl did not know it was an earthquake but thought it was some attack of her nerves — The big lamp your Mom gave her almost went over the mirror slammed and pictures swung she thought it was something in her head like a paralytic attack again and Harry had a deuce of a time till Mom went in to see her Mom-grandma and I were in the grill and did not notice it — but on the upper floors it was fierce — It would take a very violent earthquake to jar your Mom she says. I was full of earthquakes when it happened that why it did not effect me —

Hotel St. George

Brooklyn
New York City
U.S.A.
Western
Hemisphere
Earth
Sky
1200 Rooms
Covering a City Block
Clark, Hicks, Henry and Pineapple Streets

Middle left spread

This is not funny! — Sam Freestone was horribly hurt — nearly every bone in his body being broken — Clipping Enclosed — It is really awful may not live — fear his skull is fractured — Dr. Nash reported from the Hospital it will be a year if ever that he will recover and get out. Its tough on the whole family. They fear his shoulder blades have pierced his lungs a His legs are driven through his skin — (the bones of his legs I mean) Bob phoned today that he his terribly hurt — Well Such is life — No never know! — Poor Sam!

Sheepshead Bay — & Peekskill

Hotel St. George

is located in one of the few remaining aristocratic sections of Old New York.

I should worry

The St. George is only four minutes from Wall Street and fifteen minutes from Times Square. and 3 days from our Darling in Miama

The Clark Street station of the Interboro 7th Avenue Subway is in the building, giving direct access to all railroad, steamship and other transit lines. and other places when we don't go except speak easys

Here is a refined home in dignified surroundings, offering delightful living conditions within the means of even a modest budget. — budget means money — modest means small — If there is any virtue in modesty of Budgets then we are pure — Our Budgets are very modest — too modest and shy — I wish they were iridescent lewed and obscene naughty and Rotten

Middle right spread

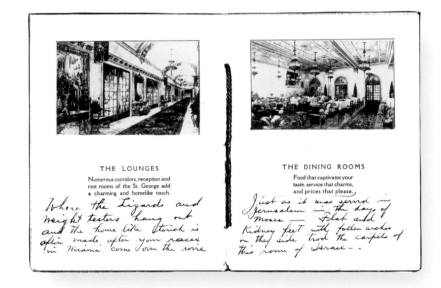

THE LOUNGES
Numerous corridors, reception and rest rooms of the St. George add a charming and homelike touch.

Where the Lizard and weight testers hang out and the home like touch is often made after your races in Miami come over the wire

THE DINING ROOMS
Food that captivates your taste, service that charms, and prices that please.

Just as it was served in Jerusalem in the days of Moses — Filat and Kidney feet with fallen arches on the side trod the carpets of this room of Israel —

Bottom left spread

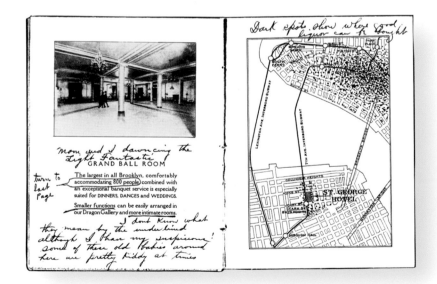

Mom and I dancing the Light Fantastic
GRAND BALL ROOM

The largest in all Brooklyn, comfortably accommodating 800 people, combined with an exceptional banquet service is especially suited for DINNERS, DANCES and WEDDINGS.

Smaller functions can be easily arranged in our Dragon Gallery and more intimate rooms.

turn to last page

I dont know what they mean by the underlined although I have my suspicions! Some of these old babies around here are pretty kiddy at times

Dark spots show where good liquor can be bought

ST. GEORGE HOTEL

Bottom right spread

Mom says to secure your reservations now — and be quick about it — We have not decided yet if any of us can come down or not yet — But at any rate we want you back as soon as it is safe — Today the weather here is Rotten Cold

MANAGEMENT
BING & BING, Inc.
AND BANG

Wet!

On days like this we are happy to know you are there away from this — Well will soon see you and can hardly wait Kiss each other and Boonskee for you lonesome Pop & Mom

I didnt know it was an earthquake — I just thought it was the usual shock —

The service in this place is Rotten

DAMN IT!

Do I weigh all I say!!

there exactly 800 of them

[we] nosed around the place. And here was this ladder laying [sic] on a low stone fence that was the perimeter of the stone porch out in back. And that was the ladder [the kidnapper used] to go up to the window. One rung was sort of cracked. I got Winsor, who was a draftsman if there ever was one, to draw a good picture of it."[36]

He sketched the house, the grounds, broken ladders found nearby, and the personnel. A rough on-the-spot drawing appeared in the March 3, 1932, issue of the *American*. Prior to the Lindbergh story, Brisbane was exploiting strained American diplomatic relations with Japan by reminding readers (and using McCay's drawings to help do so) "about the cunning and the avarice of 'our little yellow brothers.'"

After the Lindbergh event, Brisbane seized the opportunity to moralize on crime and similar subjects. "His editors were ordered to print stories of kidnappings and murders of other days, thus fanning the flame of public indignation," wrote Oliver Carlson. "But it remained for Arthur Brisbane to conceive and execute the most disgraceful piece of journalism connected with the whole tragic affair. He scooped the country in interviewing Chicago's notorious gangland chief and racketeer, 'Scarface' Al Capone, in Cook County jail about the kidnapping." An eight-column headline announced: "Capone Asks for Release to Hunt Lindy Baby, Tells Brisbane He Will Seek No Reward."

For the rest of his days, McCay was resigned to his daily task of turning out editorial cartoons for the *American*. Katje de Gorog worked in the newspaper's business section on advertising contracts; she began at the Hearst organization when she was a teenager in the early 1930s and remained until the *Journal-American* folded in 1966:

> Everyone in the old days was terribly afraid of losing their jobs, because there was no union to protect you. The women were scared out of their wits. We could be fired on the whim of the bosses, who were hideous, awful!

Whenever Hearst visited the offices, the men acted like they had a ramrod up their backs. Everything was moved off of the desks, everyone looked very busy. Hearst would walk from the elevators down the hall past the secretaries and then the salesmen into the manager's office. He wouldn't say a thing, just have that horse-face and his eyes looking back and forth."[37]

To escape the oppressive atmosphere within the *American* building, employees from all areas—secretaries, editors, pressmen, truckers, and cartoonists—headed after work for the Rain House. According to Ms. de Gorog, the Rain House was "a broken-down, filthy bar that held a fascination for our crowd. They drank like fishes at the Rain House. The absences at work were something fearful. Many a Friday night, which was payday, many of us would enjoy ourselves at the Rain House. It was the only place to cash our checks since there were no banks, only tenements, on South Street."

The bar had no name when it was owned by a gangster who wore colorful socks and died a syphilitic. It passed into the hands of the Irish/German Graff brothers, Harry, Jim, and Al, who lived in the neighborhood. A leaky roof in the bar's loft inspired the *American's* editorial staff to name the place. The small establishment offered a generous lunch at moderate Depression prices, including corned beef and cabbage, goulash, baked ham, and hamburgers. After five o'clock P.M., a snack table was set up at the far end of the bar, where customers helped themselves to that staple of the Depression "the Free Lunch," which in this case consisted of salami and liverwurst sandwiches and lunch leftovers. The main attraction after work was the drinks at thirty-five and fifty cents apiece. On Friday nights, over forty newspeople packed the little place to "whoop it up!"

Stern-faced Mike, the Irish bartender, worried about the secretaries nursing sloe-gin fizzes and tried (without success) to make them stay by themselves in a little room off the bar, away from the men. Sonny Bradley, a four-foot-high truckdriver who delivered the newspapers, had "a voice like a fog horn and loved to burst into song." Since only top management at the *American* was allowed a free copy of the newspaper (employees were expected to buy their own), Sonny Bradley made sure a bundle of papers would "fall off the truck" on Friday, so he could distribute them to the Rain House crowd.

Winsor McCay was a popular personage at the Rain House because of his elfin charm and generosity. "He'd walk in," recalled Ms. de Gorog, "put some greenbacks down on the bar and say, 'Drinks all around!'" McCay himself drank very little, preferring to "nurse one drink for hours." Sometimes he would ask for a jigger of water and with each sip of the whiskey, he would pour some water from the jigger into the whiskey to dilute it.

"He was as strange a man as I ever saw," remarked one bartender, "and absolutely the strangest drinker I ever served":

> He could sip a drink longer than any man I ever served. He always had a party with him and each one of them drank about five drinks to his one. But he insisted on being served a drink on every round. And it was nothing at all to see seven or eight drinks lined up in front of him. He would never gulp a drink down or even hurry to catch up with his friends. He'd sip, sip, sip. Naturally, when he'd leave the place, there'd be from six to ten untouched drinks on the bar. And it got to be quite a racket for the bums that hang around here to watch him like a vulture. The minute he left the bar, they'd rush up and snatch the free drinks. He drank often, but never much. And he never came into my place until he had finished his work for the day. He knew how to drink all right. He could handle his liquor like he handled his pen—plenty smart.[38]

Ms. de Gorog felt McCay came to the Rain House because "he wanted to be away from the office, not to drink." McCay enjoyed the camaraderie and fun of the place. "I remember 'Winn' McCay well," said Ms. de Gorog:

> He looked much older than he was by ten years, but he was spry and very dashing looking, and he always carried a portfolio. He always wore a scarf and a slouch hat like an artist and carried a cane, more for effect because he really didn't need it. He never mentioned his wife, but always his daughter. "I gotta meet my daughter," he'd say at the end of an evening.
>
> On holidays, Winn might climb on top of the bar to recite. On the Fourth of July, he would stand and declaim patriotic poems, or the *Star-Spangled Banner* with wild gestures, everything going! On Thanksgiving, he might recite something about a turkey or the American flag. Course at Christmastime, he would do "The Night before Christmas," and I remember him stamping his feet on the bar imitating Santa's reindeer. After he finished, people would applaud loudly and he would jump off the bar to the floor—by himself!

In order to relax at home, McCay avidly read poetry, novels, and plays, which inspired him to fill his diaries with experimental dialogue from futuristic dramas of his own invention. He could quote the Bible and Shakespeare as well as Brisbane, and he knew Shelley and Keats and particularly admired Yeats. "There's no race on this earth that can write lyric poetry that sings except the Irish," wrote McCay in his diary, Christmas 1928. ". . . And Yeats has poured genius into the Irish Sea until now its flood-level

A MERRY CHRISTMAS HAPPY NEW YEAR

RAYMOND
WINSOR
MONIZ

MAJOR
RAYMOND T.
MONIZ

MRS. MAJ.
RAYMOND T.
MONIZ

WINSOR
McCAY
THE KID HIMSELF

MRS.
WINSOR
McCAY

waters threaten to engulf the birthplace of Shakespeare with every wave . . . . There is no doubt in my mind that 'The Tower' represents the finest poetry of the 20th century. I don't think the powers that be will recognize the importance of this work in this generation. But historians will certainly sing its praises a century from now."

McCay took joy in his family. He and Maude may have had their problems, but after forty-three years of marriage (in 1934) he had come to depend on her as much as she did on him. After their children married, Winsor and Maude were rarely alone. On Fridays, Marion and her son would drive down from Peekskill, meet Winsor at the Rain House after work, and spend the weekend in Sheepshead Bay, later to be joined by Ray Moniz, Sr. Robert and Tedda McCay and their children, Janet and Robert, lived down the block and would often drop by and stay over, so a constant family reunion kept the McCay brood close. At holiday gatherings, Winsor would sometimes look over his family and chuckle to himself, "Lookit my wonderful, crazy family!"[39]

Winsor was adored by his grandchildren and their young cousins. Janet McCay Trinker remembers, "He was like a child himself of about eight or ten years old."[40] Ray Winsor Moniz recalls the gentle way

Winsor helped him overcome his fear of the dark. His grandfather took the boy's hand and led him through the darkened rooms of the house on Voorhies Avenue. As they came to a mysterious object or shape, Winsor would comment about what horrible thing it might possibly be. Then he would shine a flashlight on the "beast," and it became a chair or a sofa or a vase.[41]

Dorothy Noonan, Maude's niece, remembers watching McCay for hours "drawing the political cartoons in the third-floor studio of the house, where there was also a movie projector to screen his films."[42]

Janet Trinker "loved to stay overnight at Pop and Nan's [Winsor and Maude's] house during school vacations. Winsor helped pay for my schooling. I loved to play with the big sliding doors in the house and watch my grandfather draw and to talk with him for hours. When I would visit him at his winter quarters at the Hotel St. George, he would tell the elevator operator that his granddaughter wanted to run the elevator. And for a few wonderful moments I would!"

Mrs. Trinker said that McCay never talked down to children; since he was so in tune with a child's world, he did not find it necessary. "Once Pop took me to dinner at an Italian restaurant on Pineapple Street near his hotel in Brooklyn Heights. After din-

This grim image of the sad fate awaiting drug addicts was published three days before McCay's death on July 26, 1934. (Collection Ray Winsor Moniz)

A notice in the New York American *announcing what would be McCay's last public appearance, at the Society of Illustrators show on April 4, 1934.*

ner, I was intrigued by two women dining together who were smoking cigars. On reflection now, they must have been lesbians, but Pop's calm and simple explanation perfectly satisfied a child's curiosity."

The pampering that McCay's own children enjoyed was extended to his grandchildren. "Nan took me to Lord and Taylor," Mrs. Trinker remembered, "and bought me complete outfits: two Easter suits, including a periwinkle blue coat and bonnet, kid gloves and even a walking stick! Then we would go to the theater to see a show and then to Schraffts' for a malted and lunch. Of course everything was paid for by Winsor."[43]

McCay's fondness for nonsense words is demonstrated in a letter sent to his beloved grandson Ray Moniz, Jr., whose nickname was "Boon" or "Boonie." The following is a brief excerpt from a very long letter:

> My darling Boonie
> Etch ee buh uh eh ee heh
> Chee uh eh shi boo ah ee poo eh
> ish ee pu eh shi boo ah ee eh poo eh
> ish ee pu eh ja boo ah a ugh—
> Cha oh uh eh ba la ulla bulla poo
> alloo foo moo eh che eh a boo ooh chee ee!!
> . . . Eh eugh see moo chee ee
> Grand pa

On July 22, 1934, four days before McCay died, the *American* published a murky editorial cartoon by the artist entitled "A Great Industry Degraded." In it, the "Spirit of Clean Movies" shows Dante saying "there is no money in decency, honor, clean living" on our nation's motion picture screens. Instead, the "stuff for the box office" in this particular inferno is "crime, degeneracy, immorality, and adultery," represented by top-hatted high-livers in a tangle of bodies, shapely legs, petting couples, and booze.

On another page, an advertisement for the Post Toasties company featured Walt Disney's increasingly popular menagerie: Mickey and Minnie Mouse, Donald Duck, and Pluto the Pup in a sprightly plug for a series of cutouts on breakfast cereal boxes. One wonders how often McCay wished his Little Nemo or Gertie the Dinosaur were as popular with modern movie audiences as Disney's progeny, whose wholesome films belied the grim picture of the motion picture industry that McCay drew that day. McCay could not have known that in 1934 Disney was already planning a full-length animated feature that would build on McCay's animation principles and iconography and would fulfill his impossible dream of art in motion.

Three days before he died, McCay drew a dour cartoon about drug addicts. It featured Death as a ticket-seller in a perverse amusement park, where the midway leads to the madhouse, the penitentiary, and the cemetery. It is a strong, compelling drawing, with a vivid death's head as the focal point of the swirling crowds spilling through the gates. Did McCay have a premonition of his own swiftly approaching fate?

Excerpt from the McCay obituary in the Herald Tribune, *July 27, 1934.*

Products of Winsor McCay's Versatile Pen, and the Noted Cartoonist at Work

"A Selling Campaign," anti-Tammany cartoon which appeared on an editorial page of the New York Herald Tribune nine years ago

Winsor McCay drawing a "Little Nemo" comic strip in the Herald Tribune office in 1926. He habitually worked with hat and coat on

Characters drawn by Winsor McCay for his "Little Nemo in Slumberland," which appeared in the Herald Tribune Sunday comic section

Probably not. Two days before his death, McCay sent a gift check of twelve dollars to his daughter with a note full of sunny, childlike humor and silly code words for the hemorrhoid problem they shared:

> Hello fat face! How's your whois and your whatis in this hot weather? Old Mahatma Ghandi [sic] says to keep cool even if you have to fly backwards like the South American Ki-oola Bird that eats tobasco seeds.
> Pink eyed pop

Marion never cashed the check, and her brother never cashed the last check he received, twenty-five dollars for his birthday on June 21—final mementos from a generous, loving father.

Winsor McCay worked at his desk at the *American* as usual on Tuesday. The next evening he had dinner with a friend in Manhattan and showed no sign of illness. On Thursday, July 26, McCay appeared at the door of his wife's bedroom complaining of a pain in his head. Then he collapsed and cried out to Maude: "It's my right arm!"

His worst fear—that one day he would lose the power to draw and thus his means of survival—had become a terrible reality. "It's gone, Mother. Gone! Gone! Gone!" he cried.[44]

He lost conciousness as the paralysis spread from his arm to his face. Soon he was in a coma and remained so until late afternoon. The artist's wife, son, daughter, and son-in-law were at his side when Dr. Philip I. Nash pronounced Winsor McCay dead of a massive cerebral hemorrhage at 4:40 P.M.

chapter 10. after mccay

"I'm lost! Mama! I'm lost! Oh! I am lost!"

—LITTLE NEMO, SEPTEMBER 22, 1907

Masonic and Elk funeral services were held for Winsor McCay in the ground-floor study fronting the

porch of his house in Sheepshead Bay. The mahogany coffin was banked with flowers from friends and

professional colleagues, including William Randolph Hearst, Sr., and his son, the American Society of

Illustrators, the editorial staff of the *American*, members of the composing room, E. D. Coblentz, the

paper's editor, and Joseph V. Connolly, editor of King Features Syndicate.

Floral pieces were sent by the local restaurants Lundy Brothers and Villepigue's, and by Brooklyn

Lodge 22 B.P.O.E., the Royal and Mystic Order of the Elephant's Nest, fraternal organization of the

Brooklyn Navy Yard, and the Cavalry Post 101 of the American Legion.[1]

Telegrams poured in to the grieving family from friends and fans of the artist all over the country,

and lengthy obituaries appeared in many national newspapers. In the July 27 "Today" column, Arthur

Brisbane wrote his tribute: "[McCay] was an unequaled

craftsman in his chosen field. . . . During his continuous

years of activity, he became known in every household as a

comic artist of quaint humor, as a crusader for just causes and

as an illustrator in whose pieces often appeared stark and

compelling qualities that were Düreresque in both conception

and execution." On August 1 Brisbane rehired Mel Cummin

to fill McCay's place at the *American*. (Brisbane died soon

after McCay, on Christmas Day, 1936.)

McCay's coffin was interred in a concrete underground casing in the family plot in a verdant section of

the Evergreens Cemetery called "The Lawn." The plot already contained the remains of Sarah Dufour

Johns, McCay's mother-in-law, who died in 1923, and her daughter, Estelle Grant, who died in 1929.

One account described Maude McCay to be "in a state bordering upon collapse," and relatives recall

that Marion Moniz "cried hysterically throughout the ordeal." At one point, Tedda McCay recalled, someone close to the family told the grieving daughter, "Oh, Marion! Stop crying. Look at all the money you're going to get."

As it turned out, however, McCay had few cash assets when he died. His savings account at City Savings in Brooklyn contained $5,000, and a checking account at Brooklyn Trust in the bay held $2,922.10. He had a bond and mortgage for $2,000 on two premises in Brooklyn's 31st Ward, and he owned three other mortgaged houses: his own and two two-story brick dwellings nearby (one inhabited by Robert McCay and his family). Market value on the properties was $31,000.[2]

McCay was actually worth more dead than alive, for the bulk of his estate was a $100,000 Travelers life insurance policy.[3] And there was another surprise: McCay did not leave a will. Or rather, none was ever found; and on September 7, 1934, a petition was filed with Kings County (Brooklyn) Surrogate's Court by Maude L. McCay "for Letters of Administration of the Goods, Chattels and Credits which were of Winsor Z. McCay." But, according to Tedda McCay, "there *was* a will left, but it was not used!" McCay specified trust funds be set up for his widow and family to provide each with a modest but steady annual income.

"A long time after," said Tedda McCay, "when the money had all dribbled away, my mother-in-law Maude asked me, 'Tedda, what would you have done?' I said, 'A human being left a will. I think it should have been used. That was his wish!' And she said, 'I wish I had taken your advice.'"[4]

Winsor McCay's gross estate before taxes, administration, and attorney's fees was little more than $140,000. "I thought the man was a millionaire," said family friend Murray Tynan, expressing the thoughts of many who assumed the same after observing the lavish lifestyle of the McCays.

Maude did not alter that lifestyle after Winsor died. Although the $30,000 share of the estate she inherited was a goodly amount for those mid-Depression years, it did not last long in Maude's hands. "She spent it like Winsor was still alive to make more," commented one relative. By the early 1940s, she was forced to sell the Voorhies Avenue place and move into an apartment

house on St. John's Street, which was a gift from an admirer (the owner of a Coney Island bathhouse and a high-rolling racetrack bettor). Maude lived on the third floor above another apartment and a drill hall used by Irish clog dancers, both of which she rented out.

Once again she went through all of her money from the house sale and was taken into her daughter's home in Peekskill, where her strong personality often clashed with her son-in-law, the equally blunt Ray Moniz. On March 2, 1949, Maude excused herself from a Sunday roast beef dinner, fainted on the stairs to her room, and died of a heart attack in the arms of her grandson Ray, Jr. She is buried next to Winsor in the Evergreens.

Robert McCay inherited his mother's cavalier attitude toward legal tender and was struggling with his own money problems soon after Winsor's death. "They thought money grew on trees," said Robert's widow, Tedda. "Maude would call up and say, 'Bobbie, I'm going down to the bank.' She'd draw out $2,000 every Saturday. 'Bob, why don't you draw out a thousand, too?' And he'd do it! A friend said to me, 'Tedda, I wish you could get that checkbook away from Bob.' Once he told me to look out the front door. I thought he'd had the Packard painted, but it was a new one. He said, 'Nan [Maude] bought a new Packard and told me to buy one, too!'"[5]

Robert's financial woes increased in the fall of 1936: returning from a steeplechase in Maryland with a friend, he was involved in a three-car accident that resulted in the death of two people. A subsequent lawsuit proved devastating to McCay's already precarious finances.

Robert McCay made many unsuccessful attempts to follow in his father's gigantic professional footsteps. His daughter, Janet Trinker, recalled that Robert "adored Winsor and was pleased to have been his Little Nemo. He wanted desperately to be an artist, but he was better at a more painterly art, rather than the fine, detailed work that Winsor excelled at."[6] Robert worked briefly for the Hearst papers, and he offered his services to the Disney studio during World War II. Walt Disney himself gently turned him down, explaining truthfully that he was firing rather than hiring during those lean years when his studio survived on training and propaganda films for the war effort.

Robert McCay eventually settled in northern California and worked as an illustrator in Training Aids/Special Services at Fort Ord until he died of cancer on April 21, 1962. His sister, Marion, died of the same ailment at Peekskill on April 2, 1965.

Shortly before Maude moved from the Voorhies Avenue house, there was a fire in the living room that slightly damaged some of a large collection of Winsor McCay's original artwork, film negatives, and prints. The collection was a formidable one, for Winsor requested all of his work be returned to him after publication. Included were items going back to his Cincinnati days: *Life* magazine illustrations, hundreds of episodes from all of his comic strips, editorial cartoons, animation drawings, and about 100 cans of film.

Maude did not know what to do with the material and was not capable of looking after it. On occasion, neighbors rescued fugitive pieces of the art, perhaps a *Nemo* or *Rarebit Fiend* strip, as it blew down Voorhies Avenue. After the fire, Robert McCay agreed to take the entire collection to his house for storage.

It should be noted that at the time original drawings used in the making of newspaper comic strips were not considered "great art." To the publishers they were only an intermediate stage to the ultimate goal: publication. After that, original drawings diminished in value in the eyes of editors and publishers and were as useless as old news. Drawings were returned to the artist, thrown away or occasionally given away to fans.

The perception of cartoons as a radical variation on fine art did not attract serious attention from the art world until the 1960s. Until that happened, original drawings used for comic strips and animation were short-lived mayflies: useful for reproduction but eminently disposable.

The family of Winsor McCay regarded the collection of his artwork with nostalgic affection. It was a souvenir, a tangible remembrance of their beloved "Pop." In a way, it became Winsor McCay for them, and so the family took care to keep as much of the art

intact as possible. But just as Winsor used his art to generate funds for the survival of the family, so it was after his death.

In March 1937, the Harry "A" Chesler Syndicate announced a revived version of *Little Nemo in Slumberland* to be released on May 15 to interested newspapers. The strip would be drawn by "Winsor McCay Jr. [sic]," who would also draw a black-and-white daily strip starring Impie. The original *Nemo* characters were to be joined by a new one, "Dino," a pet dinosaur for the Imp. McCay was quoted as saying, "My one ambition is to carry on my father's name."

Chesler also published *Star Comics* and *Star Ranger*, both comic magazines in four colors, distributed by Macfadden. McCay drew a *Nemo in Adventureland* strip for the comic book format, featuring a grown-up Nemo and Princess. "When the era of the comic book began in the late 1930s," wrote James Steranko, "Harry 'A' Chesler was one of the men who helped fashion a life for the colorful new form. . . . Chesler employed a staff of artists and writers . . . from young kids who loved comics to older, syndicated newspaper strip men who couldn't find a job anywhere else."[7]

McCay's association with Chesler proved short-lived, and by the mid-1940s, Robert formed the McCay Feature Syndicate, Inc., with Irving Mendelsohn, a fabric salesman and sincere, long-time admirer of Winsor McCay and his work. In 1947, the pair managed to interest C. R. Richardson of the Richardson Feature Syndicate in yet another revival of *Little Nemo in Slumberland,* this time using the original artwork. In order to make the large-size original art fit into a modern newspaper format, Robert cut out panels and rearranged a number of his father's old *Nemo* strips and pasted new dialogue balloons over old ones. This desperate, ghastly, sacrificial mutilation of the original art for the purpose of earning cash was mercifully brief. Once again, the revived strip failed.

Also in 1947, C. R. Richardson, acting as "sales agent" for the McCay family, sent a letter to actor James Cagney in Hollywood suggesting he use his newly formed production company to mount and star in a film biography of Winsor McCay, with the artist's son as consultant. No such film was ever made, and a book biography of Winsor, commissioned by Robert McCay from Padraic O'Glasain, a newspaper crony, was written but never published.

Robert moved to California and entrusted the bulk of his father's original art into Irving Mendelsohn's care, except for a few items sold for quick cash or bartered for favors. In the early 1960s, Mendelsohn returned most of the original drawings to Marion Moniz; the bulk of the art of Winsor McCay remains in the family's possession, with occasional pieces loaned for gallery exhibits or sold through comic art dealers and galleries.

The survival of Winsor McCay's films has its own strange history. Robert McCay burned the contents of some film cans in his possession in the Brooklyn city dump in an effort to create space for the entire collection of McCay works, both film and paper. The rest were given to Irving Mendelsohn, along with the drawings. Over the years, Mendelsohn carted the art and films from Brooklyn to his fabric loft on White Street in Manhattan and finally to his home on Long Island.

In 1947, Mendelsohn's son Jack, a young animator, brought to the Long Island house a friend named Robert N. Brotherton (1925–1989). Twenty-two-year-old Brotherton had recently formed Television Cartoons Inc., one of the first studios to produce animated television commercials. He was knowledgeable about the history of animation, and when he heard that Jack Mendelsohn's father had original films by Winsor McCay, Brotherton was "eager to take a look at them."

Mendelsohn took the two young men out to his garage, and there, from floor to ceiling in a corner, were about 100 rusting film cans. "I opened one," Brotherton told this author, "and saw it was turning to powder. These were old 35mm nitrate films. When that stuff deteriorates, it first turns to jelly, then to powder, and then watch out—it explodes! It's highly flammable, so I asked Irving to fill a barrel with water. All afternoon and part of the next morning I looked through every can. Most were rotten and I threw those immediately into the waterbarrel. I managed to save around sixty cans. Most were prints of *Gertie,* but there were examples of all of McCay's animations represented, including the hand-colored *Little Nemo.* Some films, like the second *Gertie [Gertie on Tour],* I could only save a small amount of footage and a few representative frames."

One discarded film was "an original negative to a film entitled *Performing Animals.* Hand examination showed that the animals were playing musical instruments," recalled Brotherton of a film that may have been a test of a planned cartoon for McCay's vaudeville act. "In connection with this negative, there was an incomplete positive reel in a very early stage of decomposition." Both were destroyed.

Brotherton convinced Mendelsohn that "something had to be done" to preserve these seminal works from disappearing. "We needed editing rooms to air the footage, inspect it and remove the deteriorating parts. And we needed storage rooms at controlled temperatures to keep the films. Irving agreed to put up his own money for this."

Before that happened, Robert McCay had 16mm reduction prints and negatives made at his own expense in 1947. Duplicate negatives and positives of

BELOW LEFT:
Winsor McCay's tombstone in the Evergreens Cemetery in Brooklyn, New York. (Collection John Canemaker)

BELOW RIGHT:
McCay's grave marker, below his tombstone, uses his signature, but the birthdate is erroneous. (Collection John Canemaker)

Little Nemo, Gertie, and some of the *Rarebit Fiend* series were made in a Long Island laboratory and taken by Robert to the West Coast. "It was understood," said Brotherton, "by Mendelsohn and myself that MGM was to look into the idea of doing a *Passing Parade* short for that John Nesbitt series about famous people and incidents. This never came to pass. Those 16s are most likely lying in the basement of the studio at the present time, overlooked and forgotten about."

Thus began a twenty-year tragicomic odyssey in which Mendelsohn and Brotherton were thrown out of editing rooms and storage houses when it was learned the film treasures they were tending were made of nitrate.[8] In the middle of the amateur conservators' misadventures, a tribute was paid to Winsor McCay on national television.

On November 30, 1955, on the *Disneyland* television series, Walt Disney included a dramatization of McCay's vaudeville act with *Gertie the Dinosaur,* on a program called "The Story of the Animated Drawing." Writer Richard Huemer had witnessed McCay's act years before, and, with Robert McCay acting as the segment's consultant, he was able to reproduce for the actor who played McCay the exact dialogue and movements of the artist (cracking a whip, tossing an apple, and so forth). This historic overview of character animation was the first time a new generation had ever heard of Winsor McCay and *Gertie the Dinosaur.*

During Robert McCay's visit to the Disney Studio when the program was in preparation, Walt Disney acknowledged his debt, and that of all other character animators, to the experiments and films of Winsor McCay. He gestured out the window toward his bustling studio complex and said, "Bob, all this should be your father's."[9]

Meanwhile, back in New York, some McCay nitrate films caught fire in a couple of storage vaults, destroying more of the material and again getting Mendelsohn and Brotherton into trouble. Finally help arrived, but not from an American museum or a grant from the United States government. These rare film masterpieces, the beginnings of the art of American character animation, were rescued by Canada. (As Maurice Sendak has observed, America "still doesn't take its great fantasists all that seriously.")

The 1967 World Animation Film Exposition in Montreal and La Cinémathèque québécoise tracked down the McCay films and offered Mendelsohn and Brotherton the chance to have the troublesome nitrates preserved on safety film and stored properly. This the two men gratefully allowed. And so the complete 35mm filmography of Winsor McCay resides today in Montreal at La Cinémathèque québécoise.

Robert Brotherton was also directly responsible for the preservation of the largest amount of animation drawings by McCay known to survive: over four hundred of the original *Gertie the Dinosaur* drawings. "Irving wanted to give me a gift," explained Brotherton, "for helping him with the films. So he told me to go up to the loft of his fabric shop on White Street. There on the floor—I'll never forget it— strewn from one end of the loft to the other among bolts of fabric, were all these *Gertie* drawings. Irving said to take whatever I wanted, so I spent the entire afternoon picking up every one."[10]

Simultaneously with the planning of the showing of McCay's films at the Canadian Animation Expo, New York's Metropolitan Museum of Art presented an exhibition entitled *Two Fantastic Draftsmen,* in the winter of 1966. Prepared by curator of prints A. Hyatt Mayor, it featured the cartoons of Winsor McCay and a contemporary, Herbert Crowley.

The McCay family provided original art from their collection for the exhibit, including *Nemo* and *Rarebit Fiend* strips and editorial cartoons. *New York Times* art critic John Canaday pronounced Nemo "far and away the star of the show," and although it was the first time Canaday had ever seen the strip, he noted that Little Nemo "has continued to hold a band of admirers and also to attract new ones through the pages that a few people were foresighted enough to clip and save."

Canaday also mused in his review about "the exceptional strength of the popular arts in the twentieth century and our unjustifiable condescension to the best of them as nothing more than amusing trifles. It took us a long time to discover jazz as important music and the movies as important theater, and the only thing we have done with the comic strip is to take it at its worst and further cheapen it by adaptation to the second-rate, giggling pseudo-estheticism of pop art."[11]

In 1968, *A History of the Comic Strip* was published in conjunction with an exhibition of comic-strip art at the musée des Arts décoratifs at the Louvre. The book, which had six authors including Pierre Couperie and Maurice Horn, isolated Winsor McCay as "the greatest innovator of the age [who] belongs within the great intellectual and esthetic current leading from Brueghel to the surrealists."

In the spring of 1971, the University of Maryland Art Gallery presented an exhibition titled *The Art of the Comic Strip,* featuring McCay's work, with a text and catalogue by then Museum Training Fellow Judith O'Sullivan, who in 1976 presented her PhD thesis *The Art of Winsor Z. McCay* to the University of Maryland.

In 1972, comic collector and publisher Woody Gelman used dozens of color tearsheets of the strip *Little Nemo in Slumberland,* acquired from Irving Mendelsohn, to produce a lavish book of that "incomparable work of art," entitled *Little Nemo* (published by Nostalgia Press and printed in Milan). The book played a major role in reviving interest in Winsor McCay and his art.

In 1974, the author of the present work produced an informational film, *Remembering Winsor McCay,* narrated on-camera by eighty-four-year-old John A. Fitzsimmons, McCay's film assistant. The film includes *Gertie the Dinosaur,* excerpts from *The Sinking of the Lusitania,* and the hand-colored version of *Little Nemo,* and it has been screened on CBS, PBS, BBC, as well as by a number of international film festivals and archives, and is now available on the DVD *Winsor McCay: The Master Edition.*

In 1975, in cooperation with Louise Beaudet, head of the Animation Division of La Cinémathèque québécoise, this author arranged and coordinated the first Winsor McCay film retrospective in the United States at the 3rd International Animation Film Festival in New York (September 30–October 4, 1975). The show attracted the interest of John Hanhardt, head of film and video at the Whitney Museum of American Art, who asked the coordinator to prepare a McCay film show there from December 28, 1975, through January 6, 1976.

Media attention to the Whitney show was intense and focused on the rediscovery of a long-overlooked American genius. "Winsor McCay," wrote Andrew Sarris in the *Village Voice,* "was more a pioneer than a primitive, and more a full-fledged artist than either. I had no idea that McCay had achieved so much in animation so early."[12]

Richard Eder of the *New York Times* wrote that "some lovely directions were sealed off when Walt Disney made his particular style into a national monument . . . [and Winsor McCay's films are] one of the loveliest, strangest and most hallucinatory of these lost stretches . . . ." Eder found a wistfulness in *Gertie* that "Disney lost and struggled mightily to recapture," but he thought McCay's films were most gripping "in their revelations of how much menace can be conveyed very directly by animation . . . . Disney's magic, though sometimes scary, was always contained; McCay's approached necromancy." To view McCay's total film output, explained Eder, was to realize "the peculiar nature of McCay's dead end [in animation, for] like William Blake's [vision], it was too strange and personal to be generalized or to have children."[13]

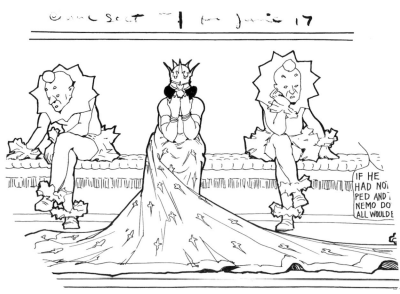

McCay established the iconography and techniques of modern character animation which were developed by others, primarily, of course, Walt Disney. If he had lived to see it, McCay would most likely have approved of Disney's 1940 concert feature, *Fantasia,* in which his dream of painting in motion was fulfilled. He would applaud the closed-form caricatures of animals, the feeling of weight in their natural movements, and realistic timing. He would admire the excellent draftsmanship in the rendering of the characters, the use of color, and the dynamic layouts and detailed backgrounds. He would undoubtedly be delighted to find character designs that were direct descendents of his early films: the centaurs and "centaurettes," for example, cavorting beneath Mount Olympus, and the anthropomorphised Gertie-like dinosaurs, some of whom engage in the kind of battle McCay talked about in 1912.

McCay's vaudeville act with Gertie the Dinosaur inspired a generation of American animators, including Paul Terry, Max and Dave Fleischer, Pat Sullivan, Vladimir Tytla, Otto Messmer, Richard Huemer, Shamus Culhane, I. Klein, and Walter Lantz, among others. McCay's international reputation and the worldwide distribution of his animated films also inspired a number of European artists.

Author Torsten Jungstedt confirms this in his 1973 book *Captain Grog and His Friends:*

> McCay must have influenced the Swedish animators [Victor] Bergdahl and [Emil] Aberg in two ways. Partly through his newspaper serials, which by 1915–16 had been reprinted all over the world, especially his *Little Nemo.* And McCay also influenced Swedish animators

through his own extremely careful, polished animations. Bergdahl mentioned one of these films, which he must have seen in the Stockholm cinema Orientaliska Teatern [in] early 1912 and which he called *Slumberland.* He studied it carefully and got from it some kind of instruction in how to start his own animation . . . the McCay animation of *How a Mosquito Operates* . . . clearly influenced the mysterious M. R. Liljeqvist in his *Negern och hunden* (1915–16).

Chuck Jones, the celebrated director of Warner Brothers cartoon shorts, creator of the Roadrunner and Coyote characters, and a developer of the personalities of Bugs Bunny, Porky Pig, and Elmer Fudd, once mused about Winsor McCay's uncannily advanced techniques: "It is as though the first creature to emerge from the primeval slime was Albert Einstein; and the second was an amoeba, because after McCay's animation it took his followers nearly twenty years to find out how he did it. The two most important people in animation are Winsor McCay and Walt Disney, and I'm not sure which should go first."[14]

Like his pioneering work in animation, Winsor McCay's great accomplishments in the comic strip field also led the way, inspiring those who followed.

Milton Caniff, whose impressionistic graphics revitalized the style of newspaper adventure strips with *Terry and the Pirates,* begun in 1934, recalled:

> When my grandfather read the Sunday comics aloud, I thought Winsor McCay's work was about real people (as in a photograph), while *Mutt and Jeff* and the others had been drawn by a cartoonist.
>
> Like all other aspiring young artists, I copied every drawing in the newspapers (rather than the magazines). I think I leaned also toward the story features, rather than the jokes. No other cartoonist of the day approached McCay's skill in holding the reader. The dream device is one I use today in *Steve Canyon.* It gives me a change of pace and the license to twist reality into my own Walter Mitty hallucinations.

In Hillsboro, Ohio, where Caniff was born in 1907, a friend who owned the village's only out-of-town-newspaper rack allowed young Caniff to "read the cartoons in copies he held back for special customers. I quickly soaked up the work of Donahey in the *Cleveland Plain Dealer,* Ireland in the *Columbus Dispatch,* and, of course, all the bright stars in the *Cincinnati Enquirer, Commercial Appeal,* and *Post.*

"None of these men attained the international stature of Winsor McCay, and I am grateful for the art education he gave a kid in the boondocks—without ever knowing the young man was enrolled in his class."[15]

Burne Hogarth, a founder of the School of Visual Arts and the artist of the dynamically drawn Sunday comic strip *Tarzan,* once asked, "Who, on looking at this kind of monumental effort, could fail to be enamored and taken over by them? McCay is not someone a cartoonist would lightly gloss over or put aside. In my view, he stands very high with the great figures of this 20th century art form."

Hogarth, like McCay, brought incredible vitality to figures in action and an expressionistic cinematic composition to his adventure strips; he believes McCay's *Little Nemo in Slumberland* was:

> . . . a remarkable development of the comic idiom, setting a high watermark in style and content. He did not hesitate to draw any subject in the world, from complicated artifacts, contraptions, inventions, conveyances, to large-scale perspectives, city views, panoramas and distant viewscapes of great complexity; these with animals, peoples of great variety, and actions and points of view, which frequently introduced a vertiginous aspect and feeling into his remarkable panels. Frequently, one had to turn a page in a number of directions to get the true "feel" and wealth of surreal illusionism he implied and introduced. Panels linked into panels as he developed enormously imposing interiors.

Hogarth "wonders at this kind of virtuosity. Where did the ideas come from—the architectural dramaturgy of Piranesi, Robert?—Rococo/Romantic Picturesque? And later, McCay becomes an editorial cartoonist for Hearst and Brisbane, with his powerful, detailed, smashing, painstaking style—big figures, cross-hatch, strong blacks. There is no credible figure today who can match this kind of output and intense artistic zeal."[16]

Some of the 400-plus original Gertie the Dinosaur drawings. Except for a few cels from the Lusitania film, no other McCay animation drawings are known to survive.

In the satiric strip *Doonesbury,* cartoonist Garry Trudeau shares the iconoclastic sense of humor that Winsor McCay displayed in *Dreams of the Rarebit Fiend.* But in writing about McCay, Trudeau is most impressed by the "validity of nonordinary reality" in McCay's work, particularly in:

> the quintessential cartoon fantasy of Slumberland in *Little Nemo* [where] a small boy dropped off to sleep and the tiniest objects of his day were transformed into the wondrous vehicles of his nights. In his dreams, Nemo floated on a milkweed seed, toppled from a colossal mushroom, and was whisked away in an ivory coach drawn by cream-colored rabbits. The scale of the objects corresponded to the importance that the boy attached to them—hence, giant raspberries and miniature furniture. Through it all, the value of Slumberland established itself through its contribution to the child's experience, and when the excitement of the vision deposited him, as it always did, in a jumble of sheets on the hardwood floor beside his bed, it was only the artist's implicit assurance that Nemo would have other dreams to explore that kept away the disappointment.[17]

Another modern cartoonist, Berke Breathed, creator of the zany *Bloom County,* discovered Winsor McCay and Little Nemo after he had "gotten into the stripper business. To say that I was blown away by the quality of the art would be a shameful understatement. Blown away with the art and blown away with the fact that newspapers once featured artists of such amazing refinement. Probably more than anything else, McCay makes me angry . . . angry that, if he were working today, there'd be no place on the American comic page for his talent . . . unless one accepts the microscopic space currently allotted to comics as any space at all."[18]

Since the original publication of this biography in 1987, original art from McCay's comic strips and films was exhibited in *Dreams in Motion* at the Katonah Gallery in Katonah, New York, from June 5 to July 25, 1988. A feature-length animated film, *Little Nemo: Adventures In Slumberland* (1990) produced by Tokyo Movie Shinsha, received mixed reviews, and quickly disappeared.

In 1991, the Library of Congress selected McCay's classic 1914 film *Gertie the Dinosaur* for preservation in the National Film Registry.[19]

2004 saw the release of a DVD titled *Winsor McCay: The Master Edition* from Milestone Film & Video.[20] It contains a refurbished and complete collection of McCay's existing films. Thus new technology assures that McCay's pioneering film works will amaze and amuse audiences in the 21st century and beyond.

Among the cartoon cognoscenti, Winsor McCay is king, and rightfully so. As fantasist, draftsman, observer, and reporter, satirist, innovator, and developer of new forms of communication, McCay must be ranked among the greatest figures of twentieth-century popular art. It is a pitiful irony, then, that this pioneer master of mass communication is virtually unknown to the public at large, and to many in the arts and communications fields as well.

That may be the ultimate paradox in the paradoxically torn life of Winsor McCay: the small man possessed of a large artistic gift whose output was superhuman; the master of fantasy who developed a social conscience; the bohemian with a wanderlust who became a classic bourgeois; the shy and private man who loved to perform on stage; the artist who embraced new technologies for reproducing his art, while remaining privately distrustful of modern machinery; the man who earned a fortune but lacked the business acumen to keep it; the visionary who never thought far enough ahead to provide substantial protection for himself in old age or his family after his death.

The one constant in the contradictory and hectic life of Winsor McCay was his implacable love of drawing. Throughout his life, he unknowingly practiced Ingres's advice to Degas: he drew many lines and in doing so became a good artist. The physical act of putting pencil or pen to paper—to use lines to separate the dark from the light, in order to make the invisible visible and reveal a private vision—filled McCay with a joy experienced only by other graphic artists.

Degas would have known and understood this delight. Indeed, McCay and Degas could have shared the epitaph Degas asked to be spoken at his burial: "He greatly loved drawing."

notes

CHAPTER 1. MICHIGAN YEARS

1. Catherine Bechard (Ontario Genealogical Society), letters to author, February 26 and August 12, 1985.
2. Ibid.
3. Bureau of the Census, *Twelfth Census of the United States* (Edmore Village, Montcalm County, Michigan, 1900), p. 212; Woodstock, Ontario, *Sentinel Review,* March 22, 1915.
4. Albert Baxter, *History of the City of Grand Rapids, Michigan* (New York and Grand Rapids: Munsell & Co., 1891), pp. 98–99.
5. Jim Van Vulpen, letter to author, March 25, 1985.
6. Letter from Robert McCay to "Winsor Maude Rob & Marion," dated August 27, 1905. Courtesy W. Robert McCay, Winsor McCay's great-grandson.
7. Padraic O'Glasain, "Winsor McCay: Little Nemo's Daddy," manuscript, 1941, collection of Janet Trinker, p. 220.
8. *Daily Wisconsin News,* May 22, 1923.
9. O'Glasain, "Winsor McCay: Little Nemo's Daddy," pp. 6–7.
10. Clare Briggs, *How to Draw Cartoons* (New York: Harper & Brothers, 1926), p. 118.
11. O'Glasain, op. cit., p. 24.
12. Ibid.
13. *Atlanta Constitution,* June 11, 1911.
14. *Daily Wisconsin News,* May 22, 1923.
15. Montgomery Phister, "People of the Stage: Winsor McCay," Cincinnati *Commercial Tribune,* November 28, 1909, Magazine section, p. 1.
16. *Pittsburgh Post,* December 19, 1912.
17. Mary S. Kitchel, *Spring Lake Community Centennial 1869–1969* (Spring Lake, Mich.: no publisher listed, 1969), p. 151.
18. Nancy Lynn Snyder, *Cleary College—One Hundred Years of Business* (Ypsilanti, Mich.: Cleary College, 1984), p. 25.
19. Kitchel, *Spring Lake Community Centennial,* p. 151.
20. Detroit newspaper clipping, c. 1912, collection of Janet Trinker.
21. Detroit Public Library, Burton Historical Collection, E&M 74D4/792 "Wonderland Theater."
22. Detroit Public Library
23. Ibid.
24. Ibid.
25. Ibid.
26. Winsor McCay, "Movie Cartoons," *Cartoon and Movie Magazine* 31 (April 1927), p. 11.
27. *Aurora 1893* (Yearbook of Michigan State Normal).
28. McCay, "Movie Cartoons," p. 11.
29. Ibid., pp. 11–12.
30. Ibid., p.11.
31. Ibid., p. 12.
32. Donald Crafton, *Before Mickey: The Animated Film 1898–1928* (Cambridge, Mass.: The MIT Press, 1982), p. 134.

CHAPTER 2. CHICAGO TO CINCINNATI

1. Charles F. Wuest, letter to McCay family, July 26, 1934, collection of Janet Trinker.
2. *New York Herald Tribune,* July 27, 1934.
3. Nicholas J. Quirk, letter to McCay family, July 1934, collection of Janet Trinker.
4. O'Glasain, op. cit., p. 29.
5. Richard Cavendish, *Man, Myth and Magic* (London: Marshall Cavendish Corporation, 1970), p. 1035.
6. John A. Fitzsimmons, interview with author, Rockville Center, N.Y., September 22, 1974.
7. Phister, "People of the Stage: Winsor McCay," p. 1.
8. *New York Herald Tribune,* July 27, 1934.
9. O'Glasain, op. cit., p. 31.
10. *Atlanta Constitution,* June 11, 1911.
11. Phister, op. cit., p. 1.
12. Ibid.
13. E. L. Hawes, "With Winsor McCay in Cincinnati," *Cincinnati Enquirer,* February 16, 1936.

CHAPTER 3. CINCINNATI YEARS

1. Phister, op. cit., p. 1.
2. O'Glasain, op. cit., p. 34.
3. Ibid., p. 31.
4. Ibid., p. 35.
5. Ibid., pp. 41–46.
6. Hawes, "With Winsor McCay in Cincinnati."
7. O'Glasain, op. cit. pp. 35–36.
8. Ray Moniz, interview with author, Highland Falls, N.Y., September 13, 1984.
9. Tedda McCay, interview with author, Pacific Grove, Ca., February 26, 1985.
10. "Marion Moniz As I Knew Her," unpublished remembrance by Maud H. Brown to author, 1987.
11. Phister, op. cit., p. 1.
12. Briggs, *How to Draw Cartoons,* p. 120.
13. Phister, op. cit., p. 1.
14. O'Glasain, op. cit., pp. 38–39.
15. McCay, "Movie Cartoons," p. 12.
16. Ibid.
17. Deanna Morse, letter to author, January 2, 1985.
18. O'Glasain, op. cit., p. 42.
19. Winsor McCay, "Winsor McCay Writes His Piece," *Newsdom,* October 3, 1931.
20. Ann Bridges, *Alphonse Mucha—The Complete Graphic Works* (New York: Harmony Books, 1980), p. 11.
21. Judith O'Sullivan, "The Art of Winsor Z. McCay" (PhD diss., University of Maryland, 1976), p. 58.
22. Robert J. Carter, letter to Winsor McCay, September 15, 1903, collection of Janet Trinker.
23. J. C. Baker, telegram to Winsor McCay, October 14, 1903, collection of Janet Trinket.
24. O'Glasain, op. cit., p. 71.
25. Tedda McCay, interview with author.
26. Briggs, op. cit., p. 121.

CHAPTER 4. NEW YORK AND THE GREAT COMIC STRIPS

1. Don C. Seitz, *The James Gordon Bennetts* (New York: Bobbs-Merrill, 1928), p. 245.
2. Ibid.
3. John K. Winkler, *William Randolph Hearst* (New York: Hastings House, 1955), p. 69.
4. "James Gordon Bennett," *Life* 30, no. 780 (25 November 1897), pp. 438–39.
5. Seitz, *The James Gordon Bennetts,* p. 360.
6. Winkler, *William Randolph Hearst,* p. 63.
7. *New York Journal,* October 17, 1896.
8. Winkler, op. cit., p. 71.
9. Maurice Horn, *75 Years of the Comics* (Boston, Mass.: Boston Book and Art, 1971), pp. 8–9.
10. *Cincinnati Enquirer,* May 11, 1906.
11. Undated contract, collection of Janet Trinker.
12. *New York American,* July 27, 1934.
13. Winsor McCay, *Dreams of the Rarebit Fiend* (New York: Dover 1973), p. ix.
14. Ibid.
15. Philippe Robert-Jones, *Beyond Time and Place* (Oxford, New York, Melbourne: Oxford University Press, 1978), p. 9.
16. Ibid., p. 8.
17. Crafton, *Before Mickey,* p. 94.
18. Judith O'Sullivan, "Aspects of Art Nouveau" (Lecture delivered at the National Collection of Fine Arts, Smithsonian Institution, Washington, D.C., 1973).
19. *New York Herald,* April 20, 1914.
20. O'Sullivan, "The Art of Winsor Z. McCay," p. 116.
21. Vincent de Sola, letter to author, June 12, 1985.
22. Maurice Sendak, "Dreams We All Had . . . ," *New York Times Book Review,* November 25, 1973.

CHAPTER 5. SHEEPSHEAD BAY

1. Robert A.M. Stern, Gregory Gilmartin, and John Montague Massengale, *New York 1900* (New York: Rizzoli, 1983), p. 249.
2. Ibid., p. 250.
3. Ibid.
4. John A. Fitzsimmons, "My Days with Winsor McCay." Manuscript, 1974, pp. 5–9.
5. Ibid.
6. Winsor McCay, letter to J. C. Baker, collection of Janet Trinker.

CHAPTER 6. VAUDEVILLE

1. *New York Telegram,* June 8, 1906.
2. *Cincinnati Enquirer,* May 11, 1906.
3. Winsor McCay, diary, c. 1906–8, collection of Janet Trinker.
4. *Cincinnati Enquirer,* June 12, 1906.
5. *Variety,* June 1906 (exact date and page unknown), collection of Janet Trinker.
6. *New York Telegraph,* October 18, 1906.
7. *Toledo Blade,* March 26, 1907.
8. *Pittsburgh Post,* April 4, 1907.
9. Winsor McCay, letter to Maude McCay and family, c. 1906, collection of Janet Trinker.
10. "Remembrance of Hammerstein's Victoria,"

New Yorker, December 20, 1930, p. 42.

11. Winsor McCay, pocket calendar/diary, 1908, collection of Janet Trinker.
12. *Brooklyn Eagle,* January 23, 1908.
13. *Brooklyn Eagle,* March 4, 1908.

CHAPTER 7. *LITTLE NEMO* ON BROADWAY
1. O'Glasain, op. cit., p. 91.
2. Ibid., p. 93.
3. *New York Telegraph,* October 23, 1908.
4. *Little Nemo,* New Amsterdam Theater program, 1908.
5. Ibid.
6. Edward Waters, *A Life in Music* (New York: Macmillan, 1955), pp. 324–25.
7. Stern, Gilmartin, and Massengale, *New York 1900,* p. 209.
8. *New York Mirror,* July 4, 1908.
9. *New York Telegraph,* August 31, 1908.
10. *New York Telegraph,* September 7, 1908.
11. *New York Telegraph,* August 17, 1908.
12. *New York Telegraph,* September 27, 1908.
13. O'Glasain, op. cit., p. 94.
14. Waters, *A Life in Music,* p. 326.
15. *New York Telegraph,* January 18, 1909.
16. Ibid.
17. Phister, op. cit., p. 1.
18. Ibid.
19. Winsor McCay, letter to unknown *Herald* employer, c. 1910, collection of Janet Trinker.
20. Undated newspaper clipping, c. 1906, collection of Janet Trinker.
21. McCay, "Movie Cartoons," p. 14.

CHAPTER 8. ANIMATED FILMS
1. Winsor McCay, *Illustrating and Cartooning: Animation.* Compiled and edited by Chas. L. Bartholomew and Joseph Almars (Minneapolis, Minn.: Federal Schools Inc., 1923), p. 18. Mail order art course book, collection of J. Michael Barrier.
2. Ritchie Calder, *Leonardo & the Age of the Eye* (New York: Simon and Schuster, 1970), p. 214.
3. Donald Crafton, "Emile Cohl and the Origins of the Animated Film" (PhD diss., Yale University, 1977), pp. 4–5.
4. Fitzsimmons, "My Days with Winsor McCay," pp. 21–22.
5. Claude Bragdon, *More Lives Than One* (New York: Alfred A. Knopf, 1938), p. 49.
6. *Rochester Post,* April 2, 1912.
7. *Buffalo Enquirer,* July 16, 1912.
8. *Detroit News,* July 22, 1912.
9. Winkler, op. cit., p. 70.
10. O'Glasain, op. cit., p. 157.
11. Ibid., p. 158.
12. *New York Telegraph,* April 12, 1911.
13. Detroit newspaper clipping, c. 1912, collection of Janet Trinker.
14. "Making Motion Pictures by Pencil," *Motography* 7, no. 4 (April 4, 1912), p. 162.
15. Paul Satterfield interview, by Milt Gray, November 30, 1977, transcript, collection of J. Michael Barrier.
16. McCay, "Movie Cartoons," p. 15.
17. John A. Fitzsimmons, interview with author, Rockville Centre, N.Y., June 8, 1984.
18. McCay, *Illustrating and Cartooning—Animation,* p. 8.
19. Ibid.
20. Satterfield interview with Milt Gray.
21. McCay, *Illustrating and Cartooning: Animation,* p. 13.
22. Al Hirschfeld, letter to author, April 9, 1974.
23. Fitzsimmons, op. cit., pp. 23–24.
24. Ibid., p. 24.
25. U.S. Patent application of John Randolph Bray, filed 9 January 1914, collection of J. Michael Barrier.
26. I. Klein, "How I Came to Know the Fabulous Winsor McCay," *Cartoonist Profiles* 34 (June 1977), p. 51.
27. I am grateful to Marco De Blois of La Cinémathèque québécoise in Montreal for providing this and other recently rediscovered documents and notebooks regarding McCay's films and filmmaking methods.
28. *New York Telegraph,* March 7, 1914.
29. *New York Telegraph,* March 8, 1914.
30. O'Glasain, op. cit., p. 158.
31. *New York Telegraph,* March 12, 1914.
32. *New York Telegraph,* February 4, 1917.
33. *Variety,* September 11, 1914.
34. *New York Times,* December 23, 1914.
35. Ibid.
36. Ibid.
37. *New York Times,* December 24, 1914.
38. *Sentinel Review,* Woodstock, Ontario, March 22, 1915.
39. Satterfield interview with Milt Gray.
40. *Detroit News,* July 22, 1916.
41. Ibid.
42. *New York Telegraph,* February 4, 1917.
43. John Canemaker, "The Birth of Animation," *Millimeter* (April 1977), p. 15.
44. I am grateful to Larry Ruppel for providing his c. 1986 interview with Jean Adams Robinson, and all quotes attributed to her are from that interview; thank you to G. Preston Brown for information pertaining to Adams and his family tree; thank you David M. Halpate, supervisor of the Maxwell Funeral Home in Renovo, Pa., for burial records of Adams and his second wife. An extensive obituary of Apthorp Adams appeared in *The Record* (Renovo, Pa.) July 16, 1952 issue: "William A. Adams, Famed Newspaper Artist, Passes Away."
45. McCay, *Illustrating and Cartooning: Animation,* p. 19.
46. Fitzsimmons, op. cit., p. 27.
47. Ibid.
48. Andrew Sarris, *Village Voice,* January 26, 1976.
49. Richard Eder, *New York Times,* December 29, 1975.
50. O'Glasain, op. cit., p. 139.
51. Ibid.
52. Robert McCay, letter to Bob Sunderland, Walt Disney Productions, October 1, 1955, collection of Janet Trinker.
53. Claude Bragdon, "Mickey Mouse and What He Means," *Scribner's* 96 (July 1934), p. 41.
54. Eder, *New York Times.*
55. Klein, "How I Came to Know the Fabulous Winsor McCay," p. 51.

CHAPTER 9. A HEARST MAN
1. Ray Moniz, interview with author, Highland Falls, N.Y., 13 September 1984; Janet Trinker, interviews with author, Pacific Grove, Ca., 26 and 27 February 1985.
   I am especially grateful to the late Ray Winsor Moniz (16 July 1918–6 December 2001) who provided many personal details about his grandfather before and after the 1987 publication of this book. Following is an interview he gave at the time of Dreams in Motion: The Art of Winsor McCay, an exhibition I curated at the Katonah Gallery in New York, June 5–July 25, 1988:
   "Windsor [sic] McCay: Artistic Pioneer at Katonah" by Felicity Hoffecker, Darien News-Review, July 14, 1988.
   "I studied art in Syracuse," Mr. Moniz told us, "and worked at the West Point Museum for thirty years. I was sixteen when grandfather died, and I remember him well. He always told me not to become an artist, that it was a thankless job. And he said of his own career that he wasn't smart but that he could draw pictures.
   "I remember going with him to his studio. He had something going all the time. My grandmother was a good cook, but as soon as dinner was over Grandfather would disappear into his studio. We would go for walks in Sheepshead Bay, and he would come back with an idea and quickly pencil it in.
   "When he'd leave the house to go to Hearst's he'd ride in a chauffeured car—he hated cars—and I would ride up front with the chauffeur. It was a beautiful Packard, and I loved it! It was kept locked up, but after he died my grandmother and I would sneak it out and go for rides.
   "I have very fond memories of him. He was a mild, meek man who loved to sit and talk. He loved people and he would sit and study them, especially on the subway."
2. Ibid.
3. Tedda McCay, interviews with author, Pacific Grove, Ca., February 26 and 27, 1985.
4. Winsor McCay, diary, c. 1906–8.
5. Ray Moniz, interview with author.
6. Ibid.
7. Janet Trinker, interviews with author.
8. O'Glasain, op. cit., pp. 182–86.
9. Winkler, op. cit., p. 73.
10. Ibid., p. 74.
11. Oliver Carlson, *Brisbane: A Candid Biography* (New York: Stackpole Sons, 1937), p. 182.
12. Ibid., p. 285.
13. Ibid., p. 198.
14. Winkler, op. cit., p. 203.

15. Jean Adams Robinson interview with Larry Ruppel.

16. William Apthorp "Thorp" Adams III was born (according to some records) on 6 September 1896; but he falsified his birth certificate by advancing his years in order to enlist in the army. His real birth date may have been between 1898 and 1900.

   Like McCay's son, during World War I he was gassed on the battlefield, which affected him personally and in business. He was legally married only once (and had two children), but he later had several "wives" and subsequently more children.

   He died 2 September 1961 in Springfield, Ma. Data courtesy G. Preston Brown.

17. "Marion Moniz As I Knew Her," unpublished remembrance by Maud H. Brown to author, 1987.

18. Ibid.

19. Carlson, *Brisbane*, pp. 284–85.

20. O'Glasain, op. cit, pp. 172–73.

21. McCay once wrote an unpublished remembrance of his visit in early September 1920 to San Simeon, William Randolph Hearst's California estate, titled "For Once W. R. was Wrong."

   It was the late, lamented L.J. O'Reilly [Hearst's secretary] who phoned me that Mr. Hearst wanted me to come out to his ranch.

   "What for," I asked.

   "I haven't the least idea," he replied. "When can you leave, so I can get your transportation?"

   After my train had crossed the California line, 'native' commenced searching out strangers to outline their state's wonders and to point out spots of interest from the car windows.

   I needed no sign hanging on me to tell that I was new. A fine old gentleman ahemmed [sic] into a seat beside me and after panting for a minute, he and I were interested conversationalists.

   Among the many things he told me was that he knew the much beloved mother of W. R. Hearst and as he told it he tipped his hat. I told him that her name was not strange to me nor any one in this broad U.S.A. and that I now felt closer to Mr. Hearst and the great ranch I was headed for.

   This was all very nice and as contemplation of my soon being in San Francisco was unnerving me slightly, I volunteered a Rickey. The narrow mirror opposite my seat reflected my face as pale, and the sighs of expectancy had my chest heaving.

   I brought forth a flask of gin and the porter did the rest. We continued on, he talking, I listening.

   "I suppose Mr. Hearst has the largest and finest store of wines and liquors on his many ranches as one could imagine," he said as we sipped on. "Mr. Hearst never drinks himself but he has thousands of old cronies whom he loves to entertain on his vast ranch, so I suppose you will get some pretty good stuff out there."

   "But," I said, "I work for him and am on an assignment, not as a guest."

   I registered at the St. Francis Hotel and phoned the Examiner *office to tell Mr. Hearst I was here.*

   I was told to stand by and they would tell me where to go. I "stood by" the hotel two days, not going ten feet from a phone or page boy, when word came to take the train for San Luis Obispo and on to the ranch.

   Mr. Hearst received me graciously. I was introduced to a score of fine laughing gentlemen thrilling me delightfully. But I was serious, for while I could see they were guests of Mr. Hearst's on this gorgeous domain, I was simply an employee on the job.

   Mr. Hearst does not play as much as one would imagine. From morning until night he is in touch with his many staff heads and his own telegraph station up on the mountain is a busy place day and night.

   And while his friends were as boys out of school enjoying every kind of sport, every hour in the day, I just stuck close to W.R. like a trailing shadow or a dog following his master, ever-ready cartoonist, as it were.

   I went no where, I saw nothing. Yet there were hundreds of places to go and thousands of things to see.

   But I sat up in the telegraph hut on the hill for hours each day near "The Chief," pen poised, ink and drawing board at the ready.

   I thought of what I was told on the train and several nights I asked faithful old George Thompson [Hearst's valet] if there was a chance of a little drink on this ranch. Each time he would answer "Sure," and bring me a couple of cold bottles of White Rock. Luckily, I had a little gin left which saved Mr. Hearst the cost of another employee's salary.

   After two weeks, I said to Mr. Hearst, "What am I supposed to do here?"

   He said, "Don't you like it here?"

   I said, "Yes, if heaven is a more beautiful place than this, I'm going to live a better life from now on."

   The next day we all went to Frisco by auto, a magnificent trip. I went to the St. Francis again. W.R. and his cronies (Guy Burham [publisher of the afternoon paper San Francisco Herald*] was one of them who I shall ever fondly remember) went to the Palace.*

   I stayed three days at this great hotel where all my expenses were paid, never going ten feet from a telephone or a page boy.

   I saw nothing of Frisco, just patiently waiting for orders from W.R. any minute. The beloved Charlie Stanton [publisher and editor of the San Francisco Examiner*] said, "McCay, why don't you beat it back to New York? W.R. evidently doesn't want you to do any work here."*

   So back I came. About a week later I received a short letter from Mr. Hearst reading: "Sorry did not see you before you left. Hope you enjoyed your vacation."

   About six months later I happened to be seen with a fine Bacardi rum cocktail in my hand by that faithful old George Thompson here in New York.

   "Oh Lordy," he exclaimed. I said, "What's the matter?"

   He replied, "Why, when you were out to the ranch, W.R. cautioned me not to offer you or even mention wine or liquor to Mr. McCay under any circumstances for he never touches it."

   For once THE CHIEF WAS WRONG!
   Undated hand-written manuscript, c. 1920. Courtesy Robert W. McCay.

22. Maud H. Brown letter to author, October 27, 1987.

23. O'Glasain, op. cit., p. 238.

24. Ibid., pp. 185–86.

25. Carlson, *Brisbane*, pp. 284–85.

26. O'Glasain, op. cit., p. 172–73.

27. Gregory D'Alessio, letter to author, June 8, 1985.

28. Lew Haskins letters to author, July 17 and 23, 1987.

29. Bill Holman, telephone interview with author, June 18, 1985.

30. Carlson, *Brisbane*, p. 251.

31. O'Glasain, op. cit., pp. 171–72.

32. Notes that McCay once drafted for an anecdote he hoped to tell on the radio circa 1927 are illuminating. They show his continuing interest in performing on stage and in animation as a new art form:

   I am going to talk on what I did today. It will not be a wonderful tale in these days when marvelous things are being done. But it will be an odd story you may like. I told it to the Radio Editor of the Journal *—he said it was a pip.*

   I arrived at this great big Lowe's Theater at 2 P.M. where I am playing a date. I went into my dressing room, changed my clothes and by the aid of powder youthful tint—rouge liner & lip stick I transformed a small pale rather weazened [sic] continence [sic] into as beautiful a rosy boyish face as only an artist could paint—combed my hairs—there are 8 of them—I went on the stage and the people in the audience gasped, for their grandfather used to read my Nemo page to them when they were kids. My stint consists of an animated cartoon.

   I am simple [sic] wild about animation drawings; I wish I had some here to talk more about animation. The new art. After my act I returned to my dressing room and with cold cream & a cruel towel I wiped out all traces of my former beauty—Donned my street clothes. Dove in to the subway and was soon in Park Row—a quick bus trip to the new Hearst Publications Building on South St., East River— The largest newspaper plant in the world—one of the elevators to [sic] me to the 5th floor and I entered the suite of offices of the greatest newspaper man in this wide world Arthur Brisbane. We had an earnest talk about cartoons he wants me to draw. He believing I had come in from my office near by—never dreaming I just came from before the footlights of Lowe's State Theater with a gorgeous big band playing in front of me.

   When I play vaudeville I am playing hookey from the office & my newspaper work. Mr. Brisbane once said McCay your business is drawing cartoons and not flopping around on a stage—but while he is strict with me he is always fair. After my talk with him which is always wonderful, I sneaked put [sic] into the subway and back to the theater here.

Mr. Brisbane's office faces the most wonderful scene in this world—on the left is the great Manhattan Bridge seeming to go up into the sky. On the right is the beautiful old Brooklyn Bridge—between the two is a continual churning of the East River by every kind of a water craft from a small launch or tug to an ocean liner or battleship. But I am painted up now and as beautiful and youthful looking as I was this afternoon and the view I get is far different than from the windows of Mr. Brisbane's office.

Here before me are clowns in every color, ballet girls in spangles and gauze—performers in tights— big scene settings—stage hands—card boys—a happy family. The Big band is playing and beyond the footlights 5,000 people are sitting, some gaping, some stern-faced, some laughing. Now the Big Thrill of the Day. I am talking over the radio to you and Thomas A. Drogan Tad—Janet & Boonie [McCay's grandchildren Janet and Ray] will you keep still.

I am not stuck on the stage. I want to promote the animation of drawings. Some day marvelous moving pictures will be show [sic] that will be drawn by artists instead of acted by artists—I will be back with my beloved boss Mr. Brisbane Monday and play hookey again later on.

Courtesy La Cinémathèque québécoise.

33. Woodstock, Ontario, *Sentinel Review,* November 26, 1927.
34. Klein, op. cit., p. 50.
35. O'Glasain, op. cit., pp. 196–97.
36. W.R. Hearst, Jr., to author, February 2, 1988.
37. Katje de Gorog, interview with author, New York City, June 17, 1985.
38. O'Glasain, op. cit., p. 176.
39. Ray Moniz, interview with author, Highland Falls, N.Y., June 20, 1985.
40. Janet Trinker, interviews with author.
41. Ray Moniz, interview with author, June 20, 1985.
42. Dorothy Noonan, interview with author, Floral Park, N.Y., September 25, 1984.
43. Janet Trinker, interviews with author.
44. O'Glasain, op. cit., p. 242.

CHAPTER 10. AFTER McCAY

1. *New York Times,* July 29, 1934.
2. Kings County Surrogate's Court Petition, September 7, 1934 and September 13, 1934.
3. Ibid.
4. Tedda McCay, interviews with author.
5. Ibid.
6. Janet Trinker, interviews with author.
7. Jim Steranko, *The Harry "A" Chesler Collection of Illustration and Comic Art,* catalogue for the exhibition at Fairleigh Dickinson University, Madison, N.J., May 18–July 12, 1974.
8. Robert N. Brotherton, interview with author, New York City, April 17, 1985.
9. Tedda McCay, interviews with author.
10. Robert N. Brotherton, interview with author.
11. John Canaday, "Little Nemo at the Met," *New York Times,* February 13, 1966.
12. Andrew Sarris, *Village Voice,* January 26, 1976.
13. Richard Eder, *New York Times,* December 29, 1975.
14. Chuck Jones, letter to author, August 22, 1985.
15. Milton Caniff, letter to author, August 18, 1985.
16. Burne Hogarth, letter to author, July 5, 1985.
17. Garry Trudeau, *The Doonesbury Chronicles* (New York: Holt, Rinehart & Winston, 1975), pp. xiii–xiv.
18. Berke Breathed, letter to author, July 7, 1985.
19. *New York Newsday,* Thurs. Sept. 26, 1991: "'Kong' Joins Film's Immortals" — "It's official: King Kong, Lawrence of Arabia and Gigi are classics. Along with 22 other movies, they were added yesterday to the Library of Congress list of American films worth preserving. The additions brought to 75 the number of films listed on the National Film Registry. Newcomers are . . . Chinatown, starring Jack Nicholson, 1974; Charles Chaplin's City Lights, 1931 . . . Gertie the Dinosaur, an animation by Winsor McCay, 1914 . . . David Lean's Lawrence of Arabia, 1962; Orson Welles's The Magnificent Ambersons, 1942 . . . and Stanley Kubrick's 2001: A Space Odyssey, 1968."
20. *Winsor McCay: The Master Edition* contains audio commentary by this author, plus the 1976 documentary *Remembering Winsor McCay,* and a stills gallery. For more information, visit: www.milestonefilms.com

chronology

1867: Winsor Zenas McKay born in Canada. According to 1870 and 1880 Michigan census records, Woodstock, Ontario, birthplace of parents Robert McKay (1840?–1915) and Janet Murray (1840?–1927).
Named after family friend and Michigan businessman Zenas G. Winsor (1814–1890), who employed Robert McKay when he first immigrated to the US in 1862 (four years before his marriage to Janet).
Family name changed at unknown date from "McKay" to "McCay."

1868: Brother, Arthur, born.

1876: Sister, Mae, born.

1886: Winsor sent by father to Ypsilanti, Michigan to Cleary's Business College, but never registers or attends classes. Instead, visits Detroit and the Wonderland, a dime museum where he draws caricatures for small change.

1888: First public mention of artistic skill: in *Ypsilanti Commercial* newspaper (February 10) exhibit of McCay drawings at post office.
Receives private art lessons (in perspective and direct observation) from John Goodison (1834–1892), professor of geography and drawing at Michigan State Normal (now Eastern Michigan University).

1889: Arrives in Chicago intending to study at The Art Institute, but financially unable to do so. Employed at National Printing & Engraving Co. (at 119 Monroe Street), which produced "Show, Commercial and Railroad Printing" and circus posters.
Joins fraternal order of Freemasonry, following in his father's footsteps; but remains lifelong agnostic who believes in reincarnation.

1890: Resides at 185 Dearborn Street, a Chicago rooming house, along with Jules Guérin and his mother. (Guérin later became a noted painter and muralist.) Also probably worked as a poster painter and caricaturist at Kohl & Middleton Dime Museum.

1891: Moves to Cincinnati to work as a poster painter/publicist for Vine Street Dime Museum, a permanent freak show owned by Kohl & Middleton.
Marries fourteen-year-old Maude Leonore Dufour (1878–1949), youngest of three daughters born to French-Canadian carriage painter John Dufour and Sarah Dufour, a hotel pastry cook.

1896: Son Robert Winsor McCay is born June 21.

1897: Daughter Marion Elizabeth McCay is born August 22.

1898: Employed as illustrator on Cincinnati *Commercial Tribune* newspaper and contributes spot gag cartoons to *Life* humor magazine.
During summer, with poster advertisement entrepreneur Ph. Morton, McCay helps create river pageant celebrating American victory in

Santiago harbor, Cuba (on July 3), one of the closing events of the Spanish-American War. In September, McCay also designs ceremonial arches for the Grand Army of the Republic's convention in Cincinnati.

Brother Arthur is admitted to Traverse City State Hospital, the Northern Michigan Asylum for the Insane, where he will remain for forty-eight years until his death on June 15, 1946.

1900: Joins staff of *Cincinnati Enquirer* newspaper.

1903: In collaboration with writer George Randolph Chester (1869–1924) McCay creates prototype comic page *A Tale of the Jungle Imps by Felix Fiddle,* which runs from January 18 to November 8, 1903. Hired by art director J.C. Baker to work at *New York Herald,* a New York City newspaper owned by James Gordon Bennett, who also publishes the *New York Evening Telegram.*

McCay arrives in October, joined by his wife and children in November; they reside in the Hotel Audubon, 39th Street and Broadway, a few blocks from the *Herald* building at Herald Square.

1904: Creates his first serial strip, *Mr. Goodenough,* for the *Telegram,* which runs from January 21 to March 4.

On April 21, sister Mae marries Clyde Disbrow in United Methodist Church in Edmore, Michigan. *Sister's Little Sister's Beau,* a McCay comic strip, makes a single appearance in the *New York Herald* April 24.

Phoolish Philipe, McCay's first color strip appears once on May 29.

Little Sammy Sneeze, McCay's first sustained and popular comic strip appears in the *Herald* July 24, 1904–December 9, 1906.

Dream of the Rarebit Fiend, McCay's first great adult dream strip, appears in the *New York Evening Telegram* September 10, 1904–June 25, 1911, drawn under the pseudonym "Silas." Revived in the *New York Herald* January 19–August 3, 1913.

1905: *The Story of Hungry Henrietta, Herald* comic strip in which female child protagonist ages visibly each week, runs from January 8–July 16.

A Pilgrim's Progress by Mister Bunion, an adult strip for the *Evening Telegram* under the name "Silas," runs from June 26, 1905 to December 18, 1910.

Little Nemo in Slumberland, McCay's masterpiece, an epic dream comic strip appears in the *New York Herald* from October 15, 1905 to July 23, 1911. (Robert McCay, Winsor's son, is the model for the boy protagonist Nemo.)

McCay's niece, the daughter of Clyde and Mae McCay Disbrow, dies in infancy.

Winsor and family move to Sheepshead Bay, Brooklyn, New York, his main residence for the rest of his life.

1906: On June 11 at Proctor's 23rd Street Theater in New York, McCay appears for the first time in his own vaudeville act (drawing quick sketches on a blackboard), commencing a decade of intermittent touring of theaters east of the Mississippi.

1908: On January 14, McCay is accused of hiring thugs to attack William Muir as he leaves the McCay home after a domestic quarrel involving Maude McCay.

On September 28, *Little Nemo,* a Victor Herbert operetta based on McCay's comic strip, opens in Philadelphia and then on Broadway on October 20.

1909: A post-Broadway tour of *Little Nemo* begins on January 25, continuing in theaters on the east coast of America until winter 1910.

McCay creates *Poor Jake,* a new comic strip for the *New York Evening Telegram.*

1910: Mae Disbrow, McCay's sister, dies in Edmore, Michigan.

1911: On April 8, Vitagraph releases McCay's first animated film, *Little Nemo.* On April 12, McCay includes the hand-colored film in his vaudeville act at New York's Colonial Theater.

On July 3, William Randolph Hearst announces that McCay has become a member of his staff of cartoonists.

From September 3, 1911 to December 26, 1913, McCay draws the strip *Little Nemo* under the title *In the Land of Wonderful Dreams* for Hearst's *New York American.* In addition, he creates several other short-lived strips for Hearst, including *A Midsummer Day Dream, Autumn Daydreams, It Was Only a Dream, As Our Ancestors Played It, Dream of the Lobster Fiend, Ain't You Glad You're not a Mormon?, Mr. Bosh, It's Great to Be a Husband, Dear Dad and Daughter,* among others.

1912: McCay's second animated film *How a Mosquito Operates* (also known as *The Story of a Mosquito*) is included in his vaudeville act during the spring and summer.

1913: W.R. Hearst forces McCay to give up drawing comic strips and concentrate on illustrating the editorial opinions of Hearst and his chief editor Arthur Brisbane.

1914: *Gertie the Dinosaur,* McCay's third animated film, premieres in his vaudeville act at Chicago's Palace Theater on February 2. The film is copyrighted on September 15 and distributed by Box Office Attractions on December 28.

In March, W.R. Hearst cancels McCay's vaudeville appearance in Pittsburgh. Later in the year, McCay is induced by W.R. not to accept vaudeville engagements outside greater New York. December 22–24, McCay testifies in court defending his wife, Maude, who is accused as the correspondent in a divorce suit filed by Irene Watkins against Harry Tobin Lambkin; Maude is vindicated when evidence proves the McCays are victims of a blackmail attempt.

1915: On March 21, Robert McCay, the artist's father, dies in Edmore.

On May 7, a German submarine sinks British luxury liner *Lusitania,* killing 1200 civilians, including 128 Americans; fired with patriotism, McCay decides to make an anti-German animated film of the disaster.

In December, W.R. Hearst opens International Film Service, an animation studio to make shorts based on comic-strip characters by cartoonists

under contract to him; McCay is listed as a future contributor but never makes an I.F.S. film.

1917: On February 4, the *New York Telegraph* announces that McCay has been forced to retire from vaudeville by W.R. Hearst.

On October 3, Marion McCay marries Captain Raymond Moniz (1879–1961) in Brooklyn; both McCay's son-in-law and son will serve as part of the armed forces in Europe.

1918: In May, Robert McCay and Ray Moniz sail with the 27th Division for France, where both men will distinguish themselves in combat. On July 16, Marion McCay Moniz gives birth to her only child Ray Winsor Moniz (7/16/18–12/06/01). *The Sinking of the Lusitania,* McCay's fourth animated film, is copyrighted on July 19 and released the next day by Jewel Productions. McCay writes a defensive editorial supporting W.R. Hearst in the *New York American.*

1920: McCay visits San Simeon, Hearst's palatial home in California at W.R.'s behest and expense.

1921: Robert McCay marries Theresa (Tedda) Munchausen on April 9.

A series of animated films, such as *Flip's Circus, The Centaurs, Gertie on Tour,* and some under the theme of "Dreams of the Rarebit Fiend" including *Bug Vaudeville, The Pet,* and *The Flying House* (the last a collaborative effort by Robert McCay and his father) are completed and sporadically distributed and screened.

1922: On November 29, Janet McCay (11/29/22–1/17/97) is born to Robert and Tedda McCay.

1924: Winsor McCay appears in *The Great White Way,* a Hearst feature film.

McCay quits the Hearst papers, rejoins the *New York Herald* (now called the *Herald-Tribune*) and revives *Little Nemo in Slumberland* from August 3, 1924 through December 26, 1926.

1926: McCay returns to the Hearst papers and continues drawing editorial cartoons for Arthur Brisbane's column.

1927: On February 23, the *Herald Tribune* transfers all copyrights for the *Nemo* strip to McCay.

1928: Robert McCay, Jr., the son of Robert and Tedda McCay, is born on October 17.

1932: McCay draws sketches on the site of the Lindbergh baby kidnapping for coverage in the *New York American.*

1934: On the morning of July 26 McCay suffers a massive cerebral hemorrhage and that afternoon dies at his home in Sheepshead Bay.

His body is interred with full Masonic rites on July 28 in lot #64 ("The Lawn" section) of Brooklyn's Evergreens Cemetery.

selected bibliography

BOOKS AND MANUSCRIPTS

Altman, Leon L. *The Dream in Psychoanalysis.* New York: International Universities Press, Inc., 1969.

Barrier, Michael. *Hollywood Cartoons.* New York: Oxford University Press, 1999.

Baxter, Albert. *History of the City of Grand Rapids, Michigan.* Grand Rapids, Mich.: Munsell & Company, 1891.

Bendazzi, Giannalberto. *Cartoons.* Bloomington and Indianapolis: Indiana University Press, 1994.

Blackbeard, Bill, and Martin Williams. *The Smithsonian Collection of Newspaper Comics.* Washington, D.C.: Smithsonian Institution Press and Harry N. Abrams Inc., 1977.

Bragdon, Claude. *More Lives than One.* New York: Alfred A. Knopf, 1938.

Bridges, Ann. *Alphonse Mucha—The Complete Graphic Works.* New York: Harmony Books, 1980.

Briggs, Clare. *How to Draw Cartoons.* New York: Harper and Brothers, 1926.

Byrnes, Gene. *A Complete Guide to Professional Cartooning.* Drexel Hill, Pa.: Bell Publishing Company, 1950.

Calder, Ritchie. *Leonardo & the Age of the Eye.* New York: Simon and Schuster, 1970.

Canemaker, John. *The Animated Raggedy Ann & Andy: An Intimate Look at the Art of Animation.* New York: Bobbs-Merrill Company, Inc., 1977.

_____. *Felix: The Twisted Tale of the World's Most Famous Cat.* New York: Da Capo Press, 1991.

_____, and Robert E. Abrams. *Treasures of Disney Animation Art.* New York: Abbeville Press, 1982.

_____. *Walt Disney's Nine Old Men & the Art of Animation.* New York: Disney Editions, 2001.

_____. *Tex Avery: The MGM Years.* Atlanta: Turner Publishing, Inc., 1996.

Carlson, Oliver. *Brisbane: A Candid Biography.* New York: Stackpole Sons, 1937.

Cavendish, Richard. *Man, Myth and Magic.* London: Marshall Cavendish Corp., 1970.

Couperie, Pierre, et al. *A History of the Comic Strip.* New York: Crown, 1968.

Crafton, Donald. *Before Mickey: The Animated Film 1898–1928.* Cambridge, Mass.: The MIT Press, 1982.

_____. *Emile Cohl, Caricature, and Film.* Princeton: Princeton University Press, 1990.

Craven, Thomas. *Cartoon Cavalcade.* Chicago: Consolidated Book Publishers, 1945.

Falk, Nat. *How to Make Animated Cartoons.* New York: Foundation Books, 1941.

Fitzsimmons, John A. "My Days with Winsor McCay." Manuscript, 1974.

Fraff, George P. *The People of Michigan.* Lansing, Mich.: Michigan Department of Education, State Library Services, 1974.

Grayson, Frank Y. *Pioneers of Night Life on Vine Street.* Cincinnati: no publisher listed, 1924. Collection of Cincinnati Public Library.

History of Muskegon and Ottawa Counties, Michigan.
Chicago: H.R. Page and Company, 1882.

Hoffer, Eric. *The Ordeal of Change.* New York: Harper and Row, 1963.

_____. *The Temper of Our Time.* New York: Harper and Row, 1967.

Hoffer, Thomas W. *Animation—A Reference Guide.* Westport, Conn., and London, England: Greenwood Press, 1981.

Horn, Maurice. *75 Years of the Comics.* Boston, Mass.: Boston Book and Art, 1971.

Illustrated Cincinnati: The Queen City of the West. New York: Acme Publishing and Engraving Company, 1891.

Inge, M. Thomas. *Dictionary of Literary Biography—American Writers for Children 1900–1960,* Vol. 22. Detroit, Mich.: A Bruccoli Clark Book—Gale Research Company, 1983.

_____. *Handbook of American Popular Culture.* Westport, Conn.: Greenwood Press, 1978.

Isbell, Egbert R. *A History of Eastern Michigan University 1849–1965.* Ypsilanti, Mich.: Eastern Michigan University Press, 1971.

Jungstedt, Torsten. *Captain Grog and His Friends.* Stockholm: Swedish Broadcasting Corporation, 1973.

Kitchel, Mary S. *Spring Lake Community Centennial 1869–1969.* Spring Lake, Mich.: no publisher listed, 1969. Collection of Grand Rapids Public Library, Michigan.

Lillie, Leo C. *Historic Grand Haven and Ottawa County.* Grand Haven, Mich.: Tri-Cities Historical Society, Michigan, 1931; reprint 1980.

Little Nemo. Edited by Woody Gelman. Franklin Square, N.Y.: Nostalgia Press, 1972.

McCay, Winsor. *Dreams of the Rarebit Fiend.* New York: F. A. Stokes, 1905; reprint New York: Dover Books, 1973.

_____. *Little Sammy Sneeze.* New York: F. A. Stokes, 1905.

_____. *Illustrating and Cartooning: Animation.* Minneapolis, Minn.: Federal Schools Incorporated, 1923.

Maltin, Leonard. *Of Mice and Magic.* New York: McGraw-Hill Book Company, 1980.

Michigan: A Guide to the Wolverine State. American Guide Series. New York: Oxford University Press, 1941.

Michigan History. Vol. LIV, no. 2. Lansing, Mich.: Michigan Historical Commission, 1970.

O'Glasain, Padraic. "Winsor McCay: Little Nemo's Daddy." Manuscript, 1941. Collection of Janet Trinker.

O'Sullivan, Judith. *The Art of the Comic Strip.* College Park, Md.: University of Maryland, 1971.

_____. "The Art of Winsor Z. McCay." PhD diss., University of Maryland, 1976.

Peary, Gerald, and Danny Peary. *The American Animated Cartoon.* New York: E.P. Dutton, 1980.

Perry, Dick. *Vas You Ever in Zinzinnati?* Garden City, N.Y.: Doubleday and Company, 1966.

Pierce, Bessie Louise. *A History of Chicago.* New York: Alfred A. Knopf, 1940.

Roberts, Keith. *Degas.* London (Phaidon) and New York: E.P. Dutton, 1976.

Roth, Leland M. *McKim, Mead & White, Architects.* New York: Harper and Row, 1983.

Sale, Roger. *Fairy Tales and After: From Snow White to E.B. White.* Cambridge, Mass.: Harvard University Press, 1978.

Seitz, Don C. *The James Gordon Bennetts.* New York: Bobbs-Merrill Company, Inc., 1928.

Simpson, Colin. *Lusitania.* New York: Ballantine, 1983.

Snyder; Nancy Lynn. *Cleary College: One Hundred Years of Business.* Ypsilanti, Mich.: Cleary College, 1984.

Sobel, Bernard. *A Pictorial History of Vaudeville.* New York: Citadel Press, 1961.

Solomon, Charles. *Enchanted Drawings. The History of Animation.* New York: Alfred A. Knopf, 1989.

_____, and Ron Stark. *The Complete Kodak Animation Book.* Rochester, N.Y.: Eastman Kodak Company, 1983.

Stern, Robert A. M., Gregory Gilmartin, and John Montague Massengale. *New York 1900.* New York: Rizzoli, 1983.

Thomas, Frank, and Ollie Johnston. *Disney Animation: The Illusion of Life.* New York: Abbeville Press, 1981.

Trudeau, Garry. *The Doonesbury Chronicles.* New York: Holt, Rinehart and Winston, 1975.

Waters, Edward. *A Life in Music.* New York: Macmillan, 1955.

Waugh, Coulton. *The Comics.* New York: Macmillan, 1947.

Winkler, John K. *William Randolph Hearst.* New York: Hastings House, 1955.

ARTICLES

Barrier, J. Michael. "Of Mice, Wabbits, Ducks and Men: The Hollywood Cartoon." *AFI Report* 5, no. 2 (summer 1974): pp. 18–26.

Bragdon, Claude. "Mickey Mouse and What He Means." *Scribner's* 96 (July 1934): pp. 40–43.

Canemaker, John. "Winsor McCay." *Film Comment* 11, no. 1 (January–February 1975): pp. 44–47.

_____. "The Birth of Animation—Reminiscing with John A. Fitzsimmons." *Millimeter* 3, no. 4 (April 1975): pp. 14–16.

_____. "1st USA Winsor McCay Film Retrospective." Program notes for the 3rd International Animation Film Festival in New York, September 30–October 4, 1975.

_____. "Dreams in Motion: The Art of Winsor McCay." Catalogue essay, The Katonah Gallery, Katonah, N.Y., June 5–July 25, 1988.

_____. "Winsor McCay Film Retrospective." Program notes, Whitney Museum of American Art, New York, December 28–January 6, 1976.

_____. "Winsor McCay Film Retrospective." Program notes, Walker Art Center, Minneapolis, Minn., March 28, 1976.

_____. "Winsor McCay Film Retrospective." Program notes for the Fifth World Festival of Animated Films, Zagreb, Yugoslavia, June 21–25, 1982.

Carlin, John, and Sheena Wagstaff. *The Comic Art Show: Cartoons in Painting and Popular Culture.* Exhibition catalogue for the Whitney Museum of American Art, New York, summer 1983.

Crafton, Donald. "Animation Iconography: The Hand of the Artist." *Quarterly Review of Film Studies* 4, no. A (fall 1979): pp. 409–28.

Deitcher, David. "Comic Connoisseurs." *Art in America* 72, no. 2 (February 1984): pp. 100–7.

Fell, John L. "Mr. Griffith, Meet Winsor McCay." *Journal of the University Film Association* 23, no. 3 (1971): pp. 74–88.

Hearn, Michael Patrick. "The Animated Art of Winsor McCay." *American Artist* 39, no. 394 (May 1975): pp. 28–33, 63–65.

Hoffer, Thomas W. "From Comic Strips to Animation." *Journal of University Film Association* 28, no. 2 (spring 1976): pp. 23–30.

Inge, M. Thomas. "Little Nemo." *Crimmer's* (spring 1976): pp. 44–49.

Kleespies, Keith. "But First, There Was Winsor McCay." *Cincinnati Enquirer Magazine,* November 25, 1973, pp. 17–21.

Klein, I. "How I Came to Know the Fabulous Winsor McCay." *Cartoonist Profiles* 30 (June 1977): pp. 49–51.

McCay, Winsor. "How I Originated Motion Picture Cartoons." *Cartoon and Movie Magazine* 31 (April 1927): pp. 11–15.

Marschall, Richard. "Comic Masters." *Horizon* 23, no. 7 (July 1980): pp. 42–51.

O'Sullivan, Judith. "In Search of Winsor McCay." *American Film Institute Report* 5, no. 2 (summer 1974): pp. 3–9.

Sendak, Maurice. "Dreams We All Had . . . ." *New York Times Book Review,* November 25, 1973, p. 3.

FILM

Canemaker, John. *Remembering Winsor McCay.* 1976 documentary, featuring an interview with John A. Fitzsimmons, and excerpts from *Little Nemo* (color version), *Gertie the Dinosaur,* and *The Sinking of the Lusitania.* Distributed by Phoenix Film & Video, Inc., New York City.

DVD

Winsor McCay: The Master Edition with audio commentary by this author, plus the 1976 documentary *Remembering Winsor McCay,* and a stills gallery. For more information, visit: www.milestonefilms.com

Walt Disney Treasures: Behind the Scenes at the Walt Disney Studios. "The Story of the Animated Drawing" recreates McCay's vaudeville act with Gertie.

index

Page numbers in *italics* refer to illustrations.

Project Manager: Céline Moulard
Designer: Robert McKee
Production Manager: Maria Pia Gramaglia

Library of Congress Cataloging-in-Publication Data

Canemaker, John.
Winsor McCay : his life and art / John Canemaker;
    foreword by Maurice Sendak.—[Rev. ed.]
    p. cm.
  Includes bibliographical references and index.
  ISBN 0–8109–5941–0 (alk. paper)
  1. McCay, Winsor. 2. Cartoonists—United
    States—Biography. I. Title.

NC1429.M474C36 2005
741.5'092—dc22

                                        2005000275

Printed and bound in China

10 9 8 7 6 5 4 3 2 1

Harry N. Abrams, Inc.
100 Fifth Avenue
New York, N.Y. 10011
www.abramsbooks.com

Abrams is a subsidiary of